Cambridge Studies in Social Anthropology

General Editor: Jack Goody

32

MUSLIM SOCIETY

For a list of the titles in the series, see page 265.

Muslim society

ERNEST GELLNER

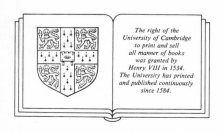

The right of the
University of Cambridge
to print and sell
all manner of books
was granted by
Henry VIII in 1534.
The University has printed
and published continuously
since 1584.

CAMBRIDGE UNIVERSITY PRESS

Cambridge
London   New York   New Rochelle
Melbourne   Sydney

Published by the Press Syndicate of the University of Cambridge
The Pitt Building, Trumpington Street, Cambridge CB2 1RP
32 East 57th Street, New York, NY 10022, USA
296 Beaconsfield Parade, Middle Park, Melbourne 3206, Australia

© Cambridge University Press 1981

First published 1981
First paperback edition 1983
Reprinted 1984

Printed in Great Britain at the University Press, Cambridge

British Library Cataloguing in Publication Data
Gellner, Ernest
Muslim society. — (Cambridge studies in
social anthropology; vol. 32 ISSN 0068-6794).
1. Islamic countries — Social conditions
I. Title   II. Series
301'.09'7'671   HN768.A8   80-41103
ISBN 0 521 22160 9 hard covers
ISBN 0 521 27407 9 paperback

Contents

Preface

The themes expounded in this book have been gestating for over a quarter of a century, ever since I first visited central Morocco, and my first debt was to those of its inhabitants who tolerated my intrusion. The central ideas are plainly stolen from four great thinkers — Ibn Khaldun, David Hume, Robert Montagne, and Edward Evans-Pritchard. The stream that started in the central High Atlas with fieldwork experience was fed, over the years, by many others — notably by systematic attention to the work of other ethnographers working in the Muslim world. Much of that work was only being produced during that period, and my next debt is to all those anthropologists who shared their ideas and data with me, very often prior to publication. (My attention to historical work was less systematic, as no doubt will be evident to readers.) During much of this period, I took part in running a seminar on the sociology of Islam. Obviously I am indebted to all those who contributed to it with papers or in discussion — often, I imagine, without being fully aware of my debt. They are too numerous for exhaustive listing. Of those who helped in running the seminar, I should single out Michael Gilsenan and Jean-Claude Vatin for special gratitude. North Africans (or persons of North African background) from whose ideas, information or impressions I have benefited are too numerous to list, but they include Germaine Ayache, Alya Baffoun, Genevieve Bedoucha-Albergoni, Lakhdar Brahimi, Fanny Colonna, Jeanne Favret, Ahmed Guessous, Ahmed Guezmir, Abdallah Hammoudi, Youssef Hazmaoui, Marie-Aimée Helie-Lucas, Elbaki Hermassi, Abdelkader Khatibi, Mouhsine Mbarek, Ali Merad, Fatima Mernissi, Taoufik Monastiri, Paul Pascon, Moncer Rouissi, Mohamed Saadani, Paul Sebag, Slimane and Souad Shikh, Noureddine Sraieb, Frej Stambouli, Larbi Talha, Lucette Valensi, and Abdelkader Zghal. Over the years, many secretaries have patiently and generously helped me with the MSS: Mrs E. Llewellyn, Miss K. Phillips, Mrs H. Frankiss, Miss Helen Wheeler, Mrs Thelma O'Brien, Miss Margaret Kosowicz and Mrs Gay Woolven. The final preparation of the main introductory essay of the volume was only possible thanks to the support of the Centre de Recherches et d'Études sur les Sociétés Méditerranéennes in Aix-en-Provence, and my thanks are due to its Director, Maurice Flory, and to all its staff. Mrs Elizabeth Wetton and Ian Jarvie

Preface

guided the MSS to acceptable form with admirable patience, and Ian also supplied the admirable indexes. I am much indebted to Jack Goody for encouragement, as Editor of this series. My wife Susan helped me over the years in more ways than I can say. My son David has read the synoptic first chapter in its penultimate draft and pointed out weaknesses in the argument which I have done my best to camouflage. Katie Platt has been most helpful in checking references. All the people listed or indicated must bear some of the blame for this book appearing at all, but not for any of its specific assertions.

Froxfield,   Ernest Gellner
December 1979

Acknowledgements

The author thanks the editors of the following periodicals, in which some of the material collected in this volume has previously appeared: Chapter 1: not previously published; an earlier and very much shorter version appeared in *Annales Marocaines de Sociologie*, 1968, pp. 5–14, and in *Philosophical Forum*, vol. 2, 1970, pp. 234–44. Chapter 2 was originally presented in Tunis in 1974 at a conference marking the fortieth anniversary of the Neo-Destour Party, and was published in the *Cahiers du C.E.R.E.S.*, Tunis, and in *Government and Opposition*, vol. 10, 1975, pp. 203–18. Chapter 3: *Daedalus*, vol. 102, 1973, pp. 191–206. Chapter 4: in Nikki R. Keddie, ed., *Scholars, Saints and Sufis*, Berkeley and Los Angeles, University of California Press, 1972, pp. 307–26. Chapter 5: *Archives de Sociologie des Religions*, no. 15, 1963, pp. 71–86. Chapter 6: *Government and Opposition*, vol. 9, 1974, pp. 277–310. Chapter 7: *Middle Eastern Studies*, vol. 14, 1978, pp. 127–30. Chapter 8: *Daedalus*, vol. 105, 1976, pp. 137–50. Chapter 9: *European Journal of Sociology*, vol. 3, 1962, pp. 297–311. Chapter 10: *Times Literary Supplement*, no. 3857, 13 February 1976, p. 164. Chapter 11: *Times Literary Supplement*, no. 3936, 19 August 1977, p. 1011. Chapter 12: *Middle Eastern Studies*, vol. 15, 1979, pp. 106–13.

Unless otherwise stated, all quotations have been translated by Ernest Gellner. References in previously published material to contemporary events have been allowed to stand. The epigraph quotations from Ibn Khaldun are drawn from the F. Rosenthal translation.

Leadership exists only through superiority, and superiority only through group feeling.

Only tribes held together by group feeling can live in the desert.

... inhabitants of cities can have a 'house' [i.e. kin group] only in a metaphorical sense. The assumption that they possess one is a specious claim ...

... while the Bedouin need the cities for the necessities of life, the urban population need the Bedouin [only] for conveniences and luxuries. Thus, as long as they live in the desert and have not acquired royal authority and control of the cities, the Bedouin need the townsmen ...

Mutual aggression in the cities is averted ... by government ... the masses are thus prevented ... from mutual injustice, save such as comes from the ruler himself.

... dynasty and government serve as the world's greatest market-place ... if the ruler holds on to property and revenue ... business slumps and commercial profits decline ... the dynasty ... suffers ... because under these circumstances the property of the ruler decreases ...

Ibn Khaldun

... the principles of religion have a kind of flux and reflux ... and ... men have a natural tendency to rise from idolatry to theism, and to sink again from theism to idolatry.

... superstition is favourable to priestly power, and enthusiasm ... more contrary to it, than sound reason and philosophy ...

David Hume

1

Flux and reflux in the faith of men

Islam is the blueprint of a social order. It holds that a set of rules exists, eternal, divinely ordained, and independent of the will of men, which defines the proper ordering of society. This model is available in writing; it is equally and symmetrically available to all literate men, and to all those willing to heed literate men. These rules are to be implemented throughout social life.

Thus there is in principle no call or justification for an internal separation of society into two parts, of which one would be closer to the deity than the other. Such a segregation would contradict both the symmetry or equality of access, and the requirement of pervasive implementation of the rules. The rules of the faith are there for all, and not just or specially for a subclass of religious specialists—virtuosos. In principle, the Muslim, if endowed with pious learning, is self-sufficient or at any rate not dependent on other men, or consecrated specialists. (If not learned, he is in a loose way dependent on those who are, which is very important.) Thus officially, Islam has no clergy and no church organisation, though it needs scholars, and church and community are co-extensive. As Tocqueville put it,

Islam is the religion which has most completely confounded and intermixed the two powers . . . so that all the acts of civil and political life are regulated more or less by religious law.[1]

Tocqueville also comments on the significant identity of training for religious and other learning, and the absence of priesthood. In traditional Islam, no distinction is made between lawyer and canon lawyer, and the roles of theologian and lawyer are conflated. Expertise on proper social arrangements, and on matters pertaining to God, are one and the same thing.

Judaism and Christianity are also blueprints of a social order, but rather less so than Islam. Christianity, from its inception, contained an open recommendation to give unto Caesar that which is Caesar's. A faith which begins, and for some time remains, without political power, cannot but accommodate itself to a political order which is not, or is not yet, under its control. Within Islam, the Shi'ite sectarian doctrine also contains devices for such accommodation, on a

1

temporary basis — not so much for giving Caesar that which is his as for telling him what he wishes to hear, whilst keeping one's own counsel. This, and a martyrdom foundation-myth, brings Shi'ism, the second-largest sect within Islam, closer to Christianity. But rapid success deprived mainstream Sunni Islam of martyrdom, and left it ambivalent *vis-à-vis* esotericism. Esotericism can be pushed to an extreme amongst sectarians, as by the Druze, where the inner doctrine is so esoteric that no one, including its adherents, appears to know exactly what it is.[2]

Christianity, which initially flourished among the politically disinherited, did not then presume to *be* Caesar. A kind of potential for political modesty has stayed with it ever since those humble beginnings. Theocratic aspirations only appear intermittently; canon law significantly means religious ordinances as distinct from secular ones, unlike the Muslim *kanun*. The most prolonged effort in the direction of theocracy was perhaps Byzantine Caesaro-Papism, which, significantly, was one of the models available to Islam.

But the initial success of Islam was so rapid that it had no need to give anything unto Caesar. The theocratic potential of Judaism has also remained muted, in comparison with Islam: though initially a charter of the conquest of the Promised Land, the achievement of the promise was neither rapid nor stable nor permanent. The conditions of the diaspora obviously did not favour aspirations to replace Caesar. (In modern Israel, the legal institutions of the Ottoman autonomous community, the 'millet' system,[3] are kept alive by parliamentary stalemate. Coalitions, in need of parliamentary support, pay the price and grant the religious interest a perpetuation of the *status quo*. Thus, ironically, thanks to proportional representation, Israel continues to be, jointly with the Lebanon, a surviving fragment of the Ottoman society.)

Two conditions favour this greater social pervasiveness of Islam: its rapid and early political success, and the idea that the divine message is complete and final. The first inhibits the handing over of some sphere of life to non-religious authority; the second makes it that much harder to offer rival versions of the blueprint. The scheme *is* to be implemented, and no new schemes are to be countenanced. Dr Michael Cook has also shown[4] how the relatively mundane and secular Jewish preoccupation with the regulation of social life, based on human legal wisdom rather than on divine authority, when fused with the God-centred, unificatory theology-mindedness of Christianity, produced the characteristically Muslim divinely sanctioned and God-centred legalism.

This social pervasiveness makes Islam specially interesting to the sociologist of religion. There are other good reasons. A European background has tended to influence the choice of questions about the social role of religion. These issues appear in a new light when looked at from a Muslim viewpoint.

Two dominant sociological questions were inspired by Christianity, more so than by other faiths. Each concerns its role, either in the rise or in the fall of a civilisation. The first question was: did Christianity contribute to the fall of the

Roman Empire? The second was: did a special segment of Christianity play a key role in the emergence of modern industrial civilisation? The first of these questions is now somewhat dated. Time was when men found this question central and compelling: their obsession was the preservation of an old civilisation, not the attainment of a new affluence. But the demise of the Roman Empire is no longer a source of current sorrow, and the attribution of blame for that disaster is not a hotly debated issue amongst us. It was not always so. St Augustine was eager to rebut any such charge. More surprisingly, the question was revived in the Augustan age; Gibbon and Hume saw the relationship of religion and civilisation in these terms, and their conclusion was not the same as St Augustine's. Later still, Sir James Frazer's *Golden Bough* contains, implicitly or explicitly, at least three theories of religion.[5] Most prominent, and as it were official, is his evolutionist, three-stage theory of a progression from magic through religion to science. This might be described as a development in the manner of seeking the connection between things, first in inherent plausibility ('sympathetic magic'), then in the caprice of spirits, whose wilfulness was better fitted to explain irregularities, and finally in scientific experiment. The manifest weakness of the theory is its intellectualism – the assumption that at the heart of religion there is a *theory* of causation, and that men shift from one style of thought to another in consequence both of cumulative and purely cognitive failures of the earlier style. Frazer's method was not so much, as later anthropologists supposed, to ask himself what he himself would think, were he primitive man; rather he asked, given the account of the human mind found in Hume's *Treatise of Human Nature*,[6] how did primitive man reach the conclusions which are reported by observers?

But when Frazer thinks of the moral and social impact of religion, he talks quite differently, and he then becomes the last of the Augustans and returns to their question:

The religion of the Great Mother ... was only one of a multitude of similar Oriental faiths which in the later days of paganism spread over the Roman Empire, and by saturating the European people with alien ideals of life gradually undermined the whole fabric of ancient civilisation. Greek and Roman society ... set the safety of the Commonwealth, as the supreme aim of conduct, above the safety of the individual whether in this world or in a world to come. All this was changed by the spread of Oriental religions, which inculcated the communion of the soul with God and its eternal salvation as the only objects worth living for ... The inevitable result of this selfish and immoral doctrine was to withdraw the devotee more and more from the public service ...

The third theory to be found in his work was one he certainly did not consciously espouse, but one which is implicit in his elegant arrangement of his material and which was subsequently exploited by others, in a spirit quite alien to his own: a kind of C.G. Jung/T.S. Eliot romp amongst the archetypal symbols dredged up from the unconscious of a wide variety of cultures:

3

To another work of anthropology I am indebted in general, one which has influenced one generation profoundly . . . *The Golden Bough* . . . especially the two volumes *Adonis, Attis, Osiris*. Anyone . . . acquainted with these works will immediately recognise in the poem certain references . . .[7]

Thus only one of the three theories in Frazer perpetuates the eighteenth-century vision and its values: an admiration for the civic and social virtues of classical religion, contrasted with the egotistic concern with other-worldly salvation which replaced it. But, in these terms, the issue is no longer alive. Those who continue to repudiate Christianity no longer sigh for the Roman Empire.

The other great sociological issue, by contrast, is very much alive. The role of ideology, religious or other, in the genesis of the modern world and of its industrial or bureaucratic institutions, is still of burning interest and at the very centre of our concern.

Each of these two questions acquires quite a different appearance when looked at from the viewpoint of Islam. Islam, unlike Christianity, was not born *within* an empire which subsequently went into a decline, a decline which a hostile observer could blame on the faith; nor did it become a kind of politically disembodied receiver of the pre-existent world empire which had collapsed, and which it could perpetuate by ecclesiastical organisation at a time when the political one was beyond recall. On the contrary, it was born *outside* two empires, one of which it promptly overran, and the second of which it conquered in the end. It was *the* basis, first of an oecumenical empire, and then of a number of others which closely identified with the faith and found their legitimation in it. This makes the question of religion as the social cement of civilisations appear in quite a different light, when considered from a Muslim viewpoint. It had not corroded an earlier traditional civilisation, nor lived on as its ghost. It *made* its own empire and civilisation.

The question concerning the origins of the modern industrial world also looks quite different from a Muslim viewpoint. Traditional Muslim civilisation was not, like Christendom, the womb of the modern industrial world. So it cannot claim the credit or blame for it as a totality, nor can the achievement be connected with any sectarian segment within it. It was the partial victim, and not the progenitor, of the modern world. But it is a rather distinctive victim.

Four major literate world civilisations were in existence at the end of the Middle Ages. Of these, it seems that Islam alone may maintain its pre-industrial faith in the modern world. The faith of the Christian world has been reinterpreted and adjusted out of all recognition. (Modernist Christian theology, with its elusive content, asymptotically approaching zero, constitutes by far the best evidence for the secularisation thesis, far more so than any overt 'rationalism'.) Confucianism is repudiated in its homeland, however much it may be possible to trace the survival of its spirit. Hinduism survives as a folk-religion, neither endorsed nor discouraged by the elite of its land. Only Islam survives as a serious faith pervading both a folk and a Great Tradition. Its Great Tradition is

4

modernisable; and the operation can be presented, not as an innovation or concession to outsiders, but rather as the continuation and completion of an old dialogue within Islam between the orthodox centre and deviant error, of the old struggle between knowledge and ignorance, political order and anarchy, civilisation and barbarism, town and tribe, Holy Law and mere human custom, a unique deity and usurper middlemen of the sacred, to cite the polarities whose linked opposition, sometimes dormant, sometimes virulent, seems perennially latent in Islam.

Thus its traditional internal differentiation into the folk and scholarly variants was actually helpful in effecting adjustment. The folk variant can be disavowed, blamed for cultural backwardness, or associated with the political machinations of colonial oppressors, whilst the 'purer' variant can be identified all at once both with pristine origins and with a revived, glorious, modern future. The old Great Tradition became the folk version under modern conditions, which also made that folk far more numerous and far more weighty in the state. The old Great Tradition, which is now its natural idiom, helps that folk to define itself against foreigners, against westernised rulers, and against its own disavowed, 'backward' rustic past. Thus in Islam, and only in Islam, purification/modernisation on the one hand, and the re-affirmation of a putative old *local* identity on the other, can be done in one and the same language and set of symbols. The old folk version, once a shadow of the central tradition, now becomes a repudiated scapegoat, blamed for retardation and foreign domination. Hence, though not the source of modernity, Islam may yet turn out to be its beneficiary. The fact that its central, official, 'pure' variant was egalitarian and scholarly, whilst hierarchy and ecstasy pertained to its expendable, eventually disavowed, peripheral forms, greatly aids its adaptation to the modern world. In an age of aspiration to universal literacy, the open class of scholars can expand towards embracing the entire community, and thus the 'protestant' ideal of equal access for all believers can be implemented. Modern egalitarianism is satisfied. Whilst European protestantism merely prepared the ground for nationalism by furthering literacy, the reawakened Muslim potential for egalitarian scripturalism can actually *fuse* with nationalism, so that one can hardly tell which one of the two is of most benefit to the other. By contrast, any attempts, for instance, to purify and modernise Hinduism must come up against the inegalitarian, hereditary and hierarchical element at its core, which cannot easily be accommodated under modern conditions.[8]

Max Weber is the greatest of the sociologists associated with the question of the affinity of faith and modern socio-economic organisation. He did not leave us a general sociology of Islam, parallel to his studies of India, China or ancient Judaism,[9] but in general he favoured the view that the *institutional* preconditions of modern capitalism were not restricted to the West, but that it was the ideological element which provides the crucial *differentia*, that extra spark which, in conjunction with the required structural preconditions, explains the miracle.

One may wonder whether indeed the Muslim case supports such a view: the *differentiae* of Islam seem institutional rather than ideological. Ideological parallels to Christianity can be found, but they operate in a contrasted institutional milieu. Whether or not he himself would have extended this general explanatory strategy to Islam, if one does try to do so, it does not seem to fit neatly. But the stability, or stagnation, whichever way one wishes to describe it, of the Muslim world, constitutes an interesting check on the theories of the origins of capitalism. Towns, trade, and an urban bourgeoisie are all highly prominent in Muslim society. Themes can be discerned in the ideology of urban trading groups which are at the very least reminiscent of those credited with a crucial role in the economic development of the West, even if a puritan sense of sin seems less well developed. The difference would seem to be less in the absence of ideological elements than in the particular balance of power which existed between the various institutions in that society. Did Muslim theology also contain that warrant for obsessional guilt and self-examination which could impel men to compulsive and 'rational' accumulation which would, in favourable circumstances, produce the modern industrial world? The experts seem to disagree. J.-P. Charnay claims:

the idea of original sin has been expunged from Islam . . . the final Revelation . . . has not condemned human nature as such . . . the absence of original sin accentuates the notion of individual responsibility . . .[10]

By contrast, Marshall G.S. Hodgson writes:

In the Qur'an it was early made clear that human beings face a fundamental moral choice. They cannot hover half way . . . they may choose to stand in awe of their Creator and accept His moral demands . . . Or human beings may . . . turn away from their Creator . . . [But] a human being cannot choose to be pure at will . . . he . . . can achieve moral purity only by the power of God. The fundamental choice . . . appears . . . overwhelmingly crucial . . . All else in the moral life will follow from this choice.

. . . This fact would be made inescapably manifest in a final cosmic catastrophe, when . . . all human beings would be visibly judged by God Himself . . .

Accordingly, Muhammed insisted on the moral responsibility of human beings. Life was no matter of play, it called for sober alertness; men dare not relax, secure in their wealth . . . all these things would avail nothing at the Judgment . . . humans must live in constant fear and awe of God, before whom they were accountable for every least deed.[11]

This state of mind — total responsibility for the consequences of a basic original choice which was yet not within one's own unaided power, and hence justified an anxiety which could never be adequately allayed by any mundane evidence — seems recognisably similar to the fashionable theory which turns the first great economic accumulation into a by-product of an unavailing attempt to reassure oneself that one's primal 'choice' has been well made. On this account, Muslim burghers too should have felt impelled to accumulate in an endless effort to persuade themselves that they were the Elect of God. Admittedly, this eloquent passage comes from the pen of an author who candidly tells one a few pages earlier that he himself is a convinced Christian and Quaker. One may well wonder whether this rather Augustinian/Kierkegaardian picture really is closer to the veritable Muslim state of mind than Charnay's more relaxed sketch of a 'morale actuelle, très humaniste'.

I like to imagine what would have happened had the Arabs won at Poitiers and gone on to conquer and Islamise Europe. No doubt we should all be admiring Ibn Weber's *The Kharejite Ethic and the Spirit of Capitalism* which would conclusively demonstrate how the modern rational spirit and its expression in business and bureaucratic organisation could only have arisen in consequence of the sixteenth-century neo-Kharejite puritanism in northern Europe. In particular, the work would demonstrate how modern economic and organisational rationality could never have arisen had Europe stayed Christian, given the inveterate proclivity of that faith to a baroque, manipulative, patronage-ridden, quasi-animistic and disorderly vision of the world. A faith so given to seeing the cosmic order as bribable by pious works and donations could never have taught its adherents to rely on faith alone and to produce and accumulate in an orderly, systematic, and unwavering manner. Would they not always have blown their profits in purchasing tickets to eternal bliss, rather than going on to accumulate more and more?

A Muslim Europe would also have saved Hegel from the need to indulge in most painfully tortuous arguments in order to explain how an earlier faith, Christianity, nevertheless is more final and absolute than a chronologically later one, namely Islam. (In fact he did it by invoking the fact that Europe was only Christianised at the time of Charlemagne, who is at least suitably posterior to Muhammed.) Had Islam, the later and by some plausible criteria *purer* faith, prevailed, no such problem would have arisen for a Muslim Hegel.[12] There would have been no embarrassing boob in the *welthistorischer* timetable. Altogether, from the viewpoint of an elegant philosophy of history, which sees the story of mankind as a sustained build-up towards *our* condition, it would have been *far* more satisfactory if the Arabs had won. By various obvious criteria – universalism, scripturalism, spiritual egalitarianism, the extension of full participation in the sacred community not to one, or some, but to *all*, and the rational systematisation of social life – Islam is, of the three great Western monotheisms, the one closest to modernity.

David Hume and Islam

The best approach to the social role of Islam is probably through the religious sociology of David Hume, notwithstanding the fact that he is not normally considered an Islamicist. His *Natural History of Religion*[13] is sometimes acclaimed as the first scientific study of the place of religion in society. It remains one of the best, perhaps the best. But the central theory found in that splendid book, and one which is quite specially relevant to Islam, seems to have been seldom noticed. For instance, the late Sir Edward Evans-Pritchard's *Theories of Primitive Religion*[14] mentions Hume and comments on some of his views, but omits to note what is most distinctive and important in Hume's sociology of religion. He only reports Hume's view concerning the historical priority of polytheism and idolatry. Philosophers do no better than anthropologists: a reader of Bernard Williams[15] might likewise easily conclude that Hume espoused and concentrated on a superficial unilinealism, which in fact he quite possibly did not even hold, but would learn little or nothing of the far more central, interesting and profound oscillation theory which he certainly *did* hold, which preoccupied him, and which is central to his argument.

The attribution of unilinealism to Hume is based on an opening remark of Hume which can just as well be interpreted as a simple assertion of *fact* rather than as a *theory*. It does indeed so happen that in the past two millenia mankind has shifted from polytheism to monotheism, on balance. But is that a law or a trend, which could justify extrapolation? Later in the book, Hume does tell us what he considers the real law-like trend to be.

The only writer who seems to have noticed this doctrine is Frank E. Manuel, but he thinks little of it. In *The Eighteenth Century Confronts the Gods*,[16] he writes:

Hume . . . could not hold fast to any theory of progressive evolution. Despite Turgot's earnest attempts to convert him, he always remained outside the ranks of . . . believers . . . in progress . . . the flux and reflux between polytheism and theism is a blunt denial of the idea of progress. Here Hume appears a sceptical cyclical theorist in the classical tradition.

Manuel considers the oscillation theory 'one of the weakest parts of the essay'. He blames Hume for failing to hold fast to the very doctrine with which Evans-Pritchard and Williams erroneously credit him. Manuel seems to grade people in terms of whether they contribute or at least adhere to the idea of progress, an idea which was emerging at the end of the eighteenth century and which was destined to dominate the nineteenth. The interest of Hume's views here hinges precisely on his refusal to adopt such a view.

Hume does indeed begin his discussion with the observation which misled Evans-Pritchard and Williams:

Behold then the clear testimony of history. The farther we mount up into antiquity, the more we do find mankind plunged into polytheism. No marks, no symptoms of any more perfect religion. The most ancient records of the human race still present us that system as the popular and established creed.

The first idea he puts forward in attempting to explain this is the difficulty of abstraction, and the tendency of the crude mind to stay close to the earthy:

the ignorant multitude must first entertain some grovelling and familiar notion

8

of superior powers, before they stretch their conception to that perfect Being, who bestowed order on the whole frame of nature.

But this evolutionist and intellectualist schema — from crude pluralism to abstract, rational, elevated monism — is soon and rightly (or regrettably, in Manuel's opinion) abandoned. It has a certain congruence with Hume's epistemology, though not with his moral psychology. It fits in well with his theory of knowledge, given its vision of the human mind progressing by gradual abstraction from sensation to abstraction, which is but a pale echo of sensation. But it conflicts with his view of human motivation, for it seems to imply that the relative success of monotheism is due to its recognition as *rational*. Hume himself apparently did, in fact, hold that monotheism, supported by the argument from design, was indeed more rational than polytheism; but he clearly does *not* suppose that the historic swings from polytheism to monotheism were due to a popular recognition of the rational superiority of the one view over the other. Not only reason, but popular religion too, is a slave of our passions, and somewhat more so (and in a different sense). The swing to monotheism, if and when it occurs, is likewise due to quite other and emotional factors. Its congruence with reason, if it obtains, is coincidental.

But, even more interestingly, Hume comes to abandon the idea of progress, of continuous unilineal change in one direction, and he replaces it by a far more intriguing and important *oscillation* theory. Men do indeed change from polytheism to monotheism, but not for rational reasons; moreover they also change *back again*, and this also from non-rational motives. *This* is the really valuable theory which is to be found in Hume. He refers to this interesting and distinctive theory as the 'flux and reflux' of polytheism and theism.

It is remarkable that the principles of religion have a kind of flux and reflux in the human mind, and that men have a natural tendency to rise from idolatry to theism, and to sink again from theism to idolatry.

This oscillation of opinion, as one might expect, has nothing to do with reason; it has to do with the politics of fear, uncertainty, deference and hierarchy. This is the heart of Hume's theory of religion.

The swing from religious pluralism to monism is activated by a kind of competitive sycophancy:

in an idolatrous nation ... though men admit the existence of several limited deities, yet may there be some one God, whom, in a particular manner, they make the object of their worship and adoration ... his votaries will endeavour, by every art, to insinuate themselves into his favour; and supposing him to be pleased, like themselves, with praise and flattery, there is no exaggeration, which will be spared in their addresses to him. In proportion as men's fears or distresses become more urgent, they still invent new strains of adulation; and even he who outdoes his predecessor in swelling up the titles of his divinity, is sure to be outdone by his successor in newer and more pompous epithets of praise. Thus they proceed; till at last they arrive at infinity itself, beyond which there is no farther progress: And it is well, if, on striving to get farther, and to represent a magnificent simplicity, they run not into inexplicable mystery . . .

Clear examples are provided of this apotheosis:

Thus the deity, whom the vulgar Jews conceived only as the God of Abraham, Isaac and Jacob, became their Jehovah and Creator of the world.

Or again:

Who can express the perfections of the Almighty? say the Mahometans. Even the noblest of his works, if compared to him, are but dust and rubbish. How much more must human conception fall short of his infinite perfections?

But this perfect, hidden, inaccessible deity, propelled beyond the reach of our ideas by our competitive sycophancy, is too distant and too inaccessible.

At this point, a contrary psychological principle comes into play. This is the principle of seeking the protection of intermediaries and middlemen when approaching the mighty and the awe-inspiring. The use of such an accredited mediator itself indicates proper respect and reverence and thus enhances the prospect of a favourable hearing. The deity itself of course then also needs such mediators, and this strengthens their position in turn. This impels the pendulum to swing in the opposite direction:

elevating their deities to the utmost bounds of perfection, [they] at last beget the attributes of unity and infinity, simplicity and spirituality. Such refined ideas, being somewhat disproportioned to vulgar comprehension, remain not long in their original purity; but require to be supported by the notion of inferior mediators or subordinate agents, which interpose between mankind and their supreme deity. These demi-gods or middle beings, partaking of human nature, and being more familiar to us, become the chief objects of devotion, and gradually recall that idolatry, which had been formerly banished by the ardent prayers and panegyrics of timorous and indigent mortals.

But the pendulum is bound to swing once again:

as these idolatrous religions fall every day into grosser and more vulgar conceptions, they at last destroy themselves and by the vile representations which they form of their deities, make the tide turn again towards theism. But so great is the propensity, in this alternative revolution of human sentiments, to return back to idolatry, that the utmost precaution is not able effectually to prevent it. And of this, some theists, particularly the Jews and Mohametans, have been sensible; as appears by their banishing all the arts of statuary and painting, and not allowing the representations, even of human figures, to be taken by marble or colours; lest the common infirmity of mankind should thence produce idolatry.

The historical material which inspires Hume's admirable theory is obvious: it is the struggle of Jehovah against the Baalim of Canaan, of the Reformation against Popery,[17] and of Islam with its own pluralistic tendencies. He comments explicitly on the parallelism:

The heroes in paganism correspond exactly to the saints in popery, and holy dervishes in Mohametanism.

This view of the *Drang* towards monotheism has a logic parallel to that eighteenth-century theory of oriental despotism, which explained it simply as a consequence of the sheer longevity of a regime, so that the mere passage of time was eventually due to bring European monarchies into line with Eastern ones. Men indulge in competitive sycophancy towards anyone in power. The longer someone holds power, the more elevated he becomes through the rivalry-in-submission of his subjects, all of them seeking to further their ends by sucking up to him. In the case of a supreme deity, superlatives soon run out, and the object of veneration becomes unique, beyond all comparison, first beyond visualisation, then beyond the reach of even conceptualisation, ineffable and inaccessibly distant.

But then the reverse process sets in. Humble petitioners know their place and dare not approach so awe-inspiring an authority directly. Hence they seek less elevated intermediaries, whether in this world (priests, living saints) or in the other (spirits, deceased saints). These however also require praise if they are to be placated and propitiated, and rival petitioners will compete in both offerings and eulogy — and so the pantheon become re-populated, until some of these secondary objects of reverence become elevated to great heights and appear to rival the supreme one. Then the stage is set once again for the contrary swing.

There are two notable weaknesses in Hume's theory: it is profoundly psychologistic, locating the mechanism of the pendulum-swing in the human heart, and rather neglecting the society within which the changes occur; and it also contains a profound contradiction. Take the contradiction first.

Hume was a Protestant Scot. He was also a man of the Enlightenment. There is no law against being either of these two estimable things. But there is a law, namely the Principle of Non-contradiction, which would seem to militate against being both of them at the same time. The Protestant observes that the heroes in paganism correspond 'exactly' to the saints in popery:

The place of Hercules, Theseus, Hector, Romulus, is now supplied by Dominic, Francis, Anthony and Benedict.
The Virgin Mary, ere checked by the reformation, had proceeded, from being merely a good woman, to usurp many of the attributes of the Almighty . . .

This is good anti-popish stuff, and the central current of argument which runs through it is the underlying identity of popery and paganism. This identification is in any case implied by Hume's oscillation theory. Popery is simply the historically specific form, in which the more exclusively unitarian worship of Jehovah slid back once again into pagan idolatry. This is indeed the standard Protestant diagnosis of Catholicism, at any rate in pre-oecumenical days. The diagnosis is independent of any value-judgement attached to it. Nietzsche abused Luther and the Reformation precisely because he saw it as such a backlash, as a manifestation of German, and English, *ressentiment* against the rebirth of noble Roman values in the Renaissance. He shared the diagnosis though he inverted the assessment.

But literally in adjoining sentences in Hume's work, we also find the eighteenth-century Augustan speaking, with his positive admiration of classical paganism and his contempt for the relatively unitarian Christianity which replaced it. Notwithstanding the fact that the heroes of antiquity are said to correspond exactly to the saints in popery, the antithesis between the two is set out as follows:

Instead of the destruction of monsters, the subduing of tyrants, the defence of our native country; whippings and fastings, cowardice and humility, abject submission and slavish obedience, are becoming the means of obtaining celestial honours among mankind.

Or again:

Brasidas seized a mouse, and being bit by it, let it go. *There is nothing so contemptible, said he, but what may be safe, if it has but courage to defend itself.* Bellarmine humbly and patiently allowed the fleas and other odious vermin to prey upon him. *We shall have heaven, said he, to reward us for our suffering: But these poor creatures have nothing but the enjoyment of the present life.* Such difference is there between the maxims of a Greek hero and a Catholic saint.

The contrast is clear. Classical paganism is civic and this-worldly. Christianity, and in particular Catholicism, is doubly harmful, encouraging selfish *individual* concern with welfare in *another* world. Much later, Sir James Frazer, when not taken up with his official, intellectualist theory of religion, which virtually equates it with a mistaken theory of causation, spoke in similar vein:

The saint and the recluse, disdainful of earth and rapt in ecstatic contemplation of heaven, became in popular opinion the highest ideal of humanity, displacing the old ideal of the patriot and hero . . . In their anxiety to save their souls and the souls of others, they were content to leave the material world . . . to perish . . . The close of the Middle Ages marked the return of Europe to native ideals . . . to romantic views of the world . . . The tide of Oriental invasion had turned at last. It is ebbing still.[18]

The contradiction between the two juxtaposed views in Hume is blatant. The major premiss is: classical paganism is admirable. The minor premiss is: Catholicism is a thinly camouflaged version of classical paganism. An elementary inference then inevitably leads to the conclusion: Catholicism is a thinly camouflaged version of something admirable . . .

But this is, of course, just the conclusion which Hume never reaches. The minor premiss is asserted in contemptuous derision, not in admiration. Perhaps the contradiction could be avoided if the derision were focused on the act of camouflage, rather than at the underlying substance. The *substrate* he would then continue to hold up to admiration — and only the lack of candour would be spurned. Such a view might indeed be consistent, but it is not Hume's. He clearly spurns the Catholic version of religious pluralism as such, and not simply because it is endowed with a thin unitarian veneer. He also on occasion has his reservations about pluralism in general:

Polytheism or idolatrous worship, being founded entirely in vulgar traditions, is liable to this great inconvenience, that any practice or opinion, however barbarous or corrupted, may be authorised by it . . .

The later critic of Christianity, Nietzsche, was more perceptive and consistent than Hume, and observed that there was something at least to be said for this religion, if only it became sufficiently corrupted by a revival of pagan principles:

in the Renaissance there was a brilliant-sinister reawakening of the classical ideal, of the noble style of evaluating things; Rome itself stirred like an awakened apparent corpse under the weight of the new, superimposed Judaised Rome, which had the aspect of an oecumenical synagogue and was called 'church . . .'[19]

Had Hume, in some such words, endorsed at least Renaissance Catholicism, in recognition of its mundane classicism, his position would have been morally consistent. But it is obvious that his revulsion for vulgar pluralist religion is at least as deep as his repudiation of intolerant other-worldly religious monism. A fastidious, intellectually puritan unitarian appears to cohabit, within his breast, with a tolerant pluralist in morals and politics. The Unitarians believe, as A.N. Whitehead pointed out, that there is at most one God.

The inconsistency and tension, however, is not merely one of attitude, of ambivalence in approval and rejection: it spills over into downright contradiction in his very interesting political sociology of religion.

The tolerating spirit of idolaters, both in ancient and in modern times, is very obvious to anyone . . . When the oracle of Delphi was asked, what rites or worship was most acceptable to the gods? Those which are legally established in each city, replied the oracle.
. . . The Romans commonly adopted the gods of the conquered people; and never disputed the attributes of those local and national deities, in whose territory they resided.

The contrast is unmistakable:

The intolerance of almost all religions, which have maintained the unity of God, is as remarkable as the contrary principle of the polytheists. The implacable narrow spirit of the Jews is well known. Mahometanism set out with still more bloody principles . . .

Though Hume is clear that *intellectual* excellence is on the side of the monist, tolerance as well as civic virtue would seem to reside with the pluralists. But a contradiction creeps in:

if, among Christians, the English and the Dutch have embraced the principles of toleration, this singularity has proceeded from the steady resolution of the civil magistrate, in opposition to the continued efforts of priests and bigots.

13

In other words, Hume notes that on his general theory, the English and the Dutch, being at least in their majority Protestants, and hence closer to monism, ought to be less, not more tolerant. As this is not so, the 'singularity' is explained by invoking the steady resolution of the civil magistrate. But this won't do. It would be a curious history of sixteenth- and seventeenth-century England which gave all the credit for the emergence of toleration to the 'civil magistrate'. Moreover, Hume himself is quite clear about this. In a fascinating essay, distinct from the *Natural History*, and entitled 'Of Superstition and Enthusiasm',[20] he distinguishes between these two religious extremes, and has much of interest to say about them, and what he says there is also echoed in his *History of England.*[21]

By superstition he means, roughly, priest-ridden pluralism; and by enthusiasm, monistic religious zeal. His three reflections or observations concerning this contrast deserve to be quoted:

... superstition is favourable to priestly power, and enthusiasm not less, or rather more contrary to it, than sound reason and philosophy.

... religions which partake of enthusiasm are, on their first rise, more furious and violent than those which partake of superstition; but in a little time become more gentle and moderate.

... superstition is an enemy to civil liberty, and enthusiasm a friend to it.

The second of these propositions anticipates the 'routinisation of charisma', though he considers this process specially characteristic of monistic faiths, in which I suspect he is right. Weber's routinisation formula does not make this distinction, and this is I think an error. In pluralistic religion, charisma is *born* routinised, so to speak, and does not *decline* into such a condition. Routinisation is more characteristic of *our* unitarian world.

The third idea is also relevant at this point: far from invoking the 'civil magistrate' to explain the emergence of English and Dutch toleration, it notes that a certain religious style itself *directly* favours toleration. (*Enthusiasm* clearly covers the unitarian and scripturalist zeal engendered by the Reformation.)

What follows from all this is of course that Hume's initial monist/pluralist schema is too simple. No generalisation about the preconditions of civic liberty can be formulated in terms of this one contrast *alone*. It would follow from that schema that monists, and scripturalist ones at that, would always be hostile to toleration (which indeed they sometimes are); and that pluralists, even when wearing a thin veneer of monism, should be favourable to civic virtue — which in fact cannot always be claimed for them. Hume rightly repudiates both these consequences for modern Europe. Unitarianism generates liberty under special conditions which obtained in parts of north-east Europe in early modern times, and spiritual pluralism often opposed it.

But one ought not simply to reject the initial schema or the oscillation theory articulated in terms of it. It only needs to be refined and elaborated. One needs to know, for instance, whether the pluralist 'priests' in the society are united in one all-embracing hierarchy, as they were in Christendom, or fragmented into many small and rival organisations, as they were in the Muslim religious orders or saintly lineages; one needs to know just why some classes of people are specially susceptible to that religious 'enthusiasm' which is so strongly hostile to priestly power, and indeed what categories of people are generally attracted to this attitude; and having identified that class, we may well ask who its enemies are and whom it has cause to fear. Do the unitarians have the motive (that of being in a minority held to be heretical by the majority) to stand up for liberty? Do they have the elbow-room to do so?

Is this group frightened, above all, of a strong central state, which in alliance with a monopolistic corporation of priests, would deprive it of its religious freedom? Or is it far more frightened of violent, tribally organised, marauding rural ruffians, who themselves normally look up to some of the freelance, and quite disunited, priests for leadership — and does it in that case look to the central power for protection from those tribesmen, whilst the central power in turn defers to this 'enthusiast' clerkly class as a moral authority, or expects it to provide and disseminate its own legitimation? Is the moral authority of this class and of its unitarian scripturalism the only check on government — and one which, if some of its members ally themselves with tribes, can threaten central authority and effect a turnover in personnel? Perhaps in such conditions, the enthusiasts are not so tolerant after all, and fulfil Hume's initial pessimistic expectation of the comportment of unitarianism — whereas they may well be champions of toleration under the alternative situation, when they only have the state and priests, not tribesmen, to fear.

In other words, an 'enthusiastic' (monistic, puritan, scripturalistic) bourgeoisie may indeed be an enemy of liberty and a friend to the state, when caught between the state and tribesmen; while it may become a friend of liberty when it is weak enough to abandon hopes of imposing its forcible views on others, and yet has nothing other than the state monopoly of religion to fear, when the state has tamed or eliminated both baron and tribesman. It was perhaps this specific constellation which converted European enthusiasts to the value of liberty.[22] Hume, by operating only with the opposition of enthusiasm/superstition, without considering the varying political constellations in which this conflict operates — notably the presence of *other* threats to the enthusiasts, and the amount of their own power relative to other segments of society — cannot get it quite right, and seems to contradict himself.

Thus in his brilliant essay 'Of Superstition and Enthusiasm', David Hume comes very close to formulating a Protestant Ethic theory of the emergence of those distinctive peculiarities which have made parts of north-western Europe the birthplace of modernity, of modern liberal society. Admittedly, he is (rightly) preoccupied more with its political than its economic aspects. What is interesting is that his observations, as they stand, are in blatant conflict with the equally brilliant insights of his *Natural History of Religion*. There, in true Augustan fashion, it is superstition, not enthusiasm (exemplified by the more extreme forms of Protestantism), which is plausibly credited with fostering an admirable classical combination of civic morality and toleration. On the unqualified argument of the longer work, the enthusiasts should have remained the sworn enemies of liberty, as indeed they occasionally were. Hume can only invoke the routinisation of their zeal to explain why they did not persist in being its enemies:

When the first fire of enthusiasm is spent, men naturally, in all fanatical sects, sink into the greatest remissness and coolness in sacred matters; there being no body of men among them endowed with sufficient authority, whose interest is concerned to support the religious spirit; no rites, no ceremonies, no holy observances, which may enter into the common train of life, and preserve the sacred principles from oblivion . . . our sectaries, who were formerly such dangerous bigots, are now become very free reasoners . . .

This won't quite do. It was not just oblivion and remissness, but a deeper continuity, which led the non-conformists to help build the modern world. It was not the *absence* as such of a special 'body of men' amongst them, but on the contrary, the fact that the duties of the special body were shifted to the inner light of all members of the community, which made them what they were and continued to be. It was not the absence of priesthood, but its universalisation, which was significant, as Weber later noted.

On the more plausible Weberian account, it was precisely their persevering zeal, and not oblivion, which eventually turned them into friends of liberty. It was the effectiveness of the inner light which helped make American democracy possible, as Tocqueville noted. But their counterparts in Islam had too much cause to fear the tribes, and were in the main too identified with the central political authority, to endeavour to limit its powers. They might occasionally help rotate its personnel. The enthusiasts with whom Hume was concerned had fewer causes for such fears, especially after the failure of the '45 (an event much closer to the world of Ibn Khaldun than that of Hume, even though it occurred in Hume's own time and country).

These refinements may make sense of the exceptions, the 'singularities', which drove Hume into so contradicting himself. These elaborations will at the same time make his excessively psychological model more sensitive to social diversity. It is interesting to carry out the required elaboration in terms of Islamic material.

Ibn Khaldun

Hume's model was psychologistic. Social factors tend only to be introduced *ad hoc*, when the system runs into difficulties. If we are to try it out in the context of Muslim societies, one may as well begin with the greatest sociologist of Islam – Ibn Khaldun.

One could never accuse Ibn Khaldun of being too psychologistic, of locating the key factors in the individual human heart. Crucial virtues and traits are forged, in his view, not in the psyche of individuals, but in communities and their social environment. Where Hume's sociology leads to the dilemma between *intellectually* meritorious monism on the one hand, and on the other the socially and *morally* meritorious pluralism (which is civic, this-worldly, non-enthusiastic and tolerant), Ibn Khaldun's basic dilemma is more deeply tragic, and also stands far more prominently at the centre of his thought. Hume could shrug his shoulders; he knew that monism was intellectually superior, but he also knew that when people embraced it, they did so for the wrong reasons, so that as far as the intellectual merit of their opinions went, they might just as well be pluralists — especially as pluralism, at least in favourable circumstances, also taught them to resist evil, to fight for their country and for liberty, and to be tolerant of the gods of others. Better civic-spirited idolators than craven unitarians, especially as the distant and hidden single deity was revered for quite the wrong reasons. It was not its elegance as an explanatory notion, and the force of the Argument from Design, which Hume respected, which led men to an exclusive God; it was fear, and the base idea that the powerful can best be placated by sycophancy — and absolute power by absolute sycophancy.

The dilemma faced by Ibn Khaldun's vision was more tragic but equally insoluble. Political, social, civic virtues were in his view fostered, not by religious pluralism as such, but by tribal life. (Tribal life may itself in turn favour religious pluralism, but that is another matter which he did not consider.) The virtues of civilisation and refinement, on the other hand, were fostered by urban life, which, however, was incompatible with civic virtues. You could have communal, civic spirit, or you could have civilisation — but not both. This is the tragic dilemma which is at the very base of social life.

Plato had once said something analogous:

We are to study not only the origins of society, but of a society which enjoys the luxuries of civilisation . . . We shall have to enlarge our state again . . . the territory which was previously sufficient will now be too small . . . we shall need a slice of our neighbour's . . . this means the addition of an army . . .[23]

For Plato, it is civilisation which makes modest self-sufficiency impossible, and hence requires the addition of a special military and governing class to the state for the defence of its inflated needs, and this generates or aggravates the problem of politics. Plato and Ibn Khaldun agree that the ordinary citizens of the civilised city will not normally fight — though for quite different reasons: Plato insists on specialisation and the division of labour — the cobbler to his last — whereas Ibn Khaldun holds urban life with its specialisation to be inherently incompatible with social cohesion and martial spirit. Plato supposes that the precivilised community did not need to fight — it does not covet, and is too poor to arouse the covetousness of others. Ibn Khaldun knows full well that, however poor, the tribesmen are objects of aggression and must fight to survive.

The contrast between the two thinkers is a contrast between their two worlds. The Ancient Greek city was a community, and it was, within its own world, the paradigm of a community. But within Islam the city is *both* the model *and* the antithesis of a community. It offers the preconditions of *piety* and contradicts those of *community*. So how is a community of the Faithful possible at all? It is certainly the antithesis of the *tribal* community, with its real or supposed links of blood and its strong cohesion. This opposition is central for Ibn Khaldun, though these are not his words.

For Plato the price of civilisation is the need to *defend* its own material pre-conditions by force of arms, and from one viewpoint, the *Republic* is a recipe for how best to pay this price — a blueprint for the political and educational arrangements which will ensure internal stability and external defence for the enriched, civilised city. It is designed to show how one can acquire the sheepdogs who will protect the flock from the wolves, without harassing the sheep. As in Marxism, domination is the consequence of a stratification which in turn has economic roots.

Ibn Khaldun is far less of a prescriptive political philosopher, and far more of a positive, descriptive sociologist; even if he does give advice on points of detail, in general he accepts society as he finds it. The political and military ineptitude of the city is simply a datum, whose implications he explores, but for which he does not expect a definitive remedy. He explains how sheepdogs emerge, but gives no recipe for their taming, and barely any even for saving them from quick degeneration.

Bedouin are closer to being good than sedentary people . . . are more disposed to courage than sedentary people . . . the reason for this is that sedentary people have become used to laziness and ease. They are sunk in well-being and luxury. They have entrusted the defence of their property and their lives to the governor and ruler who rules them, and to the militia which has the task of guarding them. They find full assurance of safety in the walls that surround them, and the fortifications which protect them . . . Successive generations have grown up in this way of life. They have become like women and children, who depend upon the master of the house. Eventually, this has come to be a quality of character . . .[24]

This is quite unlike the Europe in which peasants existed so as to be oppressed, whilst burghers were at least potentially free.

In the world which Ibn Khaldun knows, city dwellers do not really seem to be citizens at all; they abdicate responsibility to their rulers, who need to be recruited elsewhere. This is the solution. Urban living and political responsibility are antithetical. This is not fair to all townsmen perhaps, but it must have been the norm. For instance, 'The inhabitants of Spain especially have forgotten group feeling . . . since their country . . . is depleted of tribal groups.' Without tribes, no civic spirit. Without towns, no civilisation. The only solution, noted but not invented by Ibn Khaldun, is to bring the two together. He is not in the business of inventing social solutions, only analysing the ones which occur anyway.

Flux and reflux in the faith of men

But it is not so easy to bring the two social elements together:

because of their savagery, the Bedouins are the least willing of nations to subordinate themselves to each other, as they are rude, proud, ambitious, and eager
to be leaders. Their individual aspirations rarely coincide.

But there is a solution:

when there is religion among them through prophethood or priesthood, then
they have some restraining influence in themselves ... It is, then, easy for them
to subordinate themselves and to unite ...
    ... This is illustrated by the Arab dynasty in Islam. Religion cemented their
leadership with the religious law ...

Plato perhaps did not expect much more from the lower order of his city either,
nor did he wish this artisan or commercial class to leave its specialisms and
meddle in things which did not concern it, such as defence or politics; nonetheless, those whose business it was to attend to those things were, very much, part
of the city itself. The striking thing about this passage from Ibn Khaldun is that
the city-dwellers are contrasted with their rulers, who are not themselves *of* the
city at all.
    The tribesmen of the desert are held up in opposition to the urban folk:

The Bedouins ... are alone in the country and remote from militias. They have
no walls or gates ... they provide their own defence and do not entrust it to ...
others ... They always carry weapons ... Fortitude has become a character
quality of theirs, and courage their nature.

This passage is just as revealing. If in Ibn Khaldun's world the townsmen have
abdicated from politics and defence and delegated these to their rulers, then by
contrast the countryfolk, it appears, *all* carry arms. Is there no militia to take
those arms from them and to keep the peace? Evidently not. Have they no
nobles, who would reserve warfare for themselves, and teach humble shepherds
and ploughmen not to have the impertinence and presumption to act as fighting
men? Apparently not: if they do have nobles or chiefs, evidently these lack
either the power or the desire to disarm their own people. (In fact, they lack
both: they *need* the armed support of their followers, and they could not disarm
them if they wished.) Tocqueville, looking at Ibn Khaldun's world some five
centuries later, observed about the tribes

Each of these little societies elects its own chiefs whom they call *Sheiks* and they
jointly discuss their own affairs.[25]

Ibn Khaldun tells us in so many words why their chiefs do not disarm them:

Their leader needs them mostly for the group spirit that is necessary for purposes
of defence. He is, therefore, forced to rule them kindly and to avoid antagonising
them. Otherwise, he would have trouble with the group spirit, resulting in his
undoing and theirs.

19

The ruler of the central state is quite a different species:

Royal leadership and government, on the other hand, require the leader to exercise a restraining influence by force. If not, his leadership would not last.

These passages give us the really crucial traits of Ibn Khaldun's world: the state is too weak to control or disarm the countryside. Hence virtually all countrymen are armed and help assure their own defence; in other words, the maintenance of rural order, for what it is worth, is in the hands of local self-help communities (i.e. tribes), within which the majority of the adult male population takes part in war and politics.

Why did this 'tribal' solution prevail on the southern and eastern shores of the Mediterranean, whereas the 'feudal' alternative, which segregates warriors/rulers from peasants, prevailed in the north? The most obvious answer would invoke the relative weight of pastoralism and agriculture in the two societies. Flocks are mobile and fields are not: hence oppression of mobile pastoralists is far harder than of place-bound agriculturalists. (Those tied to both land and water, in the use of irrigation agriculture, are of course doubly vulnerable). Labour-intensive societies tend to be hierarchical; defence-intensive ones tend to be egalitarian. (Capital-intensive ones, a new species, seem to lead towards a widespread convergence in consumption-styles, giving an impression of equality, combined with great inequality in power; but the reality and/or illusion of social mobility normally prevents this power-inequality from ever congealing into a permanent, frozen hierarchy.)

Tribes, in the sense intended here, are defined by a near-universal male participation in organised violence, by a very high Military Participation Ratio, in S. Andreski's phrase. In other words, virtually everyone is a soldier. But what is the first precondition of military life? It is, obviously, the ability to run away. You can't win them all: and for any participant in this life-style who cannot run, any unsuccessful encounter — and chance must ensure that, for most of them, defeats occasionally occur — is the last one, destined to end in death or enslavement. Hence soldiering, as a tolerably attractive career, is open only to those who have the ability to escape.

But escaping is not such a simple matter, and requires more than sound limbs. A single man running away without companions or resources cannot easily start again. This is where the mobility of shepherds comes in. Pastoralists can not only escape, they can do so with a substantial part of their wealth intact. (Pastoralism is not the only way of achieving this. When the Mamluks fought Napoleon's army, apparently many of them carried their jewellery on their bodies under their armour, as an insurance against the consequences of defeat, a form of liquid mobile capital which would enable the owner to restart in business somewhere else if he made good his escape.) Their inherent mobility makes it harder to oppress shepherds, which weakens the state in their territory, which in turn strengthens *them* and their mutual-help collectivities, and so on in a self-maintaining circle.

Flux and reflux in the faith of men

The pastoral vocation to violence has a number of sources, over and above the mobility of shepherds and their herds. To seize the *land* of others is only an advantage when land is scarce, or when you can enslave the previous owners and compel them to work it for you. But this raises considerable problems of labour relations and management. Or, of course, you can seize the harvest; but that is a single-shot operation. Raiding for cattle is far more advantageous. If successful, you seize both capital and interest; your booty is self-propelling; and in so far as pastoralism is not labour-intensive, you can assimilate the increment in productive wealth without either over-stretching your own manpower resources or saddling yourself with a recalcitrant alien labour force. All these factors incline pastoralists not merely to dissidence *vis-à-vis* the state, but also towards a life-style which incorporates raiding, and of course the defence against raiding by others. This in turn provides the training which makes shepherd tribes state-resistant, and yet at the same time turns them into potential state-founders. Pastoralism is not labour-intensive but it is defence-intensive.

Pastoralism and literacy

The world of Ibn Khaldun, of traditional Muslim civilisation, combines pastoralism and (often vicarious) scripturalism. It is a world in which pastoral ecology on the one hand, and reverence for the Book, have been pushed to their limits, and in a way fused. When the pastoral way of life predominates, it produces a kind of chain reaction, not only, as the Russian scholar Khazanov notes, by converting others to nomadism, but also by causing non-nomads to adopt a similar form of social organisation. Thus pastoralism leaves its mark even on communities which are partly or predominantly agricultural, but which are bound in self-defence to emulate the social organisation of nomads or semi-nomads, whether as protection against the pastoralists or against the tribally based state. For instance, writing about the Seksawa, one of the longest-established sedentary groups in North Africa, Jacques Berque writes:

Those old established sedentaries, those patient villagers are above all shepherds ... the flock ... occupies the major place in all that economy.[26]

The shepherd is the protector of flocks against raids (when he is not himself a raider); he must needs combine in the mutual-aid groups known as tribes; and his warlike role within them, and his own mobility and that of his flocks, make it difficult to dominate and oppress him excessively. It is certainly much harder to do this to him than it is to oppress an agriculturalist, whose normal task is to work rather than to fight, and whose worldly goods are immobile. Ibn Khaldun cites the tradition according to which the Prophet himself observed that the plough brings submission in its train. By contrast, pastoralism tends towards an at least relatively egalitarian society, which does not normally or seriously segregate a specialised stratum of warriors.[27] The distinction sometimes found in the Sahara, between tribes of the sword and tribes of the Book, is largely a social fiction. It may govern recruitment of religious personnel, but does not dominate the life of the entire collectivities so designated.

At the same time, however, this civilisation came at the end of a long cultural development in the arid zone, in the course of which both literacy and the enjoyment of the products of craftsmanship and trade became recognised parts of life. Only towns, concentrations of traders, craftsmen and scholars, could provide the cultural and technical equipment which had become habitual and normative. Ibn Khaldun stresses the interdependence of urban luxury and intellectual tastes, which encourage literacy and provide the social underpinning of Platonism, in the sense of worship of the uncreated Word. Reverence for the written Word, as expressing an independent authority, was a cultural possibility ever inherent in the very discovery of writing, in the separability of the word from the speaker, the context and the time — even if early scribes on occasion restricted themselves to tax-accountancy, as in Crete. The central social role of the written Word is not to convey a message, but to nail down a contract. The best way of making the crucial contract stick is to turn it into a divine Message. In its Platonic form proper, as the cult of the *concept*, the potential for reverence of the socially disembodied Word was never exploited very effectively in actual social practice, perhaps because our concepts are too loose and ill-defined to serve as real arbiters of conduct, and much too shadowy in outline to inspire awe in non-philosophers. (Ideal concrete *human* models seem to be more appealing and socially effective than pure abstract ideals.) But in its Koranic form, as the cult of a delimited and final set of propositions, uncreated, eternal and divine, this cultural possibility received its purest and most striking expression. Plato divinised the word; Islam attributes the Word to the deity. This has proved socially more effective. Presumably it both reinforced, and was sustained by, the need of the shepherds for urban products, made and distributed thanks to skills which formed a kind of matrix of literacy, and which were visibly continuous with it.[28] A clustering of such skills in a sense *is* a town. The town favours literacy as one further specialised skill and at the same time an endorsement and encouragement of all the others. Specialisms benefit from being recorded in writing, and require it more than an occupation which is the dominant and more or less universal employment of a tribal society, such as, for instance, pastoralism. Hence a scriptural religion comes more easily to an urban population, and has more scope within it. What mattered in the history of mankind was not the moment when the Word became flesh, but rather the instant when the Word *ceased* to be flesh, by being incarnated in writing in a social milieu which valued writing and came to revere it. It was then that the Word could sit in judgement on men and societies.

So the original Platonism Mark 1 divinised the isolated concept, whereas the socially more effective, Koranic Platonism Mark 2 attributed a carefully delimited set of normative propositions to the deity. The interpretation of propositions, though also contentious, is incomparably less so than that of an open class of undenumerated concepts: so in this version the Norm is not only transcendent, but it is also sustained by the ultimate Power, and it is at least relatively precise and bounded. A self-sustaining, undelimited class of normative *concepts* is less persuasive and clear-cut than a delimited set of divinely uttered propositions. Its authority is socially sustained by the social classes which have privileged access to it through literacy, and an interest in invoking its legitimacy against such groups as would threaten it, and which can elaborate and uphold a corpus of interpretations and applications of the initial set of revealed assertions.

Platonism Mark 2 was superior to the earlier prototype not merely in being propositional, underwritten by God, and finite; it also guaranteed its own completion. When Bertrand Russell discussed the doctrine of logical atomism, according to which both the world and our characterisation of it broke up into final atoms such that each member of the set of atomic propositions as it were captured, married, mirrored one atomic fact, he noted that nonetheless, the set of all atomic propositions would not *exhaust* truth and our knowledge of the world: we would need at least one further proposition, namely, that the set was *complete*, that these were all the propositions which were available. Islam, through the doctrine that the line of Prophets was completed, satisfies this logico-philosophical requirement. No further increments to the Normative Truth are either possible or allowed. The logical point does not perhaps matter much. But sociologically it is extremely important. By firmly closing the door, in principle, to further additions to the Revealed doctrine, it enormously strengthens the hand of those who have access to the delimited truth through literacy and who use it as a charter of legitimacy. They cannot be outflanked by new Revelations.

Anticipating the argument somewhat, one may observe that there was also Platonism Mark 3, improving the product yet further. This consisted of adding to the reification and deification of the Word, the Platonic doctrine that sustained education of a well-selected, individually recruited elite, trained in war, administration and the recognition of Norms, is, more than tribal life, the right recipe for social cohesion and a stable polity. The longevity and power of the Ottoman empire testified to the excellence of this recipe. But this recipe was only developed relatively late in the history of Islam, and is in my view a variant within it rather than of its essence. But if Muhammed implemented Platonism by teaching an entire society to revere the Word, the Mamluks and Turks carried the job further by systematically training and insulating Guardians from corrupting kin links, rather than relying on tribal life to produce a wild variety, which depends for its growth on those very kinship bonds which Plato distrusted.

Thus the discovery of writing contained the potential for an ideological device greatly favouring such social groups as are capable of literacy. But literacy flourishes best among specialists; it is itself a specialism, initially, but it also encourages and helps to codify, transmit and delimit other specialisms. Specialists of various kinds in turn are mutually interdependent and thus tend to congregate, thereby creating urban centres. Literacy appeals to them, suits and helps

23

them, and becomes their shared badge. The present stress on this socially reinforced transcendence may obscure another very important feature of this Norm
— its capacity to serve as the basis for a fairly minute regulation of the details of
social life even among an anonymous and mobile urban population. Mark 2 is
also, so to speak, a talmudic Platonism. Such codified regulation once again has
an affinity with urban life. Regulation by *un*written tradition is only feasible
amongst fairly stable, non-anonymous, non-urban populations.

Platonism Mark 1, which divinises the Word, is flattering to us intellectuals.
We like to hear that the main tool of our trade should be sacred. The magic rubs
off on us. But ordinary people prefer the personal touch, and even, or especially,
in a monotheism, prefer that residual human warmth in the universe which it
retains by the attribution of the Word to God, as taught by Platonism Mark 2.

The doctrine that the line of Prophets is closed firmly circumscribes the
Sacred and thus saves it from devaluation. Plato himself was not sufficiently
aware of the Quantity Theory of Ideas. The proscription of innovation protects
a scriptural faith from inflation.

Thus scripturalism gave the townsmen and the tribesmen a common idiom,
even if they used it differently, and made them into parts of what certainly was
one continuous moral order. So the cult of the Word is pushed to an extreme
point where it endows the carriers with great moral authority and, at the same
time, pastoralism is developed to a limit at which it endows pastoral mutual-aid
collectives ('tribes') with great cohesion, and fatally weakens any polity other
than one based on some coalition of such tribal collectives. This fusion of
scripturalism and pastoralism, the implication of each pushed *à outrance* in one
continuous system, *is* the classical world of Islam.

The consequence of this is the difference between European and Muslim
dynasty-founders. After the initial *Völkerwanderung*, European kings were
recruited from leading barons rather than from tribal leaders; Muslim ones are
either tribal chiefs or the men of religion who weld tribes together under a
religious banner.

In some ways, tribalism is a far hardier plant than feudalism. In England, the
Wars of the Roses could decimate a feudal class and help strengthen the monarchy.
In Persia, by contrast, the complaint was heard that however many tribal *khans*
you killed, new ones always emerged from the chiefly lineage; the killing could
not keep up with their proliferation so that try as you would you simply couldn't
suppress tribes by liquidating their leaders. A more or less self-insulated feudal
class can be massacred *en bloc* (as happened in nineteenth-century Nepal), or
worn out by prolonged conflict, or corrupted by fun-and-games at some
Versailles; but segmentary tribal leadership has a truly Dragon's Teeth quality.

This rural tribal wilderness in which no militias keep the peace is not at all a
Hobbesian anarchy, a war of all against all. Long before modern social
anthropology made the same discovery, Ibn Khaldun knew full well that the
state of nature is not individualistic, but tribal. This courtier knew more about

tribesmen than did the European political philosophers; in his society, it was rather difficult to ignore them. He was deeply imbued with the sense of pastoral/tribal life:

Those who have no one of their own lineage [to care for] rarely feel affection for their fellows. If danger is in the air ... such a man slinks away ... Such people, therefore, cannot live in the desert ...

So in the wilderness, the state of nature *is* a reality: the maintenance of order and the righting of wrongs is in the hands of an armed population itself, and not of a specialised law-enforcing agency, i.e. the state. But this statelessness is not individualistic. Those who partake in it feel affection for their fellows of the same lineage. Order is maintained, at least in some measure, by the mechanisms of stateless *tribal* organisation.

The weakness of the state — the militia is far away — both permits and obliges these rural units to be strong; and their strength, in turn, keeps the state weak. Once established, the system is self-perpetuating. Moreover, Ibn Khaldun's observations about the tribesmen and the townsmen are complementary: it is just because the townsmen have such good cause to fear the tribesmen that they cannot dispute with their rulers and share in the control of the city: they need the rulers too much to be able to afford such defiance, even if they had the stomach for it. And who are these rulers?

Plato gave the answer as to who the rulers should be, and how they should be trained so as to be good rulers, so that they should not need further rulers to check them in turn; how to make them be of such noble, incorruptible metal as to evade, at least for some time, the need to face the endlessly regressive political question — who guards the guardians?

Ibn Khaldun does not indulge in any such philosophical speculation or prescription. The corruptibility of rulers is a central datum and it is not contested. In the end, the only solution lies in the fact that there is an ever-ready supply of new ones. These are produced, not by philosophical training, by that judicious, Platonic blend of music and gymnastics, but by the natural conditions of tribal life, that ever-fruitful womb, not of philosopher-kings, but of tribesmen-kings.

He gives a straightforward, factual account, telling us who the rulers actually are, where they come from, and how they acquire the spirit which enables them to rule and defend the city:

Leadership exists only through superiority, and superiority only through group feeling.

This is perhaps the most important single sentence in Ibn Khaldun's sociology: domination, authority, are the rewards of social cohesion. Everyone aspires to authority and its rewards, very few can attain it, and they are selected from among the cohesive. Government is by tribe, and only the cohesive deserve to rule. Government is the gift of the tribe to the city. In a sense, the state *is* a tribe, which has moved from the desert to the citadel, and milks the town instead of its herds, and protects the mosque; the market—citadel—mosque trio constitutes the political system. The Soviet anthropologist Khazanov has put forward the hypothesis that nomads become less egalitarian in proportion to their involvement with the state (whether as its agents, victims, or both). The capture of the political citadel by a tribe or group of tribes then constitutes the extreme position along this spectrum: the tribe becomes extremely stratified in so far as one of its number becomes the sultan, and his clan his ministers, who also constitute the pool of his potential successors. At the same time, its political institutions, having been intermittent or 'dispositional' in their natural habitat — only activated into being by the need arising from conflict — acquire a state-like permanence and continuity.

It is not, as Plato thought or recommended, a sound philosophical education which fits one for authority. Quite the reverse: education emasculates one politically.

those who rely on laws and are dominated by them from the very beginning of their education and instruction in the crafts, sciences, and religious matters, are thereby deprived of much of their own fortitude. They can scarcely defend themselves at all against hostile acts. This is the case with students, whose occupation it is to study and learn from teachers and religious leaders . . .

Education and law-abidingness are politically debilitating; they undermine that social cohesion which alone confers authority. This is slightly embarrassing for Ibn Khaldun as a Muslim, and he has to indulge in a little special pleading:

It is no argument that the men around Muhammad observed the religious laws, and yet did not experience any diminution of their fortitude . . . When the Muslims got their religion from Muhammad, the restraining influence came from themselves . . . It was not the result of technical instruction or scientific education. The laws were the laws and precepts of religion which they received orally . . . Their fortitude remained unabated, and it was not corroded by education or authority.

In this way, his view that education and authority are politically and martially corrosive is squared with the pieties, with an acknowledgement of the fact that the Companions of the Prophet were cohesive, yet received the law from him.

If only cohesion is the basis of authority and alone constitutes qualification for leadership, and if it is not to be had from education — quite the reverse — then from where is it to be had? The answer is clear:

Only tribes held together by group feeling can live in the desert.

and

Group feeling results only from blood relationship or something corresponding to it.

In other words: cohesion is engendered in groups living in a rough natural environment, far from the law-enforcing militias of the state, and in groups which are bound to each other by *ideas* of consanguinity; or, more briefly still, it arises only amongst tribesmen. Although Ibn Khaldun seems on occasion to take seriously the terminology of 'blood' — 'respect for blood ties is something natural among men' — he really knows better than this. 'Blood' is neither a necessary nor a sufficient condition of cohesion: it is merely a way of *talking* about it. It is not necessary:

Clients and allies belong in the same category. The affection everyone has for his clients and allies results from the feeling of shame that comes to a person when one of his neighbours, relatives, or a blood relation is in any degree humiliated.

Nor are kin links sufficient, when the social preconditions of their effectiveness — survival in a rough, ungoverned or ill-governed environment — are absent:

Isolated inhabitants of cities can have a 'house' [i.e. kin group] only in a metaphorical sense. The assumption that they possess one is a specious claim ... Many inhabitants of cities who had their origins in noble Arab or non-Arab 'house' share such delusions.

The Israelites are most firmly misled in this delusion. They originally had one of the greatest 'houses' in the world ... because of their group feeling and the royal authority which God promised them and granted them by means of that group feeling. Then, they were divested of all that ... Still, the delusion ... has not left them. They can be found saying: 'He is an Aaronite' ... 'He is a descendant of Joshua'; 'He is one of Caleb's progeny' ... Many other inhabitants of cities who hold [noble] pedigrees but no longer share in any group feelings are inclined to similar nonsense.

It is obvious that Ibn Khaldun considers the invocation of genealogies, and claims to the membership of kin groups by townsmen, to be a kind of sociological fraud, *nonsense* to speak bluntly, not because the genealogies themselves are necessarily false — which is neither here nor there — but because they no longer correspond to the social reality which they were meant to express, i.e. effective group cohesion, engendered by self-reliance in rude and lawless circumstances.[29] He who allows order to be maintained for him by a ruler may not truly claim to be part of a 'house'. A *real* 'house' looks after its own defence. Genealogies without a real 'house' are just verbiage. Submission to law is political emasculation. He makes this very plain:

A tribe paying imposts did not do that until it became resigned to meek submission with respect to paying. Imposts and taxes are a sign of oppression and meekness that proud souls do not tolerate ... In such a case, group feeling is too weak for its own defence and protection ... When one sees a tribe humiliated by the payment of imposts, one cannot hope that it will ever achieve royal authority ...

The motto of a proud soul, evidently, is not so much 'No taxation without representation', but rather, 'No taxation *at all*'. And indeed, well into this century, there were tribes which took great pride in never having submitted to the humiliation of taxation. But those tribes who submit to authority and taxation thereby join the townsmen and belong to the number of those unfit to rule. Only those who refuse to be governed are themselves fit to rule: political education is to be had in the wilderness alone. If you wish to command you must not learn to obey. And if prophetic status also requires a period in the wilderness, this way the two elements of political renovation – tribe and prophet – may meet.

Thus an urban civilisation depends for the provision of its own rulers precisely on those whom it cannot itself rule, and who acquire the toughness and cohesion required for government in the wild lands beyond the pale. Thus, politically, the civilised are dependent on the barbarians, and not only in politics:

When sedentary people mix with the Bedouin in the desert or associate with them on a journey, they depend on them. They cannot do anything for themselves without them. This is an observed fact.

But economically, the dependence is reversed.

while the Bedouin need the cities for their necessities of life, the urban population needs the Bedouin [only] for conveniences and luxuries. Thus, as long as they live in the desert and have not acquired royal authority and control of the cities, the Bedouin need the townsmen . . .

The economic dependence of pastoral tribesmen on urban artisans and commercial specialists, eventually symbolised by their religious dependence on the crucial specialism of literacy, spring from their conspicuous non-autarchy: they are not windowless nomads. This is the reverse of what one would expect, or of what is taken for granted in Plato's world, in which the rude rural population is economically so self-sufficient, and only the desire for luxury and civilisation brings in its train the need for acquisition and defence of territory, and thereby the problem of politics. Here, this is reversed: the townsmen seem economically self-sufficient and only need the tribesmen of the wilderness for luxuries, and more significantly, for political and military services, whereas the opposite holds in economic matters. Speaking of traditional Algeria in 1840, Tocqueville noted the same:

Virtually all manufacturing industry was enclosed within the towns.[30]

The article on *Algeria* in the *New American Encyclopaedia* of 1858 modifies this picture only slightly, making a partial exception of the Berbers:

The Kabyles are a hardworking people who live in real villages; excellent agriculturalists, they also work mines, smelt metals and have workshops in which they weave wool and cotton. They make gunpowder and soap . . . Faithful to the customs of their ancestors, the Arabs lead a nomadic existence, moving their camps for pasture and other reasons.

The author of the entry was Friedrich Engels.[31]

Ibn Khaldun might have added that much the same is true in what could be called religious ecology: when the tribesmen adhere to a religion of the Book, they are dependent, in the end, not only on urban artisans and traders but also on literate religious specialists.

The division of labour is the essence of urban life. It is the key to the capacity to supply those services, economic and cultural, which the tribesmen are unable to provide for themselves. The tribal ethos spurns specialisation: the economic specialist is despised, the ritual and political specialist viewed with suspicion, ambivalence and irony, even if he is respected, feared and revered.[32] Under European feudalism, only a relatively small upper stratum spurned trade or economic activity. In Muslim tribal society, it is the very broad middle stratum of ordinary tribesmen, above craftsmen and below the religious nobility, which is the carrier of a specialism-spurning ethos. But if this fact were to be invoked for explaining a relative lack of economic development, it should also be remembered that, notwithstanding the ethos, tribesmen take to trade with alacrity and without compunction the moment political circumstances permit it — and sometimes even sooner.

The economic and religious—cultural need by the tribesmen of the towns, in the traditional social order, is profoundly significant, and constitutes presumably the second most important fact in Ibn Khaldun's world, alongside the *political* dependence of towns on tribes. This mutual dependence holds the overall society together in its peculiar form, and helps explain what may be the greatest puzzle of all: why a society so fragile politically should be so very coherent and homogeneous culturally.

A type of society

The society brilliantly sketched out by Ibn Khaldun could also be summarised in other terms, which would highlight the contrast between it and other social forms. Ibn Khaldun's own perceptiveness is all the more remarkable in so far as he evidently thought he was describing the only kind of human society, society *as such*, anywhere. His analysis is evidently meant to follow from basic human or social traits, and not to be dependent on any cultural idiosyncrasies. In this he was mistaken: it is all the more noteworthy that he should have seen that which, within his own horizon, lacked any contrast. His perceptiveness refutes the view that to exist is to differ, and that only what is differentiated from other objects within one's horizon can ever be perceived.

It is worth sketching, in terms other than his own, the outlines of this world. It is a tribal world, or rather, one in which much or most of rural life is tribal. What does this mean? It means that the maintenance of order in the countryside, in the desert and in the mountains, is in the hands of local groups defined in terms of real or supposed kinship, or of kinship-surrogates such as clientship. It means that these local groups are relatively unstratified politically: they do have leaders, but these leaders depend on the support of their armed followers, and hence cannot tyrannise them.

29

The tribes are of three kinds: in Platonic terms, the wolves, the sheep and the sheepdogs. There are the tribes strong enough to defy authority and resist taxation, and thereby maintain their cohesion and spirit, and they retain what Ibn Khaldun calls their fitness for royal authority, though this can generally be attained only when religion confers cohesion on a whole group. These are the wolves. There are also those, originally drawn from amongst the wolves, who have been successful enough to *attain* royal authority, by conquering the areas in which it can be exercised — the town and sedentary regions. These are the sheepdogs.[33] And finally, there are the sheep who have submitted to authority, thereby betraying a loss of that moral fibre which might make them royal, and losing it ever more completely through the habits of submission.[34]

Implicit in this classification of tribes there is also a political sociology, which Ibn Khaldun spells out. Government is by cohesive tribes, by sheepdogs, erstwhile wolves, wolves-turned-sheepdogs, and it is exercised over cities and over sheep. Government by the people of the people and for the people is poppycock. When modern conditions lead to the fusion of democratic jargon with the spirit of Ibn Khaldun, we get a distinctive species of 'totalitarian democracy', in which populist verbiage covers kin-patronage politics. Under modern conditions, it is often noted that government is by patronage network, which in turn has a communal or territorial base. This is no longer an instance of an Ibn-Khaldunian regime proper, in which a whole conquering kin group share as of right in the benefits of the acquisition of royal authority. (Perhaps such a system never did exist in an absolutely pure form. Reciprocal services must always have counted for something. It is unlikely that privileges were ever accorded quite mechanically by virtue of men's position on a genealogy, without the intrusion of other considerations.) But this system does have something in common with the old pattern. The links of patronage are not created arbitrarily and freely, in a, so to speak, open market of corruption. Their formation is weighted in favour of pre-existing group links. Such systems, which are now common, should perhaps be considered a mixed or intermediate political form, a neo-Ibn-Khaldunian type of government.

It is remarkable how very much Ibn Khaldun is a positive sociologist rather than a normative political philosopher. He wastes little time on moralising. He tells us what political authority is, gives its natural history, and there's the end of it. It is the rule of some cohesive groups over others which are less so, or which are less fortunate, *and* over the towns and detribalised peasantry, if any is available. Amongst free tribes there is little justice or law other than such as the group ensures for itself; in governed territory there is the rule of law, which simply means that the governors have the monopoly of large-scale injustice (though not, interestingly, of legitimate violence):

Mutual aggression of people in towns and cities is averted by the authorities and government, which hold back the masses under their control from attacks and aggression upon each other. They are thus prevented . . . from mutual injustice, save such injustice as comes from the ruler himself.

The problem which Plato and modern liberals share, and which they solve so very differently (by seeking perfection in rulers, or by pluralist mitigation of inevitable imperfection) — how can one prevent injustice *by* authority itself, as well as that which is perpetrated *between* its subjects — does not seem to pre-occupy Ibn Khaldun very much. Morally speaking, there is little to choose be-tween wolves and sheepdogs. They differ only in their position, good fortune, or cohesion. This too would seem to be a fact about the society of which he was part and which he was describing. In his argument one does find prudential rules and advice to monarchs — for example, great harshness is counter-productive, and not in the king's own interest — but no more.

Ibn Khaldun's model is not static. Its dynamics, the theory of a kind of tribal circulation of elites, is its best known part. This theory is of course already implicit in the classification of tribes, and in the view that sheepdogs are erst-while wolves, and are destined to end as sheep.

Political authority and the privileges which go with it corrode that very cohesion which had bestowed authority on a group and its leaders in the first place. As cohesion is whittled away, the ruler comes to rely on mercenaries rather than kinsmen. As his authority and territory dwindle, even severe taxation brings in less revenue than mild taxation once had done, in the halcyon days of expansion; and so the ruler's demands alienate his subjects at the same time as the quality of his support declines. Eventually some new grouping of cohesive, warlike wolves, well suited for authority by their qualities, replaces the exhausted sheepdogs — only to suffer a similar fate some four generations later.

The rotation-within-an-immobile-structure is perhaps inherent in a certain general ecology, or mode of production and reproduction if you prefer. It is an ecology in which extensive nomadic and/or mountain pastoralism co-exists with trade and urban centres of artisan production, and within which cohesion and mobility confer dominance on those nested groupings of mutual-aid associations, which we call tribes. At the same time the general level of cultural and technical equipment confers a different kind of centrality or legitimacy on the towns. They are economically indispensable; scripturalism confirms and reinforces their standing. The consequence is the kind of rotation of leadership, and the kind of symbiosis between rude tribal cohesion and urban sophistication, which Ibn Khaldun described.[35] Tribes provide rulers and some luxuries, towns provide essential tools and moral legitimation.

The pattern as such is not necessarily Islamic: it seems inherent in this kind of ecology. It was found in the arid zone before Islam, and it is significant that this circular or 'reversible' pattern has also been noted by scholars who, as Marxists, might be expected to seek basic structural transformations, rather than the mere perpetuation of a fundamentally identical pattern. Apparently arid zone nomadism does not support any such expectations of profound change. A.M. Khazanov, a Soviet authority on the Scythians and on nomadism generally, who suggests that the Scythians may have been among the first to initiate the pattern by creating a nomad conquest state,[36] observes:

In the course of nearly three thousand years, within the nomadic world of Eurasian steppes, circular developments clearly predominated over cumulative ones, and if the latter nevertheless had their place, this was largely due to stimuli emerging from the agrarian world.[37]

Another Soviet specialist on nomadism, G.E. Markov, spells out this conclusion as firmly:

agrarian government is an irreversible phenomenon. It changes its type, but cannot disappear, as long as antagonistic class contradictions remain.

But when we come to nomads, the facts bear this testimony: the transition in social organisation from 'communal-nomadic' to the 'military-nomadic' and vice-versa are reversible phenomena. After the disintegration of nomad empires, new governments appear in the agrarian regions subject to them; with the mobile pastoralists, the communal-nomadic organisation reappeared in one form or another.[38]

By 'communal-nomadic' the author evidently means a social form corresponding to tribal-segmentary, and by 'military-nomadic' the assumption, by such a grouping, of a politically dominant role in wider society including townsmen and agriculturalists. Thus, though Ibn Khaldun is not quoted, his views seem fully vindicated.

But if this is so, what is the significance of Islam as such? Its diffusion in the arid zone has meant that this cyclical or 'reversible' process was henceforth carried out by partners who spoke the same moral language, who could leave visiting cards with each other, which was not possible when Scythian steppe nomads traded or fought with Greek townsmen in the Crimea or Iranian agriculturalists in Transcaucasia. Henceforth, the barbarians could arrive by invitation; a dissident cleric from the town could lead them to the city to replace a morally exhausted dynasty. And when the new rulers were installed, they could promptly be provided with secretarial, clerical and administrative assistance, and in some measure with moral guidance or even constitutional limitation, by a class of scholars who spoke an idiom which the newly arriving tribal rulers already understood or at any rate respected. So one might say that Islam provided a common language and thus a certain kind of smoothness for a process which, in a more mute and brutalistic form, had been taking place anyway.

In Eastern Asia, nomads also notoriously on occasion acted as conquerors and formed states. But the areas which they ruled would have been politically centralised anyway: the nomads were, from the viewpoint of state-formation, redundant. Their political role was superfluous. The state, well-established anyway, was not a tribal gift. This differentiates them from the world of Ibn

Khaldun, in which they were indispensable and ever-recurring. There they did not, in Markov's terms, create an irreversible agrarian state. So the gift of the state had to be periodically renewed. East Asian nomads are contingent, Muslim ones are necessary.

An argument exists in the work of Germaine Tillion which attempts to explain the well-known traits of these tribal communities, of these 'republics of cousins', traits such as the relative egalitarianism, diffusion of civic and military responsibility, and possessiveness towards womenfolk of the lineage, in terms of the discovery and diffusion of agriculture and the need for manpower it implies.[39] It is strange to find an authoress attributing to early Mediterranean man such a mercantilist and anti-free-trade attitude towards women and their exchange. On this theory, it would seem that, in defiance of C. Lévi-Strauss, they preferred to define their groups by the retention rather than the exchange of women. Why should they assume that exchange cannot be beneficial, that the boarding of parallel cousins inside the group leads to a quicker accumulation of a labour force, than a judicious exchange of manpower-generating brides? But above all, if this were the explanation, why do non-Muslim peasant societies seldom display a similar structure?

It seems to me more plausible to credit the republic of cousins to pastoralism, the need to combine for the defence of pasture and the difficulty of oppressing shepherds, and the chain-reaction which obliges adjoining communities to organise in a similar way. I cannot pretend to solve the problem of parallel-cousin marriage, but there is no doubt but that it aids clan cohesion. For a tribesman, the clan means not only access to pasture, but also to brides. Without your clan, where could you graze your flocks and whom could your son marry?

It would be an exaggeration to say that pastoralists are predestined for a 'segmentary' form of social organisation, and pastoral societies do exist which do not display this form; but it seems that they are strongly predisposed towards it. A single shepherd is at the mercy of any group of other shepherds, or even of an ambush by another single shepherd. His most natural insurance against such danger is to form or join a mutual-aid association, which can jointly defend pasture, watering-place and so forth, and avenge him should he be killed. But such a small group is, once again, at the mercy of larger associations of such groups: in other words, the argument is repeated at each level at which a shared interest or danger can arise. At the same time, the mobility of both shepherds and their wealth inhibits centralisation and a politico-military division of labour inside these groups: it is normally difficult to extract much surplus from such populations, for as their members retain their arms for external defence these arms are also available for their internal defence against oppression. But without surplus, there are no specialised military—political agencies. The circle is complete. The result of all this is that characteristic superimposition of 'nested' groups of various sizes, fairly egalitarian and uncentralised internally, and with

33

no one level of size being clearly more important than others. There is no privileged level for the articulation of political units.

This also helps explain the predilection of nomadic or semi-nomadic populations for genealogical self-definition. For sedentary segmentary populations, genealogy, though often used, is optional. People who have a clearly defined address can be identified in terms of it. But nomads, people of no fixed abode, cannot be defined, or have their nested social units defined, in terms of their locality. They need genealogy. Genealogy or group membership is their only address. In so far as their mobility is regulated, as generally it is, territory is defined in terms of social group rather than vice versa. A pasture is the pasture of such and such a people (membership of which grants access to the pasture), rather than people being defined by the locality.

Trade cycle and dynastic tribal cycle

It is interesting that in the course of his account of the decline of dynasties, Ibn Khaldun also elaborates a Keynesian theory of economics, clearly containing the concept of the multiplier. There is a crucial difference: where for Keynes it is the middle class, with its greater propensity to save, which receives blame for inadequate effective demand and thus for economic depression, in Ibn Khaldun's world it is the court and government, which constitutes not merely the possible remedy, but also the initial cause of the down-swing of the trade cycle. It is *governmental* propensity to save at times when investment opportunities do not take up the slack, which leads to that defective aggregate demand which in the Keynesian version is blamed on the middle class:

Curtailment of allowances [expenditure] . . . by the ruler implies curtailment of tax revenue. The reason for this is that dynasty and government serve as the world's greatest market-place . . . if the ruler holds on to property and revenue . . . the property in the possession of the ruler's entourage will be small. The gifts which they, in . . . turn, had been used to give to their entourage . . . stop, and all their expenditure is cut down. They constitute the greatest number of people [who make expenditure], and their expenditure provides more of the substance of trade than that of any other [group]. [When they stop spending], business slumps and commercial profits decline because of the shortage of capital. Revenues . . . decrease, because . . . taxation depends on cultural activity, commercial transactions, business prosperity . . . the dynasty . . . suffers . . . because under these circumstances the property of the ruler decreases . . . The dynasty is the greatest market, the mother and base of all trade, the substance of income and expenditure. If government business slumps and the volume of trade is small, the dependent markets will naturally show the same symptoms, and to a greater degree. Furthermore, money circulates between ruler and subject, moving back and forth . . . if the ruler keeps it to himself, it is lost to the subjects.

This must be one of the most eloquent inflationary, expansionist, anti-Milton-

Friedman pleas ever made. But although Ibn Khaldun was an expansionist, clearly he was no lefty. He was unambiguously opposed to state enterprise:

Commercial activity in the part of the ruler is harmful to his subjects and ruinous to tax revenue.

Nor did he hold with any kind of price control or tinkering with the market:

the ruler . . . will be able to force the seller to lower his price . . . he forces the merchants or farmers . . . to buy from him. He will be satisfied only with the highest prices or more. The merchants and farmers . . . will exhaust their liquid capital . . . an oft-repeated process. The trouble and financial difficulties and the loss of profit . . . take away . . . all incentives to effort, thus ruining the fiscal structure.

Evidently, Ibn Khaldun held that government should restrict itself to a Keynesian propping up of aggregate demand, but leave the rest to the market, without itself dabbling in enterprise.

But to return to the main theme: partly through this depression, the economic consequence of political decline, and mainly through the political weakening itself, the ruling personnel rotate, though the structure itself remains the same. To say that Ibn Khaldun is a pessimistic thinker would be to give the wrong impression, to suggest that a sense of sadness pervades his political sociology, that he was seized by a yearning for some total consummation in which the merits of civilisation and those of cohesion and authority were fused, and endowed with stability to boot. Neither the platonic aspiration for arresting decay, nor the modern idea of continuous improvement culminating in some radical transformation of the human condition for the better — i.e. 'progress' — seems to be present. He accepts the socio-political world as he finds it, and tells it like it is.

A convergence

The model which is here offered of traditional Muslim civilisation is basically an attempt to fuse Ibn Khaldun's political sociology with David Hume's oscillation theory of religion. Hume's theory will not do on its own and as it stands: it is far too psychologistic and not wholly coherent. It describes the phenomena with elegance, precision and insight, but it is too narrow when it specifies their roots. These are not to be sought exclusively in the human heart, in its tendency towards competitive sycophancy of the powerful and the timid use of brokers— intermediaries when soliciting favours from the unapproachably great. These traits are indisputably present in us and no doubt they play their part in generating both the idea of an ineffably distant and hidden God, and conversely in producing the spiritual patronage-networks which mediate between Him and humanity. But these are not the only considerations which impel men towards one end or the other of the religious spectrum which Hume sketched out. There are also social factors, the requirements of the types of social organisation within which men find themselves. Social organisation is not indifferent to religious style. One kind of organisation needs and favours one style, and another, a different style again. These social aspects must be added to Hume's account before it becomes adequate. In other words: what is the natural religious bent of townsmen and of tribal wolves?

As indicated, the characteristic form of social organisation of Muslim tribal peoples of the arid zone is what social anthropologists call 'segmentary'. Muslim tribesmen, in the largely arid zone stretching roughly from the Hindu Kush to the Atlantic and the Niger bend, are generally segmentary, though this form of organisation is also found elsewhere and amongst non-Muslim peoples. To describe a tribal grouping as segmentary is not merely to classify it − it is also in large measure to explain its organisation. More than most classificatory terms, perhaps, *segmentation* contains a theory. The theory is simple, elegant, and, in my estimation, to a very large extent correct.

A characteristic Marxist-style criticism of the theory occurs in R. Gallisot and G. Badia's *Marxisme et Algérie* (Paris, 1976, p. 238):

the approach through segmentarity . . . remains purely descriptive, and causes societies to hang in thin air, through neglecting the analysis of their productive activities . . .

The supposition that the 'segmentary' account of certain tribal societies is 'purely descriptive' presumably springs from the assumption that genuine explanation *must* be in terms of the mode of production. In fact, segmentation is an explanatory model, and one elaborated in answer to the question: how is order maintained in the absence of a central law-and-order-enforcing agency? The assumption is, indeed, that the basic problem is *political*, and moreover political in a sense which does not necessarily involve exploitation by one 'class' of another: the problem is that of attaining co-operation, in pasture utilisation, trade, etc., without recourse to an effective sovereign, who is generally neither necessary nor possible. The manner in which this political problem is analysed does not in the least ignore the productive activities and economic needs of the segmentary units, but on the contrary stresses and highlights them: transhumant pastoralism, for instance, requires complex regulation of pasture use at diverse seasons; ecological diversification presupposes trade and markets. Hence there must be organisation − the agreement of complex arrangements and their implementation and enforcement, and the protection of trade, but without centralisation, without concentration of authority and power. This is precisely what segmentation achieves.

The whole idea that a system of political organisation is not explanatory but descriptive presupposes not merely some kind of economic determinism, but the logically deeper, far more contentious idea that the economic and political spheres can in general be distinguished. (The contrary view is, precisely, that this

36

ability to distinguish these two spheres is the distinctive trait of one kind of society. In other words, the separability of these spheres is a specific and not a generic trait.) In acephalous or near-acephalous segmentary society, what you own and what you can effectively defend can hardly be distinguished. The productive and the property-defending groups are largely congruent. The producer is himself the nightwatchman and does not delegate to a nightwatchman state. The 'nested' units which are the carriers of ownership rights, which are in turn 'nested' and do not preclude specific individual family rights within this context, are also the agents of order-maintenance and enforcement. (The individual family owns a field but cannot dispose of it outside the segmentary group without the consent of the members of the group, and the same applies to disposal of women.) Contested ownership claims do, of course, occur; but the legal procedures for settling such conflict are virtually indistinguishable from the procedures and rituals governing inter-group diplomatic relations generally.

The view that the notion of segmentation is purely descriptive also presumably springs from the fact that the notion itself happens to be borrowed from indigenous self-conceptualisation. This in itself makes it neither true nor false as an explanation: false consciousness is not the universal human condition, it is merely a common one. Not all local beliefs are false. The criticism that 'segmentation' is not explanatory at all must be distinguished from the view that, though explanatory, it is false.

What are the features of segmentary societies, and how does the implied or stated theory explain them? Perhaps it is best to use the words of the man who is, above all other, responsible for elaborating the theory of segmentation, the late Sir Edward Evans-Pritchard:

Each section of a tribe, from the smallest to the largest, has its Shaikh or Shaikhs. The tribal system, typical of segmentary structures everywhere, is a system of balanced opposition between tribes and tribal sections from the largest to the smallest divisions, and there cannot therefore be any single authority in a tribe. Authority is distributed at every point of the tribal structure and political leadership is limited to situations in which a tribe or a segment of it acts corporately. With a tribe this only happens in war or in dealings with outside authority ... There cannot, obviously, be any absolute authority vested in a single Shaikh of a tribe when the fundamental principle of tribal structure is opposition between its segments, and in such segmentary systems there is no state and no government as we understand these institutions.[40]

In segmentary society, power — and other advantages — are fairly evenly diffused. Generally speaking, the entire adult male population, or a very high proportion of it, bears arms and is legitimately involved in the maintenance of order and in group defence. The *feud* is a characteristic institution: it means that the group of kinsmen are co-responsible for the conduct of any one of their number, sharing in the risk of becoming objects of retaliation, or of contributing to blood-money as an alternative to feud if any one in the group commits an act of aggression against a member of another group, and similarly, being morally bound to avenge aggression against any fellow member, and standing to benefit from compensation. It is this risk and this obligation which sustain the cohesion which, in Ibn Khaldun's estimation, made such groups fit to become rulers, and endowed them with the ability to acquire royal authority when conditions were propitious.

The division of the male population into warriors and agricultural producers, so characteristic of feudalism, is alien to such a society. The European discovery and exploration of Muslim tribal society occurred in the main after the French Revolution, and was often carried out by men — long before T.E. Lawrence — who were possessed by a nostalgia for a Europe as it was prior to the diffusion of the egalitarian ideal. General Daumas, French consul to Amir Abd el Kader, or Charles Henry Churchill, his English biographer, were among the first to prepare the Valentino image of Arab society. They sought, not the noble savage, but the savage noble. But whether or not he possessed the traits they required, he was not really an aristocrat in the proper feudal sense, that of belonging to a legally distinct, jealously insulated warrior stratum. Rather, he was a Big Man of the tribe, or one of them, linked to fellow tribesmen both by kinship and status, needing their military support as much as, or more than, their surplus product.[41] But the romantics who sought a military nobility because they longed for it are now followed and quoted over a century later by leftists, wishing to find the same thing because they do *not* like it or because their theory requires its existence. *Les féodaux* is now a term of political abuse.

Segmentary society is of course not normally perfectly symmetrical and egalitarian, with power neatly diffused over all segments and all heads of households within segments. Big Men do arise, and sometimes reach such heights that it makes sense to speak of tyrannies. Robert Montagne's theory of an oscillation between tribal republics governed by assemblies of elders and temporary despotisms, inspired by southern Morocco early in this century, no doubt sometimes applies. Elsewhere, there is a more gradual spectrum from rule by assemblies with elective chiefs, to relatively small Big Men, to really powerful Big Men and to eventual subjection to a state. At one extreme, the tribe is a mechanism both for resisting the central state and for avoiding having a mini-state internally; elsewhere, it indulges in partial centralisation 'at home' so as better to resist the state, or to benefit from being its agent; one and the same chief may pursue either strategy at diverse times, or use one to complement or hide the other. Characteristically, the tribe is both an alternative to the state and also its image, its limitation and the seed of a new state. These transformations and ambiguities are of the essence of the socio-political history of Muslim lands. Nevertheless, decentralisation, diffusion of power, generalised participation in violence and order-enforcement, mutual opposition of groups similar in scale and occupation, and occurring simultaneously at a number of levels of size, the absence of a specialised and more or less permanent class of warrior-rulers — all this is what predominates, and justifies the 'segmentary' picture.

The concept of segmentation has an interesting history which antedates the work of Evans-Pritchard, in which it found its best expression. Leaving aside the folk formulations of the theory which abound within the very societies in which it flourishes, segmentation made its big entry into social theory with Emile Durkheim. Durkheim was in fact inspired in part by North African material, and Phillipe Lucas and Jean-Claude Vatin argue that probably the same is true of Marx and Engels, through M.M. Kovalevsky.[42] From the viewpoint of one who accepts the Evans-Pritchard notion of segmentation, Durkheim's version is incomplete in one important respect. It is basically, so to speak, *lateral*: Durkheim has a strong sense of the similarity of *adjoining* groups, and also of the similarity of individuals within the group to each other. For him, segmentary society is endowed with the cohesion of likeness, which is contrasted with 'organic solidarity', i.e. with cohesion based on *dis*similarity and mutual complementarity. But what he did not stress sufficiently in segmentary societies was the *vertical* likeness: groups resemble, not only their co-ordinate neighbouring groups, but also the super-ordinate groups of which they are parts, and the sub-ordinate groups which compose it. The clan resembles the tribe of which it is a clan. It also resembles the minor class and lineages of which it is itself composed. Groups are 'nested'; but the various levels of size or nesting resemble each other in function, ethos, terminology, and internal organisation.

This is an enormously important point, and one without which the idea of segmentary social organisation could not perform its explanatory role. Segmentary theory explains the cohesion and co-operation of groups, notwithstanding the fact that they are devoid of strong leadership or effective central institutions; it explains this cohesion by invoking the threat of other, similar and rival groups. The unifying effect of external threat is something which of course operates in all societies; what distinguishes 'segmentary' ones is not just that it is present, but that it is proportionately far stronger and becomes, if not the only principle in operation, at least the main and dominant one — or very nearly the only one. Segmentary groups are internally divided into smaller segments still (and so on), but they cohere at any given level (if and when they do) only through the threat of similar neighbouring groups of comparable size.

But this principle can only operate if indeed there are (at least latent) groups available at each and every level at which conflict is liable to arise. If there were only groups at *one* level of size, then what could contain conflicts arising between adversaries larger or smaller than the units at that one level? If this system is to work, groups are required at each level at which conflict may arise. And this is precisely what in fact we do find. The 'nesting' of groups is fairly dense. The jumps in size between various levels are not very great. A group subdivides into n segments — where n is a fairly small number, very seldom in double figures —

in fact seldom over seven, and usually less. The village will be a unit, capable of co-operating in the defence of its field and pasture; but it will also be internally segmented into groups capable of acting in defence of their share of, say, the water flowing through the village's irrigation ditches. But the village will also be part of a larger segment, collectively defending pasture areas, and so on.

Actual reality is seldom if ever quite as neat as the tree-like pattern of social organisation displayed by an ideal-typical segmentary society. Inequalities of wealth and power indisputably occur, and these of course can become particularly acute if the big man of the tribe also doubles up as agent of an encroaching central state; or again, kin and territorial criteria of segmentation often cut across each other, complicating the system further. Nevertheless, despite all such and similar qualification, the segmentary system does function, sometimes astonishingly well. The major and conclusive proof of this, to my mind, is the fact that very complex tasks, involving extensive territory and large numbers of people, such as an intricate pattern of seasonal pasture utilisation, or conflict containment or even resolution, can be performed by such tribal troups, without yet either producing or presupposing any kind of strong political centralisation or permanent social stratification, or any overt and stable hierarchy of authority.

What matters here is not so much segmentary organisation as such but rather, granting that it exists and is or was pervasive, the religious style which it engenders or which at least it favours, and which in turn aids it in the performance of its tasks. The system works, without the benefit of political centralisation, through the cohesion-prompting presence of violence at all levels: it is society and all its groups, and not the state (which is absent or distant or weak), which possess the 'monopoly of legitimate violence'. This threat can only be effective if it is at least sometimes actualised. This is of course what in fact occurs: observers are generally struck or appalled by the pervasiveness of violence, the threat of which is actualised often, perhaps too often. Nevertheless, the system does not disintegrate into total chaos. How is this attained?

The most characteristic religious institution of rural, tribal Islam is the living saint (naturalised in the English and French languages as the dervish and the marabout). But once again, a European background is liable to mislead one. Within Christianity, sanctity is an individual virtuoso performance. Sanctity, like genius, is unpredictable in its appearance. The notion of charisma, popularised in and by sociology, transmits this idea: the saint is the possessor of charisma, which is, precisely, the kind of aura and authority which knows no rules, which appears unpredictably, and which is contrasted with authority bound by precedent or regulation. Of course charisma does get routinised, but it is thereby tarnished and diminished. Routinised charisma is shop-soiled and has lost its glamour.

All such associations must be eliminated when dealing with Muslim sanctity. Of course, full-blown unroutinised charisma can also occur within Islam. But the typical saint is routinised, and is in no way tarnished thereby: it is the justification of his charisma (and *not* its diminution) that it is hereditary, and explained in terms of descent, notably from the Prophet. The saint is such in virtue of being part of a saintly lineage. Freelance, *ab initio* sanctity is proportionately much rarer, and when it succeeds in establishing itself, tends then to create its own lineage *ex post*, and thus it actually emulates and aspires to routinisation. As in other societies, the invented genealogy is the compliment of talent to privilege.

All this neatly dovetails with segmentary tribal society, which is a compromise between the state and anarchy. At all its many fissures it has a great need for arbitrators and mediators, and these can only function well if they are in it but not of it. Saintly status and, very often, obligatory pacifism, makes the mediators both viable and authoritative, standing as they do outside the web of alliance and feud; and selection by birth endows them with the same continuity and stability as that which is possessed by the segmentary groups. The roles performed by such saints include:

Supervising the political process in segmentary groups, e.g. election or selection of chiefs.

Supervising and sanctioning their legal process, notably by collective oath.

Facilitating economic relations, by guaranteeing caravans and visits to the markets of neighbouring tribes; trade and pilgrimage routes may converge.

Providing spatial markers for frontiers: a saintly settlement may be on the border between lay groups.

Providing temporal markers; in a pastoral society, many pasture rights may be bounded by seasons and require rituals for their ratification. What better than a saintly festival for such a purpose?

Supplying the means for the Islamic identification of the tribesmen. The tribesmen are no scholars. Not to put too fine a point on it, they are illiterate. They have neither the taste nor the equipment for the scholarly piety of a scripturalist urban faith. The reunions which mark the high points of agricultural pastoral and tribal life need to be *occasions*, with a heightening of consciousness if not ecstasy; not extramural theology classes of some tribal W.E.A.

All these factors clearly conspire to one end: the faith of the tribesmen needs to be mediated by special and distinct holy personnel, rather than to be egalitarian; it needs to be joyous and festival-worthy, not puritanical and scholarly; it requires hierarchy and incarnation in persons, not in script. Its ethic is one of loyalty, not of rule-observance.[43]

The urban scene is quite different. There is no need for mediators or arbitrators; for here the ruler assumes responsibility for justice, and appoints literate judges. No stable corporate groups face each other, such as would need both mediators and rituals for asserting their identities and boundaries. No such groups are allowed to persist. The well-heeled urban bourgeoisie, far from having a taste for public festivals, prefers the sober satisfactions of learned piety, a taste more consonant with its dignity and commercial calling. Its fastidiousness

41

underscores its standing, distinguishing it both from rustics and the urban plebs. In brief, urban life provides a sound base for scripturalist unitarian puritanism. Islam expresses such a state of mind better perhaps than other religions. Thus the political micro-sociology of the world of Ibn Khaldun provides us with the social basis for the polar-oscillation theory of religion found in Hume.

A faith in which theology is scarcely distinguishable from law, and in which the central corpus of law is sacred, thereby also acquires a kind of built-in separation of powers. The legislature is distinct from the executive power, for the simple reason that legislation is in principle ready-made and in theory complete, and pertains to God alone. This also gives a certain measure of independence to the judiciary: though they may be appointed by the ruler, they apply a law which cannot be the ruler's. For if legislation is God's, it is not the sultan's. The entire corpus of the law, and not just the constitution (which is absent), stands above the ruler. As only the literates have access to this Law, this also automatically confers a certain authority on the literate clerkly class in society. They have access to a set of norms which, in principle, the ruler cannot manipulate. Judges do not in theory make law, but a consensus of interpretation can in fact extend law.

Though physically defenceless *vis-à-vis* the ruler — indeed caught between him and the threat of tribal aggression, and needing the ruler's protection, and hardly inclined to defy him — yet the inherent hold of the literate class over the symbols and content of legitimacy, i.e. divine law, does give it, and the urban stratum from which its members are drawn, a position of some strength.[44] The social norms and ideals are in its keeping and outside the ruler's reach. They are available, in final and definitive form, to anyone who can *read*. The Norm is extra-ethnic and extra-social, and not too easily susceptible to political manipulation. This is of very great importance.

Within Shi'ism, there is a special nuance. On the one hand, through the martyrdom foundation-myth, vigorously internalised through the prominent and regular passion plays, the scholars are not merely jurists but also and above all experts in the founder-martyr's biography. But the fact that he was a victim of an at least putatively Muslim ruler makes it even easier for the religious leaders to de-legitimise political authority and mobilise opposition, in a way which must be the envy of more self-consciously revolutionary ideologies. The crime supplying the Foundation Martyrdom of Christianity was perpetrated by non-Christians, and consequently could only be used to justify persecution of a minority which was in any case politically disfranchised. The Shi'ite Martyrdom was perpetrated by Muslim rulers, and its symbolism can be used to de-legitimise Muslim rulers, and not just a powerless minority. The martyrdom was fiercely avenged, and revenge is also required when the politico-religious drama is re-enacted.[45] (Christianity, in any case not a peaceful civilisation, would presumably be less ambivalent about its own bellicosity if St Peter had organised a posse which in due course fearfully avenged the Crucifixion on Pontius Pilate and all those implicated in it, and if *this too* were remembered at Easter.) The Pahlevis, unlike the Romanoffs, were overthrown without prior defeat in war, with their military power intact and whilst endowed with enormous financial resources – an astonishing feat, and an impressive testimony to the capacity of Shi'ism for revolutionary mobilisation. The rioting crowds in Iran saw the Shah as Yazid, the murderer of Hussein.[46] Whether the religious scholars, when they have overturned the state, can run it themselves (as opposed to merely providing it with certain secretarial and bureaucratic services, at any rate in pre-modern conditions), is another question. Significantly, Iran even in the past had two different kinds of *ulama*, religious scholars: on the one hand, administrative-bureaucratic ones, and on the other, populist-mystical ones – the former serving religion and state, the latter catering to the religious needs of the masses.

The contrast between reverence for the Law and for the sacred person, which emerges in Sunni Islam as the opposition between scholar and Sufi, is within Shi'a Islam incorporated as an internal distinction into the scholar class itself. (Of course, even with Sunnism it is all a matter of stress and proportion: there are scholars among Sufis and Sufis among scholars.) But this inclusion of the distinction in the corpus of learned men in Shi'ism is perfectly logical, given that a cult of the martyred personality is at the very core of this sect. In our time, the complexity and technicality of the tasks facing a modern state and economy will no doubt affect the circumstances in which the two kinds of scholars, the Shi'ites with Ph.D.s and the populist mullahs, come to fight it out for the inheritance of the Iranian revolution.

It is interesting that in Iran modern conditions helped the urban *bazari* class, for once, actually to make a revolution without significant rural help; it is less likely that modern conditions will also help it actually to rule. In the past, in more traditional circumstances, the scholars did not always fully benefit from the revivalist, reformist revolutions which they helped bring about. In the Mahdia, for instance, it seems that they were displaced by the tribesmen when the state was established, though they were prominent when it was being erected by enthusiasm and conquest.[47]

The occultation of the Christian God was more conducive, one feels, to the civic training of the faithful than that of His Islamic counterpart. The Hidden God amongst the Christians was characteristically revered by groups such as the Nonconformists, amongst whom literacy was widespread: every man his own *alim*, you might say. Hence the occultation, jointly with the lack of provision of detailed divine regulation of social life, encouraged such communities of literates to attend to their own social arrangements, and thus to learn to manage them on their own, and to do it in a sober, scholarly and egalitarian manner. Religion thus provided civic-political training. This style then also came to be reflected in the polity, when they had the opportunity to form one, or to influence the organisation of an existing one. By contrast, the occultation of the Muslim God in Shi'ism does indeed, until the return of the Hidden Imam, push responsibility

43

into the path of the *ulama*: but they are a minority elite amongst an unscholarly turbulent majority, and this makes it more likely that they would have to aid the ruler in his governing the rest, or alternatively rouse the masses against him, than that they should turn to democratic self-government. It can however lead to a kind of separation of State and Church, by depriving the ruler, in the absence of the Hidden Imam, of the right to invoke *religious* legitimation. So all this provides another contrast with Christianity, in which scholar—puritans often belonged to a dissident, urban, egalitarian, self-governing minority and their religious life provided them with civic training in preparation for the liberal law-abiding state. Their very religion habituated them to committee work. The clerics in Islam belong to the religious majority and are used to serving the state, rather than administering themselves or their little nonconformist community, except of course for those exceptional situations when they condemn the state. But on those even rarer occasions when they denounce it successfully, when it topples, they are not ready with some new and different technique of (liberal-democratic) government. They often serve the state, and sometimes lead the people; but they do not form self-governing communities.

Orthodox Islam does of course also have its permanently dissident sub-communities, but they are characteristically segmented, or consist of religious 'orders', which provide mediation with God whether or not brokerage is warranted by the strictest theology of *this* faith. These orders, or the holy lineages which provide religious services for tribes (and the two can of course be linked in single or overlapping networks), are notoriously *not* egalitarian, but make a cult of submission and authoritarianism (far beyond, in fact, their power of actually implementing it). They are not recruited from scholarly, sober, urban strata. The consequence is of course that this kind of dissident religion does not provide civic training either. Tribesmen do have a kind of training in their own lay communities, often egalitarian; but religion is for them a hierarchical *complement to* their community, rather than continuous with it or part of it. Submission to Saint is discontinuous from tribal custom agreed by equal elders. Where tribal custom is consensual, the authority of Saint is (ideally, if not in fact) absolute and validated by a higher extraneous source.

If one divides this overall society into its four components — rulers, un-governed tribesmen, townsmen, and governed semi-tribal rural population — one sees that the first two elements are politically active and the latter two passive. It is profoundly significant that, whereas many non-Muslim enclaves survive within the latter two categories, they are almost completely absent from amongst the first two. Islam is a precondition of active political participation. Non-Islamic status can of course be a positive advantage and enhance the usefulness of a group, notably amongst urban specialists: quite apart from the obvious feature of making it liable to special taxation, the political disfranchisement of a group makes it a more attractive partner for special purposes. A financier who cannot aspire to political power is less dangerous and hence more appealing than one who can. (The forging of a tribal confederation can sometimes be achieved by urban money and supply of arms, not just by piety — as happened in southern Iran.) It is their political harmlessness, not some theological niceties about the permissibility of usury, which causes rulers to use minorities for financial and commercial operation. The selection of the palace guard is liable to be governed by similar considerations. But whilst exclusion or abstention from Islam does open these special doors, it closes the main one: the hope of becoming the ruler or part of his dominant group, when a new dynasty is born of the overlie of religious fervour and tribal spirit.

What would happen normally in traditional conditions if the scholars inside the city found the ruler gravely wanting when judged by the Norm? Nothing at all, for they are powerless, unarmed and lacking in the habit of cohesion. What would happen if bellicose tribesmen outside the walls had designs on the city? Most often likewise nothing at all, for these tribal wolves are generally at each other's throats, and their endless mutual feuds, often fostered by the ruler, neutralise them. They lust after the city anyway, but their internal divisions prevent them from satisfying their desire.

But what would happen if *both* these conditions were satisfied simultaneously, and if some authoritative cleric, having with some show of plausibility denounced the impiety and immorality of the ruler, thereby also provided a banner, a focus, a measure of unitary leadership for the wolves? What if he went into the wilderness to ponder the corruption of the time, and there encountered, not only God, but also some armed tribesmen, who responded to his message? This ever-latent possibility hangs over the political order, and is perhaps the Islamic form of the Permanent Revolution. Thus the purer form of the faith suits some people all the time (i.e. upper urban strata), but all of them some of the time (i.e. during the revivalist movements when it crystallises an ephemeral unity amongst the rustics who sustain the movement).

Of course, such fusions of nomocratic legitimacy and tribal cohesion do not always succeed. In fact, it does not even succeed frequently. Life would be even more unstable than it is, if it did. Crystallisation does not occur easily, even if the required elements are present. When they fail, as so often they do, they are retrospectively seen as frauds. (Justified reform never fails, for when it does, no one will deign to call it such.) Ibn Khaldun noted all this:

revolutionaries from among the common people and ... jurists ... undertake to reform evil practices. Many religious people who follow the ways of religion come to revolt against unjust amirs ... most of them actually do perish in consequence of their activities ...

Rulers and dynasties are strongly entrenched. Their foundations can be undermined and destroyed only through strong efforts backed by the group feeling of tribes ... Many deluded people took it upon themselves to establish the truth. They did not know that they would need group feeling for that.

For instance:

At the beginning of this century, a man known as al-'Abbas appeared among the Ghumarah. The lowest among the stupid and imbecile members of those tribes followed his bletherings . . . He was then killed, forty days after the start of his mission. He perished like those before him.

There are many similar cases. Their mistake is that they disregard the significance of group feeling . . .

Both truth and the support of tribal cohesion are required for success. And even if you have both, of course, you still can't be sure of success. Friedrich Engels, near the end of his life, summed it all up very well in an article published in 1894/5 in *Die Neue Zeit*:

Muslim risings, notably in Africa, make a remarkable contrast [with Christendom]. Islam suits Orientals, especially the Arabs, that is to say, on the one hand townsmen practising commerce and industry, on the other hand, nomadic Beduin. But there is in this the seed of a periodic collision. Townsmen, growing opulent and ostentatious, become lax in the observation of the 'Law'. The Beduin, poor and hence austere in their manners, contemplate the wealth and enjoyment with envy and lust. They unite under the direction of a prophet, a Mahdi, to punish the faithless, to re-establish the ceremonial law and true faith, and by way of recompense to appropriate the treasure of the faithless. A hundred years later, naturally, they find themselves at exactly the same point as their predecessors; a new purification is required; a new Mahdi emerges; the game re-starts. So it has come to pass since the wars of conquest of the Almoravides and the African Almohades in Spain till the latest Mahdi of Khartoum . . . It was the same, or very nearly, during the convulsions in Persia and other Muslim lands. These movements are born of economic causes even if they have a religious camouflage. But, even when they succeed, they leave the economic conditions intact. Thus nothing has changed, and the collision becomes periodic. By contrast, for the popular risings in the Christian West the religious camouflage is only the banner and mask for an attack on a crumbling social order: in the end, that order is overturned; a new one emerges; there is progress, the world moves on.

It is obvious that by then Engels had come across Ibn Khaldun's ideas. The availability of a translation dispensed him from the need to learn a Semitic language, for which, as he wrote to Marx, he had an aversion. In fact, Marx had annotated Kovalevsky, whose chapter on Algeria contained de Slane's translation of Ibn Khaldun in its bibliography.[48]

Engels's general picture is admirable. He is less than convincing on details, where he tends rather to jump to conclusions. Muslim burghers were unlikely to be ostentatious: who wishes to attract taxation or confiscation? It was the European bourgeoisie which could give itself such airs and get away with it. And the tribesmen, though possibly poor, did not generally practise moral austerity at home; this did not prevent them from invoking sinfulness and infidelity in the towns when coveting urban wealth, though the actual ostentation was probably governmental rather than bourgeois.

Thus, this state was not engendered by internal class conflict within either the conquering or the conquered society; and the theory that this is the origin of the state cannot be saved by the *Hilfshypothese* of the presence of 'embryonic' or 'early' class relationships among either conquerors or conquered. The conquerors were only stratified in the sense that, for once, for the duration of conquest and domination, they accept firm leadership, usually only engendered by success in this enterprise and growing in snowball fashion. The conquered urban and sedentary population may indeed be stratified and unequal, but this only indicates that it is well worth conquering, but it is not otherwise part of the preconditions of a conquest state, which arises, if anything, from lateral rather than horizontal strife.

It is interesting to see Engels subscribing so late to the thesis of the socially stagnant East — and an East embracing the Muslim West, and even paradigmatically exemplified in it. This throws some doubt on the argument[49] that Marx and Engels after 1881 overcame the European prejudice concerning Oriental stagnation (and, incidentally, the very notion of an Asiatic Mode of Production). Young Marxists[50] tend to see the idea of a stable or stagnant social structure in the Maghreb as a colonialist projection. If such it is, Engels appears to have shared it with great emphasis.

The stabilising, un-'progressive' role of religion, which Engels so deplored, is connected with its three more specific functions in this society, and its adaptation to them: it is the only available civic rights charter for the burghers, in some measure protecting them from arbitrary rule; it is the only social catalyst of unity on a sufficiently large scale for the pastoral tribes, in so far as the potential for the unification of local shrine and saint seems to have a ceiling not high enough to cover enough men to found a state, and they can unite only in the name of something Other and Better than their normal selves and piety; and its scholars provide secretarial services for the state when it is established. These roles are intertwined: the dynasty, owing its existence, power and authority to the faith, cannot disavow it and is vulnerable to criticism in its name, and its name only. Its agents naturally think in its idiom, for that is their only training. No other agents are available. Its subjects can only appeal to it if they want wrongs redressed or prevented. Thus, being linked to the natural bent of each of the participants, the system and the faith perpetuate and fortify themselves. Only by sinning against the faith, or by seeming to do so, can one provoke that urban/tribal alliance which can bring forth a new dynasty.

This helps to explain why the traditional Muslim state is simultaneously and without contradiction both a Robber State, run for the benefit of a dominant group, and a moralistic state, bound to promote good and proscribe evil. It is carried by and identified with a dominant group, yet it also has an inbuilt vocation towards the implementation of a sharply identified divine order on earth.

In the days of the Prophet, the rules of inheritance were said to constitute half of the Law. In pastoral or pastoral-dominated societies, based essentially on family ownership of herds and collective tribal ownership of pasture, the central concern is no doubt — *who inherits what*. Industrial society is incomparably more complex, and claims on resources and advantages in it have more devious forms. But the urge to impose a severe moralistic rule on the distribution of advantages in industrial society is known as socialism. It may be for this reason that the moralistic tradition inherent in Islam, its vocation to uncompromising and implemented righteousness, has its curious elective affinity for modern social radicalism. It can still be combined with the presence of a dominant group. The totalism of both ideologies precludes institutionalised pluralistic politics and thus protects the rulers. So 'Islamic Marxism', which no doubt would have astonished Engels, is only superficially paradoxical.

Urban saints

But the towns do not provide a base only for the scholarly, unitarian, puritanical faith of the bourgeoisie. Not everyone living in the city is comfortable, sober and contented; not everyone looks to religion for a ratification of his own cherished place in the world and the cautious, orderly life-style which goes with it. Some, on the contrary, look to it for an escape from an unsatisfactory or even intolerable condition. The city has its poor; they are uprooted, insecure, alienated, with little inclination towards the more abstract and arid branches of theology. What they require from religion is consolation or escape; their taste is for ecstasy, excitement, stimulation, an absorption in a religious condition which is also a forgetting. They crave the audio-visual aids of faith, whether in the form of music, dance, intoxication, trance or possession. Mystical states, with or without pharmaceutical aids, appeal to them more than scholarly precision or learned distinctions. So, like the tribesmen, but for other reasons altogether and in a different style, they need a religion externalised in ritual and personality. For the tribesmen, the festival is an externalisation and highlighting of their effective social groups, in true Durkheimian manner. For the urban poor folk, it is a compensation for the *absence* of such groups.[51]

Islam officially has no 'church'. The community of the faithful is not, in theory, internally differentiated into a lay society and the body of the extra-specially faithful. In practice, however, it does possess a multitude of mini-churches, variously characterised as religious orders or brotherhoods and centered upon their specific saints. They do not, however, *fuse* into one overall organisation, which could thereafter monopolise and rationalise sanctity and magic. These orders possess a fairly standard terminology for their constituent units (lodges) and for the hierarchy of their leadership.

This homogeneity of nomenclature is however profoundly misleading. The underlying social reality is in fact quite diversified. At one extreme, there may be urban lodges which are in effect religious clubs, recruited individually, by voluntary adherence and enthusiasm; at the other extreme, there may be a tribal holy settlement, whose members are recruited exclusively by birth. You can join a *lay* tribal group simply by placing a shame compulsion on it, by making a 'sacrifice to it' and thereby placing yourself under its protection; but it is not so easy to enter a lineage through which there flows a current of hereditary holiness, and if one does join it at all, it is not on terms of equality. The lay followers of such a holy settlement tend to adhere to it not as single converts but in tribal battalions.

Moreover, one and the same 'order' or 'brotherhood' will contain units of quite diverse kind, ranging from those approximating to a purely voluntary urban religious club or association to kin-selected hereditary tribal segments. Its diversity may be its strength. The leadership which unites the various units, territorially dispersed and spread out along this organisational spectrum, will tend to be hereditary; but spiritual lineages, in which the links are those of teacher and disciple, will also often be intertwined with the more literally genetic ones of father and son. Furthermore, these movements are of course not always stable. Either success or decline will affect their internal structure. An expanding movement with an urban base may be relatively 'bureaucratic' — i.e. the central leader, when nominating representatives at new centres, may be inclined to select talented disciples rather than sons. By contrast, a stabilised, so to speak routinised, movement is more likely to rely on well-tested links of family, and is in any case liable to be swayed by the need to place the offspring of the current leader or leaders.

The original nucleus of such a movement may be located at either end of the organisational spectrum. A successful tribal thaumaturge may acquire urban followers and then found urban clubs; or an influential urban saint may be successful in his missionary work among tribes, and establish centres amongst them which eventually become tribal units with a hereditary religious vocation — padre segments, so to speak.

Those who approach these phenomena through texts alone are liable to be misled in a variety of ways. As stated, homogeneity of nomenclature may hide a great diversity of structural forms. In so far as all these movements tend to seek filiation to prestigious points of origin, and in so far as all these spiritual filiations tend in the end to converge on great Middle Eastern saints/mystics, there is a tendency to class all the movements together as branches of 'Sufism'. This interpretation, based on their own internal view of origins, is further reinforced by the fact that the brand-differentiating, diacritical totems of these movements tend to be special, distinctive spiritual practices and techniques. No doubt the more serious ones amongst these movements are indeed schools of mysticism, perpetuating sophisticated and complex mystical techniques which, as such, may perhaps have a definite point of origin, and whose diffusion can be studied like that of an intellectual idea. Others amongst these movements are mystical only in the loose sense that their assemblies promote heightened excitement — and, to this end, they simply draw on the practices currently available in the local folk culture.

Another point at which the textual scholar may be misled concerns the authoritarianism of these movements. At the level of doctrine, there can be no doubt about their severe authoritarianism. The oft-quoted assertion about the relationship of leader to followers is: the disciple must be in the hands of his shaikh as the corpse in the hands of the washers of the dead. But, here as elsewhere, doctrine often compensates for the imperfections of reality, rather than reflecting it faithfully. These movements are inevitably loose associations, territorially discontinuous, and mostly devoid of any physical means of imposing their will on subordinates. The head of a minor lodge does of course owe his position and prestige to his endorsement by the more general leader at the central lodge, and to that extent, sanctions are indeed available to extract reverence and tithes from him for the centre: without the endorsement of the prestigious centre, he might receive neither respect nor donations from his own underlings in turn. But these sanctions are not absolute. There exist rival movements soliciting followers, and securing a defection from the clientele of another movement may constitute particular-choice demonstration or the superior sanctity of the leader . . . So, in practice, the reciprocal services and advantages of leaders and followers are reasonably well balanced, and do not encourage leaders to make excessive, peremptory or provocative demands.

The fundamental fact is that these movements, associations of ranked saint-worship and mystical practice, satisfy the various and often quite distinct needs for personal leadership, for incarnated holiness, for the cult of personality, as it arises in both tribal and urban contexts. But whilst this is the fundamental truth of the matter, even this calls for a certain qualification. Within the enormous mass of these movements, some are much nearer the ecstatic, non-scripturalist end of the spectrum than others. Some, on the other hand, are close to the sober urban—unitarian—puritan—scripturalist end, and these then constitute a kind of compromise between the egalitarianism of the scholarly puritan style — the idea that all believers have equal access to the Sacred through Holy Writ — and the requirements of a minimum of *organisation*. The orthodox solution of this problem, which relies on nothing more than loose guilds of scholars—jurists, on the Schools of Law, may not always be adequate. For instance, in the savannah belt of West Africa, the values of the puritan end of the spectrum are represented by some of the big religious orders, possibly because a minimal central organisation was required in missionary circumstances.[52] Or again, the work of the Sanusiya order in the Eastern and Central Sahara was primarily missionary in kind, and missionary on behalf of 'proper' learned Islam — but it *was* nevertheless carried out by an order, rather than under the banner of anti-Sufi, anti-saintly, anti-mediation puritanism. Conversely, one should remember the Palestinian story of the pious man who preached against shrine worship with such fervour that

50

he became venerated, and on his death his tomb promptly became a revered shrine.

Tribal puritans

So, whilst the faith of the scholars sets the tone in the cities, reality is more complex. The same is also true in the tribal world. But in the towns, the complexity was introduced, first of all, by social stratification, by the differences in the religious taste of diverse urban strata. It would also be an exaggeration to say that the faith of the scholars and of the mystics is always in opposition. No doubt there are times when their opposition remains latent, and then the two styles permeate each other. The scholars too will have their shaikhs, spiritual mystics, leaders: 'He who has no shaikh has the devil for his shaikh', as they used to say in Morocco. Nevertheless, the latent opposition remains, ready to be activated.[53] The Wahabis, for instance, activated it in the eighteenth century:

> Wahab's rebel brood who dared divest
> The Prophet's tomb of all its pious spoil . . .
> Byron, *Childe Harold*, Canto II, LXXVII

It is interesting to note that apparently the Wahabis saw their task in virtually the same terms as the Reformers of modern times:

When Muhammad ibn Sa'ud . . . decided in 1744 to champion the religious revival preached by . . . Muhammad ibn 'abd al-Wahhab . . . Orthodox Islam, especially among the bedouin of Najd, had degenerated into a multitude of superstitious practices, cults of tree and stone worship; tribal and customary law, for the most part, prevailed among the bedouin and sedentary population . . . and had eroded the influence and primacy of Islamic Law . . .[54]

The Wahabis were a little premature for the major wave of neo-puritanism, which was to receive its stimulus from the colonial impact of Europe. When the impetus came, in North Africa for instance, those who were sensitive to its appeal were nevertheless liable to repudiate the Wahabi connection, which had in the meantime acquired a bad name. Timing may be important. Beware of being a premature Reformer.

Foreign aggression, one might add, is liable to have a different impact according to the scale on which it comes. The first wave of Iberian aggression against North African Islam — before Iberian energies were diverted into the New World and the Indian ocean — is said to have provoked an upsurge of the marabouts, in the so-called 'maraboutic crisis'. (The argument for this is not entirely conclusive, but is widely accepted. As Dr Magali Morsy has pointed out, the geographical distribution of the saints does not support the view that they arose as leaders of resistance at the frontier with the infidel.) Even the initial French aggression in the 1830s helped crystallise what was essentially a maraboutic state around Amir Abd el Kader.[55] On the other hand, the qualitatively quite different and incom-

51

parably greater impact of industrial society powerfully impelled Egyptian and North African Islam, as well as, for instance, the Islam of South-East Asia, towards the scripturalist end of the spectrum.[56] Pure scripturalism is thus caught between two enemies: lax pre-literate tribesmen, and modern townsmen, ultra-literate to the point of scepticism. Scripturalism flourishes nowadays in the area between the two, amongst partially urbanised ex-countrymen, not yet at home, secure and well placed in the modern city,[57] eager to disavow all at once both their own rustic past and those socially above them, who have gone too far and done too much too enviably well out of modernity.

Amongst the tribes, by contrast, it was normally the hereditary holy lineage which set the tone; but the nuances and complexities of the picture are not due to any differences in religious consumption between tribal shaikhs and humble tribesmen. Their tastes in this matter, as in others, do not differ significantly, if at all. Here the complexity enters in quite a different manner. Amongst the tribes, difference in religious taste is not a matter of class or status: it is a matter of time-scale and political occasion.

Religion in the tribe serves different purposes at different times and on different occasions. Perhaps, following the idea of Thomas Kuhn in the philosophy of science, one should distinguish between Normal religion, and Exceptional or Revolutionary religion. *Normal* religion is indeed that of the dervish or marabout. It is highly Durkheimian, concerned with the social punctuation of time and space, with season-making and group-boundary-marking festivals. The sacred makes these joyful, visible, conspicuous and authoritative, and not too much else is expected of it. In fact, were it to attempt *more*, it might not normally be tolerated.

But the sacred which performs these tasks is generally a rather petty form of it. This is entirely appropriate. The sanctioning of a village festival, the underwriting of a frontier between two petty tribal segments, is a job well suited for a little holy man whose settlement barely if at all exceeds in dignity those of the parishioners who call on his services. Corresponding to a proliferation of these little requirements, there is a similar multiplication of little shrines and holy personnel associated with them. These holy men are not only numerous, they are also inescapably and vigorously in competition with each other. There is a kind of second-level segmentation: tribal groups of diverse size keep each other in check by mutual competition, and, similarly, their spiritual shepherds balance or neutralise each other in turn in mutual rivalry. They may not fight (ideally), but they can and do compete for reverence.

What follows, however, is that they are most ill-equipped to provide inspiring leadership on a grand scale, should the occasion for it arise. They are too divided and mutually competitive. Under normal conditions, there is no call for such large-scale leadership; the petty local feud, the problem of co-ordinating pasture use, and so forth, can be and are dealt with by the little holy man, and normal religion prevails. But suppose there is some larger task, requiring concerted action by an entire region, transcending tribal boundaries? Such occasions do arise, when there is an alien invasion, or when the nominal overall ruler provides the opportunity and warrant, by his decline in authority and religious propriety, for an attempt to turn the political wheel of fortune, for a rotation of the tribal circulation of elites. Then a distinctively different and superior kind of leadership is required, and has its chance.

Thus we return to the question — what happens when a ruler's internal loss of moral authority (whose evaluation is in the hands of the students of the Law), and the crystallisation of external opposition by the tribal wolves, come to pass simultaneously? The manner in which demanding, puritan unitarianism *also* enters tribal life, and the manner in which tribes are induced on special occasions to accept overall leadership, are the *same*. The exceptional crisis in the tribal world provides the opening, the opportunity, for that 'purer' form of faith which normally remains latent, respected but not observed.

It is a curious but crucial fact about the social psychology of Muslim tribesmen that their normal religion is for them *at one level* a mere *pis aller*, and is tinged with irony, and with an ambivalent recognition that the real norms lie elsewhere. Thus the tribal holy man will claim, amongst his legitimating traits, the fact that his ancestor was a great scholar — though he himself makes no very serious efforts in this direction. Under normal circumstances, this recognition is ambivalent, ironical and ineffective. It would perhaps be good if the local marabout were also a scholar, but, between ourselves, who cares? The implications of this latent norm do indeed remain latent. But for all that, the norm does provide a hold, a *prise*, an entry-point, for that special appeal in an exceptional situation, when an unusual, outstanding, more general and demanding leadership, activating a wider unit, is possible and required. There is an underlying shared current of unitarian iconoclasm in the religions of the God of Abraham, but felt with special tension perhaps in Islam, which makes even the most uncouth, ignorant, heterodox, sybaritic, Dionysiac marabout look rather like a fastidious Quaker, when compared with the folk shamans or priests of non-iconoclastic religions such as, for instance, those of South-East Asia.

This latent recognition of a purer norm thus provides that major premiss for the exceptional preacher, who is needed for the special mission and the activation of a wider loyalty. It helps him who had come from town to denounce, all at once, the laxity and backsliding at the centre, the ignorance of the tribesmen, and the heterodoxy of the normal, petty, humdrum religious attendants. The tacit recognition of the more rigorous, exclusive, unitarian ideal provides such a personage with something to invoke, something already present and occasionally ready for activation in the hearts of his listeners. It is his scholarship and unitarianism which distinguish him from the normal and petty forms of the sacred, and allow him to supersede them for a time. Of course, there are many who try this. Mostly they fail. But some do succeed.

Church and state

It is in this manner that the polarity and oscillation found in Hume's sociology of religion can be welded to the political sociology of Ibn Khaldun, giving a composite but adequate picture of traditional Muslim society. The impulsion towards personalised, organised, hierarchical, ecstatic, unpuritanical, unscriptural religion comes in the first instance from the needs of tribal society, and, secondly, from the needs of the less privileged urban strata. Tribal society requires that the Word should become flesh; it needs human mediators, tribal frontier posts, spatial and temporary markets, masters of ceremonies; it recognises an ethic of loyalty rather than an ethic of rules; and the urban poor, on the other hand, need ecstatic consolation. Sufism is then the opium of the people.

But traditional Muslim civilisation is an urban one, in which towns dominate economically and culturally, but *not* politically. This urban ethos finds its expression in scholarship, sober unitarian piety, and aspires, not so much towards theocracy, as towards divine nomocracy, in Professor Montgomery Watt's suggestive expression.[58] It has a much smaller need of opiates. This reverence for an extra-ethnic, extra-historical Law becomes part of the power balance of the society:[59] it provides the burghers with an ideological sanction against authority, and one which can become seriously menacing if and when a puritan scholar succeeds in rousing and fusing some of the tribal wolves. It thus has a role in the tribal world, too – it provides it with Exceptional Religion, fit for special and literally revolutionary, wheel-of-political-fortune-moving tasks. It is thus that Ibn Khaldun's famous tribal version of the eternal circulation of elites, and David Hume's strangely neglected theory of flux and reflux in religion, are aspects of one and the same process.

This civilisation seems a kind of mirror-image of traditional Christendom. In Islam, it is the central tradition which is egalitarian, scripturalist, devoid of hierarchy or formal leadership or organisation, puritanical, and moralistic; whereas it is the marginal, questionably orthodox movements which are fragmented, ritualistic, hierarchical, ecstatic and deeply implicated in, if not compromised by, local political structures. In Europe, it was the big, national or trans-national religious organisations which were most deeply involved with one social order or another; whereas the small fragmented sects which were the least involved and most severely moralistic, theocratic or world-defying. Churches were disembodied states. *The* Church was a disembodied super-state. They monopolised, systematised and bureaucratised magic, or at any rate did their best to do so. At the same time, strong states, in the literal sense, pacified the countryside, and thus freed the townsman of the fear of baron or tribesman. So dissident burghers, finding the magical end of the religious spectrum already pre-empted by an international or national church, and having in the main only the central state to oppose, were inclined to turn to the scripturalist style of religion – which may in any case have been more to their taste – and to use it in efforts to wrest a

share of power and political security. (Where towns were in any case independent, as in Italy, this tendency may have been correspondingly weaker.) In
Islam, this is inverted. The hierarchical associations, which most resemble
churches, were not shadow states but only disembodied *tribes.*[60]

Such spiritual dissidents were more prone to provide leadership for rural,
tribal groupings, and less so for any urban attempts at civic resistance to government. Urban *frondes* looked more characteristically to scholars for legitimation
and leadership. The towns, eager to distinguish themselves from the rustics, were
more inclined to identify with the literate Great Tradition, which in this civilisation is central and not normally dissident. In any case towns, fearing tribal
pillage, had less incentive to defy the central power which was their natural protector. This scripturalism could lead to some measure of egalitarianism — at least
to the extent of a reluctance to endow social inequality with a religious stamp,
terminology, authority, rigidity and depth, a reluctance partly modified in
differing degree in various times and places, in favour of the alleged progeny of
the Prophet. It also led very significantly to an attempt to impose moral criteria
on government, but not to participatory politics or the demand for public
accountability for policy. Instead, it contented itself with the requirement that
the ruler should both fulfil and enforce moral norms. So the state was subject to
Law, and the Law had its learned guardians, but there were no permanent, institutional arrangements for enforcing it against an evil ruler, still less for ensuring
real or symbolic general participation in such sanctions. There was no impeach-
ment machinery. For ultimate sanctions, the system had to rely on the occasional
and exceptional alliance of inspired scholar with cohesive tribes.

This structure is also sharply contrasted with that once fashionable model of
Eastern society, 'hydraulic' oriental despotism. That model assumed the existence of isolated and insulated rural communities, combining crafts and agriculture, all endowed with similar but competing interests, and supinely subject to a
well-centralised, bureaucratic state. The traditional rural Muslim world did
indeed contain mutually competitive rural communities; they were not supine,
but on the contrary were addicted to violence amongst themselves, and did not
delegate enforcement and politics to a central state. They did not combine
crafts with agriculture or pastoralism; instead, they practised and valued the
dominant agrarian or pastoral pursuit and delegated crafts to artisans whom they
despised, whether they lived in towns or amongst the tribesmen. The central
state did indeed exist, but the hold it had — for what it was worth — over tribesmen did not arise either from the maintenance of indispensable irrigation works,
or from terror. Generally there were no such essential public works, and the
state, though perfectly willing, was not able to apply so much terror. The hold
which the central state did have was rather cultural/religious; it protected the
towns, and the towns were the centres of both sacred learning and of trade and
crafts, without which the tribesmen evidently could not manage.

A weak state and a strong culture — that seems to be the formula.[61] The cul-

55

ture was in the keeping of a relatively open, non-hereditary and thus non-exclusive class, but without a central secretariat, general organisation, formal hierarchy, or any machinery for convening periodic councils. Its authority, though in part explicable by the need in such a society for urban services, the capacity of clerkly faith to express the urban ethos, and by the ever-present threat of a reforming-preacher/tribal-*fronde* alliance, nonetheless remains a sociological mystery. *Because* this religious culture had such a hold over the people, *therefore* urban religious services were essential, and *therefore* also the spectre of a preacher leading the tribes had to be present to the mind of the ruler, enjoining *him* in turn to enforce the good and prohibit evil. But this theory explains the hold of culture by invoking it one step further back. Perhaps we cannot go beyond describing this self-perpetuating circle.

The unhinging of the pendulum

With the coming of modernity, the stability of the structure and its internal rotation end. The picture ceases to be adequate, the swinging pendulum becomes unhinged, and finally flies off in one direction, perhaps for ever. This in itself does not undermine the usefulness of the model — rather the reverse, for it illuminates the manner in which the pendulum does become unhinged under modern conditions.

Modernity means, first of all, effective centralisation and so the end or decline of tribalism. The traditional Muslim state may have been absolute more in pious aspiration than in fact.

The sovereign, who before found his power (despotic in name) circumscribed, because with all the will, he had not the real art of oppressing, by the aid of science finds himself a giant.[62]

The modern state (whether colonial or post-colonial) can, must and does monopolise legitimate violence. In other words, it undercuts those local military and political mutual-help associations which, whether self-conceived in terms of kinship, territory or compact, are known as tribes.[63] It thereby also removes the need for that religious unguent which oiled the friction in their joints and between them, in other words the revered saintly personnel who mediate between men by claiming to mediate with God. Moreover, keeping the peace, the state enables travel for purposes of trade to be carried out without let or hindrance, and thus frees it from the need of saintly protection, or of doubling up as a pilgrimage. The commercial traveller need no longer be a pilgrim.

One might almost say that the existence of a politically independent *zawiya* proves that in the place in question, tribalism has bested the authority of officials (*caids*).[64]

When this happens, the petty saints, like French nobles, in the late stages of the *ancien régime*, are seen to retain some of their perks but to perform little or no social function, a combination well calculated to provoke a good deal of resentment against them. The time is then ripe to denounce them as pious, or impious, frauds, battening on popular superstition, a public disgrace, and indeed an accomplice of the colonialist foreigners in the degradation of the true Muslim culture of the country. The theological prohibition of mediation, long and conveniently forgotten, can suddenly be recalled, and the message now sounds compelling. Clearly this is a case of

> The law hath not been dead,
> though it hath slept.

But the new situation does more than all this. It tilts the entire balance in favour of urban styles of life as against tribal ones. In Morocco during the colonial and immediate post-colonial periods, the world of Ibn Khaldun overlapped with the world of Karl Marx. Tribes were still mobilisable *as* tribes, and in fact, on occasion, as late as the 1950s they joined political parties, and swore an oath of loyalty to them, *as* tribal units. The first study of Moroccan political parties, Paul Rezette's, stressed the manner in which their organisation followed that of the religious orders. At the same time, the shanty-towns outside the industrial towns house a new, raw and explosive proletariat. In the Yemen, contrary to the development prevailing elsewhere, the political significance of tribes increased in the twentieth century rather than declined. The traditional Imamate is remembered as a period of strong and effective government, which, within the limits of the constraints under which traditional government operates, it certainly was. Since then, the hold of a would-be modernising government at the centre over the tribal periphery has weakened, partly because the tribes receive support and encouragement from outside forces. In consequence, in the northern part of the country at least, the entire tribal system can be seen functioning in full pristine vigour right into the 1980s. (Personal communication from Shelagh Weir).

The traditional 'Sharifian Empire' in Morocco, nominally perpetuated by the French protectorate, had been unable to cope with the tribes, though it had little trouble from the urban poor. Unlike the Roman Empire, which apparently had to import slaves to replace and appease the plebs,[65] Muslim empires did not normally need to appease the lower orders of the towns. (Characteristically, the most significant use of slaves in Islam was not at the bottom of the social scale, but at the top. They were imported, not to replace the lower classes but to rule them, to replace the tribal groups which had previously intimidated and/or ruled them. Slaves, ideally torn from their kin context, can be more rationally deployed than free men, burdened with all their social bonds. It looks as if Romans could use such systematic and rational deployment of manpower at the bottom, whilst Turks required it at the top. Systematic — as opposed to occasional, domestic — slavery is indeed *rational* in that it permits the use of manpower for single and hence calculable aims, as opposed to the tangled, incommensurate criteria

57

applied to the work of men enmeshed in reciprocal obligations of kinship or loyalty.)

By contrast with the traditional state, the colonial authorities could cope with tribes, and indeed used them as sheepdogs, but were unable to cope with the new urban poor. The new Moroccan urban proletariat was both large and, unlike the lowest urban strata under the *ancien régime*, indispensable for an emerging industrial order; it resembled the English working class observed by Engels in the 1840s; and there was no way of controlling it when it went into violent dissidence, short of a level of brutality no longer open to a European power at that time. The colonial state could cope fairly easily with what had been the nemesis of the traditional one, namely the tribes, but could not cope with what had been no serious problem for its predecessor, the numerically swollen urban poor. The traditional state did not fear the towns; the colonial one did not fear tribes.

Population under the new dispensation does not merely grow, it becomes increasingly urbanised, either by actual migration, or by rural imitation of urban models. The tribal style of religion loses then much of its function, whilst the urban one gains in authority and prestige from the great eagerness of migrant rustics to acquire respectability. And there are also considerations of general ideology, which become particularly pressing when Muslim identity is crucial in an overall political conflict, notably with an alien colonial power. The scripturalist style of faith is modernisable; the tribal and saintly one is *not*. The scripturalist version can be presented as a national ideology, defining all Moslems in a given territory as one nation (even if that, as in Pakistan, leads to a dilemma as to whether faith or nation is the basis of the state). It is also possessed of an international ideological dignity: petty hereditary saints and their market-place profane festivals lack it. What a nation uses for attracting tourism it cannot also invoke for workaday and serious identity. Better far to see the old tribal forms as corrupt aberrations, which had been introduced or encouraged by the foreign occupying power.[66]

There are two outstanding models of modernisation by Muslim states — *against* religion and *with* it. The first is of course that of Kemalism, the second of Muslim Reformism. Nationalism and modernist political movements may be anti-religious if previously religion has been closely tied to the old order. As Serif Mardin observes about Turkey:

Shackled to the state, official Islam could produce no original solution to the problems raised by the impact of the West.[67]

Another case of Islam-shackled-to-the-state, and thus leading to an at least relative secularism, was Tunisia.[68] By contrast, where a colonial authority imposed itself and tolerated or utilised unregenerate traditional forms, Reform overlapped with nationalism; Reformism indeed appeared to be the early form of nationalism.

Flux and reflux in the faith of men

The strong Ottoman state had favoured the development of autonomous, self-administering, quasi-national communities (millets). Under modern conditions, when rapid occupational mobility and technical innovation make peaceable co-habitation of specialised communities difficult or impossible, each of these communities attempts to capture or create its own state. In other words, nationalism becomes dominant. (In one case only, the eccentric and perhaps tragic case of Lebanon, were the communities obliged, by an unstable balance of power, to continue to coexist under a political roof not belonging to any one of them. The Ottoman state was strong and could rely on the various communities to run their own affairs internally. This was convenient for rulers and ruled. But modernity meant a new kind of division of labour, incompatible with the political or economic specialisation of entire communities. So the state reclaimed its full prerogatives and at the same time each community tried to capture or create its own state. The lucky ones had, or acquired, their own territorial base. The succession states were thus *national* states, within each of which culture and polity were congruent and minorities were absorbed, expelled, or reduced to some degree of more or less irredentist submission. Only in the Lebanon did the process go the opposite way: the communities took over the role of the state. The state for once really did wither away, but not to make room for a classless, let alone community-less harmony, but rather, making way for a precarious, explosive balance of communities. All power is to go, not to the Soviets, but to the communities.) At the same time, puritan/radical Islam replaces the plural and socially enmeshed form of religion which had mostly preceded it; and this happens with special virulence in places where the struggle with a dominant foreign power (or, in Iran, a Westernised ruling class) is acute and bitter. The two processes, 'purification' or radicalisation of religion, and nationalism, are often intimately intertwined, to a degree that it is hard to say which one is 'merely' the external form of the other.

It is interesting that Balkan Muslims constitute one of the fairly rare cases in which the spokesman of the 'cult-of-personality-and-mediation' type of Islam dares to polemicise vigorously with the representatives of 'Reform'. (Elsewhere, the representatives of this, now apparently discredited form tended rather to trim their position so as to meet the criticisms levelled at them and to satisfy in some measure the norms of their critics.) The explanation of the Balkan idiosyncrasy is easy: these Muslims were in any case minorities within their national communities, whether they were Sufi *or* scripturalists; hence the puritans could not intimidate their opponents by the implicit or overt threat of branding them as national traitors.

In practice, the Kemalist, anti-religious style of striving for progress can drive the previously opposed wings of Islam into an alliance against its own secularising policy, and thus find itself landed with a permanent religious problem.[69] Much of post Second World War Turkish political history seems to hinge on the dilemma facing the Westernising secularist elite: either to have free elections, and thereby to hand over electoral victory to parties willing to play up to the religiosity of the countryside and small towns, or to uphold the Kemalist heritage, but only at the cost of overruling the popular vote. It seemed that they could have democracy, or secularism, but not both: the version of the modernist package which they had adopted and internalised turned out surprisingly to contain incompatible ingredients. The Army as guardian of the Kemalist legacy may then intrude and proclaim a *nuancé* version of the social contract to the religious interest: you may win the elections, and benefit from your victory in moderation, but if you push your luck too far we'll step in again and hang you. One distinguished Turkish social scientist even went, in the attempt to resolve this dilemma, so far as to contemplate seeing support for the forces of progress in the Eastern Anatolian rural and permissive ('Alevi') Islam.[70] He was not a solitary case. If disabused Marxists sometimes turn to Buddhism, disabused Kemalists (or Nasserites) may turn to Sufism (but refined, urban-apartment Sufism is no longer the same as the annual pilgrimage/festival of a tribal segment).

The first generation of Kemalist modernisers embraced secularism in an unwittingly Koranic, puritanical and uncompromising spirit. Professors would issue secularist *fatwas* through the press, confirming the legitimacy of a political coup. They still knew their Islam inside out, and also had to fight it in their own hearts, and unwittingly fought it in its own style and by its own rules. They were the *ulama* of Kemalism, and taught and thought like *ulama*. The next generation knew much less about Islam and had no need to fear it inwardly, and hence are far more willing to find accommodation with popular sentiment.

By contrast, Muslim states modernising in the name of Reformed Islam seem to escape much of this painful *Kulturkampf*, though the demonstration effect of Khomeiny's revolution may encourage new pressure from their own extremists. But hitherto, at any rate, they seem to have been spared much of this strain. For instance, Algeria has a semi-legal Communist Party, weirdly symbiotic with the regime, notwithstanding the fact that only the F.L.N. is formally recognised. This C.P. is tolerated subject to good conduct and abstention from excess of zeal. The Central Committee of this party on occasion suspends its debates for a Muslim prayer session (*sic*). An official of the party, explaining and defending this practice, claimed that Marx only said that religion was the opium of the people *before* he became a Marxist — a most remarkable case of the use of the *coupure*, of the alleged crystallisation-point of Marxism, for determining what is and is not truly part of the doctrine.

In Soviet Central Asia, the Russians have combined the two approaches.[71] Reformism (Jadidism) is proscribed, but its ideas are stolen and assigned to the official Muslim cult. Thus the orthodox permission to suspend the fast in wartime is invoked: is not the struggle to erect a socialist economy also a war, which warrants a similar exemption for those actively engaged in it? Contemporary Sufism is likewise proscribed, but its historic manifestations acclaimed as achievements of local culture. Only a dead Sufi may be a good Sufi, though he may indeed be officially certified as good. In 1964 in Tashkent, the Grand Mufti of Central Asia made a speech in Uzbek to a delegation of visiting anthropologists explaining that Islam held there was but one God; hence all men were brothers; hence they ought not to throw nuclear devices at each other. The Soviet government, he added, adopted a similar position on this matter, and so there was a happy convergence between Islam and the views of the Soviet authorities. Margaret Mead, self-appointed Grand Mufti of the anthropologists, promptly stood up to reply, and assured him that anthropology, too, held that all men were brothers and ought not to bomb each other, and so we could all rejoice in a triple convergence between Islam, the Soviet authorities and anthropology.

The Reformers generally first sweep away rural superstition, or at least sweep it under the carpet, in the name of a purer and truer Islam (which may in fact never have existed locally); and when they assume the mantle of orthodoxy, they do not subsequently seem to offer very much opposition to the new national state, which in any case may be quite inclined to ensure that the moral tone of the community conforms to their requirements.

The ideal of divine nomocracy, of the pure application of divine law which they uphold, has its enemies or obstacles on two flanks: the traditional rural tribal society on one side, not normally quite capable of living up to so demanding a code, and modern secularism on the other. The first impact of the modern world, with its greater political centralisation, mobility and literacy, is to aid the Law against the old kind of tribal heterodoxy. The old rival weakens long before the new one has time fully to assert itself.

The outcome of the second conflict — fundamentalism against modernism — is far from clear. The elective affinity of scripturalist rigorism or fundamentalism with the social and political needs of the period of industrialisation or 'development' is fairly clear. It is a period which calls for much discipline and self-sacrifice, for self-discipline above all, and for orderliness and literacy, the obedience to abstract rules, imposed by central and as it were disembodied authority. One has to perform one's duties *religiously*, as the significant English locution has it. (The rival religious style was always incarnated in local personalities and more tangible, immediate, yet more pliable, social pressures.) The actual content of the doctrine imposed by fundamentalism also makes few unpalatable demands, though it may make some such demands, which seem archaic or barbarous to the modern mind, and thus impose a certain strain; but it may well be that, for the viability of a religion, its specific doctrines on faith or morals matter far less than their spirit. Whether that spirit can also remain compatible with an economically developed society, as opposed to a developing one, remains to be seen.

Joseph de Maistre observed somewhere that superstition constitutes the outer bulwarks of religion. His point was of course that the abandonment of such strong points may eventually endanger the central citadel itself, and so they ought not to be relinquished lightly. Religions in which the outer bulwarks and the central bastion form one integral whole face a terrible dilemma in modern times: if they defend those exposed outer positions, the entire system may fall when the outposts become indefensible, as nowadays they often do. If, on the other hand, they are abandoned and disavowed, the remaining inner redoubt is so narrow and constraining and minimal, and its retention seems so opportunist, that it barely looks worth defending, and inspires little enthusiasm.

In Islam, it is all different. The traditional situation engendered tension and intermittent hostility between the outer bulwarks and the central citadel, between rural superstition and urban scriptural unitarianism. This opposition was not invented for the sake of avoiding modern criticism — it was always there, and thus doesn't have an air of arbitrariness and opportunism. The perforation is ever ready, marked 'Tear off here when modern world arrives', for the tearing-off of superstition . . . So, when modern conditions did make it socially and intellectually attractive to separate a true, pristine, pure faith from the superstitious accretions, it could be done with real conviction. The inner residue is sharply defined, and can be ascribed that absoluteness which distinguishes it from those rather shifty adjustments which make modernism so unconvincing in other faiths. Hence the purified residue can be rousing, and can also be fused with other demanding, total attitudes, such as the burning zeal for a new and juster social order, with the mystique of the Revolution.

Diverse paths

Tribalism itself is still on occasion significant. Independent Somalia proscribed tribal identification and made it illegal for men to proclaim or inquire after it. Hence men would ask or tell each other about each other's *ex*, meaning ex-clan, the units themselves being officially held no longer to exist. (Somalia is not unique in this respect.) So a Somali referring to his *ex* did not mean his ex-wife. This usage became so widespread that eventually the authorities also proscribed the use of the term *ex*, because it had virtually come to mean 'clan'. When an anthropologist then enquired whether one could ask a man about his 'ex-Ex', he was invited to keep his jokes to himself.

The accident of geology and oil wealth has on occasion allowed the puritan version of Islam to be applied with a rigour which would have been difficult under ordinary economic constraints — as in modern Libya. In recent years, Gaddafy has pushed the logic of scripturalism further than earlier puritans had dared in practice, restricting the fount of legitimacy to unambiguous Revelation only — i.e. to the Koran — and denying the authority of humanly and historically tainted extensions of it, such as arguments based on transmitted oral 'traditions' only, or on the example of the Prophet's life. In consequence, Gaddafy's case was considered by a theological commission in Saudi Arabia, under the chairmanship of the Qadi of Medina, and it found him guilty of apostasy.[72]

It is clear that, if such an extreme scripturalism were established, it would free the ruler — already endowed with much elbow room by the miracle of oil wealth — from the restraint imposed on him by the normal legal–theological corpus. The abstract and general, and hence in practice ambiguous, precepts and assertions of the Koran would restrict him less than the highly elaborated body of scholarly consensus. Just as the extreme cult-of-personality of the Ismailis gave the Aga Khan great freedom in choosing paths of modernisation for his community — for it caused him to be unhampered by either scripture or scholars — so a very narrow scripturalism could have a similar effect, at the opposite end of the religious spectrum. Gaddafy is the first Sunni ruler to go so far as to suspend the Sunna (the codified traditions, as opposed to the Koran itself), and incidentally to reform the Muslim calendar, basing a new version on the Prophet's death rather than the Hijra.[73] The idea that the Koran alone, without the 'Traditions', defines true Islam, was articulated in this century in Egypt as early as 1909. But only recently has an attempt been made to implement it by a political authority.

Gaddafy's suspension or pruning of the Sunna thus undermines much of the position and authority of the *ulama*, and in a way constitutes a disestablishment of the *ulama* class. (The Shah's erosion of the economic and moral position of the mullahs proved fatal for him, but perhaps oil wealth can afford to be more arbitrary in a country with such meagre population.) Participatory democracy in effect undermines their standing; populism then becomes a kind of ultra-protestantism, which sweeps away not merely priests and saints but even the open class of representative scholars. 'Neither mufti nor marabout nor shaikhs', proclaimed an article in the only Libyan daily. One could hardly call day-to-day Sunnism the opium of the people, given its orderliness and sobriety, and that of its preferential consumers: it was much closer to being the protecting charter of the burghers, and the *ulama* were something like its judicial committee. But Gaddafy's extremist rigorism deprives the burghers of such defences.

This kind of society, when it seeks and affirms its own roots in defiance of the outsider, does not generally (as European cultures did in a similar situation) turn towards that which is rustic. Traces of such rustic populism can be found, as for instance in Anouar Sadat's autobiography; but it is equally significant that the term *fellah* is still, so to speak, a living and vigorous term of abuse. In America, populism was a reaction of rustics against urban slickers, notably lawyers; in Russia, it was a vicarious reaction of intellectuals on behalf of muzhiks. In Muslim countries, it was more often than not doubly vicarious, a reaction of foreigners on behalf of the carriers of the little tradition of the society. The local reactive self-definition, without stressing urban life as such, chose features — notably scripturalist puritanism — which in fact had an urban base.

It is interesting that those attracted by this extremism should also frequently move towards a socialist radicalism and a rather mystical, highly nebulous notion of *the* Revolution, which is entitled to make all demands but whose promises remain wholly unspecific. But the convenience of such a combination from the ruler's viewpoint is obvious. The socialist radicalism destroys any social bases of opposition which depend on wealth independent of the state. The ultra-Reformism, reducing the extra-social Norm to the absolute minimum, to an exigous and hence ambiguous Text, abrogating the existing accumulated tradition of exegesis, deprives the clerical class of its basis of censure and opposition. At the same time, the democratic radicalism, the creation and encouragement of local committees which can overrule officials, means that no official can be secure of his tenure, and is thus all the less able to afford any independent stance *vis-à-vis* central authority. For instance, in Libya recently a local official was subjected to censure for failing to carry out instructions issued from the capital, *and* those emanating from the local elected committee – and as the two were not necessarily congruent, this was liable to keep him on his toes and mend his fences in all directions. The traditional image of the good sultan was indeed one who was in direct contact with 'the people' and who checked and overruled his own officials. The curious blend of Maoism and Islamic Reformism seems to achieve the same end by modern means, attaining a kind of neo- and super-Mamlukism in which neither wealth nor pious learning nor technical competence nor administrative apparatus nor kin group can defy the ruler. Thus no one is left with an independent power-base, and at the very same time, the extent of the specific, concrete, *identifiable* content of the Law, transcending the ruler and restraining his caprice, has shrunk. Divine nomocracy mediated by a law-interpreting guild of scholars once imposed greater checks on political arbitrariness than does the new combination of centralism, theocracy and populism.

Like other contemporary societies, Muslim countries are divided on the issue concerning whether industrial society should be organised in a socialist or liberal manner. Unlike other societies, they are also divided about the status of Islam in social life. The consequence of the fusion of these two sets of questions is a complex situation, such as would arise in Europe if twentieth-century issues were superimposed on those of the sixteenth. One spectrum or dimension separates traditionalists, with a ruling elite still based on an Ibn-Khaldun-type kin-recruitment, from real or would-be modernists, amongst whom the very notion of tribe or clan is proscribed. Another dimension separates the religious rigorists from the religiously lax. No simple line or curve connects the two dimensions. Rigorism is found at one end with some traditionalists with quasi-tribal elites (such as Saudi Arabia or Northern Nigeria), and at the other with some neo-Mamluk regimes, where soldiers and technocrats, recruited for competence, use religion partly to enforce social discipline, and partly in an attempt to buy off a petty bourgeoisie which is traditional in part for lack of educational access to anything else, and which might otherwise invoke religion to express its resentments against Mamluk privileges. In between these extremes, relatively liberal or socially plural regimes tend to be less preoccupied with the faith.

One might suppose that these two high points of religious enthusiasm represent two successive swings of the old pendulum analysed by Hume, and that the trough between them is occupied by tired old regimes. But in modern conditions, there is more to it than that. The very latest puritans no longer arrive from the desert, unlike the last-but-one-wave, who came with Ibn Saud or Osman dan Fodio. And it is unlikely that the pendulum will swing again, for one of the two forces which used to swing it − rural autonomy and its needs − is now decisively weakened. For another thing, the regimes in the trough, lax and 'old', may yet positively benefit from their condition. It is not clear so far whether modern conditions really favour laxity and liberalism or rigorism and centralisation, in the long run. The question remains open, and need not have the same answer everywhere.

The distinctive pattern of distribution of scripturalist puritanism and of hierarchical ecstatic mediationist styles in Islam may help to explain *both* why industrial society failed to be born within it, *and* why Islam may be in the end so adaptable to industrial society, perhaps more so than the faith which provided it with its historical matrix. Egalitarian scripturalism is more suited to a mobile technical society than ascriptive, mediationist, manipulative spiritual brokerage. To *engender* industrialisation, it is presumably best if the scripturalism is insulated and protected in a more or less peripheral part of the older society, within which a new world can emerge in a relatively undisturbed way. But to *survive* in conditions of emulative industrialisation, it may be better if the scripturalism is at the very centre rather than at the periphery, and can slough off the peripheral styles as superstitions and unworthy accretions − thereby simultaneously affirming its own continuity and local roots *and* explaining away its political and economic retardation. It can then simultaneously affirm an ancient identity *and* justify a strenuous Leap Forward.

The penultimate wave of old-style puritans—fundamentalists, in Saudi Arabia or Northern Nigeria, did still come from the desert or savannah (even if their leadership was not rustic) − or their ancestors came that way, with the Wahabi conquest or with Osman dan Fodio. The latest wave, however, no longer arrives in this fashion. The neo-puritanism of the Algerian or Libyan variety emerged in countries which had suffered real colonial domination − unlike Northern Nigeria or central Arabia, where British and Turkish suzerainty operated through or even strengthened local elites − and this may be highly significant. The Islamic rigorism may be nominally similar in the two types of society, but its psychological feel is rather different. In the countries endowed with continuous, hereditary elites, which had come to power in the hallowed Ibn-Khaldunian fashion, for all the severity of the imposition of the Law − lapidation of adulteresses by tipping a truckload of stones on them, for instance − the divine nomocracy nevertheless remains tied to an old and established social order, and hence does not quite have that inward intensity which characterises the other and genuinely new type. The religious culture remains political rather than individualist. (Members of this kind of elite are even more easily tempted to sin when abroad and away from social surveillance.) The neo-puritanism of the other type, on the other hand, emerged under colonialism, that is to say in a condition of political impotence. This spared those who elaborated it from having to worry about the implementation of orthodoxy in the political sphere, for they did not control it. They did not, at that time, need to worry about whether to cut off the hands of thieves or to wage the Holy War at least once every ten years, for they lacked the power to do either. (That perplexity was yet to come.) But the very fact that they were deprived of external, political sanctions, quite apart from the fact that this was a *reactive* national religiosity, gave an extra intensity to their inward compulsion, and, in the long run, inner sanctions are more powerful than outward ones. The inner sanctions continued to operate when those subject to them attained political power, at least in fair measure. Complaints of corruption are of course heard even in and about the neo-puritan regimes. No doubt the elite has many privileges and perks, and does not always live by the book. But this is a matter of degree. This kind of corruption and conspicuous affluence simply is not comparable, either in scale or in brazenness, with that which occurs amongst the elites with traditional roots.

Thus ironically, though the theocratic or 'divine nomocratic' impulse was historically born of great political power, it could also in a later age be endowed with special intensity by temporary political powerlessness. Colonialism could do for Islam something similar to that which the dispersion effected for Judaism. And, as stated, this inner intensity can be kept alive even after independence, fed by the jealousy felt by the lower urban orders when contemplating their co-national, co-religious, but nevertheless inevitably more or less westernised rulers. These lower urban orders continue to be politically impotent even after independence, and can only console or express themselves in terms of their Islamic purity: for a nationalist expression of the *ressentiment* is no longer open to them. A sociologist, Dr Riaz Hassan, interrogating people about religion in Teheran in 1980, was told simply, it is *the poor* who are the Muslims. Contrary to Marxist theory, class conflict tends to irrupt into revolution only if it can conceptualise itself in ethnic or religious terms. By its secularised cosmopolitanism, the Persian ruling class aided a social revolution by making it a gift of a religious idiom. Thus Iranian Shi'ite neo-puritanism seems also to be of this kind, notwithstanding the fact that Iran had not suffered colonial rule in the literal sense. But the Persian ruling class evidently managed to provide a pretty good imitation of it, especially when it came to exacerbating fundamentalist sensibility. It is ironic to reflect that had Iran been colonised, rather than retaining its independence, its ruling class would probably have been *less* offensively westernised. One imagines that the British Raj would have ruled indirectly through rural tribal khans (as it worked through Nigerian emirs), who would thereby have been encouraged to maintain their local responsibilities and their links with the old culture, instead of hitting the *dolce vita* quite so hard.

So the revolutionary potential shifted from the desert to the bazaar. But it kept the same, all in all, unitarian, puritan ideology, but with a new stress and role. Once this had legitimated a new set of rulers, tribesmen or religious leaders with a tribal power-base, and had at the same time provided some measure of protection for trading burghers. Now it legitimates a new type of ruling class, emerging from below rather than from outside the city walls, a mixture of new Mamluks and new *ulama*, technocrats and religious revivalists; and the creed legitimates and above all provides self-definition for them, as against foreigners and/or a corrupted old local elite. It now inspires furtive shame, and through it loyalty, in the technocrats rather than in the tribesmen, as of old. It dissociates the society both from the Westernised old upper stratum, which it secretly envied, and from its own rustic past of which it is openly ashamed.

Thus the puritan version of Islam has enjoyed a considerable revival and vogue, in conjunction with quite diverse forms of modernising policy, ranging from militant socialism to a rigid traditionalism based on clan leadership. It would be quite wrong to explain this success in terms of whatever oil-financed subsidy it may receive. Not much would be achieved, I suspect, if B.P. chose to divert a comparable part of its North Sea oil revenues to finance a Methodist revival, including a film spectacular of the life of John Wesley, with Omar Sharif in the title role. The fact that Muslim neo-puritanism does have such a widespread impact shows that it does have a deep resonance in the psychic and social needs of contemporary Muslims.

The fusion of 'Reform', i.e. of Koranic fundamentalism, with social radicalism of a loosely Maoist kind is particularly potent, when it occurs. (It can hardly occur in countries in which the fundamentalist elite is itself a kind of extended clan, owing its position to the old type of Ibn-Khaldunian rotation, and hence having too much to lose to play with social extremism; it does occur in places where the present rulers emerged from below in some form of anti-colonial struggle.) The Islamic element offers a form of collective self-identification which is more positive and satisfying than the mere notion of the 'damned of the earth', of the disinherited proletariat, whilst yet broad enough to encompass all those other than the Western foreigners and the culturally alienated, westernised upper class; and at the same time, the vaguely Marxist element allows a far more plausible identification and diagnosis of the current enemy than could conceivably be extracted from Islam alone. The joint appeal of these attractions makes it likely that diverse forms of Koranic Marxism will be a powerful force in the coming years. Its potential for identifying one's own charismatic community, *and* the enemy, of exculpating the community from blame for its own recent backwardness and shifting the guilt and resentment to the Other, is remarkable. It restores dignity, canalises resentment, and provides a plausible explanation, all at once. We may well be entering a period of Che Khomeiny revolutionary movements.

Developing countries — whether European ones in the nineteenth century or Third World ones in the twentieth — in general face the painful dilemma between Modernism and Populism. The former is the key to wealth and power, but involves a˙denial of the local identity and a recognition of the authority of an alien model. The latter implies an idealisation of the backward masses, the *Volk*, *narod*, etc. In fact, the painful dilemma between on the one hand development and self-transformation, and hence self-contempt and repudiation of local tradition, and on the other maintenance of cultural identity at the price of economic and military weakness, is the general formula for the predicament of 'backwardness'. Muslim societies can escape this fork. Populist idealisation of the fellah or the bedouin is mainly perpetrated vicariously by foreign romantics. The society itself, on the other hand, can at this point identify with one important strand within itself, its own Great Tradition, which is simultaneously indigenous and yet appears, to a considerable extent at least, to be usable as a banner of modernity, as a spur, standard and chastisement of local slovenliness, superstition, lethargy and immobility. They are not obliged to choose between Marx and Muhammed. Without necessarily invoking the former by name (leaving the matter vaguely formulated, or invoking one of the lineal descendants in the spiritual *silsila* of Marxism, say from the Korean branch, as in the case of the Somalis) .they can have it both ways. Psychologically, the blend seems very viable.

Modernity or economic development, whichever way it may be conceived, is then very liable to be endowed with a moral—religious aura. It is interesting, and perhaps symptomatic, that the one Muslim state which has autonomously opted for secularism, Turkey, practised it, at least for a generation or so, in a markedly didactic, so to speak Koranic, manner. But Reformist Islam may be preferable to didactic secularism from the viewpoint of wide urban strata other than the top ruling elite. It enables such strata to differentiate themselves, all at once and self-approvingly, from three different and unfavourably viewed outside groups: the non-Muslim West; the questionably orthodox, licentious and turbulent rustics; and the local ruling class, whom the need for 'development' and technocracy inevitably pushes towards religious laxity. Didactic and nationalist secularism only satisfies about one and a half of these needs.

One may well wonder whether, in this general Islamic tradition, it is possible to see the state in a simply instrumental manner, as an institution doing a job at the least cost, as opposed to seeing it endowed with a permanent moral trusteeship for society, obliged to promote good and suppress evil. No doubt there is also an egalitarian and consultation-enjoining element in Islam. But if this is invoked in attempts to establish a connection between Islam and democracy, one must bear in mind that there is a great difference between popular sovereignty against a background of scepticism, and against the background of the assumption that the Truth has been revealed and is available. Tocqueville may have been right in saying that American democracy was facilitated by religious conviction and self-discipline; but there was also the view that rival interpretations had to be allowed to co-exist. The fusion of popular sovereignty with the availability of truth (also characteristic of Marxist states) is more awkward. Kemalist didactic secularism is complicated and paradoxical, in so far as it internalised a modernism, a Western model, at a time when parliamentarianism and plurality of parties were themselves inherent in it.

One might sum up the situation as follows. Old-style puritanism prevails where a traditional elite survives but is still fairly close, in time and spirit, to its own origins in one of those Ibn-Khaldunian swings of the pendulum, which had brought it to power in a fusion of religious enthusiasm and tribal aggression. New-style puritanism, with its elective affinity for social radicalism, prevails where colonialism had destroyed old elites and where a new one had come up from below, rather than from the outer wilderness. The one Muslim state which was a colonial power in its own right also opted for political secularisation. Iran seems to be a case of neo-puritanism directed not against a literally foreign ruler, but against a local ruling class so alienated from the indigenous ruled population that it might as well have been foreign.

If we contrast fundamentalism with laxity along one dimension, and social radicalism with traditionalism along another, we get the following schematic representation of some of the available options. 'Social radicalism' is here

	Socially radical	Politically conservative/traditionalist
Fundamentalist	e.g. Algeria, Libya	e.g. Saudi Arabia, Northern Nigeria
Religiously moderate or secular	e.g. Turkey	e.g. Morocco

allowed to have different content according to period: in the days of Ataturk, it meant Westernisation *à outrance*, but nowadays it incorporates socialism. The most interesting contrast is probably between the socially radical and the conservative fundamentalists. Khomeiny has clearly taken Iran out of the lower right-hand box; it remains to be seen just where along the upper level spectrum the country will end.

Problems

The model has now been sketched out. What are its difficulties and problems?

One of them is this: Is the segmentary model a good account of the internal organisation of Muslim tribal societies? This has been challenged, along the following lines: The segmentary model is indeed an *idiom*, and a way in which members of these societies conceptualise their situation. The Arabs do indeed say: I against my brothers, my brothers and I against our cousins, my brothers, cousins and I against the world. The idea of internal rivalry, overruled by a simultaneous cohesion against an outside group, and so on at a number of levels, with no effective centralisation or external interference at *any* level, is indeed an idea which they habitually invoke. Moreover, it receives further encouragement by the neat tree-like genealogical patterns which simultaneously also symbolise the internal divisions, sub-divisions and so forth of a tribe. But the actual reality of alignment and opposition is far more flexible, complex, loose and opportunist. The protagonists of the segmentary model, on this view, have mistaken the ideal or the idiom for reality.[74]

Some who have put forward this criticism are not always fully clear about what they envisage as an alternative theory, or whether indeed they have one at all. Sometimes one has the feeling that a stress on, almost an intoxication with, the idea that concepts and conduct are mutually intertwined in a complex and subtle manner, as indeed they are, acts as a substitute for theory, notwithstanding the lack of specificity or precision of such assertions. On other occasions, one does find a relatively specific theory, such as that the reality of personal relations in a given Muslim society is of a dyadic-patronage kind, with unequal partners exchanging benefits and support, as opposed to egalitarian, fraternal, 'nested' communities envisaged by the model. This at least is a theory with sufficient meat and concreteness in it to make it possible to discuss it.[75]

The truth of the matter seems to me to be that with the expanding power of the central state, unsymmetrical patronage relations do indeed become the norm. A man's prospects and security now depend on his connections; what he needs is to have a friend at court, and there is a multiplicity of linked courts at local, provincial and national levels. But this kind of system has successfully replaced an earlier, relatively symmetrical and 'brotherly' or 'cousinly' one, in which a man's security lay not in his patron(s) but in his kinsmen. Under modern, centralised conditions, the kinship-segmentary idiom survives and continues to be used, but the reality of conduct becomes different.

But if one treated it as always and inherently an idiom which masks reality, one would have no way of saying that things have in recent times changed from a tribal-segmentary system to a loosely centralised and patronage-ridden one.[76] One would have no way of saying this — for what is a perennial and inherent illusion can hardly become even *more* of an illusion — and yet one wants to say it, for the simple reason that it happens to be conspicuously true. Scholars who take the 'illusion' view of the segmentary egalitarian idiom tend to have done their field research fairly late in the development of these societies; I suspect they mistake what is indeed a correct account of the present, for one which was also valid in the past.

There are also good positive reasons for considering the segmentary model to be at least in good measure an accurate representation of traditional reality. Complex patterns of co-operation, in warfare and feud, pasture utilisation, leadership selection, self-taxation, prestations to saints, and other activities, occurred in many tribes without leaving any permanent or profound social hierarchy or stratification. Some men were indeed richer and more powerful than others, but this did not seem to congeal into different *kinds* of people, into conceptually separable categories of men. This kind of society moreover was actually conscious of when it deviated from the segmentary model. For instance, in his remarkable book *Honneur et Baraka: les structures sociales traditionnelles dans le Rif* (Cambridge University Press, 1981), Raymond Jamous describes how certain North Moroccan tribes made a distinction, within their customary law, between situations in which there was a dominant Big Man in a tribal segment, and situations when no such men existed. This contrast is already prominent in the work of Robert Montagne, but Jamous shows that instead of a stark contrast between egalitarian/oligarchic tribal republics and ephemeral absolute tyrants (who do sometimes emerge), we should rather think in terms of a spectrum allowing many intermediate possibilities. But the symmetry and diffusion of power does seem to be a kind of base-line for which the society seems destined by the nature or poverty of its means of coercion (until the modern world strengthens them), and towards which it tends to return, without generating a stable or pervasive aristocracy other than a religious one. Feudal Europe had both a military nobility and a religious class (the latter theoretically more open); Muslim tribal society only had the latter, and it was theoretically closed.

The diversity of customary law from tribe to tribe, and the recognised divergencies between tribal custom and Koranic law, also enabled such tribes to be conscious of the human, social roots of their own customary law. It had a Divine contrast, within their own world. In modern times, this issue of course became politically septic in some countries. The tribal-human fringe of Divine law is reduced or demolished, as the modern, urban-human fringe is, inevitably, expanded.

Those who are above or below in the old tribal system — by virtue of faith, special religious status, specialised craft occupation, pigmentation — constitute relatively small minorities. But the bulk of men are of the same kind. Profound political differentiation is either absent or ephemeral. Yet there was no chaos. What, other than the segmentary principle of balanced opposition of groups at a variety of levels, could possibly have helped bring this about?

Moreover, there is a variety of very conspicuous, widely diffused, well-documented and important institutions, such as the feud, the collective oath, the definition of pasture or preferential rights to brides, and others, which simply do not make sense without the assumption of reasonably stable segmentary groups, with unambiguous and not too fluid membership. The feud, like football, makes no sense if you do not know which team you are in. Of course people could, and often did, re-allocate themselves; this was obvious both to participants in the system and to observers of it. Transfer procedures were well recognised. There were and are familiar rituals for such an end. This was part of the system and one of its sanctions. In the course of my fieldwork in the central High Atlas of Morocco, I was struck by the firmness and emphasis of one principle which tribesmen invoked when discussing their own social organisation: it is absolutely essential for a man to have his place amongst his *Ait Ashra'a*, his

People of Ten, the people who will be co-responsible with him in case of collective oath, and pay or receive blood-money should the occasion arise. He may indeed re-allocate himself. If he moves to a new location it is in fact his first and crying need to find such a place, to secure it by imposing a shame obligation on his hosts or some of them.

But whilst re-allocation *is* possible, double citizenship is *not*. A man will always lose his previous place by finding a new one, and the publicity of the ritual by which he obtained it will help ensure this. At any given moment a man's unique place in the system of rights and duties must be unambiguously clear. The model requires, not that the system be absolutely rigid — on the contrary, it requires that it should not be such — but merely that at any given time, there should be well defined, identifiable groups which can be and are activated.

The notion of segmentation in social anthropology, used to explain cohesion and order-maintenance in stateless tribes, should be distinguished from the extended application of this term in political science, as in John Waterbury's *Commander of the Faithful.* [77] The mutual checks-and-balances of superimposed tribal segments, devoid of strong leadership, operating in field and pasture, are one thing; the fluid intrigues of rival patronage networks, played off by a trimmer king, are another. There may be similarities between the two phenomena, and the extension of the terms was certainly suggestive: but the two things are nonetheless distinct.

A somewhat related criticism is the following: the model assumes a tribal countryside (irrespective of how the internal organisation of the tribes is interpreted). It assumes the interaction, in the overall drama, of three sets of characters — rulers, townsmen, tribesmen. This in turn suggests that tribal life extends up to the city walls. But is that not a myth? Was there not also a peasantry, oppressed and without far-flung tribal organisation and cohesion, which played its part in the wider society?

No doubt there was. Ibn Khaldun himself comments on its existence and notes how its presence facilitates government. In a country such as Egypt, nomads formed less than one-tenth of the total population and of course the proportion has fallen even lower in modern times. It obviously varies a great deal from country to country and from period to period. Areas in which the population which can reasonably be described as tribal (i.e. capable of administering itself and of acting as a corporate body in self-defence) falls very low, such as Egypt or the north-western parts of the Ottoman Empire, no doubt do elude the model; and this helps to explain the relative strength and stability of government in those areas. But the very existence of a peasantry, caught between towns and tribes and often harassed by both, somewhat complicates but does not fundamentally change the model. Such peasantry was no doubt more common in the Fertile Crescent than in the Maghreb or the Arabian peninsula, and in the Maghreb commoner in Tunisia than in the other two countries. Its presence, and the inapplicability of the towns-and-tribes-only model, is argued in an interesting article by H. Munson Jr ('The mountain people of north-west Morocco: tribesmen or peasants?', *Journal of Peasant Studies*, forthcoming) for the north-western part of the Moroccan Atlantic plain. It is amusing to note that what counts as evidence of the existence of peasants in Morocco — individual land tenure, the buying and selling of land, the absence of effective corporate groups, mobility — is precisely what a very important book has invoked in support of the thesis of the *absence* of peasantry in England, argued by Alan Macfarlane in *The Origins of English Individualism* (Blackwell, 1978). Evidently it depends on whether you are contrasting peasants with tribesmen or with capitalists. Quite clearly, peasantry — subjugated agricultural producers — did exist, but in most places, not in such numbers as to modify the basic rules of the game.

The Terrible Turk

Another objection to the theory, of quite a different order, arises from the very existence of the Ottoman Empire, and also from that of the Mamluk regimes in the Middle East which preceded it and overlapped with it, and anticipated some of its principles. Without any doubt, the Turks are an embarrassment. To ignore them because they seem to defy Ibn Khaldun's theory would seem both discourteous and unscholarly. The Ottoman Empire contradicts the model on a number of important points.[78] It was stable, strong and long-lived, by any standards, not only those of Muslim society. Except for its early period, when Turkic principalities in Anatolia, not yet united, exemplified the required pattern, it offered the example of a political system of great authority which was not based on the cohesion of a pre-existent tribal group, but on the contrary relied on a conspicuously non-tribal elite, recruited individually (by slave purchase, or taxation requiring subjugated non-Muslim populations to supply male offspring as recruits). This principle it shared of course with the Mamluk regimes. In brief, political cohesion at the top was attained by the artificial creation of a new elite, technically 'slaves', ideally free of kin links to distract them from their duty, and formed, not by the shared hardships of tribal life, but by systematic training and education for wars and administration. Thus its solution of the political problem was closer to Plato than to Ibn Khaldun, but containing elements of each. As in Ibn Khaldun, these rulers were often recruited from a tribal background; but as in Plato, they were moulded by systematic training rather than by the practice of tribal life and, at least theoretically, insulated from temptations of wealth and of partiality to kinsmen. Being in theory slaves, at any rate initially, they ideally had neither kin nor wealth, thus satisfying Plato's, but not Ibn Khaldun's, qualifications for authority. In fact, of course, they eventually acquired both, and their decline followed the lines foreseen by Plato, of seduction by special interests and the love of gain. For instance, in eighteenth-century Egypt (as described by André Raymond, in work to be published) men of the sword and those of the market eventually intermingled, soldiers going into trade and tradesmen buying their way into the military corporations. This is a fine example of the Platonic transition from timocracy to plutocracy. It also shows that even the Turkish solution to the problem of the Guardians does not, in the end, escape the ravages of time, any more than the tribal solution described and accepted by Ibn Khaldun, though the Turks did succeed in giving themselves a very long innings. The logic of Ibn Khaldun's world precludes any effective solution to the problem of decay. The Turks at least attempted to find one.

Whereas a modern society functions only if the rulers seem culturally similar to the ruled, it actually benefits a traditional state if the rulers have or are credited with a cultural distinctiveness; and the Mamluks tended to lose it. It seems (as suggested in yet unpublished work of Robert Mantran) that in the early Ottoman Empire there were, so to speak, Mamluks *de robe* as well as Mamluks *d'épée*: there were slave bureaucrats as well as slave soldiers. In other words, the novel form of elite-recruitment enabled the state to dispense with each of the two key elements in the Ibn Khaldunian state (i.e. the tribal army and the urban clerics). It is almost as if the Ottoman polity endeavoured deliberately to make itself independent of the two customary social bases of the Muslim state. This innovation, together with the fact that at its centre it faced sedentary peasants rather than nomadic pastoralists, was presumably what enabled it to become so very exceptional.

Paraphrasing Oscar Wilde, one can do anything with a counter-example except explain it. The trouble with this exception is that it is such a big one. Other powerful Muslim states in history do not present the same difficulty for a theory inspired by Ibn Khaldun. (There is an irony in the fact that the Turks were eager students of Ibn Khaldun and the first to rediscover him, but apparently they turned to him to seek an understanding and remedy of their own decline. In the case of the other great Muslim powers, the brevity of dynastic survival and the manner in which they succeed each other do, all in all, fit the classical pattern.)

If one did attempt to explain away the Ottoman Empire in terms of special circumstances, there are indeed some special features which one could invoke. It did perfect a very special technique for recruiting and training an elite. At its centre of gravity in Western Anatolia and the Balkans, it faced settled peasantry rather than tribal populations. Ibn Khaldun knew about this kind of phenomenon:

it is easy to establish a dynasty in lands that are free from group feeling. Government there will be a tranquil affair . . . This is the case in contemporary Egypt and Syria. They are free from tribes and group feeling . . . Royal authority in Egypt is most peaceful and firmly rooted, because Egypt has few . . . tribal groups. Egypt has a sultan and subjects. Its ruling dynasty consists of the Turkish rulers and their groups. They succeed each other in power, and the rule circulates among them.

In a dynasty affected by senility . . . it sometimes happens that the ruler chooses helpers and partisans from groups not related to the ruling dynasty but used to toughness ... That was what happened to the Turkish dynasty in the East. Most members of its army were Turkish clients. The rulers then chose horsemen and soldiers from among the white slaves [Mamluks] who were brought to them. They were more eager to fight ... than the children of the earlier white slaves who had grown up in easy circumstances as a ruling class in the shadow of the government.[79]

Better still, the Ottomans frequently faced populations excluded by their own religion from aspiring to replace the rulers. One of the most revealing episodes in Ottoman history is that of the Balkan population which consented to embrace Islam, but only on the condition that it would *not* thereby become exempt from the male baby-tax (*devshirme*) normally imposed on non-Muslims. They wanted to retain their connection with a nominally kin-less elite. Evidently they thought of this institution more as a meritocratic scholarship system than as an onerous tax.

Alternatively, one could appeal to the fact that, although Ibn Khaldun's model did not apply to the centre of the empire, it did apply to its tenuously governed and extensive peripheral regions. This argument, alas, cuts both ways. Though it applies to some provinces, in others the central system was emulated on a local scale, with an alien, Mamluk or Turkish or 'Circassian', individually recruited elite performing the political function. It could work well.[80] One could argue that the areas where it did work, such as Tunisia or parts of the Fertile Crescent or Egypt, were those in which the ratio of exploitable peasantry to tribal population was high. This may be true, but fails to explain why the system worked in Algeria.

The Turks developed their own political philosophy to rationalise their system, and codified it by the fifteenth century under the suggestive title of 'Cycle of Equity'. This circle was not at all the same as Ibn Khaldun's. It was very simple: subjects could only amass wealth if there was law and order. Only the state could provide these. But the state needs money to live. Prosperous subjects could be taxed and thus sustain the state. A strong, well-fed state could protect them so that they could produce more wealth, available for taxation. To modern minds, the theory is offensive. It excludes producers from political participation, and rulers from economic concerns. But that does not matter from the viewpoint of assessing its applicability for the time for which it was formulated.

What does matter is this: wherever, or in so far as, the Ibn Khaldun version applied, this two-term theory of the circulation of resources is a case of false consciousness, a misrepresentation, an omission, through a kind of political *pudeur*, of a third, essential and offensive element: the dissident tribal groups beyond the pale, who did not contribute to the wealth of the state. The theorist averts his eyes from this reprehensible fact. The real balance of power, the effective complementarity, is at least triangular. The urban traders and artisans pay taxes to the ruler not merely because they fear him but because they fear

75

the tribal wolves even more. The ruler lives off the townsmen and the subjugated peasantry near the towns, to the extent to which it is available, and, when all's well, is strong enough to protect them from tribal depredations. The tribesmen have a sufficient need of urban products to be involved in the urban market economy, and thereby they help the town artisans to survive. The tribesmen are obliged to trade because the state is, normally, strong enough to prevent them from pillaging the town which is, in effect, a market and a mosque with a citadel to protect them. The mosque and its scholars/teachers ratify the entire arrangement, and provide those who take part in it with a common idiom, even if it is spoken with a different accent and stress by the diverse parties. If the fear inspired by tribesmen helps to make the towns governable, the moral authority conferred on city and state by the learning of the town scholars inspires some measure of at least awe in the tribesmen, though this is double-edged: the unitarian scripturalism which teaches the tribesmen their place allows, and on occasion legitimates, a revivalist revolution which they assist and from which some of them benefit.

Thus this particular nightwatchman state has quite a job on its hands. It does not merely maintain order within the ring; it needs to protect the ring from the outside. The Faith is both an aid and a menace. It damns the impiety of aggressors, but the ruler himself can be impeached for impiety by a coalition of revered scholar and cohesive tribal group.

What need of the town and state at all, you might ask, if the tribes can exist on their own? Why the city? And why the state? The complementary answers must once again be sought in Ibn Khaldun's crucial remark to the effect that the countryside needs the towns, but not vice versa. The general ecology, cultural and military as well as more literally productive, of the arid zone has come to presuppose artisan production and trade. A really small group of petty artisans and traders can live simply under the protection of a single tribe, as coloured blacksmiths, potters, dyers, etc., lived under the walls of a tribal collective fort in the Atlas. But such petty settlements are insufficient. A really large market, with serious trade and massive artisan production, is what is known as a city; it needs more effective and continuous protection than that, and this cannot be provided by merely *ad hoc* tribal levies, or by the tribal obligation to avenge aggression against those who live under its protection. The organised force which offers such protection is known as a state. The only source which can produce such a force (until the invention of the Mamluk and *devshirme* system as alternative models of elite-recruitment) was the tribal world itself. A tribe or tribal coalition is a potential ruling class. Islam provided an admirable language for the maintenance, and occasional personnel-rotation, of this system. But it is indisputably true that, at the centre of their empire, the Turks managed for a long time to eliminate one of the three partners and to arrest the rotation of the political wheel. They escaped the Ibn-Khaldunian fatality, at least for quite a time.

One could follow Perry Anderson,[81] and treat the Ibn-Khaldunian and the Mamluk–Turkish state as two stages of one process, the latter being only 'the most developed and sophisticated example' of something 'found all over the Muslim world'. The Ottoman solution is, on this view, the only natural completion of the tribally-founded state because it is the only solution for its problems. As rulers, tribesmen simply don't *keep* well, so they need to be replaced by personnel secured by purchase, taxation, or any other available method. Anderson's way out unfortunately does not explain why it worked well only in the Ottoman case. It is part and parcel of the world of Ibn Khaldun that recruiting non-tribal mercenary or slave armies only aggravates the disease of a declining state.

It is probably best not to make any attempt to explain away the phenomenon at all, but simply accept it as an alternative model: within the general conditions imposed both by nature and the technical and cultural equipment of Muslim civilisation, there exist at least two possible solutions to the problem of political organisation. One is explored by Ibn Khaldun, and in it political talent is supplied by tribes, whilst the cultural and technical equipment is supplied by towns, and the symbiosis of these two elements leads to the characteristic rotation of personnel which he described. The exclusive cohesion-engendering power of kinship is in a way confirmed by the fact that in pre-modern times, bureaucracy, which is the antithesis of kinship, is recruited by preference from priests, eunuchs, slaves or foreigners – people deprived in one way or another of real, avowable or socially relevant ancestry of posterity. It is only in our modern world that everyone becomes employable on bureaucratic terms, that the Mamluk condition becomes universalised.

Thus the other model which gradually emerged in the Middle East – Ibn Khaldun had indeed seen its beginnings and noted them – was brought to its greatest degree of perfection by the Ottomans. 'Slave soldiers . . . had by the eleventh and twelfth centuries become the predominant military and administrative elite in all Middle Eastern states.'[82] The emulation of this system outside the empire was not generally successful: for instance, the attempt by the Moroccan monarchy to rely on a black slave army rather than on privileged tribes for its basic support proved abortive. The slave army only survived in the form of a mounted black palace guard. During the French period, this ceremonial corps occupied a place of honour in the annual parade on 14 July – a bizarre piece of symbolism.

Trade, town and sobriety

Or again, it is possible to object to the general theory outlined on the grounds that it assumes too easily the connection between the importance of urban centres and commerce on the one hand, and a taste for sober, scholarly, unitarian religion on the other. Such a connection seems natural, whether under the influence of the long tradition of Abrahamic monotheism, or Weberian sociology, or both:

> This religiosity of bourgeois strata seems to originate in urban life. In the city the religious experience of the individual tends to lose the character of an ecstatic trance or dream and to assume the paler forms of contemplative mysticism or of a low-keyed, everyday piety. For the craftsman, steady work with customers can suggest the development of concepts like 'duty' and 'recompense' as basic orientations towards life.[83]

The elective affinity between the bourgeois style of life and religious sobriety and strictness may well, however, be a piece of Judaeo-Protestant ethnocentrism. Perhaps, far from being inherent in the nature of things and thus capable of explaining why a given culture exhibits this conjunction of traits, it is distinctive of that culture, or present in it in a particularly marked degree. Such seems to be the view of Marshall G.S. Hodgson:

> Islamicate high culture was ... even more urban than most citied agrarian cultures ... in its urbanness, Islamicate culture was also heavily conditioned by an urban populism which held a monopoly of cultural legitimation.[84]

Such a monopoly, or near-monopoly, of legitimation, very seldom if ever accompanied by a monopoly of power, or indeed by much power, is the central problem of a sociology which would aspire to explain it.

But not all commercially enterprising and successful urban populations are in fact averse to ritual excesses. The Nepalese Newars are *the* commercial success story of the Gurkha empire, but they must be one of the most festival-addicted peoples of the world. Kathmandu has a certain resemblance to Venice, its palaces and temples cry out to be the setting of a carnival, and indeed neither Italian city-state nor Greek commercialism fits the model. Or again, consider the contrast between the Muslim Malays and the overseas Chinese. A Malay village mosque looks like a well-kept cricket pavilion out of season — clean, empty, and with a conspicuous absence of graven images. By contrast, Chinese village festivals are strongly reminiscent of a village fair in one of those Central European countries which were dominated by the Counter-Reformation before they fell to Communism, and which used to exhibit brazenly that characteristic conflation of the sacred, the profane, and the commercial, with the conspicuous presence of every form of irrationality, ranging from the opera, gambling and over-eating to systematic attempts at bribing the supernatural, and moreover rival forms of the supernatural at the same time. Such a confusion, one would think, whatever it may do for religion, could hardly benefit the long-term interests of trade and the rational commercial spirit. From all this, a sociologist of Weberian orientation should rapidly conclude that, clearly, the Malays must be the Calvinist-type successful entrepreneurs, whereas the spiritually manipulative, eclectic and opportunistic overseas Chinese must obviously be economically inept and feckless.[85] Ah well.

In brief, the commercial/puritan link has an inward plausibility which is not fully sustained by all facts. *Verstehen* may on occasion help us to understand connections which then, irritatingly, turn out not to be the case in the first place. This being so, it may be improper to use this kind of 'meaningful' connection as a self-sustaining premiss.

But it is not only the very nature of the scholarly/commercial bourgeoisie which constitutes an issue. There is also the remarkable problem of its homogeneity within Islam over many countries and continents, and of the source of its astonishing authority. This scholar class cannot choose between one ruler and another, one dynasty and another, but must needs accept the strongest; nor can it by its own resources keep the tribal wolves from the city walls; but it can and does nonetheless impose its tone and values on the society. In the towns, they set the tone with a good measure of effectiveness. Within Shi'ism, the 'occultation' of the sacred leadership may on occasion strengthen the authority of the scholars.[86] Sacred leadership when identifiably incarnate may supersede scholars, but when, so to speak, authoritatively hidden it leaves effective authority in their hands and uncontested *pro tem.*, until the next divine appearance. The Shi'ite deity is not so much a hidden God, as one given to playing hide and seek with men.

Amongst the tribes, the scholars set the tone, at least to the extent of securing a recognition of an abstract ideal which, even if honoured in the breach rather than the observance, is nevertheless accepted as ultimately valid and worth following on occasion, if/when there is some booty or political advantage in it as well, and which thus plays a supremely important if intermittent part in their lives. It has no power of veto over personnel, but it does seem to have and to exercise it over institutions and styles. All this unity and influence is secured without control over any means of coercion, without any head, formal hierarchy, central secretariat, without even any kind of conciliar movement or orthodoxy-determining assembly or college. It is astonishing that this sociological miracle is not more emphatically invoked as evidence for the truth of the Faith.[87]

Those of us who nevertheless also seek mundane explanations can only indicate the directions in which it may be found. The central position of the pilgrimage helps to ensure quick publicity for eccentricities. The insistence on the uniqueness and, above all, on the finality of the message helps establish a reasonably unambiguous and trans-ethnic, trans-political norm of propriety, beyond at least easy reach of opportunist manipulation. The trans-ethnic quality of the Word was perhaps reinforced by the fact that for many Muslim states, the Holy Places and hence the pilgrimage were beyond the political boundary and power of the local ruler, thus in a way symbolising the social transcendence of the fount of legitimacy. In Shi'ism, the fact that the holiest place of pilgrimage was often outside the territory of *the* Shi'ite state, and that a certain embryonic separation of state and clerisy (or of a political and populist clerisy) occurred, may have had a similar effect. But the main key is perhaps sociological, and is to be sought in that surprising remark of Ibn Khaldun's, when he observes that the tribes need the towns, but not vice versa. The entire society appears to live on the assumption of a technical and cultural equipment which makes the towns indispensable; whilst the perennial presence of an external and unsubdued tribal proletariat ensures that there is a potential reservoir of military power which can on occasion be mobilised if the ideological situation warrants it. An independent ideology, in the hands of the burghers, and an independent sword-arm of the tribes . . . The possibility of these two forces fusing provides a sanction on rulers, encouraging them to enjoin good and suppress evil. The fact that the two elements required to activate the sanction can really on occasion come together does constitute a check of a kind on some versions of social and political eccentricity, and in turn discourages political interference with the sacred Word, and thus reinforces its authority.

This is perhaps the overall characterisation of an Ibn Khaldun civilisation: it is a continuous and far-flung society, with a technical and cultural equipment which presupposes trade and towns, and which makes the rural population dependent in some measure on urban production and services. A scripturalist faith expresses and reinforces this condition. The towns cannot survive without a measure of political protection and hence centralisation, and they pay the price of submission and sustain the ruler. At the same time, however, the military and administrative equipment available to the civilisation does not allow the state to dominate the countryside effectively, particularly given the arid and/or mountainous nature of the terrain and the pastoral ecology encouraged by it. This brings into being those nested and segmented mutual-help associations we call tribes; the common Mediterranean agnatic ethos causes them generally to use the patrilineal principle for their self-definition, whatever inner adjustments also occur in reality. (The emphasis on patriliny with its exclusion of feminine inheritance produces some conflict with the literal application of Koranic law, with its provision of half-shares for daughters.) The strength of these groups in turn perpetuates the system, by helping to keep the state weak. It also provides a sanction for the upholding of the faith, for a ruler who could plausibly provide grounds for accusations of religious laxity thereby also risked crystallising an alliance between the urban guardians of legitimacy and orthodoxy, and the extramural reservoir of political-military talent.

And there is another problem, related to the above but not identical with it, and which is only now becoming conspicuous, as a result of the accumulation of social anthropological research: it is not only the urban and literate Great Tradition which is significantly similar in Islam, despite geographical distance and lack of means of enforcement: the rural and folk tradition also displays astonishing similarities. In the past, there was a tendency to explain this questionably orthodox Little Tradition in terms of local 'pre-Islamic survivals'. But it would be strange if the pre-Islamic stratum in, say, Southern Arabia and the Moroccan Atlas were as similar as the non-orthodox elements of custom in these regions, and others, seem to be. Perhaps heterodoxy of practice was diffused like the orthodoxy of theory; or perhaps, as I am inclined to suspect, the complex of cultural and organisational traits, great and little, formed one unity which, if diffused at all, was diffused as a whole, and in which the less orthodox elements are a kind of socially necessary complement to the orthodox, and are naturally engendered by it.

Saintless nomads

Objections to the model can also be raised at the rural or tribal end. For instance, the argument connecting segmentary tribal organisation with use of specialised religious personnel and a taste for ritual occasions seems cogent, and certainly fits some Muslim tribal agrarian societies. But it seems at least superficially in conflict with the paucity of both ritual and holy personnel reported of some Muslim nomadic communities.[88] Here the data are probably open to diverse interpretation. Cyrenaican bedouin, for instance, both had their own petty *marabtin bil baraka* and also welcomed the Sanusi religious leadership.[89]

It is pastoralism which inclines, without forcing, societies towards segmentary organisation, which then spreads towards adjoining agrarian communities by a kind of osmosis, impregnating them with the pastoral ethos and obliging them to emulate a form of organisation which helps them defend themselves. My argument stressed the manner in which pastoralism favours segmentation, and segmentation favours a cult-of-personality religion, in so far as it needs holy personnel to mark the boundaries of segmented groups and to mediate between them. Perhaps the argument needs to be refined by the insertion of a further step, in so far as the cult of living saints flourishes most among sedentary or semi-sedentary groups, amongst whom admittedly pastoralism is an important but not an exclusive occupation. In North Africa, sanctity seems more developed among transhumant Berbers than amongst more nomadic Arabs, and where the tribes mix, as they do in some parts of the Sahara, it is the Berber ones who are ascribed the status of people of the Book, and the Arab ones who are the people of the sword. (This is a theoretical or ideal ascription rather than a genuine division of labour. Tribes of the Book provide religious specialists but otherwise fight like anyone else.) There is also the curiously under-explored question of the social organisation of oases, which combine elements of urban, tribal and oppressed peasant society.

Or again, it is sometimes claimed, in contradiction of the present model, that there is such a thing as 'puritanism of the desert', distinct from burgher puritanism. It sounds plausible, at least to a townsman scholar, who imagines that if he were in the desert, he would also be a puritan, if only for lack of alternative forms of entertainment. Arguments of the form of what-I-would-feel-like-in-the-desert go back at least to Herder. In fact, though puritan-revivalist movements often derived their military strength from pastoral populations, the leadership comes from elsewhere. The Wahabis originated in the townships of Najd.[90] The Fulani were the sword-arm and (some of them) the beneficiaries of Osman dan Fodio's puritan jihad, but *chez soi*, in the savannah, they continue to be noted for their laxity. It was *he* who provided the strictness. *They* recognised its authority when it legitimated their conquest of the Hausa towns.

Counter-examples, apparent or real, can also be found outside the desert and savannah. The tribal Zaidis (a kind of Shi'ism) of the Yemenite uplands appear to be less, not more, shrine-addicted than the orthodox Sunni populations of the more centrally controlled lowlands.[91] But the role of hereditary religious personnel amongst them seems considerable, nevertheless, as mediators, arbitrators and leaders of the ordinary tribes. Or again, Kharejites, normally classed as puritan, are prominent among the tribal populations of upland Oman. There are also contemporary phenomena which appear to contradict the model. There seems to be a religious revival in post-Nasserian Egypt, in middle-class strata, which turns not to the scholasticism of El Azhar, but to refined philosophical Sufism, enjoyed in the privacy of individual consciousness and apartment rather than in public space, as was the case with the more immediately socially functional cult of personality of rustic or popular Sufism.[92] This by contrast is Sufism in the *personnaliste* style. Here one might say that inwardness of this kind, though no doubt always constituting one element in Muslim mysticism, has become so separated from the public, *social* ecstasy of the traditional saint-cults and their associated practices that it should really be considered a different phenomenon altogether. When new-found puritanism had gone socially radical, as it had in Nasser's Egypt, perhaps it was natural for a revived liberal bourgeoisie to turn to inwardness?

Or once again, though strict Reformist Islam is the state religion of modern Algeria, rural elections, at any rate in Kabylia, appear to be dominated by men drawn from the old maraboutic lineages.[93] But there is no evidence that these neo-marabouts act *as* marabouts. (Similar evidence could be drawn from the Aures mountains or from post-Independence elections in the Moroccan central High Atlas.) When a centralising state creates or recruits petty local patrons in its attempts to control the countryside, it cannot but draw on the existing pools of political talent and the habit of leadership. In tribal segmentary areas, such talent will come disproportionately often from the holy lineages. This indicates not so much a revival of the old religious style, as the adaptability of its personnel to new tasks.

At another level, the model is in conflict with various rival efforts at a general interpretation of Muslim society. There have been attempts for instance to include it under the category of 'oriental despotism' in the Wittfogelian sense. The absolutist pretensions of much official Muslim political theory provide such a view with some support at least. But it seems to me that rulers of these states were total in aspiration rather than in fact, and that to take such pretensions at face value is to mistake the wish for the reality. In practice, they were limited both by the divine legislature and by tribal autonomy. The striking thing is that this seems on occasion true even in the Middle Eastern river valleys which one might expect to provide paradigmatic material for the Wittfogel thesis. Apparently, it is possible to run even the complex irrigation or drainage system of southern Iraq by means of uncentralised tribal leadership, without use of a central 'hydraulic bureaucracy'; and moreover, that decentralised management was more efficient than the central control which succeeded it.[94] Or again, there have been attempts by neo-Marxists to approach a model of a distinctive North African mode of production, parallel to the alleged oriental and African ones. A model of that kind, stressing distinctive local methods of surplus-appropriation, such as piracy at certain periods, would seem to me to assume just that which is central and needs to be explained: the existence of that local balance of power between state, town and tribes which, precisely, prevents too much surplus being extracted from the rural population, the tribes.

The various objections need to be assessed in diverse ways. The argument from the stability and elite-recruitment procedures of the Ottoman Empire (and perhaps some of the Mamluk polities) seems to me by far the most serious, and to imply that there are (at least) two distinct types of traditional Muslim socio-political organisation. At many places and times, these two ideal types appeared in mixed and intermediate forms. The objection concerning the proportions of myth and reality in the segmentary model is less serious, though well worth pursuing, perhaps in a more sustained manner than has been done hitherto. The 'mythicality' thesis seems to me misguided, but the issue deserves further debate. Puritanism of the desert, on the other hand, seems to be a myth, though the ritual poverty of some nomads is an interesting anthropological problem, as is the occasional ritual restraint of some agrarian tribal populations. These points, if valid, seem to me more in the nature of occasional exceptions, which sadly haunt all sociological theories, than something calling for the scrapping of the theory itself. And one must of course repeat that the model is not meant to apply to Muslim communities outside the arid zone.

The theory has been constructed partly on the assumption that any intelligible model is better than none: at the very least, it highlights data which are in conflict with it, and raises problems. The assumption is made that one or possibly two types of balance between political, religious and economic institutions prevailed in the arid zone for many centuries, between the crystallisation of the early Khalifate and the impact on the Muslim world of the modern West; and that this continuity was more fundamental than changes within it. This may seem a strong claim, and it has recently become fashionable to challenge it; neo-Marxists eager to extend the thesis of perpetual change, young anthropologists keen to defy the functionalist paradigm, historians anxious to stress the indispensability of their own craft in an age of expansionist social sciences, nationalists or guilt-expiating Westerners intent on denouncing the stability/stagnation doctrine as a piece of colonialist denigration, have all questioned it.[95]

For my own part, I have not been persuaded that it is fundamentally false: when I read Ibn Khaldun, I feel myself in the very same world as the one described by social anthropologists who are, in effect, recording or reconstructing a society such as it was just before modernity made its full impact. Perhaps changing patterns of military technology have effected transformations in the overall social structure;[96] the striking thing to my mind is that firearms do not seem to have changed radically the balance of power between the central state and tribal organisation. The baronial power of the Glawi in the western High Atlas has been attributed to his possession of a Krupp cannon; but very similar crystallisations of power occurred elsewhere without the benefit of the fruits of German engineering. (A lineage in the central High Atlas attained eminence within its tribe and attributed it to being the first to own a fast-loading rifle, but one suspects this was a symbol rather than a cause of its position.) An anthropologist working in southern Arabia in the 1950s was astonished to find, in the course of the usual cost/benefit accountancy operation between two feuding clans, that the deaths entered on the balance sheet, which for honour's sake always had to come out even in the end, included men who had perished by *arrows*: in other words, that these accounts were kept up over centuries and dated back to before the introduction of firearms.[97] Thus institutions survived across a revolution in military technology, without, apparently, any profound change in themselves. This of course is a token, not a proof, of continuity; but I believe that this continuity did obtain.

The Maghrebin data which initially inspired the general model may seem an exiguous base for such ambitious claims. They have of course been supplemented by other available ethnographic data. Every attempt has been made to record data, and interpretations, which do not support it, with fairness. In the past few decades, social-anthropological material on Muslim societies has been accumulating at an ever-increasing rate, and has come to cover a wide variety of geographical contexts. If there is one lesson, one moral, which appears to emerge from this ever-growing mass of data, it is that, albeit with modifications, the world of Ibn Khaldun persisted at the micro-social level for a very long time. No doubt anthropologists are suspect: have they not a preference for the archaic, whether this springs from being lackeys of colonialism or from simple nostalgia for a lost *Gemeinschaft*? Notwithstanding this suspicion, it seems to me that their accounts of rural and urban life add up to a coherent and convincing picture, and I have tried to spell out what it is.

When all is said and done, however, it remains a picture inspired by data which are either Maghrebin or anthropological, or of course both, and which draws its ideas from any sociologists who seem to be relevant, and which makes correspondingly less use of orientalists and historians.[98]

One may well ask: why treat the Ibn Khaldun model as basic, and the Ottoman social formation merely as a variant or a superimposition on it? Is this not arbitrary? Is it justified by a statistical preponderance of the one type over the other, whether one counts political units or populations? For instance, Marshall G.S. Hodgson's *The Venture of Islam*, which is probably the most ambitious and sustained modern attempt to offer a sociological *and* historical account of Muslim society, observes:[99]

Ibn Khaldun's *Muqaddima* ... no doubt the best general introduction to Islamicate civilisation ever written ... illuminates very effectively the political state of Islamdom in the Middle Periods ... he was unable to appreciate the role which civil political forces could play in better circumstances, and did play in earlier and later times.

To say this is in a way to treat the 'middle periods' as a kind of aberration, and hence Ibn Khaldun's work as the account of something aberrant. It seems to me more fitting to treat these long middle periods as sociologically typical, as evidence for the really relevant ideal type of Muslim society. Does the period which preceded it have much in common with that which followed it (other than that it is often invoked by way of justification of reforms attempted in our time)? Does the *post*-middle, in other words the modern, period really display the triumph of *civil* political forces? And is it not significant that when social anthropologists burrow in the micro-structures of Muslim societies, they generally come back with a picture very compatible with that of Ibn Khaldun?

The real justification of the commended view seems to me this: inside every Mamluk state, there appear to be many Ibn Khaldunian social formations hidden away and signalling wildly to be let out — and very frequently succeeding, whether uncovered by a political upheaval or a probing anthropologist. It is only in modern conditions, when the central state is endowed with new and really unprecedented means of coercion, and a new economy with quite novel means of seduction, that these old forms genuinely begin to evaporate; but even then, the constellation of the old forms at the moment of the impact of the modernity, the particular point at which the pendulum was located, helps explain the specific path towards new forms adopted by each Muslim land.

So in the end, whilst the model is propounded in part because any model is better than none, this modesty, or hedging of bets, if you wish, is a good deal less than total. The model is also put forward with the conviction that, all in all, it does capture the way in which ecology, social organisation, and ideology interlock in one highly distinctive civilisation; that it explains *how* their distinctive fusion produced its stabilities and tensions, and continues to influence the various paths along which it is finally entering the modern world.

2

Cohesion and identity: the Maghreb from Ibn Khaldun to Emile Durkheim[1]

Ibn Khaldun, like Emile Durkheim, is primarily a theorist of *social cohesion*. His central problem is: what is it that keeps men together in society? What is it that leads them to identify with a social group, to accept and observe its norms, to subordinate their own individual interests to it, in some measure to accept the authority of its leaders, to think its thoughts and to internalise its aims? This is a question which sociologists, moralists and political philosophers share. One of the interesting traits of Ibn Khaldun, however, is the extent to which he is a sociologist rather than a moralist: modern sociologists may preach *Wertfreiheit*; he practised it. Even when, as a kind of Maghrebin Machiavelli, he offers advice to princes, it is basically technical advice on points of detail, or on the wisdom of knowing things for what they are: but when it comes to the basic features of the social system, he indulges in no preaching. No advice is offered to the social cosmos as to how it should comport itself. Things are as they are. The thinker's job is to understand them, not to change them. Marx's contrary opinion would have astonished Ibn Khaldun. In this sense, Ibn Khaldun is *more* positivistic than Durkheim, whose thought is far more often at the service of values and of the concern with social renovation.

If Ibn Khaldun and Durkheim shared their basic problem, and if their moral attitude differed in its stress, then, however, in their *solution* of the problem they stand diametrically opposed. Their respective accounts of what binds men together in societies are radically opposed. Each of them *knew* about segmentary societies, and indeed Durkheim initiated the use of the expression; Ibn Khaldun knew them at first hand, from prolonged personal involvement in Maghrebin politics, and Durkheim was familiar with the North African specimens of it from contemporary ethnography. But though their material overlapped, their use, interpretation and evaluation of it differed very profoundly. Durkheim, as is well known, considered mechanical solidarity, exemplified by segmentary societies and based on *similarity* (of social sub-units and indeed of individuals) to be *a* form of cohesion, but an inferior and less effective one than 'organic' solidarity, which is based not on similarity but on *complementarity*, on mutual interdependence, and is exemplified by more complex, non-segmentary societies.

86

Cohesion and identity

It would be an understatement to say that Ibn Khaldun inverted or contradicted this evaluation. Had he used Durkheim's terminology he would have said, not that organic solidarity was less effective than mechanical, nor even merely that it was not effective at all, but that, far from being a form of cohesion at all, it was a form of social *dissolution*.

This is of course the central fact in Ibn Khaldun's sociology: in Durkheimian language, it is the contrast between mechanical solidarity, which he might as well have called solidarity *tout court*, and the organic *lack* of solidarity or cohesion. The ethnographic material on which this crucial dichotomy is based is of course primarily North African. On the one hand there is the cohesion, the capacity to identify with the group and internalise it, which is exemplified by tribal society; and on the other, the lack of cohesion in urban society, despite or indeed because of its 'organic' character, i.e. its highly developed division of labour. Unlike Durkheim, Ibn Khaldun saw no way to moral and social salvation in such a complex division of labour. On the contrary: he held urban life as such to be so inherently inimical to social cohesion, that he considered any town-dweller who used the idiom of kinship, who claimed membership of a 'house' (in the clan sense), to be perpetrating a sociological fraud. For Ibn Khaldun, kinship is the idiom of true cohesion; for a townsman even to use that idiom is to pass counterfeit coin!

Almost everything in Ibn Khaldun's sociology follows from this conviction: almost everything, but not quite everything. One further key premiss is required: the cities, though offering very little by way of *political* contribution to society, are *economically* indispensable. The rulers may perhaps be economic parasites, but the townsmen are not: far from being parasitic, the townsmen performed functions essential for the society as a whole. And one might add – the *economy* can here be interpreted in a very wide sense, as including the cultural as well as the productive equipment of the society. Not merely agricultural and military implements, but equally the ritual and conceptual tools of the society require urban specialists for their production and maintenance. Tribesmen may view the towns as politically redundant and parasitic and may opt out from central-urban control whenever they have the chance, but they do not view the town as *economically* parasitic.

Ibn Khaldun, Durkheim and Weber

It is interesting that Ibn Khaldun's cold sociological eye views so dispassionately each of the principal partners in traditional Maghrebin society – tribesmen and townsmen – seeing each from the viewpoint of the other; the contempt which each of them feels for the other is transmuted by him into an unflattering analysis. His comments on the havoc wrought by nomads are well known and often quoted, but they ought really to be cited alongside his similarly condemnatory observations on the fraudulent nature of urban kin affiliations. They were fraudulent not because they might be 'genetically' untrue — Ibn Khaldun knew that this was also often so in tribal society and was of no importance — but because they were *sociologically* untrue, i.e. corresponded to no effective social cohesion. This sociological contempt, so to speak, for the cohesion-potential of towns, is a kind of translation of the disdain of the tribesman for any specialist — the revulsion of mechanical solidarity for the organic kind. To this day, tribesmen in the recesses of the Atlas will use outsiders for the performance of various economic specialisms which are essential for them — blacksmiths, dyers and such — but which are yet somehow socially suspect. Only the non-specialist is morally whole. This is the voice of mechanical solidarity, viewing the 'organic' principle with revulsion, and Ibn Khaldun echoes this reaction as much as he echoes urban contempt for lack of tribal civilisation. The possibility that organic solidarity is also one way of attaining cohesion, another and perhaps a more powerful way, is something which is no part of his experience.

So the difference between Durkheim and Ibn Khaldun is this: Durkheim's account of social cohesion is worked out in terms of the contrast between mechanical and organic solidarity, and presupposes an awareness of these two paths towards cohesion, whereas Ibn Khaldun knows *only* mechanical solidarity. He is aware, of course, of 'organic' society (i.e. one based on diversification and a complex division of labour), but though he holds it to be the indispensable and necessary precondition of *civilisation*, he does not consider it to be the basis of any *solidarity* at all. From a political or 'cohesionist' viewpoint, he holds its specialist citizens in contempt; this is a feeling which can still be encountered . . .

This is of course the very heart of Ibn Khaldun's sociology, of his vision of man's social condition: the preconditions of civilisation and of cohesion are mutually antithetical. These two plants will not grow in the same soil. The society he knew was neither a purely tribal one, such as could do without civilisation, nor a properly town-dominated one, such as could do without tribal cohesion. Each of the two elements was ever-present and essential. The story of the interplay of these two elements, of this repetitive stalemate position, is at the core of Ibn Khaldun's vision.

There is a number of very remarkable things about Ibn Khaldun. For one thing, he is a superb deductive sociologist, a practitioner, long before the term was invented, of the method of ideal types: what he has to say about human society follows neatly from a small set of premises concerning the causes and hindrances of cohesion. But, whilst worked out in this elegant and economical manner, the end result corresponds to and illuminates the full richness of concrete societies — at any rate of those societies which he knew well. The economy of explication comes to meet the diversity of actual manifestations, and it does not travesty it.

But there is a further remarkable fact: Ibn Khaldun was in error when he supposed, as evidently he did, that he was analysing human society as such, anywhere, any time. In fact he was offering a brilliant account of *one* extremely important kind of society — namely, one in which tribes and towns co-exist, in which the general technological and economic level is such as to make the towns indispensable, but *without* giving them the means of dominating the tribes, and in which this relationship is expressed by a religion which in its official formulation stresses urban literacy and individualism, as opposed to tribalism, but which also possesses less individualist and less scripturalist institutions for the *encadrement* of tribesmen. To put this point more simply, he was the sociologist of Islam; notably of Islam as manifested in the arid zone, an environment which encourages tribalism by favouring nomadic or semi-nomadic pastoralism and which hinders centralising political tendencies. But even within Islam, it is not obvious whether Ibn Khaldun is universally applicable. Leaving aside for a moment the special case of 'modern' conditions, does he apply to those Muslim societies which recruit their rulers not by the 'new dynasty' method, in which new princes come in with their entire tribal 'tail', but by individual purchase (Mamluks) or — interesting measure of political parsimony — through taxation. Recruiting infants in such a way is obviously much cheaper than market purchase. Does it apply to a long-lived and relatively stable system such as the Ottoman Empire, at least at its centre?

This point — there are societies to which Ibn Khaldun's account does not apply — is not made by way of criticism. One must be grateful to him for having offered so splendid an account of one important kind of society. The point is made rather in a spirit of admiration and of puzzlement: how could a man, who did not really know or even conceptualise any other type of society, come to analyse that one kind of society so brilliantly? Max Weber's *Protestant Ethic*, for instance, is a masterpiece not for its highly debatable and much debated contribution to the aetiology of capitalism, but for its superb sketch of what it is that distinguishes the modern world from the other possible and actual social worlds. But Max Weber was aroused to ask the question about the specificity of the modern world precisely because he knew full well that the modern world was but one of many possible ones, and very different from the others. It is platitudinous to say that the same is true of modern Western sociology as a whole: it was born of an attempt to understand a very big *difference*. Even the proliferation of American sociology after 1945, and the particular form it took, can be explained in part by the fact that Americans found themselves with the White Man's Burden thrust onto their shoulders and were obliged to seek for ways of thinking about societies other than their own or the Red Indians. All this is a truism: people generally take their own society and culture for granted, except when they are shaken into an awareness of it by the conspicuous presence of some contrasted social form. Often, even the presence of such a contrast fails to awake their sociological sensibility.

Now this may be a truism, but it is a truism contradicted by the very existence of Ibn Khaldun. What is so curious and remarkable about him is precisely this: though he did quite mistakenly suppose his kind of society to be the only kind, and a paradigm of the general social condition of mankind, he was somehow fully aware, in an explicit way, of just how it worked. Ibn Khaldun at any rate cannot be explained in the same way as modern sociology, as a reaction to the awareness of a big, conspicuous contrast. He saw no contrast. He saw only the one un-contrasted thing, but nevertheless he understood it perfectly. This remains a mystery.

The present relevance

The contrast which concerns us now is one of which Ibn Khaldun could not possibly be aware: that between Maghrebin society as he knew it, and as it is *now*. To say this is not, of course, to criticise him: indeed, even the observations about his lack of awareness of social forms other than those of the Muslim world were made more to highlight the brilliance of his analysis of that particular world, than to comment on his limitations. But our present topic is national and cultural identity: and it seems to me that the principles underlying social cohesion and cultural identification in the Maghreb of the twentieth century are radically different from those which operated in Ibn Khaldun's world.

North Africa in the twentieth century takes part in the global trends of the age. If these can be summed up briefly at all, then two terms must be used: industrialisation and nationalism. The principles which underlie these two processes are new, and though they have been discussed endlessly, yet their implications for social cohesion are not yet fully understood.

Industrial society is defined by a very distinctive kind of division of labour. It is incompatible with mechanical solidarity, for the simple and obvious reason that productive specialisation is pushed to a very extreme degree and is a precondition of that high productivity which has enslaved humanity to the industrial ideal. At the same time, *cultural* specialisation or differentiation is much diminished. In other words, industrial society could not possibly resemble the kind of tribal society in which only one kind of activity — say, herding or agriculture — has dignity, and in which specialists are suspect, for the very simple reason that such an ethos would, absurdly, deprive the overwhelming majority of the producers of their dignity ... In industrial society, the man with highly specialised qualifications is at the very front of the dignity ranking and not in the rear.

Nevertheless, it is by no means enough to say that industrial or industrialising society exemplifies organic solidarity, that its cohesion is based on the mutual interdependence of specialists. Durkheim is a better guide to industrial society than Ibn Khaldun — not surprisingly, given that he had experience of it — but he is not fully adequate either. There have been *other* 'organic' societies, i.e. such as exemplify a complex division of labour and a consequent mutual dependence: for instance, Indian caste society. But industrial society differs from them in at least one important and radical way.

In those societies, the division of labour is complex, but relatively stable. In consequence, diverse economic specialisms can be attributed to various social groups — castes, millets, guilds, estates, i.e. groups which may be defined in a ritual, legal, ethnic or other way — and which then charge themselves with reproducing the appropriate skills over generations. The groups themselves transmit the specialisms. They also differentiate themselves culturally and this helps the identification, protection and perpetuation of the productive specialism.

In industrial society, this is not so. It is no accident that industrial or industrialising societies possess centralised educational systems which induce cultural homogeneity: the state seems more jealous of its near-monopoly of education than it is of its monopoly of legitimate violence. In England, for instance, many secondary schools bear names which testify to their origin as *guild* schools — but the social reality is quite different: the educational content, the output, of such schools is controlled by centrally imposed norms (even when these are not legally enforced, but depend on informal mechanisms), and bear not the least mark of any guild specialism. For instance, the products of Haberdashers' School have not the slightest bias, in their training or ethos, towards haberdashery . . . Or again, if a country like Algeria recognises a cultural dualism and deals with both traditional ('original') and modern education, it still ensures that both of them are centrally supervised.

The reason for all this is not far to seek. Industrial society is not merely complex in its division of labour, but also occupationally and otherwise highly *mobile*. Notoriously, manpower planning is difficult or impossible, because new kinds of employment turn up all the time, and the numerical proportions between existing types of jobs change all the time, in a largely unpredictable manner. In consequence, all economically useful citizens need a certain basic training — literacy, numeracy, a certain cultural and technical all-round minimum — which allows them to shift occupations and be re-trained. Moreover, the very texture, so to speak, of the division of labour conveys a kind of expectancy of these shifts of employment, and a readiness to receive newcomers: the tasks may be highly specialised and diversified, far beyond the point known in caste or guild society, and yet the idiom in which these most diversified tasks are specified is a *common* idiom. The operating manuals of most diverse kinds of machines or techniques are written not only in the same language but in accordance with similar conventions.

Suppose we took Ibn Khaldun's theory of social cohesion to be *universally* applicable, for any kind of society: it would follow that an industrial society, one in which the division of labour is pushed to such extremes and accompanied by such mobility, is quite incapable of any kind of cohesion. How could individuals, indulging in such diverse activities and never together for very long, let alone bound to each other by a shared experience of hardship — how could such individuals ever acquire that sense of identity which makes a community? Like the city in Ibn Khaldun's world, they might need to import some super-tribe to rule over them . . . Some phenomena in industrial society, such as the collapse of American cities, lend support to such expectations. But by and large, contrary to the logic of Ibn Khaldun's premisses, industrial society — a mass of mobile, atomised, highly specialised individuals — *has* exemplified its own kind of social cohesion and identification, working on a new principle which has not infrequently been capable of arousing the fervour of broad masses and of leading individuals to make extreme, self-denying sacrifices. The name of that principle is 'nationalism'.

To put all this another way: from Ibn Khaldun's viewpoint, nationalism is wildly paradoxical. It operates in a milieu and on individuals who, from Ibn Khaldun's viewpoint, should exemplify the very opposite of any social cohesion. It operates on people far removed from segmentary or mechanical solidarity, the only kind of solidarity he knew, and who are deeply sunk in an urban-style life of specialism and individualism. And yet, nationalism and the principle of nationality have proved a powerful social bond, often operating spontaneously, without official encouragement, or in the face of official discouragement and of powerful legal or economic deterrents. How is this to be explained?

The truth of the matter is that industrial society has its own principles of cohesion, its own centripetal forces, which work very differently from the type of social bond that dominated Ibn Khaldun's world. Durkheim's notion of organic solidarity provides at least a starting point for understanding that new-style cohesion, though as formulated by him it does not get us quite all the way. One deficiency of his formulation we have noted already: he does not see clearly enough that industrial society exemplifies a *very* distinctive and specific kind of organic solidarity, rather than organic solidarity in general. Another deficiency of his is his tendency to underrate the, so to speak, 'Protestant' tendency of modern industrial society. Durkheim, especially in *The Elementary Forms of Religious Life*, stresses with emphasis the community-defining, cohesion-enhancing role of ritual, and the importance of ritual within religion. But a mobile modern society does not wish to encourage sub-groups to fortify themselves by rituals or in any other way — a point which Rousseau sensed even if he expressed it in a confused manner — and it is itself too large to have rituals of its own, in the literal sense which would require or allow the presence of all members. It can at best simulate them either by synchronising local rituals, and pretending they all add up to a kind of unity, or by simultaneity-through-mass-media. It is partly for this reason, I suspect, that modern societies prefer to rely on the 'inner forum' of individuals, on the effective internalisation of loyalty, rather than on rituals in the 'external forum'. This in turn helps to explain why contemporary religion tends, whatever its nominal doctrine or history, to move in a 'Protestant', sober direction, away from ritual and towards the cultivation, effective programming and strengthening of the inner light.

The real cohesion of modern society

But where are these general cohesion-engendering factors of a modern society, which escaped Ibn Khaldun with his over-concentration on the segmentary form of cohesion, and which Durkheim only partly understood? It is I think fairly easy to sketch the general relevant traits of such a society:

(1) It has a hold over its members through the promise or the reality of wealth. In societies which have achieved affluence, the 'revolution of rising expectations' constitutes a promise of *more* wealth to come; and except for the rather ambiguous phenomenon of the 'opting-out' of youth in very affluent societies, there is as yet no sign of satiety. The combination of rising expectations and democratic and Keynesian government has now produced the spectre of uncontrollable inflation, but that is another story. Industrial society has refuted de Maistre: the washing machine, not the executioner, stands at the basis of social order.

(2) But access to this growing wealth is restricted to those who are employable. Only the educated are employable. Only the literate are educated. And one can only be literate in some definite medium, some language and some script. Hence employability is not unqualified, but tied to the catchment area of an educational system and to a language. Hence the world tends to settle down into a number of discontinuous linguistic areas, within which there is mobility, but *between* which mobility is restricted. (Between them, mobility tends to occur only at the top — outstanding, creative specialists — and at the bottom — unskilled labour.)

(3) Within each such area, the occupational and geographical mobility, the atomisation of the population, the dependence of status on individual qualification rather than on group membership, all tend to erode clear-cut, sharply symbolised inequality. Such inequality as remains, and of course much remains, tends to be economic, to allow of gradual transitions, to be devoid of legal or ritual sanctions, and to remain semi-observed. In other words, there tends to be no rigid caste system. Formal equality and a certain openness prevail. On this point, Tocqueville was right.

Anything else would be incompatible with that flow of labour-power, that centralised and reasonably homogeneous educational system which is inherent in the industrial pattern of the division of labour.

These, I think, are the general traits of industrial society, traits which also appear in large measure in *industrialising* ones. My way of sketching this out is designed to bring out the intimate relationship between the new ecology, the new division of labour, and nationalism, the principle of nationality as the prime criterion of political legitimacy.

We can see how very much a world in which this is true has changed, in contrast with the world of Ibn Khaldun. The type of cohesion which he considered paradigmatic — the cohesion of a tribal unit, forged by shared hardship in desert or mountain, reinforced by the ever-present threat of tribal enemies, and symbolised by the idiom of kinship — is neither necessary nor even tolerable for a modern society. Such a society will not allow peace-keeping by feud, by local

93

private wars, and its armoury enables it to impose its will fairly easily on any surviving tribes; its administrators can control desert and mountain, its labour market can seduce the young men, its culture can replace the tribal ritual . . . But this is merely the negative aspect of the matter. On the positive side, by promising affluence and security to all those who acquire its culture in a literate manner, it can also secure popular loyalty.

Thus industrial society can win the loyalty of its citizens and attain cohesion, *provided* there is a basic cultural homogeneity between its various loose strata, such as will permit the reality and the hope of employment and betterment for individuals. If, on the other hand, there are deep, impassable or hard-to-pass cultural cleavages, a new nationalism is likely to be born on the less favoured shore of such chasms.

So much for a general theory of nationalism, or the manner in which it has merged with industrialism and the aspiration to industrialism, and the manner in which it replaces the cohesion of the tribal group by the cohesion of a shared literate culture. To understand this change is important in itself. But it has various implications for the question of 'national identity'.

For one thing, it seems obvious that we have here (at least) two quite distinct questions: (1) What *kind* of community, with what kind of cohesion, shall we live in? and (2) Just what territory, or demarcation, geographical or linguistic or historical or whatnot, shall we employ?

The answer to question (1) is, I think, dictated by our overall socio-economic situation. Whilst fully aware of the pitfalls of sociological determinism, I do not think any society today has the option of return to 'mechanical solidarity'. We can, indeed, try to work out the balance-sheet of gains and losses — but only as a kind of theoretical, philosophical exercise, not as a preliminary to any realistic choices. We shall return to this theme.

But under (2) there are, of course, choices. We are destined for a definite species of organic solidarity, but it does not dictate the criteria of boundaries. This, I take it, is the context in which a country or its intellectuals may wonder about the option amongst diverse possible identities — local, pan-Arab, Ottoman, Maghrebin, French. And here, as far as I can see, the nature of contemporary social reality does *not* dictate anything. The specific type of division of labour, of 'organic solidarity', imposed by the modern mode of production, requires educational homogeneity, near-universal education in a shared medium, absence of rigid and deep cleavages between segments of the population, and above all between it and the ruling elite; but within the limit set by these sociological imperatives, there seems to me to exist a variety of possibilities. An ideal-typical national state, with a national language shared by the administration and the people, and one whose political boundaries correspond to the linguistic one — so that *all* its citizens, *and* no one else, speaks that language as both their first and their working language — is only one possible solution. One can think of others.

Cohesion and identity

There is the Swiss solution: a plurality of languages, but unaccompanied by any domination by any one of them, and associated with a level of education and a degree of equality such that no one language correlates with an 'area of discontent or under-privilege' which would make that language into the symbol and dia-critical mark of a new nationalism; the Indian solution: a great linguistic frag-mentation accompanied by the official use of an alien language, but with a great underlying cultural homogeneity based on a shared religious tradition, and a fair amount of symmetry in the access to that alien language and hence to the advan-tages it offers; the 'small nation' solution, exemplified by many of the smaller European countries, in which an internal linguistic homogeneity is accompanied by the widespread and efficient use, for commercial or academic purposes, of an outside world language in the interest of the advantages it offers in international communication. Perhaps calling this the 'small nation' solution is a misnomer, in so far as my impression is that at least one populous and economically very powerful country — West Germany — is in effect adopting this solution.

It would be impertinent for a foreigner to offer advice to Tunisians on their choice of identity. But my impression, no doubt inevitably based on superficial knowledge, is that the problem is less than acute in Tunisia. The French motto after 1871 was said to be, in connection with revenge, *toujours y penser, jamais en parler*. After 1945, it was said that the West German attitude to the reunifi-cation of Germany was: *toujours en parler, jamais y penser*. My impression of Tunisians and identity is that the motto might be: *y penser et en parler un peu, mais pas trop*. They give me the impression of feeling quite at home in their own cultural skin. It seems an enviable condition to me, and one must hope that my impression is well based.

The transition from an Ibn Khaldun style of social cohesion and community-definition to a Durkheimian one is not always so fortunate. One should not, perhaps, idealise the earlier situation. The fact that order was maintained by local kin-defined groups made collective retribution morally acceptable — in other words, people managed to 'live with' the feud. Did this make premature death any less tragic? We need not ask the question, for we do not have the option of returning to a tribal and feuding society.

But it is true that there are aspects of Maghrebin society which tempt one to idealise the traditional situation. The Maghreb possesses what must be the most dramatically beautiful folk architecture in the world. But the beauty of moun-tain or oasis villages is complemented by what can only be described as the social aesthetics of the traditional forms of organisation: the intricate patterns woven by the simple themes of clanship, shrine, festival, market, pilgrimage, lead to social designs of great beauty, which achieve complex ends of human co-operation with the most elegant economy of means.

This is a beauty to which one cannot return. But sociologists should do what they can to preserve an accurate memory of it.

The price of nation-building

The transition from a decentralised, locally-articulated society, such as pervaded the Middle East and the Maghreb traditionally, to a centralised, culturally homogeneous one — to a 'national' state, whatever its precise boundaries — can on occasion involve a terrible price. Cultural and religious pluralism, previously tolerated or exploited by the weak traditional state, is difficult to sustain in the modern, post-independence situation. Under such conditions, the old pluralism can hardly survive. Let us not idealise it: it was often accompanied by hate, sometimes by oppression and brutality. But for better or worse, whatever its merits, it seems not to be a current option.

Industrial society presupposes a mobile population with a shared literate culture; in other words, it generates 'national' states whose symbol of identity is the culture which is shared by most of its citizens. Such a state supervises the transmission of that culture, *at a literate level*, from generation to generation. Though not generally egalitarian to a degree that would satisfy a convinced egalitarian, it is nevertheless more egalitarian than most pre-industrial societies. It is hostile to deep, unbridgeable, culturally-marked chasms between its own sub-groups and between its own social strata. To return to the narrowly local theme — Tunisia would not appear to have any such deep chasms internally, nor would it have them if it combined with its neighbours in some larger unit. Hence, if I interpret the inherent dictates of industrial society correctly, they leave Tunisia ample leeway: it is a viable unit as it stands, and would also sociologically remain such within a larger unity. The precise boundaries are left to human choice or historical accident: they do not impose themselves.

The major social tragedies in our time occur in those situations arising when the transition from a pluralistic, locally or otherwise sub-divided world of Ibn Khaldun, to the culturally more homogeneous but economically more diversified world of Durkheim, cannot be completed in a peaceful manner. Communities which previously were culturally differentiated sub-groups in a wider society are suddenly transformed into culturally homogeneous, territorial and exclusive societies.

But that is not the end of the story. The tragedy is accentuated by the peculiar international situation of our industrial or industrialising world. Internationally, the politics of today's world are almost the same as those which held for inter-tribal relations in Ibn Khaldun's day. There is, as he put it, no militia to keep the peace. Each community relies for its own defence partly on its own power, partly on a system of alliances, fluid, shifting and unreliable, just like the precarious alignments of clans. Voting at the inter-tribal shrine on the East Side of Manhattan Island is not unlike the performances of collective oath of traditional Maghrebin tribes at the tombs of saints. The cohesion of rival groupings, the intensity of their internal differences, is brought to the test by challenging them at the vote, at the collective oath . . .

Cohesion and identity

In such conditions, modern societies which are internally quite centralised, and not at all Ibn-Khaldunian, are obliged to rely on *the feud* for the settlement of their disputes. The feud is a mechanism by which groups constrain each other to constrain their own members, by wreaking vengeance indiscriminately, anonymously, on *any* members of the rival group.

Let us not idealise this method even for tribal society. It would be arrogant to suggest that death is less tragic for a tribesman than for us, because his kinsmen will provide (always?) continuous support for his offspring and dependants. It is not easier to face death because one has a life insurance, even if that insurance is provided by a tribal structure. Moreover, let us not idealise the efficiency of this mechanism either. At its best, it may have provided very large tribes with relative peace and stability at very small cost in lives. One has the impression that balance sheets of tribal feud could stretch literally over centuries, and not run into double figures. I remember an anthropologist doing fieldwork in the Hadramaut, observing negotiations for the settlement of a feud, and hearing to his astonishment that one of the deaths had been caused by *an arrow* — a weapon not in use in the region for a long, long time. In other words, the accountancies of reciprocal killing stretched back right into an age of long-past military technology, without straining anyone's arithmetic. This clearly was an economical and relatively humane system. At other times and places, feuds could escalate uncontrollably.

But when all this is said and done, in Ibn-Khaldunian tribal conditions, the feud seemed the only mechanism for the maintenance of order between tribes, and apart from seeming to be the only option, it also appeared morally acceptable.

The tragedy arises in our day when Durkheimian societies face each other in an Ibn-Khaldunian feud: when communities, which were previously segments of a wider world, become 'national' states as we have defined them, controlling an exclusive territory and a relatively homogeneous population (thanks to migrations, forced or voluntary, and educational 'acculturation'); and when at the same time, the conflict between them has to be carried on — owing to the absence of external peace-keepers — by the method of the feud, i.e. by revenge which selects its victims anonymously from the opposing camp. This is no longer morally tolerable.

As everyone knows, situations of this order have arisen in many parts of the world: in the relationship of Catholic and Protestant in Ireland, Turk and Greek in Cyprus or, previously, on the mainland of what are now modern Turkey and Greece. But the most tragic and intractable version of this kind of confrontation is of course the present 'Middle Eastern conflict'.

That it should have occurred was perhaps inevitable. In the transition from a *millet* or segment society to a territorial 'national' culturally homogeneous one, it is inevitable that 'rights' should conflict. In a simplified model, one can imagine both sides to the conflict aspiring all at once to all the territory of the previous plural society *and* at the same time to all the privileges and honours of the top segments in it. By a kind of optical illusion, a community may suppose that it can have all the advantages, and none of the losses, involved in the transition from the world of Ibn Khaldun to that of Durkheim. The erosion of the old ranking must mean a loss of prestige somewhere, and hence a sense of humiliation for some; the drawing of boundaries between the new culturally homogeneous units must inevitably mean a 'loss' of territory by some old criteria.

That the conflict should have occurred was perhaps inevitable or, at any rate, with sociological hindsight it can be made to seem so. Those who advocate a return to some absolute *status quo ante*, corresponding to the pre-modern solution, may well speak in good faith, but I fear they may be pursuing an illusory hope. But, whether inevitable or merely plausible, the situation in which two modern, literate, industrial communities confront each other with the methods of tribal society, remains unspeakably tragic. If we can understand why it had to happen, perhaps we can also come to understand why it need not continue.

3

Post-traditional forms in Islam: the turf and trade, and votes and peanuts

Orientalists are at home with texts. Anthropologists are at home in villages. The natural consequence is that the former tend to see Islam from above, the latter from below. I remember an anthropologist specialising in a Muslim country telling me of his first encounter with an elderly and distinguished Islamicist. The old scholar observed that the Koran was interpreted differently in various parts of the Muslim world. The young anthropologist remarked that this was indeed obvious. 'Obvious? Obvious?' expostulated the older man angrily, 'It took *years* of careful research to establish it!'

The story has various morals, but one of them is that the diversity of Muslim civilisation is now a well-established fact, amply documented by scholars and by field-workers, and it no longer requires further documentation. In its day, it was no doubt a useful corrective to the simplistic view which took Islam at face value and assumed that, because Muslim life is the implementation of *one* Book and its prescriptions, therefore Muslim civilisation is homogeneous. This view need no longer be fought. The time has come to re-assert the thesis of homogeneity, not so much as a thesis, but as a problem. For all the indisputable diversity, the remarkable thing is the extent to which Muslim societies resemble each other. Their traditional political systems, for instance, are much more of one kind than were those of pre-modern Christendom. At least in the bulk of Muslim societies, in the main Islamic block between Central Asia and the Atlantic shores of Africa, one has the feeling that the same and limited pack of cards has been dealt. The hands vary, but the pack is the same. This homogeneity, in as far as it obtains, is all the more puzzling in the theoretical absence of a Church, and hence of a central authority on Faith and Morals. There is no obvious agency which could have enforced this homogeneity.

It is worth trying, rashly but tentatively, to identify some of the main cards in this pack, as a preliminary to an examination of some curious examples of what happens when hands drawn from that pack are dealt in a modern context.

The elements which go into what one may call the Islamic social syndrome fall into two main groups: the ecological/technological, and the ideological. All this refers to the traditional context, defined loosely and summarily (and

99

perhaps question-beggingly) as the conditions preceding the impact of the modern and Western world on Islam.

Ecology and technique: Muslim societies between the Hindu Kush and the Atlantic were characterised by the symbiosis of urban, literate, centrally governed, trade-oriented communities, with tribal ones. Tribes may be defined as rural communities which partly or totally escape control by central government, and within which the maintenance of order, such as it is, is left largely to the interplay of local groups, generally conceived in terms of kinship. What is so striking a characteristic of Muslim civilisation is the numerical and political importance of tribes. Tribes were not unknown on the margins of Christendom or Hinduism — but they were far less important. This fact is mirrored to this day by the popular Western stereotype of the Muslim as a fanatical turbaned tribesman on a camel — what one may call the T.E. Lawrence, North West Frontier or Beau Geste image. This is of course in striking contrast to Islam as seen from inside, as an urban faith, practicable only with difficulty in an illiterate milieu of desert or mountain.

One may rephrase this characterisation in terms of the technical and institutional equipment of Muslim societies. They assumed literacy, urban life, long-distance trade, and central authority. But they also assumed, or had to live with, the fact that the central power and the towns could not effectively control outlying tribes, though at the same time they constituted, economically and religiously, one community with them. All this assumes a level of population which has forced enough people to live in marginal mountain and desert regions, and to be sufficiently numerous out there to constitute a threat. The central power does not possess adequate technical and organisational resources for the effective subjugation of the tribes; at the same time, the general ecology of the tribes is such that they need urban markets and specialists, and remain in sustained contact with the towns. (In Platonic terms, the tribes resemble the inflated rather than the self-sufficient and simple city, and hence autarchy is not open to them. As Ibn Khaldun noted — and it sounds surprising to Western ears — economically, the tribes need the towns, rather than vice versa.) This economic need is reinforced by what may be termed moral ecology: the tribesmen identify with a religion which, through literacy, ultimately must have an urban base. These factors lead to that characteristically violent symbiosis of tribe and urban-based government.

What are the ideological cards which are dealt by Islam? The crucial ones are: a scriptural faith, a *completed* one (the final edition, so to speak) is available, and there is no room for further accretion or for new prophets; also, there is no warrant for clergy, and hence for religious differentiation; and, third, there is no need to differentiate between Church and State, between what is God's and what is Caesar's, since it began as a religion of rapidly successful conquerors, who soon *were* the state. These are the basic data, as they emerged when Islam shook down, so to speak, to its settled form in the early centuries of its existence.

100

Post-traditional forms in Islam

Islam is trans-ethnic and trans-social: it does not equate faith with the beliefs of any one community or society (even the total community of the faithful). But the trans-social truth which can sit in judgment on the social is a Book, plus the traditions — a recorded Revelation, rather than an institution. Thus by implication Islam is not clearly tied to any one political institution or authority. But at the same time, this implication fails to obtain reinforcement or support from any tradition of state/church opposition. The early community was both church and state, and thus this differentiation never fully developed, as it does in a faith which organises itself long before it captures the state. The Shi'ites, who did need to organise before they captured the state, and organised in order to do so, did develop a theory, not so much concerning what is God's and what is Caesar's, but concerning the permissibility of telling Caesar what he wished to hear, while keeping the truth to oneself.

The consequence of all this is that the trans-social standard which judges the social is a Book, and not a Church. This can then be socially incarnated either in the corporations of literate interpreters of the Book, or in such spiritual leadership which emerges as best it can, notwithstanding the lack of a clear charter for it.

This is the setting, these are the elements in the power game which limit the available political and doctrinal moves. Within the limits thus set, what were the options? The dominant notions available for political legitimation, in these circumstances, were:

Communal Consensus   The Book   Organisation,
                                                      Leadership, Ancestry

These are the three central ideas that were available, arranged along a spectrum, from a kind of Left to a kind of Right. The Book is, on the whole, shared ground: few extremists go so far as actually to suspend its authority in favour of either spiritual leadership (on the Right) or of Communal Consensus (on the Left). Though such extremist deviations do occur on the Left and on the Right (particularly on the Right), they remain relatively rare. An extremist Left deviation, in this sense, would allow the consensus of the community to override the Book; an extremist Right one (and this has been known to happen) would deify an individual and allow *him* to overrule the Book. 'Left' and 'Right' are here in effect defined in terms of egalitarianism versus hierarchy and hereditary inequality. The tension between these two is endemic in Islam: the egalitarian element is inherent in the universalist, scriptural, no-clergy, proselytising elements of the Faith. The inegalitarian element is inherent in large and complex organisation, and the articulation of inequality in terms of heredity follows from the fact that the societies incorporated in Islam were and remained kinship-oriented societies. Conventionally, two somewhat contradictory theories are given by historians of the *origin* of this conflict: one, that the impetus to inequality came from the early conquerors and their desire to maintain their privileges against the conquered and the later converts; the other, that the egalitarianism was rooted in Arab tribal traditions, while the inegalitarianism originated in the monarchic inheritance of the Persian converts.

Origins need not concern us in the present context. What does concern us is that the tension is inherent in the situation. In practice, extremism was rarer than either the moderate Left or Right positions – which are the fusion of a cult of the Book either with a cult of the Community, or of Leadership (and hence, of hierarchy and organisation).

The interesting thing is that the tension and conflict can be played out in two different ways – which I shall call the Unbounded and the Bounded. Chronologically, the Unbounded comes first, the Bounded becomes more common later. The reason for this sequence seems straightforward. The Unbounded way of playing out the conflict is the consequence of the *early* situation when no bounds, no limits, had yet clearly emerged, and hence protagonists were easily pushed into relatively extreme positions. No markers were there to signpost danger and to encourage caution. The Bounded style, on the other hand, is a consequence of a certain maturity, of the emergence of well-known and recognised limits which protagonists respect and which they cannot and will not easily violate. At the start, they could hardly help violating them, for the boundaries were not laid down. Later, when the boundaries became well-known and revered, the average participant in the religious-political game – and the vast majority of the participants are, naturally, rather ordinary and unexceptional people – will hardly dare brand himself as a heretic by transgressing them. A scriptural religion which believes its Revelation to be complete has a natural tendency towards delimiting the possible moves in the game.

In concrete historical terms – in the early years of Islam, the plugging of either the egalitarian or the inegalitarian card led to the crystallisation of the Kharejite and the Shi'a sects of heresies respectively. Neither of these tendencies need in normal circumstances be extremist, nor push either communal consent or the cult of personality to its utmost limits (though in Shi'ism, the tendency towards deification of personality was present and on occasion emerges). In normal times, either principle can be fused with a recognition of the Book and the Traditions.

But it is characteristic of the early period that, for the lack of established and familiar bounds to the game, these two tendencies did end up as outright sects – heresies from the viewpoint of the main community and of each other. If we are right in the claim that the tension between the egalitarian and the organisational principles was inherent in the situation, what happened to it in later centuries?

Basically, people learned how to keep it within limits: clear bounds emerged and, being clear, were more easily enforceable. The tension which, at the beginning, emerges as that between the two *heresies*, one each at either end of the spectrum, the Kharejites and Shi'ites, appears at a later stage *within* the fold, between the *ulama* and the Sufi. Sociologically speaking, the Sufi is an addict of leadership, of the cult of personality, who does not allow it to run away with him, or whose leader knows how to remain within the bounds of orthodoxy. The member of the corporation of the *ulama* is a member of a tradition which has found a compromise between the sovereignty of the community and the sovereignty of the Book, by having within the community a non-sacramental guild of scribes—lawyers—theologians, guardians and interpreters of the social norm, who yet do not claim deep or hereditary differentiation of spiritual status.

All this, though no doubt contestable, is not original. But it was necessary to rehearse the manner in which the traditional, pre-modern situation generated a certain possible span of religious-political attitudes, of styles of social legitimation. There were, as stated, two spans — one broader, one narrower, both were generated by the same basic tension between an egalitarian faith and inegalitarian social requirement, but one span *dépassait les limites* and was articulated in terms of rival heresies, and the other managed to stay within bounds. As far as I can see, the main reason why the same tension sometimes did, and sometimes did not, break out of limits was simply the clear demarcation of those limits, and this in turn was a matter of age and maturity. Movements which in the early days of Islam would have made a bid for a total take-over of the whole community, and would in consequence have ended at outright heresies, in *later* centuries, when the Community as a whole seemed too stable and well-established to be available for take-over, generally contented themselves with more modest claims *within* the faith.

There are various common theories of the origins and roots of the Sufi movement within Islam: the influence of mystical traditions springing from Christianity; India; pre-Islamic Middle Eastern thought; local cults; a reaction to the aridity of scholastic Islam; a reaction to foreign encroachment. There are no doubt important elements of truth in these various theories. But the most important factor, at least sociologically, seems to be the inescapable requirement of religious *organisation* and *leadership*. Formal Islam is capable of providing this only to a limited degree: it can do so when the state is strong, as in the Ottoman Empire, by linking religious organisation with political authority; and it can, and does, provide the legal 'schools', the corporations of scribes—teachers—jurists, who moreover can provide leadership of a limited kind only. Being numerous, they can ratify better than they can initiate, and being scholars, they can make their weight felt only in the kind of milieu in which they are respected and in which they flourish. But if we reconsider the ecological and military balance of Muslim societies, the manner of the symbiosis of tribe and city, we see that the Muslim world does not *everywhere* provide a milieu which favours the scholarly legal schools and makes their members adequate for the problems of leadership. Nor does it always favour a strong state. Sufism provides a theory, terminology, and technique of leadership, far more generally usable, in tribe, village or town, under government or in anarchy, but one which, unlike Shi'ism, does not normally transcend the limits of orthodoxy. Sufism is a kind of Reformation-in-reverse. It creates a quasi-church.

So much for traditional society. What is especially interesting are two well-documented specimens of adaptation of old Islamic movements to *modern* conditions. Each of our two specimens is drawn from the 'Right' end of the spectrum, from organisationally complex and inegalitarian movements. One is Shi'a, one is Sufi: in other words, one is older and operates, conceptually, outside the bounds, and the other can claim to have remained within the orthodox, Sunni fold. Both are conspicuous success stories in the modern world, and in each case the success is highly paradoxical: for, generally speaking, the conditions of the modern world favour literacy, sobriety, rationality, formal equality, all of which are found on the moderate 'Left' of the Islamic religious spectrum. The modern world has not favoured Sufism; and Shi'ism, though it holds its own relatively speaking, has all in all not been an active political force, and its characteristic, distinguishing features have not been conspicuously displayed. One suspects a tacit shift to the left within it.

Here we have two relatively extreme movements, neither of them particularly attuned to the allegedly rational, production-oriented, and egalitarian spirit of the modern world. Each of them, one should have said, was doomed to fare ill under the cold wind of either colonial commercialism or the subsequent cult of economic development. Neither had any good reason to welcome the modern world, and each of them had good cause to fear it. Any resemblance between these particular Shi'ites or Sufis, and the puritanical entrepreneurs of popular sociological theory, is not so much coincidental as downright unbelievable. Yet, strange to tell, each of these particular movements is not merely famous for the success of its adaptation to modernity, but owes this success, above all, to brilliant *economic* performance. This paradox deserves consideration.

Within the Shi'ite part of the Muslim spectrum — in other words, the segment of Islam turning towards a cult of personality rather than consensus mediated by scholars — there were further internal differentiations and dissensions. The *Ismailis* tended to extremism. Of the Shi'a as a whole, Bernard Lewis writes: 'A recurring feature is the cult of holy men ... who were believed to possess miraculous powers ... Among the beliefs attributed to them are those of reincarnation, the deification of the Imams ... and libertinism — the abandonment of all law and restraint.'[1] Expectation of miracles and a suspension of all Law — of such material successful orderly entrepreneurs are *not* made!

Within this general tradition, the Ismailis are not among the moderates:

The imam is central to the Ismaili system of doctrine and of organization, of loyalty and of action ... The imams ... were divinely inspired and infallible — in a sense indeed themselves divine ... As such, [the imam] was the fountainhead of knowledge and authority — of the esoteric truths that were hidden ... and of commands that required total and unquestioning obedience.[2]

These were large claims. Their implications for political theory are plain:

For men to think of electing an imam is . . . blasphemy. He was revealed by God . . . the imams are perfect sinless beings. The imam must be obeyed without question . . .[3]

The implications for political practice are even plainer. If you believe that you, or your Leader, is 'infallible . . . [and] the executor of the word of God', you possess a fine legitimation of revolution against current rulers who are not so remarkably qualified. Hence, from the viewpoint of those rulers, you are not merely a heretic, you are also a most disagreeable political danger. And as you constitute such a menace to others, your own chances of survival must be correspondingly small.

And so it was. Not surprisingly, many of the varous lineages of pretenders to the Imamate were violently eliminated and became extinct (quite unlike those very numerous lineages that also claim descent from the Prophet, but without extravagant political or theological pretensions, and which have multiplied exponentially in the Muslim world). The various sub-segments of the Shi'ites have diverse beliefs covering the disappearance of the Imam: some believe that the last Imam known on earth is still living incognito and will reappear, others believe that the Imam is incarnated in a different person in each generation, but remains concealed. But as luck would have it, *one* at least of these lineages survived, or is believed to have survived, and is represented not by someone hidden or transcendent, but by a living and identified person. At the same time, the theological claims made on his behalf remain undiminished.

The sect which, presumably by the hazard of history, has survived with a concrete, tangible Imam is the *Shia Imami Ismailia* which, thanks to the activities of recent Aga Khans, its leaders, is well known and incorporated into popular English (and perhaps now international) folklore. The modern history of the movement begins in 1840 when 'the first Aga Khan . . . fled from Persia after an unsuccessful rebellion against the throne.'[4] Nothing unusual or interesting about this: this is the normal stuff of Muslim history. A leader endowed with a religious aura and some tribal support tries his hand at challenging the central power. Normally such efforts fail. If the leader is unfortunate, his severed head is displayed on the city gate by way of demonstration of the inefficacy of his charisma. If he is fortunate, he manages to escape. This one did: to British India. There he rendered some valuable service to the British Raj, and was awarded a pension and the title of Aga Khan. In due course, he settled among some of his followers located in Bombay.

But all was not well. Certainly not as well as one might expect, if one remembers the absolute and total claims made by members of the sect for their Imam. If he was truly infallible, sinless, and the executor of the word of God, in a sense indeed divine, the followers behaved in a manner which can only be characterised as impious. Divine or not, they disputed the payment of tithes, and forced the sinless one to take them, not to the Last Judgement, but to the High Court of Bombay. Moreover, these litigants against their own living Imam had some very interesting arguments on their side, in defence of their practice of using Sunni, non-Shi'a officials to officiate at their weddings and funerals: this practice had begun in the days of *taqiya*, the officially sanctioned Shi'a double-think permissible in the face of a hostile unenlightened government, and they felt they could continue it now, though Caesar was no longer hostile, but neutral.

The dispute remained unsettled and went to the courts again in 1866. The opponents of the Aga Khan among his supposed followers put forward something that was, in substance, a non-Shi'a position, one which shifted sovereignty, and in particular the control of communal funds, to the community rather than the divine leader. Under the Pax Britannica, of course, religious sovereignty could no longer signify temporal power – but it could still signify financial power. The decision was now in the hands of a British judge.

His judgement was the crucial event in modern Ismaili history. From the viewpoint of Shi'a Ismaili theology, his judgement was impeccable, and resulted in the absolute transfer to the Imam of communal property, without responsibility of trusteeship. Given Ismaili theology, he could hardly do less. Whether Mr Justice Arnould's sociology was as sound as his theology is a question we may leave aside.

With the wealth he now controlled, thanks to Shi'a theology and British law, the then Aga Khan had the means to live in a princely Indian style which gave him, and his successors, social access to the British rulers. The third Aga Khan went to Europe in 1897 and dined with Queen Victoria. He maintained his position as somehow a member of the British ruling class, of the international aristocracy of title and wealth, and as the divine reincarnation of his own sect. His story and that of his successor is familiar from the world's press. What is surprising is that its sociological morals have been so seldom spelt out, though they are not hard to discern.

Shi'a theology is a kind familiar on the 'right' wing of Islam, whether that right wing goes beyond the limits of orthodoxy, or stays within it (as with the Sufis). By stressing a person at the tacit expense of the Book and at the open expense of the Community, it verges on, or reaches, anthropolatry. But the significant thing is that under the 'normal' conditions operating in the traditional Muslim world, the extreme claims of obedience are balanced by the social reality of power. The claims to absolute and total obedience (though not the approximations to divine status) are made even by minor little Sufi shaikhs. But the 'normal' religious movement within Islam is constituted of dispersed pockets, tribal and urban, physically separated from each other and operating in a partly anarchic environment. The government may be hostile, and, whether or not it is, travel is perilous and arduous. Under such circumstances, whatever the theology may say, the effective control by the leader of his followers and lodges is inevitably loose and precarious: effective control rests, if it rests with anyone,

with the local representatives of the leader. The leader himself can only maintain his leadership, and hope to receive some tithes, if he skilfully manages and
plays off the various local leaders – if, in effect, the prestige pay-off for *them*,
of their connection with *him*, is greater than the loss they incur by submitting,
more or less, to his authority. Of course, he may try to seize political power, so
as to strengthen his position. For that particular end, he will value and cultivate
his tribal supporters rather than his urban adherents. Urban adherents may come
on pilgrimages and pay tithes, but to reach the throne one must be carried by a
cohesive tribal group, as was stressed by Ibn Khaldun.

The weakness of the then Aga Khan *vis-à-vis* his urban followers was only too
clearly demonstrated by their willingness to take him to court. So was the fact
that their urban position evidently tempted them in the direction of theological
moderation and of Sunni orthodoxy, with which they were blatantly flirting. All
this is true to type, as was his attempted rebellion against the ruler of Persia.

But now a completely new set of circumstantial factors begins to operate:
British India was an effectively centralised state, in which the verdicts of the
courts were properly enforced. So when Mr Justice Arnould found in favour of
the Aga Khan, this was not an empty verdict, nor a mere preliminary to endless
further litigation. On the contrary, it settled the matter. Moreover, under the
Pax Britannica, the more taxable Ismaili traders of Bombay, with a greater tithe
potential, so to speak, were *far* more valuable adherents than the tribesmen
driving their flocks somewhere in the Persian mountains. With luck, the tribesmen might once have carried their Imam to the throne, but that throne was now
out of reach, and from the viewpoint of long-distance tithe collection, those
tribesmen were probably, if not a dead loss, at least not a very impressive asset.
The traders of Bombay were a different matter. No one could ever have ridden
to a throne with their help, but when it came to tithes – a different matter
altogether.

So far, however, only theology provided a sanction for the payment of those
tithes. Mr Justice Arnould's verdict added the existing communal wealth, and
thus the means for adopting a style of life which gave the leader access to the
topmost British rulers. And at this point, we witness a crystallisation of a new
social form.

After the court verdict, presumably the Ismaili traders of Bombay could do
little to recover their existing communal property, now handed over without
accountability to the Aga Khan. There was nothing to stop them from drifting
away. But this they did not do, or at least a significant proportion of them did
not do. At some point, the reality of a new situation must have dawned on
them, and converted them to a more pious and deferential attitude, however (if
at all) they may have articulated it to themselves.

They were a trading community in a well-governed state, and their divine
Imam had access not merely to God but also to the otherwise very distant and
not fully intelligible British rulers. Every little holy man claimed privileged

access to God, but Lord Dufferin, the British Viceroy, was socially more exclusive. Under an effectively centralised colonial regime, such as British India, where countless communities competed in a very complex society, real direct contact with the rulers was an incredibly valuable asset. So, evidently, the Ismailis of Bombay overcame their egalitarian, orthodox, Sunni leanings, and reverted to a theology whose exaggerations of human divinity had been elaborated in so different, and near-anarchic, a context (for the anarchy and indiscipline of which they had indeed been intended as a kind of over-compensation). But now, there was no chaos to compensate: British India was well governed. So the exaggerated claims, effectively enforced by the courts, gave the communal leaders the financial and social means for doing something quite different — namely, meeting the rulers on the turf and the polo ground. And this was no matter of mere worldly frivolity. Who was better placed to protect and aid his community than one who had the ear of the rulers, one who had access to the centres of power and information?

This remarkable combination of an ideology, worked out in one set of circumstances (and seldom effective there, though it may have been the best thing available), with a completely different and unforeseen set of circumstances, is the real sociological clue to the familiar story. No doubt, the remarkable women — Persian, British, or jet-set — whom the successive Imams married and who busied themselves with the movement's affairs, were a great help. The success was not possible without some individual ability and energy. But the real clue remains elsewhere. The Ismailis could not have brought it off without the historical accident of possessing a living and manifest, rather than a hidden and transcendent Imam. The fact that they possessed, within their ranks, an urban trading population, as well as some tribal populations in the Iranian highlands, was not an accident. Most movements do have such a diversified following. But among the Ismailis, under the new order, the centre of gravity of the sect moved to this part of the followership.

The 'right wing' theology, in terms of the Islamic spectrum, continued to be invaluable. A 'left' community which requires consensus, mediated by the guild of scholars, makes reform, and in particular drastic and rapid reform, extremely difficult or impossible. Some of the scholars will always see heretical innovation in any change, and if you try to push through some reform, the community will tear itself apart in inner conflict. But if the leader is authoritative and near-divine, if the person of the leader, rather than Book or consensus, is the heart of the faith, reform becomes relatively easy, always assuming that the leader is inclined in that direction. The social contacts of the Aga Khans aided their perceptions of the direction of the winds of change. Who could challenge the leader's innovations? We have then the preconditions for a kind of purely spiritual Stalinism, or a spiritual Peter the Great, for dramatic development made possible by the concentration of leadership in one centre. And, in this case, the Stalinism could indeed be spiritual, and employed means quite other than physical compulsion: a trading population, operating under a centralised colonial regime, had every motive for following a leader who could, through his political contacts, do so very much for them, and who was ideologically legitimated for doing this. They did not need to be compelled. If Paris is worth a Mass, then the trading opportunities of the British Empire were surely well worth the Shi'a principles of incarnation, succession, and divine leadership, all the more so if you are already nominally committed to them anyway. And so it was. The Ismailis prospered famously, displaying entrepreneurial virtues and an ideology which is virtually an inverse Weberian paradigm.

With the end of colonialism, the situation changed again drastically. Minority trading communities, now even more dispersed and minoritarian through their very trading success, could no longer rely for protection on a leadership with contacts primarily with the erstwhile colonial rulers. On the contrary, as a minority, and a rich one, they found themselves the natural targets of economic and social nationalism. It is a curious feature of the 1972 Uganda crisis that the present Aga Khan, who combines divinity with an official position as U.N. Commissioner for Refugees, has not been openly and *visibly* conspicuous as a protector of his followers. But it is an indication of the remarkable success of the movement in the preceding era that it is by now so well established that it may salvage a good deal even from the present, far more unfavourable, circumstances.

The Murids of Senegal are the objects of a recent brilliant study.[5] Like the Ismailis, they too are famous for a specific *Wirtschaftswunder*. They are not as famous as the Ismailis, but nevertheless, fame of their economic exploits is part of Africanist folklore, and the religious-authoritarian manner in which they appear to achieve it arouses the indignation of the international Left. The power they appear to have to cause peasants to cultivate a new cash crop in arduous circumstances, opening up new lands in the process, for very meagre material rewards, must also inspire much envy among economic developers. These Muslim holy men appear to have succeeded where the British Groundnut Scheme failed so notoriously. How do they do it? As in the case of the Ismailis, a simplistic answer is available and is indeed current: they persuade their followers that they will go to paradise if they work like blacks growing groundnuts in this world, and their credulous followers do as they are told, thus enabling their 'feudal-religious' leaders to live in opulence. Were it so simple!

The followers of the Murid religious brotherhood are recruited mainly from one ethnic group, the Wolof. The Wolof had a strong state organisation within what is now the Republic of Senegal. Their society was sharply stratified with a middle stratum of peasantry and a top stratum of royalty, court, and warrior class, and a low or perhaps ambiguous stratum of slaves or servants. This latter class is normally classed as *low* in the literature, but it seems possible that, like military or administrative slave personnel in some Middle Eastern states, their position could vary considerably. Be that as it may, it was the top and the slave strata which were most affected by the French destruction of the state of Kayor in 1886.

Prior to the French conquest, the Wolof were already strongly but not completely Islamised. The diffusion of Islam in the societies of black Africa takes many forms: Islamic scribes may be imported as administrative technical aids to government: or they may exist to justify opposition to government. Islam may be carried by nomads, or by traders.[6] Amongst the Wolof, it would seem that Islam appealed to the classes resenting the oppression by the warrior aristocracy. Nevertheless, warm relations evidently existed between the ruler and Muslim religious leaders.

The man who was destined to found this brotherhood, Amadu Bamba, had but a handful of disciples at the time of the battle of Dekkilé in 1886, when the French finally destroyed the native state. After some peregrinations and two exiles, and a religious revelation around 1891, his movement, formally an off-shoot and segment of the great Qadiriyya brotherhood, came to have 70,000 followers by 1912, the date at which it began to have good relations with the French authorities. It continued to grow and became one of the greatest economic, social and political forces in modern Senegal.

How was this achieved? Anyone can claim to have the key to salvation, and ambitious preachers and thaumaturges are not lacking in West Africa. What concatenations of circumstances, what special crystallisation accounts for this most remarkable success?

Donal Cruise O'Brien's excellent study documents the answer admirably. The French thoroughly destroyed the old local state and the social hierarchy sustained by it. At the same time, their conquest increased the opportunity for marketing cash crops: they encouraged such cultivation, and of course colonial taxation in itself creates a need for a cash income. Inside the land of the Wolof, there was a socially displaced population, which had lost the roles it had enjoyed under the old order. Re-creating the old order was impossible: the chiefs tolerated or created by the French were small fry, not comparable with the old rulers. As in the case of displaced populations in many parts of the world, religion offered the most plausible alternative form of organisation. The most easily available model and leadership was that of a Sufi religious brotherhood.

Inside the Wolof area there was a dislocated population; but outside it there was uncultivated and under-used land, well suited for groundnut cultivation, and owned in an ambiguous way, as these things go, by Fulani pastoralists. An obvious solution would be for the uprooted Wolof to settle these new lands, prosper with the help of a new and desired cash crop, help the new rail lines to flourish, and bask in administrative approval for this economic enterprise. But it was not quite as easy as that. An individual Wolof settler-squatter on Fulani territory would soon find himself attacked and destroyed by the Fulani. Even if he could stand up to them, which was unlikely, he probably would not know *how* to produce groundnuts successfully. The erstwhile aristocrat or slave from a Wolof state did not necessarily possess either the required skill or the equipment. Before the human need and the physical opportunity could meet, some *organisation* was required which would bring them together.

Here was the basic key to the Murid success. It possessed the framework of an easily understood — because familiar — type of organisation, and a kind of organisation which can easily be expanded when recruits are available. The loose hierarchy of shaikh and follower, with a ranking of leaders in a pyramidal federation, is familiar in Muslim lands and can easily be emulated. But, of course, this advantage was shared by other religious orders. A special, and as it happens, both an ideological and organisational twist was required, to adapt this religious brotherhood for the particular task for which it was destined.

One of the earlier important converts of the founder of the movement was Shaikh Ibra Fall, a Wolof aristocrat with a strong personality, no scholarly leanings whatever, and a curious, indeed idiosyncratic, penchant for physical work. He did not seem inclined to the scholarly and/or mystical initiation which is the stock in trade of Sufi religious leaders. It was he who started and organised the *working* novitiate, which turned out to be such a crucial innovation in the structure of this Order.

There is nothing inherently novel in the performance of a voluntary corvée by the devotees of a religious leader, either as a substitute for or a supplement to voluntary tithes. To cultivate the living saint's field, or help build his house, are perfectly familiar notions in, for instance, North Africa. What was original was the systematic organisation and expansion of this principle by a lieutenant of the leader, himself of prestigious lay origin, who somehow canalised the enthusiasm which his class had once felt for their status and for warfare, into a positive ethic of work. It is not true, apparently, that the Murids believe work to be a substitute for prayer: but they do lay unusual stress on work as the form taken of the submission which is required by the follower *vis-à-vis* the leader. This submission, theoretically total, is a common trait of these religious orders or brotherhoods. The follower, it is characteristically claimed, must be in the hands of his shaikh as is the corpse in the hands of the washers of the dead. Otherwise no mystical illumination will come. What was novel here was that the submitting 'corpse' was required or encouraged not to scholarship and mystical exercise, but to the planting of groundnuts without much or any remuneration.

But this 'ethic of work' did not achieve this remarkable human and social transformation unaided. More mundane motivation, more concrete circumstances were also operative. The population was uprooted. It knew that land was available, if only it could be seized, and that a profitable cash crop could be grown and marketed, if they learned how to grow it. The religious kibbutzim, so to speak, at which the novitiates worked so selflessly, with apparently nothing but spiritual salvation in mind, were in effect agricultural training centres, and the adepts took no vows for life, but could look forward, after some years of service, to the reward of an individual holding. Furthermore, a family with one represen-tative at the Murid agricultural labour settlement was thereby linked to a power-ful movement and system of protection and patronage. In the meantime, the organised kibbutz, protected by a religious aura and a powerful, extensive, well-organised and well-connected religious Order, favoured by the administration (which could look forward to economic development through its activities), had an incomparably better chance of seizing Fulani land – and making it prosper – than individual squatters could ever have had.

We have here something very similar to the Zionist movement, with a religious brotherhood performing the role of the Jewish Agency, and the Fulani in the role of the Arabs. Freelance Jewish settlements in Palestine, without organis-ation, could hardly have withstood Arab opposition. Moreover, they could hardly have transformed a nation of non-farmers into farmers in difficult and initially most unrewarding circumstances. Zionism was fortunate in having, in Socialism, an ideology which already and independently pervaded the mental climate of nineteenth- and twentieth-century Europe, and which, through its populist elements, prized collective work on the land without individual remuneration, and which thus ratified a human transformation which had to be accomplished anyway if Jewish resettlement of the land of Israel was to become a reality. (Without the presence of such an ideology, that resettlement might have resembled those European settler populations in Africa which were either driven out, as in Algeria, or forced into repellent extreme measures of a caste society, as in South Africa.) The Murids could not draw upon any such general socialism; they were fortunate in the accident of the enthusiastic enlistment of a secondary leader who was ill-suited for normal Sufi pursuits, but who had a splendid penchant in the right direction, and great organisational ability.

It is worth noting that in certain senses, Muridism is Zionism-in-reverse. The Wolof once had a state, and Muridism gave them a religious organisation instead – where Eastern European Jewry had had a religious organisation and exchanged it for a secular state. Jewry had been occupationally specialised and Zionism diversified it; the Wolof had possessed a state with a diversified stratification and the Murid movement (though it created a leadership of its own) turned this diversified population into a more homogeneous set of groundnut-growers.

It is useless to try and explain the success of the order by simply invoking the authoritarian traditions of Sufism. For one thing, all the countless other orders share them. For another, the cult of submission is very deceptive. It is the equivalent, in Sufism, of the tendency to deify the leader found in Shi'a Islam. In neither case can it normally be taken at face value. It is precisely because organisation is normally so very weak, that the doctrine of discipline is so very exaggerated. Ideological excess tries, vainly, to compensate for organisational weakness. The typical Sufi order is a loose and dispersed federation of holy centres, where the minor ones balance the losses inherent in submission against the advantages gained from the spill-over of prestige from some famous centre.

Post-traditional forms in Islam

Sanctions of central authority are weak. The Murids, however, had unusual incentives and opportunities for making the submission more significant, and they had some special doctrinal and organisational features which could bring motivation and opportunity together.

Their opportunities did not end with the settlement of land and the extensive cultivation of groundnuts. Senegal was one of the first of the French overseas territories to become involved in French electoral politics. The Murids could and did peddle votes as well as peanuts. With the approach of Independence and the struggle for power in the early years of Independence, votes were particularly valuable. Thus the organisation resembled not merely the Jewish Agency, but also the American Democratic Party. It is not only immigrants who need aid and protection, and repay it at the voting booths. Colonial dislocation had made the Wolof migrants in their own lands.

As in the case of the Ismailis, the favourable circumstances were not to last forever. New lands for groundnuts were not unlimited. Novices cease to be such, and in the end must be rewarded. Once power crystallises in a new African state, elections cease to be serious and votes become less valuable. Recent reports suggest that groundnuts have lost much of their economic attraction. All the same, a powerful organisation, once established, has its own momentum, and its fame and past achievements are in themselves valuable assets. It is too early yet to speak of the fate of the movement in post-colonial conditions. It is not without resources and may yet deploy them to good effect.

These are two striking cases of 'post-traditional' social forms. Both are paradoxical, not to say piquant. In each case, a fortunate combination of circumstances has enabled a particular set of organisational and ideological elements, inherited from a tradition in which they were but slight variants of a standard pattern, to make a marked impact in novel circumstances. Shi'ism is an unpromising candidate for the Protestant Ethic, but the followers of the Aga Khan are famed as entrepreneurs, and it seems unlikely that, without their Shi'a faith, they could have been as successful as in fact they have been. Sufism does not resemble socialism and looks like most unpromising ideological equipment for the formation of agricultural kibbutzim, but, in its Murid form, this is just what it has achieved. It too was essential for an unusual achievement. In either case, an explanation in terms of the faith alone and its preaching is woefully inadequate, but in either case, the faith played a crucial part.

113

4

Doctor and saint

Accounts of societies in terms of the beliefs and values of their members often assume that each member has *one* set of beliefs about the world, and *one* set of values. This seems to be a major mistake. Any professional sports team invariably has more than one reserve in addition to the set normally presented to the public, ever ready to replace the first lot, either one by one or, if necessary, as a whole. The same is generally true about our cosmological picture or about our moral values. There is, of course, an interesting difference. When the cosmological picture or the moral values claim unique and exclusive validity, the overt possession and display of rival alternatives would be shameful, heretical, and scandalous. Apart from anything else, it would undermine confidence in that unique cosmological picture or set of moral values. One of the points of having the picture and the values is, of course, to reassure both oneself and others, and to proclaim that certain ideas and certain attitudes are simply not negotiable. A person who made it plain that his confidence in his own supposedly unnegotiable basic positions is less than total, and that he is keeping an alternative ready and available, would thereby undermine the credibility of his own stance and encourage intransigence in others. This would never do.

Thus the alternatives are decently hidden away. There is nothing unusual about this, and there are many parallels in social and political fields. For instance, a government recognises the legal and legitimate authorities in a neighbouring country, and it would be a hostile and provocative act to recognise at the same time some 'government in exile', heading a revolutionary movement which hopes to dislodge the present rulers of the neighbouring state. But, of course, it would be most unwise to have no relationships at all with that revolutionary movement: after all, they might win. So, while the department of state charged with diplomacy entertains cordial and exclusive relationships with the official government, the covert intelligence services are at liberty to maintain just as significant relationships with the revolutionaries.

The importance of the *ulama* is that they are the openly displayed, official first eleven of Islam. They are the norm-givers of the community of the faithful; they

114

are the repositories and arbiters of legitimacy. So much for theory. There is one well-known manner in which reality diverges from theory: the verdict of the *ulama* regarding legitimacy, like the flight of that much overrated bird the Owl of Minerva, takes place only after the event, and hence in effect ratifies the actual power situation, rather than sitting in judgement on it. From the viewpoint of understanding the general social structure of Islam, this particular limitation does not matter too much, perhaps: it does mean that in general the *ulama* cannot do very much about determining the identity of the ruler, but are constrained to ratify whichever ruler prevails by force of arms. This is indeed so. But while they cannot determine the specific identity of the ruler, and must bow to superior strength, whether they like it or not, it does not preclude them from being extremely influential on the general *kind* of society over which the ruler presides. A group of men may be powerless with respect to filling individual roles in a society and yet extremely influential with respect to what kind of system of roles there is to be filled. This, I suspect, is indeed the role of the *ulama* in Islamic society: not very powerful in deciding between one ruler or dynasty and another, they were most influential in determining the general nature of the society.

But there is another limitation on their influence of quite a different kind: the limitation not on their choice of personnel, but on their influence on the general social structure. This limitation is notoriously well attested by the fact that such large segments of Muslim populations look not only, and not so much, towards the *ulama* for spiritual guidance, as they do towards other types of religiously significant groups, whom there is a tendency to lump together under the heading of Sufism.

It should be said that this kind of indiscriminate lumping together of what is in effect a residual category is probably a mistake. Under the general category of Sufism, people tend, for instance, to group together genuine mystics and tribal holy men whose connection with mysticism is minimal. Both may be classified by the same kind of terminology, not only by scholars but also by the local population, but this does not mean that the two phenomena are homogeneous and deserve to be classed together, either from the viewpoint of social significance or from that of religious phenomenology. Roughly speaking: urban Sufi mysticism is an *alternative* to the legalistic, restrained, arid (as it seems to its critics) Islam of the *ulama*. Rural and tribal 'Sufism' is a *substitute* for it. In the one case, an alternative is sought for the Islam of the *ulama* because it does not fully satisfy. In the other case, a substitute for it is required because, though its endorsement is desired, it is, in its proper and urban form, locally unavailable, or is unusable in the tribal context.

There are within Islam three major types of legitimation: the Book (including its extension by Tradition), the consensus of the community, and the line of succession.

The Book is a repository of the divine word, publicly available, not incarnated

115

in any one person, group, institution, or policy, and hence capable of sitting in judgement on any one of them. This trans-ethnic and trans-social quality of the Book is, of course, of the utmost importance in understanding the political life both of Muslim societies and of the expansion of Islam. Even if the sociologists were right in supposing that the divine is merely the social in camouflage, it is a fact of the greatest importance that the camouflage (if such it be) is so rigorously maintained, and hence emphatically ensures the non-identification of the divine with any *one* concrete human or social representative of it.

Another important form of legitimation, in Islam and elsewhere, is, of course, the consensus of the community. In Islam, this approach has complemented rather than opposed the Book. Islamic societies have never been what might be called 'pure' democratic societies; they have not maintained that the *only* sort of legitimacy is the consent of the community. That consent was invoked only for the supplementing of divine truth by interpretation where interpretation was required, rather than as an independent and equally powerful source. In practice, the Book required scholars to read it and consensus to interpret it, and hence, concretely speaking, the authority of the *ulama* as religious scholars, and that of the community as interpreters of the Word, were in harmony.

But there is a third type of legitimation within Islam, that of Succession. Succession can be either physical or spiritual, and sometimes one genealogical line may employ both physical and spiritual links. The physical links, of course, arise from the fact that there is no requirement of celibacy on religious leaders. The spiritual links are made possible by mystical doctrine: mystical illuminations can be passed on from teacher to disciple in a legitimacy-preserving way, analogous to the manner in which paternity maintains legitimacy of authority from father to son.

This third principle of legitimation is, of course, not always in harmony with the other two. In Shi'a Islam, it becomes the main principle bringing with it the possibility of overruling the other two. But even within Sunni Islam, which does not have the same stress on locating religious legitimacy in a lineage, succession can become extremely important, and particularly so in social conditions that display a particularly strong requirement that the Word should become flesh. There are such milieux. The most obvious examples are tribal societies, cut off from the Book by the fact that their members are illiterate (and, one should add, that they do not possess the means for sustaining or protecting a class of literate scholars), and in some measure cut off from the wider Islamic consensus by a relationship of hostility (and yet of economic interdependence) with those urban centres which are somehow the visible incarnation and centre of gravity of the Muslim civilisation. In such tribal milieux, there is a shift of stress in legitimation from the Book or the abstract consensus, toward the lineage. The stress is, of course, exemplified in practice rather than expressed in any kind of theory.

This, then, is the general setting: the significance of the tribal holy lineages is that they satisfy a need for the incarnation of the Word in a milieu that through

116

lack of literacy and of towns cannot use the *ulama*. Thus the lineages of holy men are an alternative to the *ulama*, an alternative that at the same time, within the wider spiritual economy of Islam, is parasitical on them. It provides an alternative and in effect serves and represents values other than those of the *ulama*, and yet at the same time indirectly endorses the values and views of the *ulama*. Tribal society has its values and attitudes, and these are served and symbolised by the tribal holy men. The tribesmen do not wish to be any different from what they are. But they are, in the eyes of their more learned urban folk, sinful and/or heretical. They know that this is how they are seen, and they do not really repudiate the judgement. They accept it, and yet wish to persist in their attitudes. At the same time, they do not in any way desire to opt out of the wider community of Islam. Their attitude really is that of Saint Augustine: Lord, make me pure, but not yet. They recognise standards of purity in terms of which their own tribal society fails, yet at the same time wish to remain as they are, indefinitely. They are quite aware of the conflict and contradiction, yet at the same time the contradiction is not articulated clearly or stressed. It is there, yet is clouded in decent obscurity.

The significance of the tribal holy men lies in the manner in which they help to perpetuate this situation.

The Berbers of the central High Atlas are an outstandingly fine example of the manner in which the Word must become flesh when incarnated in a tribal society. In addition to factors frequently found elsewhere in Islam, there are here some additional ones, which perhaps once operated throughout the Maghreb, but which in any case are most deeply preserved here. These local factors are a most remarkable case of tribal separation of powers, inspired not by either modern or any political theory, but tied in beautifully with the requirements of religious representation.

The political and social system of these tribes is segmentary, which is to say, each tribe divides and subdivides again and so forth until family units are reached. At each level of size, all segments are equal and there is no division of labour between them, either of an economic or of a political nature. Neither within segments nor between them are there any specialised political institutions or groups. Thus, from the viewpoint of the tribe as a whole, the tribe possesses a tree-like structure, dividing and subdividing in the manner of the branches of a tree — though there is no central and pre-eminent trunk, all branches being equal. From the viewpoint of any one individual or family, this means that he or it are at the centre of a number of concentric circles — the intra-village clan, the village, the group of villages forming a local clan, the larger clan, the tribe, and so forth. None of these superimposed groupings, from the individual's viewpoint, ever cuts across another and thus ideally they give no rise to conflicting obligations. Conflict at a lower level in no way precludes cohesion and co-operation at a higher level: in other words, two clans may be hostile to each other yet co-

117

operate jointly as members of the tribe against another tribe. Everything is symmetrical and egalitarian: although, of course, some men and some groups manage temporarily to be richer or more influential than others, this gives no rise either to a permanent, or a symbolically ratified, stratification. Only complete outsiders to the tribe can be located, socially speaking, above or below: negroid or Jewish artisans and holy men are the only significant exceptions, in the traditional system, to the pervasive symmetry and equality.

The general features of such segmentary societies, with their diffusion of power and the maintenance of order by the opposition of groups to one another at all levels, are well known. The only remarkable thing about the Berbers of the central High Atlas is the degree of perfection to which they have brought the system. They approximate more closely to an ideal type of segmentary society than do most other societies of this kind, including those most frequently cited when the principles of segmentation are expounded.

A crucial feature of the society, which conveys its general nature, is chieftaincy. Chieftaincy among these tribes is elective and annual. Moreover, the manner of election is remarkable: it observes the principles of what I call 'rotation and complementarity'. These work as follows: suppose a tribe to be subdivided into three clans, A, B, and C. Any given year it will be the turn of one clan only to supply the chief. But the clan that supplies the chief does not elect him. Suppose clan A supplies the chief: then it is the turn of the men of clans B and C to be the electors. In other words, any given year, a clan can supply either candidates or voters, but not both.

This system of rotation and complementarity operates at a number of levels of segmentation at once, so that the political system as a whole could be compared to a number of rotating wheels-within-wheels. The system is somewhat modified at the top and at the bottom ends of the scale, in terms of size. At the top, the wheel may turn only if there is need of it: in concrete terms, a topmost chief may be elected only if there is need of him, if there is some issue of concern to the topmost unit. There will be no filling of chieftaincy posts for the sake of continuity alone. At the very bottom, rotation and complementarity may not be observed. If it is a matter of choosing heads of tiny segments, say, of the three sub-clans within a village, the total population of which is in the neighbourhood of two or three hundred people, then the chief of these minuscule sub-segments will be chosen from the segment as a whole and not from a restricted area of candidacy, so to speak. At that level, the number of people available with suitable talents may be so small that such restriction would prove too cumbersome. But for the village of about two or three hundred inhabitants, rotation and implementing will be observed.

The relationship of lower-level chiefs to higher-level chiefs is obscure and eludes the categories of neat political or administrative theory. The lower-level chiefs are at once elective heads of their units, and representatives within their units of the higher-level chiefs.

A particularly bewildering feature of the system is what I call leap-frogging in the hierarchy. It works as follows. Suppose there are four levels of size of segmentary units. It may happen that top chiefs of units at the level of size 1 will have their agents and representative chiefs at level 3, whereas chiefs at level 2 will act through representatives at level 4. In other words, there will be two hierarchies which, as it were, pass through each other without affecting each other, articulated as they are in two different media. In an ordinary, centralised, non-segmentary society, where the maintenance of order is the concern of some specialised agencies in the society, this would be madness. It would be inconceivable for the government, or for the courts, or for the police to be concerned with conflicts and violence only selectively, according to the level of size at which they occur, with one police force concerned with conflicts at one set of levels and another police force concerned with conflicts at another set, the two sets being related to each other like alternate layers in a cake. In a segmentary society, where violence and aggression are a tort and not a crime, and where conflicts of units of different size are kept apart and do not implicate one another, this kind of arrangement makes perfectly good sense.

The political system of the lay tribes of the Central Atlas does not concern us directly, but only for its implications for the holy lineages. What are the relevant features of this political system? Its most obvious features are weak chieftaincy and lack of continuity. All chiefs are lame ducks. As soon as elected they are within a year of the termination of their office (even if, rather exceptionally, their tenure may be prolonged). Moreover, they depend on the votes of the members of the rival clans, in a society built upon the rivalry of clans. They have no agents or sanctions, other than minor chieftains elected in a manner similar to their own: they have no secretariat and no police force. The only backing they have are the moral pressures of public opinion and the normal mechanisms of segmented societies — the anger of the offended sub-group in the case of an offence against it.

All these factors militate against the emergence of permanent and tyrannical chieftains and privileged political lineages, and indeed, their political system did enable the Berbers of the central High Atlas to escape the kind of ephemeral but harsh tyranny which characterised, for instance, the western High Atlas in this century.

But if the merit of the system is to provide checks and balances against tyranny and political ambition, its corresponding weakness is, as indicated, a lack of continuity and of order-maintaining agency. Yet these tribes do need a measure of order. They are not made up of small, inward-turned communities. They are ecologically most diversified and complementary. The natural environment is highly diversified, with extremes of climate and season between the Sahara edge and the high pastures of the Atlas mountains, whose highest point rises above 4,000 metres. The shepherds and their flocks can survive thanks only to a complex pattern of transhumance, involving movement over large distances and the drawing up of complex pasture rights, synchronised use, and deferment of use, of the better pastures, and the drawing of boundaries in time (seasonally) as well as in space. Many tribes must trade if they are to survive, being grossly deficient in their production of staple cereals, and all of them trade if they are to procure salt, and what might be called the essential luxuries of sugar and tea, and, in the olden days, firearms and ammunition. At the same time, order is not maintained, in the traditional situation, by the central government: on the contrary, the tribes ensure that central government does not interfere in their affairs. In brief, we have a situation of great ecological and economic inter-dependence, combined with only very weak and, in themselves, inadequate political institutions for the maintenance of the order required by economic life and for purposes of communication. How is this paradox resolved?

This is, of course, the point at which the holy lineages enter the argument.

It might be best first of all to describe them briefly. The holy men (*igurramen*, in the local Berber dialect) live in settlements generally centred on the shrine of the founding saintly ancestor. They possess a genealogy linking them to this ancestor. In the central High Atlas, the genealogy generally stretches back beyond the founding ancestor and leading, finally, to the Prophet through his daughter and his son-in-law, Our Lord Ali.

The settlements around the shrine may be quite large and have up to something like three hundred inhabitants. In some cases, virtually all the members of the settlement may be descendants of the founding saint (in the sense of believing themselves to be such and having the claim generally recognised). Nevertheless, even in these cases in which this genealogical qualification is widely diffused, by no means all of them will actually perform the function ascribed to *igurramen*. This function will only be performed by a small number among them, and in a limiting case, by only one of them. The others may be described as laicised or latent saints. Presumably their ancestors were once effective saints, but the off-spring were pushed out into a lay condition by demographic pressure and by the crucial fact that it is of the very nature of this kind of sanctity that it is con-centrated in a small number of people. It is incompatible with excessive diffusion.

What is the role of the effective saints? They provide the continuity and the stable framework that the political system of the lay tribes so conspicuously lacks. For instance: the lay chiefs are elective. But elections are procedures that require some kind of institutional background, and this society, needless to say, has no civil service or secretariat or anything of the kind that could look after these matters. So the elections take place at the settlement and near the shrine of the hereditary holy men, which is, of course, also a sanctuary within which one must not feud. Thus the saints provide the physical locale and the moral guarantee that make it possible for rival clans to assemble and carry out their elections. They also provide the means of moral persuasion and the mediation that help ensure that the elections, in the end, arrive at a unanimous conclusion.

120

Doctor and saint

Or again: the saints provide the cornerstone for the legal system (or perhaps one should say, arbitration system) of the lay tribes. The legal decision procedure is trial by collective oath, with the number of co-jurors dependent on the gravity of the offence. A theft might require two co-jurors; a rape, four; a murder of a woman, twenty; a murder of a man, forty. The rule is that issues requiring less than ten co-jurors are settled on the spot, among the lay tribes, but issues requiring ten or more co-jurors are taken up to the shrine of the founding saint of the holy lineage, and settled with the moral assistance of the saints who are the progeny of the enshrined founder.

The saints and their settlements are thus arbitrators between tribes, and between their clans, and they are physically located on important boundaries. This indicates a further important function performed by them: their physical location at important boundaries indicates and guarantees those boundaries. Their moral authority also helps to guarantee the complex seasonal arrangements connected with transhumancy between the high mountain pastures and the desert edge. Their location on the frontier also greatly assists trade. Tribesmen visiting markets in neighbouring tribes can pass through the settlement of the saints, deposit their arms there, and be accompanied on their way to the market by a saint from the settlement or a representative of an important saint. This holy fellow-traveller then provides simultaneously a guarantee of their safety from their hosts and a guarantee of their good conduct towards their hosts.

The political life of the saints is quite different from that of the lay tribes. There is a neat contrast in almost every respect. Lay chiefs are chosen by the people: saints are chosen only by God. Lay chiefs are, in principle, annual: saints are permanent, and in principle permanent over generations. Lay tribesmen are addicted to feuding and litigation: saints are obligatorily pacific and must not litigate. (In the tribal mind, litigation and violence are very close to each other. The collective oath is the continuation of the feud by other means.)

The basic contradiction in the life of the saints arises from the fact that there must not be too many of them: their role and influence hinges on the one—many relationship between them and the tribes, for one saint must arbitrate among many tribes or tribal segments. At the same time, saints proliferate, and yet they have no rule of succession to decide the inheritance of saintly role. The rule of inheritance among the saints is the same as among the lay tribes, and is symmetrical as between brothers. There is only a very slight predisposition in favour of primogeniture, a predisposition that is certainly not decisive.

How then is the succession decided? In the local mind, it is only God who decides. It would be presumptuous indeed for men to decide where grace, *baraka*, is to flow. God makes his choice manifest through the possession by the elect of the crucial attributes of pacifism, uncalculating generosity and hospitality, and prosperity.

In reality it is, of course, a kind of unconscious choice by the tribesmen which decides the succession. By using this rather than that son, by using this rather than that rival saintly lineage, the tribesmen in effect choose and elect the given son or lineage as the 'real' saint. But the fact that the voice of God is really the voice of the people is not made manifest and explicit. The voice of the people manifests itself through making feasible the possession or attribution of characteristics which are then seen as signs of divine election. A man who is used by the tribesmen as a saint and revered as such can afford to be pacific, to turn the other cheek, with impunity. A man who is not respected as a saint would, if he behaved in this kind of way, only attract aggression. A man who is revered by the tribesmen as a saint will receive plentiful donations and can afford to act with what appears to be uncalculating generosity, and yet also retain that other attribute of election, namely, prosperity. A man, on the other hand, who did not receive adequate donations from the tribe but who behaved as if he were in effect a saint would impoverish himself and thereby make most manifest his lack of divine grace.

Thus the choice of the tribesmen externalises itself and comes to appear as a divine choice. The mediating factor is, of course, the stress of the specifically saintly virtues of pacifism and of uncalculating generosity. The possession of these virtues is the test: one can acquire them only with the co-operation of the lay tribesmen. Pacifism and a consider-the-lilies attitude among the saints cannot be explained as some kind of diffusion or survival of values derived from the Sermon on the Mount. They are much too inherently and visibly a necessary corollary of the local social structure, of the role performed by saints within it and the manner of attributing sanctity within it. They are in no way generalised beyond the role that requires them.

Thus both the conceptualisation and the rhythm of political life are quite different among the saints from those that are found among lay tribes. The political life of the saints is a game of very slow musical chairs, played out over generations not by the removal of chairs but by the addition to the number of contestants. Success and failure in it are in principle for keeps and are seen as the consequences of supernatural, divine favour. By contrast, election to chieftaincy among the lay tribes is in the hands of men, not of God, and is for a limited period only. There is a belief among non-anthropologists that tribesmen generally see their tribal arrangements as supernaturally sanctioned. Berbers of the central High Atlas do not: they know their own tribal arrangements to be secular and based on the will of men, and they have the conceptual equipment that enables them to be clear about it. This equipment is, of course, derived not from secularist philosophers, but simply from the fact that within their own society, they need to distinguish between the divine factor in political life, represented by the saints, and the secular factor, complementing it and represented by themselves. What the saints decide is, in local belief, a reflection of divine will: but what the tribal assembly decides, though deserving of respect as perpetuation of ancestral custom, springs from a human source and can on occasion be consciously and deliberately changed by consent.

There is, however, one further function performed by the saints, over and above the invaluable role they visibly fulfil in the local socio-political structure. This additional role is to anchor the local society in the wider system of Islam. The saints are not merely saints: they are also, in local belief, the descendants of the Prophet. The tribesmen know that in the eyes of inhabitants of the urban centres of literate Islam, they are held to be at worst heretical and sinful, and at best sadly ignorant of religion. They know that only Muslims may own land, and that a tribe convicted of not being Muslim would provide a most enviable justification for all its neighbours to dispossess it. Admittedly, the city dwellers would not have the means to deprive a mountain or desert tribe of its land, but they could encourage other tribes to combine in a joint act of aggression against it. So every tribe needs, and in any case wishes, to display its Muslim status. They can hardly do this through Koranic scholarship. They are illiterate. But they *can* do it by showing due reverence to those supposed descendants of the Prophet who are so conveniently settled among them, helping to guarantee tribal frontiers and in other ways assisting the tribes to manage their affairs.

This, then, is one further function of the holy lineages. Though the holy lineages are often assimilated to Sufism, their real life and function has little to do with mysticism and the diffusion of mystical ideas. (On the contrary, some supposedly Sufi practices may in fact derive from tribal customs, tribal styles of dancing, and so forth.)

The political system in which permanent and pacific saints divide the political role with elective, secular, and feud-addicted tribal chieftains is elegant and, *structurally*, sufficient unto itself. But it is not *conceptually* sufficient unto itself. Conceptually, it is other-directed and looks towards the wider world of Islam. Spiritually speaking, the holy lineages are lords of the marches. They represent the religion of the central tradition of the wider society for the tribesmen, and guarantee the tribesmen's incorporation in it. As described, they also help the tribesmen to avoid being saddled with physical, military lords of the marches, by giving continuity and stability to a system otherwise possessing only minimal political leadership.

How is this local other-directedness concretely manifested?

The manifestations vary in kind. They are found both among the lay tribes and the holy lineages. Take, as a simple example, some legends circulating both about and among one of the most backward, savage, and religiously ignorant among the Atlas tribes, the Ait Abdi of the Ait Sochman. When I say that this tribe is particularly backward, savage, and ignorant of religion, I refer to a stereotype held of it not just by outsiders to the region, urban folk and such, but by other tribes *within* the region itself, and, most significantly, by the tribe itself. Though all mountain tribes without distinction may seem to be licentious, violent, heterodox savages to the bourgeoisie of Fez, once you get in amongst the tribes you find, as so often, that further subtle distinctions and nuances can be made by anyone with local knowledge. All tribesmen may seem savages from Fez, but for the connoisseur, some are much more so than others, even, or especially, in their own estimation.

The Ait Abdi are at the end of the road, literally and figuratively speaking. Or rather, literally speaking they are a good way beyond the end of the road, for no road at all makes its way to their desolate and stony plateau. Even nowadays, you can get there only on foot or on the back of a mule, and the plateau is held to be almost inaccessible in winter. Figuratively speaking, they are at the end of the road, for almost anyone can look down on them as savages, and as far as I know there is no one more savage on whom they can look down, though there are some who are perhaps their equals in this respect.

The interesting thing is that the Ait Abdi themselves share this view. There is one legend that circulates among and about them which is particularly suggestive. This legend is something utterly familiar to every child among the Ait Abdi as Father Christmas is to a child in Western society.

The legend runs as follows: a false teacher of Islam, in fact a Jew, appeared among the Ait Abdi, and was received by them and recognised as a true religious leader. He made a good living among them as a *fqih*, that is to say, scribe and Koranic teacher. He was in fact quite devoid of the religious knowledge he was supposed to teach, but he did not allow this to dismay him: instead of reciting the Koran, he simply rattled off various well-known local place names, ending this recitation with the words — I show you your land, O heads of asses — *ichfau n'ighiel.* Despite this blatant effrontery, it took the Ait Abdi quite some time to unmask him — and the rest of the legend does not concern us.

Note the point of the story: it illustrates, of course, the perfidy, cunning, and effrontery of the infidel—foreigner, but it also illustrates, indeed highlights, the stupidity, gullibility, and total religious ignorance of the Ait Abdi themselves. Yet they themselves tell the story!

This is not the only legend in which the Ait Abdi display a kind of joking relationship to their own image and history. Another story, as popular and familiar among them and their neighbours as is the story of the scurrilous religious teacher, concerns a man, Ohmish, and his wife, Tuda Lahcen, whose intransigence and pugnacity triggered a murderous chain-reaction of feud and killing, all started by a trivial quarrel on a pasture. It is actually *forbidden* among the Ait Abdi to tell this story, on the assumption that its recounting will bring bad luck and perhaps a repetition of such episodes, yet at the same time the story is utterly familiar to all of them. The moral of the situation is: we know we ought not to be so quarrelsome and feud-addicted, and we know at the same time perfectly well that this is just how we are.

Another legend — this one told about rather than among them — explains why it is that they find themselves on their particularly bare and stony plateau: the reason is that they fought so ferociously against their rightful Sultan, Mulay Hassan (referring to the nineteenth-century monarch of this name, and not to the present king). It is a curious explanation, insofar as they were by no means the only tribe, or even the most important one, which joined in resisting the attempts of that ruler to penetrate the mountains. But, as so often in these legends, the explanation is, so to speak, differential: what counts as an explanation in one case would not count as such in another. Explanations are not universalised.

What concerns us of course is that the legend underscores once again the recognition of a value — submission to the central state — which is in fact not practised by the very tribes who repeat the story (or rather, was not practised till the modern world forced them to practise it, and of course the legend antedates the centralisation imposed under modern conditions).

So much by way of illustration of the kind of self-ironising attitude, the joking relationship with one's own image, as manifested in legends circulating among the lay tribes. The situation becomes even clearer and more conspicuous among the holy lineages.

Here nature has arranged a nice experimental situation. All other factors being held constant, one factor alone is varied, as if for our benefit. This independent variable is: the proximity to the plain and hence to the urban centres from which scripturalist, puritanical, and reformist Islam emanates.

In the central High Atlas, there are a number of centres of sanctity, of holy settlements that act as sanctuaries, centres of arbitration, and pilgrimage, for the surrounding tribes. In many ways, these centres are very similar to one another (though of course they differ in size, influence, and one or two other associated features). On their own account they ought indeed to resemble one another, insofar as they all have the same ancestor: within quite a wide area of the mountainous terrain where the Middle Atlas fuses with the High Atlas, most holy men, and virtually all holy men of influence, are descended from one founding saint, Sidi Said Ahansal. They are, or believe themselves to be, of one flesh and blood, though this does not preclude bitter rivalry amongst them.

But as stated, they are geographically separated, living as generally they do on important frontiers *between* tribes. Some of them are in the very heart of the mountains while others are not far from the edge of the plain. For purposes of comparison, we shall take the dramatic contrast between the founding and central lodge, Zawiya Ahansal, and another lodge, somewhat to the north and much closer to the plain, named Temga.

The holy men of both lodges agree on one important point of faith and morals — namely, that dancing (*ahaidus*) is immoral and un-Islamic. This point is widely accepted in Morocco and has received much support and endorsement from the Muslim Reform movement. At the same time, of course, this form of dancing is a well-established and extremely popular part of the folklore of the Berber tribes. The issue of the dance has all the potent emotive colouring that the theatre had for seventeenth-century Puritans. What urban Muslims and those under their influence find particularly shocking is that in the course of this kind of tribal dance, men and women mingle and it can even happen that they dance shoulder to shoulder! This reaction was shared by the great leftist leader Mehdi Ben Barka, later kidnapped and presumably murdered, who was a great champion of the equality of women. For instance, he rejected with scorn the argument that Muslim polygamy was acceptable because it was merely a legalised version of the informal polygamy current among Europeans, with their habit of having mistresses. As he put it, polygamy, whether legalised or informal, was wrong. In consequence of his nationalist activity, Mehdi Ben Barka had at one time been imprisoned by the French and placed for safe custody among one of the central High Atlas tribes, the Ait Haddidu. In the course of his imprisonment in the mountain fastness, he had opportunity to witness this form of dancing. Yet even he, left-wing modernist, was shocked, as he later told me, by these dances and the possibility of women, even married women, being involved!

This perhaps illustrates the deep feeling that is invoked in this rejection of tribal dancing. Anyway, to return to our saintly lineages: the two centres, both the founding lodge and Temga, agreed that dancing is highly improper. Some time probably before the turn of the century, the two saintly settlements held a joint meeting to discuss such theological and no doubt other outstanding issues, and in the course of it decided that henceforth, as good Muslims and descendants of the Prophet, they would refrain from dancing. As a matter of fact, Temga and its group of lodges have kept to this self-denying ordinance to this day, at least to the extent of imposing and enforcing fines on any of their own number who are caught dancing. The meeting at which this was agreed, and the subsequent events can be roughly dated; they occurred when a man named Ahmad u Ahmad was leader in the main lodge, and his 'reign' overlapped with the passage of Father de Foucauld through the area of Ahansal influence — though he was unable to visit the lodges in question. Father de Foucauld's passage through the area took place in 1883 and 1884.

As stated, the saints of Temga and their group stuck to the agreed principles. Not so the saints of the main or founding lodge. Soon after the agreement, a male infant was born in one of the leading families. The overjoyed family and their kinsmen simply could not restrain themselves, and in no time, as anyone who is familiar with the habits of the main lodge would indeed expect, they were off, dancing like nobody's business.

This blatant transgression of holy law *and* violation of solemn agreement did not, of course, pass unnoticed. Such a combination of religious transgression and violation of solemn agreement was too much for the men of Temga, and they took up arms against their lax, irreligious, and self-indulgent cousins. The conflict and feud are said to have lasted seven years (a suspect figure, which with some other evidence suggests that the whole episode is now on the borderline of history and legend). In the end, the conflict was brought to a close by the intervention and arbitration of the surrounding lay, feud-addicted tribes. The irony of this part of the story of course in no way escapes the attention of either

126

the lay tribes or the saints. The ferocious, savage, feud-addicted lay tribes had to exercise strong moral pressure and arbitration to bring to an end murderous violence between holy, obligatory and essentially pacific saints.

One should add that another feature of the situation is quite obvious to all the locals: they are not at all taken in by the theological occasion of the conflict between the two saintly centres. 'Everyone knows' that, however emotively septic the issue of dancing may be, the real underlying cause of the conflict was a rivalry between the two lodges for influence — a rivalry that normally is kept within the bounds imposed by the obligation of pacifism on saints, but which on this occasion transcended those bounds.

The whole story is highly instructive from a number of viewpoints. It illustrates our general argument in the following way: everyone concerned endorses and formally accepts the values that are believed to be those of urban, central Islam, exemplified above all by Fez. In particular, those values prohibit dancing. There is no disagreement at the level of theoretical endorsement.

But some are under greater pressure to conform to these values than others. The Temga group of lodges is close to the edge of the plain, and some of its client tribes are right on the edge of the plain. In other words, they have to satisfy a tribal clientele who are also close to urban centres of religious propaganda, and they have to compete for the favours of this clientele with other religious leaders, some of them actually urban, who can exemplify values and ideals closer to the scriptural and puritanical ideals of the *ulama*. To meet this competition and answer its arguments, the holy men of Temga and its groups have no choice but to try to emulate those standards.

The main lodge is in quite a different position. It is much older established than Temga and thus, not being on the make, does not have to extend itself to establish its own holiness. More important, it is located right in the depth of the mountains, within half a day's march of the main Sahara—Atlantic watershed. The tribes that form its clientele are likewise overwhelmingly drawn from the heart of the mountains, and from the area between the mountains and the Sahara. Though these saints also need to compete for their followership with other saints, they do not need to compete with any urban-based religious centres. In other words, the urban puritanical ideals are far away and have no local anchorage or sanction. No wonder that there was so little countervailing power available in the hearts of the men of the main lodge, to help them to resist the temptation of the dance!

In the purely tribal context, exemplified by the main lodge, the 'central' values are endorsed but not practised. The local tribesmen require the holy lineages, the incarnation of Islam, mainly for purposes such as arbitration, mediation, social continuity, facilitation of trade, and so forth, and are not at all interested in purity. On the contrary, they are interested in a kind of cover for impurity. If they can have their own, very own, local saints, who like themselves dance but at the same time, being descendants of the Prophet, can claim

127

to be as close to the source of Islam as the learned men of the city, so much the better. That way, one can legitimate one's Muslim status and persist in the ancient practices, and no very serious tension need be felt by anyone.

Things become a bit different as one comes closer to the plain, or when for one reason or another the urban world exercises stronger pressures. The hereditary holy men of Temga still perform the same functions as do their cousins of the main lodge, but they have to do so in a context that in part is open to the influence from the plain.

Thus the same ideals are proclaimed throughout, but the way in which a compromise is reached with the exigencies of tribal life differs according to circumstance.

Or take another illustration. In the area of Ahansal influence there is one legend that is particularly popular and which with some variation in detail is often recounted. I shall call it the Kingmaker story.

Its hero is Sidi Mohamed n'ut Baba, an ancestor of the effectively saintly sublineage within the main lodge. If this legend is true, he would have had to have been alive toward the end of the seventeenth century. The story begins during the reign of the Sultan Mulay Rashid. This sultan apparently sent a messenger to the saint, to inquire how he managed to acquire so much holiness. The saint impressed the messenger by additional displays of saintly powers, such as making a mule give birth to a young mule. In return he asked the monarch to liberate some tribesmen from among his client tribes, whom the monarch had imprisoned. The monarch refused, and the incensed saint decided to punish the monarch by magical means. He hammered a magical *tagust* into the ground. A *tagust* is a metal peg used for attaching animals, and as it is hammered into the ground it is extremely phallic in appearance and function. The word is in fact also used to mean 'penis'. But I shall not dwell on the obvious and suggestive Freudian aspects of the story.

As a result of hammering the *tagust* into the ground the monarchy came upon a troubled period and in the end Mulay Rashid died. This was not the worst: his death was followed by one of those anarchic interregnums which are not infrequent in Moroccan history.

The next sultan-to-be, Mulay Ismail, failing to overcome these difficulties, came to the saint for advice. He stayed at the main lodge for a few days, presenting his case. The saint, evidently convinced by the strength of this pretender's claims, in the end gave him advice. The details of this advice and Mulay Ismail's adventures in carrying it out do not concern us, but they involved his finding the magical *tagust*, pulling it out of the ground as prearranged by the saint, and finding himself at that moment back in Fez, acclaimed by the populace as King!

Given the Freudian undertones of the liberated *tagust*, the legend is a fine specimen of a 'Waste Land' story, in which the peace and prosperity of the kingdom depend on the virility of the monarch. But this is not the aspect I wish to dwell on.

Doctor and saint

The aspect that is interesting from the viewpoint of our theme is a certain ideological naïveté of the story. The manifest purpose and moral of the story is obvious: it is meant to heighten the prestige of the local holy lineage by turning it and its ancestor, contrary to all historical probability, into a kingmaker and arbitrator of the political fortunes in the distant capital of Fez. (The legend is unhistorical to the extent that the striking feature of this particular holy lineage is its stability and continuity in its mountain homeland, and its abstention, in the main, from interference in or impact on politics at the urban centres of the country. The two things may well be connected.)

This is the only too obvious purpose of anyone telling the story: the story wears its heart on its sleeve, and it would be almost impossible to retell the story without empathising its moral. Yet unwittingly, in its simplemindedness, the story also endorses the ultimate legitimacy of that central monarchy, which had no effective power locally and which the local tribesmen defied, and from whose power they had collectively seceded. The local tribesmen paid no taxes to Fez and received no officials from it: if the peripatetic court and army attempted to enter their territory, they fought to stop it. In order to raise the prestige of their own little local holy men and their link with Islam, they retell the story showing how influential and crucial those holy men are. Yet in telling the story, they unwittingly recognise the ultimate authority of the centre. The story does not even hint that its hero, the saint, should have himself become a sultan: it only hints that by magical means it was he who enabled the sultan to rule effectively.

These various legends and situations illustrate, though of course they do not by themselves prove, the main contention of this argument: Islam embraces various types of social structure, and while the *ulama* are its ultimate and most important expression, its constitutional court, so to speak, yet many of those social structures, notably tribal ones, cannot accommodate or use these learned scribes, and need other anchorages for religion. A typical specimen of these anchorages are the holy lineages, so highly developed among the Berbers, but by no means unparalleled elsewhere. These holy lineages are tied by links of terminology and even organisation to mystical urban clubs, but despite the similarity of terminology, and sometimes organisational relations, the two phenomena are quite distinct in nature and function. Thus very little is explained by any simple reference to the diffusion of Sufi ideas. It is important to understand just what the saints do and what they mean in their context. In the case of the holy lineages of the recesses of the mountains, their acquaintance with or interest in Sufi ideas is negligible. What they do and what they mean can only be understood by reference to the tribes whom they serve.

But while these lineages are very unlike urban *ulama*, and sadly deficient when the standards proclaimed or even practised by urban *ulama* are applied to them, they should not be seen as unambiguously hostile to them. Their role is inherently ambiguous. They must serve tribal, non-urban ends, but they must also link the tribes with a wider and urban-oriented ideal of Islam. They serve both local and tribal needs and universal Islamic identification. They hamper the diffusion of good and proper Islam, in a way, by giving the tribesman an excuse for pretending that they are *already* good Muslims, that they already possess the institutional framework of faith; and yet at the same time, they keep the door open for the propagation of 'purer' Islam by endorsing it in the course of those very practices in which they deviate from it.

5

Sanctity, puritanism, secularisation and nationalism in North Africa: a case study

The most characteristic social institution of North African religious life is the saint, the holy personage. As Islam does not enjoin celibacy, saints proliferate and form lineages and dynasties. 'Nepotism' would be a misnomer, as the North African saint does not need to bequeath his spiritual power to a nephew, for there is no reason why he should not have or should not admit to having a son. Moreover, no condemnation attaches to such a family succession, for spiritual merit and role are expected to be passed on in the family line. But such genetic-spiritual lineages, so to speak, are not the only possible bond between successive generations of holy personages: there are also spiritual–spiritual lineages, in which the links are formed not by father–son relationships but by teacher–disciple ones. Thus living saints and dead, enshrined ones are connected by a complex net of two kinds of 'kinship'.

The saints are not all of one kind, of course. One interesting spectrum is that between rural and urban ones, the former operating in tribal contexts, the latter amongst city populations. It is still possible — though it will not be possible for much longer — to study the functioning of rural saints by observation. I studied one saintly lineage intermittently during the 1950s, and am publishing the findings elsewhere. By way of contrast, it would also have been interesting to see something of the working of their urban counterparts, but by the middle of this century whatever was left of this phenomenon — and no doubt, something remained — was extremely difficult or impossible to study. In any case, such attempts as I made in this direction soon discouraged me.

Fortunately, a book appeared recently which assembled a good deal of documentation concerning one urban saint.[1] The book is written from the viewpoint of interest in religion as such rather than religion as a social form. The present paper is an attempt to interpret the material sociologically, and to place it against a general picture of the role of religion in North Africa, traditionally and in transition.

In religion, the southern, Muslim shore of the Mediterranean is a kind of mirror-image of the northern shore, of Europe. Europe is, or was, Christendom. Within Western Christianity, one has become habituated to the opposition be-

131

tween the central tradition and the deviant splinter churches and sects which, even when relatively large, remain small in comparison with *the* Church. The central tradition has certain marked features: it has a hierarchy, it makes use of personal mediation between the ordinary believer and the deity, it verges on a cult of personality or personalities, it has a strong rural appeal, it stresses and uses ritual a good deal, it incorporates or is tolerant of a good deal of rural superstition or rites, it possesses an organisation economically dependent, at least in part, on the donations of the faithful, it satisfies the emotional needs of its believers. By contrast, the deviant splinter groups tend to dispense with personal mediation, with ritual, with emotional and sensuous accompaniments of faith, with hierarchy; they tend to be puritanical, stress *the Book* and hence literacy rather than mediators and ritual, and so forth.

In North Africa, all this is reversed. It is the central tradition which has the 'protestant' characteristics — a tradition without clergy in the full sense (but rich in lawyer—theologians) or personal mediation; based on trading towns, stressing literacy and learning, sometimes hostile to shrines and popular cults. It is the deviant cults which are hierarchical, employ personal mediation with the deity, indulge in greater ritual richness, personal cults and so forth.

Moreover, in Europe with its strong states and long-established freedom from tribalism, *the* Church is or was a kind of disembodied (and not always disembodied) state. In North Africa, where states were weak and tribalism strong, the deviant religious organisations were a species of disembodied (and not always disembodied) tribes.

This is the reality under the apparent religious homogeneity of North Africa. Statistically, disregarding the European and Jewish minorities, virtually all North Africans are Sunni Muslims of the Maliki rite. (The only significant exception is the Ibadi minority, with such strong 'protestant' features as to have been described as 'the Calvinists of Islam', and who, thanks to trade, manage to wrest a living from their desert base in Mzab and their island base in Djerba. This group still awaits its Max Weber. There are also a few non-Maliki survivals of the Turkish elite.) But this appearance of homogeneity is only superficial. Underneath, there is, or was, a rich and varied world of religious associations, of living traditions of sanctity, perpetuated and reproduced by both physical and spiritual lineages of saints ... The saints whom one can find on the map of Europe from (say) St Andrews to St Tropez no longer represent a living social form. The map of North Africa is richer in *Sidis* than the map of Europe is in saints, but the type of personage commemorated by place and shrine is still to be found in life.

But here some qualification is required. In very recent years, even in North Africa there has been a decline in this form of popular religious life, Uprooting and industrialisation, a new wave of Muslim Reformism and purification, and finally nationalism have all significantly diminished the extent and importance of these religious manifestations. In this respect, there is a striking contrast with West Africa. There, Europeans were identified with Christianity, and so all forms

Sanctity, puritanism, secularisation and nationalism

of Muslim religious life could continue to flourish, whether orthodox or not: none were tainted by association with colonial powers. In North Africa, Christian proselytism was not significant: in as far as the colonial power worked on the indigenous masses through religion, it did so not through Christianity but through the more archaic and segmented religious traditions. Partly for this reason, national revival also meant a decline of the saints, and special cults. Today, they are on the way out: the day is probably near when a 'Sidi' on the North African map will, like a 'St' on a European one, merely be an echo of a past form of life.

Except for the occupying French and Spaniards, Europeans have on the whole not had much contact with this sanctity — at least for some time. (Outside Tangier there is a shrine of a saint who became such for fighting the English when they held the town — and of course a far greater number became sanctified for fighting the Portuguese.) In the twentieth century, more Europeans in Europe have probably been in contact with these forms of North African religious life unwittingly, *in the circus*, than in any other way: Southern Morocco exports circus acrobats, and it is not generally recognised that these form something between a clan and a guild and attribute their skill to the saintliness (transmitted charisma) of their patron saint . . .

The literature on this subject in English is scanty (the most important item is probably the book by an Englishwoman who married into one of the saintly lineages — Emily Shareefa of Wazan, and one sociological masterpiece — Professor E. Evans-Pritchard's study of the Sanusi Order), and Mr Lings's book is a most welcome addition to it. Mr Lings is interested in religion and mysticism as such, rather than specifically in the social manifestations of it. But this in a way makes the sociological material all the more valuable: it is assembled quite unselfconsciously.

Shaikh Ahmad al-'Alawi was born in Mostaganem in Western Algeria in 1869, and died in 1934. He was an extremely interesting example of the living tradition of sanctity as it is conceived in North Africa. Mr Lings remarks that he remains wholly unknown 'outside the precincts of Islamic mysticism'. Within those precincts he did however acquire enough fame to attract the interest of French scholars concerned with Sufism, notably of A. Berque and of Massignon. The former of these published an article about him two years after his death, entitled *Un Mystique Moderniste*. This article curiously reproduces as fact an emergent legend about the Shaikh's supposed travels in the East, including India. A legend is a fabrication or, as Mr Lings more charitably puts it: 'these ten years in the East were no more real than a dream, . . . [but correspond] to what the Shaikh would have chosen for himself if his destiny had allowed it'. Mr Lings's charity suggests that there is something like a Mystic's Licence which permits some vagueness in differentiating between real and imaginary travels. In my own experience, North African saints are indeed addicted to mystical travels to the holy places of Hejaz, travels frequently unaided by normal means of transportation (though sometimes aided by sprouting wings for the purpose) and

133

extremely speedy. As Mr Lings remarks in another context, Sufis (Muslim mystics) visit Medina in spirit every morning and evening; and, it appears, the distinction between spiritual and material peregrinations is sometimes blurred.

Mr Lings polemicises with A. Berque's earlier study, but not so much on account of such insufficiently critical use of material: just as the imaginary journey becomes validated *qua* 'dream', so Berque's contention that the Shaikh hypnotised his disciples is accepted, but re-interpreted by the assertion that the disciple's passivity, as that of 'a corpse in the hands of the washer of the dead', really presupposed 'an undercurrent of extreme spiritual activity' and led in the end to independent spiritual perception on the part of the disciple. Mr Lings's real disagreement with Berque concerns the fact that the latter describes the Shaikh as a *moderniste*. In Lings's view, he was, on the contrary, 'essentially very conservative'. He goes on to remark that the Shaikh's 'so-called "modernism" appears to have been nothing other than the great breadth of his spiritual interests'.

This brings us to what, from the outside, is really the most interesting thing about the Shaikh: his position on the range of alternative possible religious positions. Sociologically, it is this range, the nature of the alternatives, oppositions and affinities in it, which is of the greatest interest. The span of the Shaikh's life corresponds roughly to the period when the French domination of North Africa was at its height, the period when the Pax Gallica was most securely superimposed on Muslim life. The pre-French period of Maghrebin life, so to speak, when saints were leaders against the infidel, was almost over: the year of the Shaikh's death was also the year in which the last tribal marabout-led dissidence against the French in North Africa came to an end. The new form, so to speak, in which Muslim puritanism provided the basis for a modern nationalism, had begun in his lifetime, but its nationalist and political aspects were hardly prominent at the time when he was most active. In view of the passivity or co-operation of the saints, the marabouts, *vis-à-vis* the French, it is curious to reflect that their historical origin lies not only in Sufism and in Berber tribal practices, but equally in military orders fighting Christian invaders, in a kind of Moslem equivalent of crusaders, Knights of Malta, etc. But in the Shaikh's own life and times, the militant aspects both of the past and the future were in abeyance.

It is difficult to agree with Mr Lings's own characterisation of the Shaikh's position (as 'essentially very conservative'), at any rate sociologically, for it too has, so to speak, primarily a spiritual significance and validity. Mr Lings agrees with certain characteristically Sufi claims — notably, that Sufism is not really a later development within Islam but that, properly understood, it is there to be found in the Prophet's own pronouncements; and furthermore, he has much sympathy with a kind of pan-mystic eclecticism, in which he goes a good deal further than the subject of his study, the Shaikh himself. Mr Lings's own attitude is a kind of 'Mystics of all religions, unite' approach. He quotes with approval a statement of Pope Pius XI to the effect that Muslims are eligible for Salvation, he recommends a re-interpretation of Jesus's words 'None cometh to the Father but by Me' to include Hindu Avatars, Buddha, etc., in the 'Me'[2] (whilst allowing that the apparent and exclusive meaning is providentially useful in being adapted to the ethnocentric attitudes of Europeans and Semites, 'incapable of following seriously a religion unless they believe it to be the only one or to be exceptionally privileged'), and he compares the Shaikh to Indian, Red Indian and Chinese mystics. Mr Lings makes some interesting observations on the relative merits, from his standpoint, of Christianity and Islam: it is 'one of the excellencies of Christianity that it has a definitely constituted spiritual authority consisting of a small minority of men' — but unfortunately this minority is pushed 'further and further into a remote corner of the community from which it can barely function and from which it sometimes seems to emerge by pandering to mundane triviality'. It is, on the other hand, 'one of the excellencies of Islam that there is no laity and every Moslem is in a sense a priest' — but the corresponding disadvantage is 'the existence of a large number of very limited individuals who imagine that the whole religion is within their grasp . . .'.

Precisely: the fundamental issue is the equality of believers. The central tradition of Christianity denies it, and the deviants affirm it. The central tradition of Islam affirms it, and the deviants deny it. The saintly Shaikh, like his very numerous North African fellow-saints, was in this sense a deviant in Islam. This conclusion of course neither he nor Mr Lings would accept, despite the fact that Mr Lings does provide the crucial premises for it. From the viewpoint of Mr Lings, the Shaikh was not a deviant: neither in virtue of being a Sufi (for he holds Sufism to have been present in Islam from the start), nor in view of the tolerant breadth of his spiritual interests (for truth is present in many religions, and their exclusive protestations are only a sugarcoating for the benefit of ethnocentric Europeans and Semites). The Shaikh's own eclecticism, one should add, is of course not nearly so sweeping, open and daring as Mr Lings's: we are told (p. 82), for instance, that 'as an extremely subtle and penetrating metaphysician, he was able to reconcile plurality with unity in the Trinitarian conception . . . [but] he rejected it none the less, [though] his understanding of it made some people (his enemies) think that he adhered to it'. It is interesting to have so striking a refutation of a widespread view — that doctrines of such difficulty have to be believed to be understood.

The kind of religious eclecticism openly advocated by Mr Lings and much more cautiously flirted with by the Shaikh, is of course generally inspired by most admirable motives, by the desire to avoid exclusiveness and intolerance whilst not cutting oneself off from the intensity and richness of specific religious traditions. Or, to put it in another way, it is an attempt to combine the symmetrical, tolerant, from-the-outside view of religions, inherent in the present pluralistic one-world society, with the exclusive claims which, alas, at least seem to be part of some religions when seen from the inside. Such syncretism is an

135

interesting phenomenon in its own right: it underlies movements such as the *Ahmadiyyah*, and academic versions of it are not unknown. Whether such syntheses can be made logically acceptable to those who do not share to the full the Shaikh's metaphysical penetration and subtlety, I am not sure. In any case, granted the premisses, the Shaikh was not, at a spiritual level, either an innovator in virtue of being a mystic, or in virtue of his breadth of interests.

But on a sociological rather than a spiritual level, one must also take him as he appeared to his contemporaries, however misguided. From their own premisses, he did sometimes seem to be a deviant (and even from his own later viewpoint, he was such earlier in his spiritual career), and he did not repudiate their premisses, for he polemicised with them in print on their own terms. Fortunately from the viewpoint of those interested in the mundane and social aspects of the saint's life, the book does contain a wealth of illuminating information about it. This is contained not so much in Mr Lings's commentary or in the saint's reproduced devotional poems, but in the saint's quite long autobiography, most of which is reproduced. This document was found amongst his papers after his death. It has an absolutely authentic ring, and constitutes for me the most fascinating part of the book.

A devotional work by one of the Shaikh's disciples tells us that, prior to his conception, his mother had a vision of the Prophet in her sleep. The Shaikh's own recollection begins with a memory of having had no schooling whatever other than being taught the Koran by his father, and he states that his handwriting remained ever unproficient. Economic pressure forced him to give up Koranic scholarship when he reached the Surat ar-Rahman. (He modestly omits to say that this entails that he knew nine-tenths of the Book by heart. Those familiar with the Book must tumble to this at once. For those who are not, Mr Lings makes the point explicit.) The pressures which prevented him learning the remaining tenth led him to become a cobbler. This eased the family's situation. The Shaikh tells us that previously they did not have enough to live on, but that his father was too proud to betray the fact to outsiders. (Again, a footnote by Mr Lings tells us that the Shaikh's grandfather was one of the notables of Mostaganem. The name 'Alawi' would lead one to suppose that he was of Sherifian descent, i.e. descended from the Prophet, and in the same wider family as the Moroccan Royal house. The book does not confirm that this indeed was one of the Shaikh's claims. One should add that the number of people making such claims, and having them accepted, is extremely large in North Africa, so that there would be nothing unusual in it.)

He lost his father at the age of sixteen. He remained a cobbler for some years and then took up trade. The precise nature of the trade is not specified. He soon acquired the habit of attending devotional religious meetings and lessons at night. At first, this involved conflict with his mother — who survived until he was forty-six — but later she gave in to his religious tendencies. Not so his wife: she complained of his nocturnal studies and habit of bringing a teacher home, and

136

claimed her divorce. (We are told of this episode, but not of the preceding marriage.)

At the time he composed the autobiography, he clearly did not think much of what he learnt in these early studies: he valued them only for giving him some mental discipline, and enabling him at least to grasp 'some points' of doctrine. (To the mystical insights he later valued he refers to as *the* doctrine.)

His first contact with esoteric religious fraternities was with what is perhaps the most exotic and notorious of all North African 'ways', the 'Isawi Tarika. Amongst the followers of this 'way', snake-charming, fire-eating and other practices are extensively used. The Shaikh himself became a proficient snake-charmer. However, one day God willed that his eyes should alight on a saying traced back to the Prophet — the Shaikh does not say which — which made him realise the error of his ways: he gave up these practices, for the time being, except snake-charming (no reason is given for making this exception). There appear to have been two stages in his dissociation from the 'Isawi followers, though he does not say this in so many words: for he says that at first he avoided the practices by making 'excuses to my brethren', but also that he wished to take the entire brotherhood away from them too. Evasion by excuses and attempted conversion of his fellows presumably followed each other.

Thus we see the Shaikh, already in the early parts of his story, oscillating between the two poles of Muslim religious life, between the specialist—esoteric on the one hand, and the egalitarian—orthodox on the other. His evaluation of his early instruction places him clearly on the side of esoteric understanding, but his rejection of the extreme and specialised 'Isawi practices, and the reason given for this rejection, imply the opposite premisses.

It is after telling us about his involvement with the ritual extremists of the 'Isawi order that he comes to speak of his meeting with his true Teacher. He had already heard of him in connection with a successful cure of an illness in his childhood, effected by means of an amulet obtained from this Shaikh. Now he met him again, apparently by accident, together with his own (our Shaikh's) business partner and friend. Gradually he came under his influence, and received instruction and encouragement, including predictions of future spiritual eminence, from the Teacher. The Teacher dissuaded him from continuing with his remaining 'Isawi practice, snake-charming, with the help of a parable (the snake in one's own body, i.e. one's soul, is far more venomous and worth charming), though apparently he had no disrespect for the founder of the 'Isawi order — in so far as the prediction of spiritual eminence for the disciple had the form of saying that one day he will become like that founder.

The instruction appears to have consisted mainly in the training in reciting litanies and the Divine Name. The Shaikh records no regret at giving up snake-charming, but he did go through a struggle when asked by the Teacher to give up attending lessons in scholastic theology. 'No order he ever gave me was so hard to obey as this.' (There are other remarks which throw light on the authoritarian relationship between teacher and disciple, as later between the disciple-become-Shaikh and his disciples.) The Teacher had a low opinion of the hair-splitting courses. The disciple had four consolations: perhaps the mystical knowledge was superior to that which he was now missing; the prohibition was only temporary; he had just taken an oath of obedience; and perhaps he was just being put on trial, as apparently was the custom of Teachers. But these consolations or arguments 'did not stop the ache of sorrow' he felt within him.

Instead of scholastic, intellectual theology, he was given mystical training. The main technique employed was 'the invocation of the single Name with distinct visualisation of its letters until they were written in [the disciple's] imagination. Then he would tell him to spread them out and enlarge them until they filled all the horizon. The *dhikr* would continue in this form until the letters became like light.' After this, the subsequent stages apparently escape the possibility of verbal description. He would reach ultimate illumination, and having attained it would be allowed to return to the ordinary world, though one now transformed by the preceding insight.

Having successfully passed through the mystical training, the Shaikh was allowed to return to formal theology by his Teacher, and when he did so, he says,

I found myself quite different from what I had been before as regards understanding. I now understood things in advance before the Shaikh who was teaching us had finished expounding them. Another result of the invocation was that I understood more than the literal sense of the text.

The subsequent quoted part of the autobiography contains a digression concerning the development of the Shaikh's Teacher himself — his travels in Morocco, his affiliation to *his* (in turn) teacher, placing him within one of the orders and its spiritual genealogy. (As North African tribes are organised around genealogies, so the fraternities are organised along spiritual genealogies. These, like the tribal, physical ones, tend to be 'segmentary', i.e. possess a tree-like pattern: but spiritual genealogies can occasionally, unlike unilineal physical ones, flow together. There is fusion as well as fission on the ancestral map: a man may have more than one spiritual father.) There are also interesting allusions to the dangers and difficulties of such mystical affiliation and proselytism: at various crucial times in his career, the Teacher, in view of opposition and hostility or on the other hand of opportunity, had to vary his strategy from proselytism to restrained silence and back again. Each of these changes in the dialectical line, as it were, was heralded and guided by the appearance to him in his sleep by the Prophet or by a prominent spiritually-ancestral saint, the latter accompanied in the dream, perhaps by way of introduction and guarantee, by one of the Teacher's real ancestors.

The Shaikh was by now initiated into the Teacher's order and qualified to receive and instruct novices. So was his business partner and friend, though he appears to have concentrated more on keeping the business going: the Shaikh gratefully remarks that but for him, the business would have been altogether ruined. His own activities made 'our shop more like a *zawiya* (religious lodge) than anything else'.

The major crisis in the Shaikh's life came, after fifteen years in the service of his Teacher, when the Teacher died. The Shaikh tells us that prior to the Teacher's death, God had put in his, the Shaikh's, heart the desire to emigrate. He gives no motive for this desire more specific than the moral corruption of his country. Thus he found himself torn between the desire to move and his obligation to stay with the ailing Teacher. He did, however, even before the Teacher's death, liquidate his property, etc. But even the Teacher's death did not resolve the conflict: difficulties arose with permits from the French authorities and through the illness and death of the Shaikh's then wife. The major difficulty now was however through the need of the local segment of the order to find a successor to the Teacher.

The Teacher had not nominated a successor. The Shaikh himself, either because he was busy at his wife's deathbed and/or because he remained determined to emigrate, and also because, as he says, he was willing to accept the verdict of the other followers, did not take part in the deliberations about succession. These discussions proved inconclusive and 'somewhat argumentative'. The Shaikh hints that this was because the members knew that he was determined to go away (i.e. no other candidate appeared generally acceptable). His old friend and business partner, who did take part in the deliberations, then proposed that the decision be postponed, in the hope that some of the brethren might in the meantime have a guiding vision. And in due course and before the day appointed for decision a good number of visions were had, and all of them — or at any rate all of them that were subsequently recorded when our saint was the Shaikh of the order — pointed to one conclusion, namely that he should be the successor. The Teacher who, when he was still alive, had refused to name a successor (perhaps on the Parkinsonian principle that subordinates are kept in order by fear of their rivals' promotion and hope of their own) and declared that such matters had to remain in God's hands, made up for his indecision in life by proferring ample and clear guidance after death. The Teacher appeared in visions to many disciples to notify them of the right succession: it appears that the theological objections he felt during his life to usurping this function no longer obtained after death. These visions, incidentally, apart from having great clarity and freshness, are it appears followed by 'a state of entire vigilance without any intermediary process of waking up': so Mr Lings was informed by the one disciple of the Shaikh with whom he had direct contact. Thus, succession was determined in favour of our Shaikh.

If one were to suspect that political motives may have been present in the Shaikh's plans for emigration, two possibilities suggest themselves: one, that a threat of emigration was a means of putting pressure on the brethren to come to reach agreement; and two, that the plan provided an alternative in case of defeat.

139

(Fraternities of this kind invariably tend to proliferate and consist of a number of dispersed centres: the Shaikh may have preferred to be No. 1 in a spiritual colony rather than hold a lower rank in the founding centre.) But whether or not these motives operated, the Shaikh also appeared to be possessed by a geuine and independent *Wanderlust*. All appeared to go well after his accession to leadership: the followers took their oath of allegiance to him (he later introduced a new style of doing so), and members of affiliated centres in other places also came in due course to accept him as leader. All the members of the order thus came to be united, 'except two or three'. This union was, as he says, 'counted by us as a miraculous Grace from God, for I had no outward means of bringing within my scope individuals from so many different places'.

Nevertheless, in due course he set off on travels. He hesitated between his duty as 'remembrancer' to his followers and his desire to travel, but after a time the latter prevailed. The actual travels are described as occurring with an apparent inconsequentiality: they begin by a desire to visit some near-by brethren with a view to curing an affliction. He then, with a companion, decides to visit some others further off: and then, to proceed to Algiers with a view to finding a publisher for one of his manuscripts. (One assumes that the possibility of such a trip may have been present in his mind from the start, for he appears to have had the required manuscript with him.) He failed in this purpose in Algiers, so he and his companion decide to proceed further, to Tunis, where 'the whole thing would be quite simple'. In fact, he did make some progress towards publication in Tunisia: he also made some converts to his order and was constantly visited by 'theologians, canonists and other eminent men'.

He was tempted by the thought of making the Pilgrimage (to Mecca), but desisted in view of the fact that it was forbidden that year by the French because of an epidemic in Arabia.[3] So, instead, he went to Tripoli, to visit his cousins who had emigrated there. He found them well and prosperous. He comments that the country was 'a good place to emigrate to, since its people [are] as like as possible to those of our country both in speech and ways'. (This is an odd reason in view of the motive given earlier for wishing to emigrate — namely the moral corruption of his own country. It may be relevant that the Western parts of North Africa have for a considerable time been exporting saints to Tripolitania and Cyrenaica, where their superior skill is recognised. Why this should be so is not clear.)

A Turkish Shaikh who was also a government official (in the department of maritime revenue) invited him to settle and offered him a *zawiya* 'and all the out-buildings that go with it'. Our Shaikh agreed — but there is no further follow-up of this offer and episode in the narrative. Instead, he reports hearing the town crier advertising cheap tickets to Istanbul — and after a terrible crossing he reached it. Whatever his plans there, he concluded that the times were not propitious for them. Here occur the only comments on general politics which are to be found in the saint's autobiography. His visit to Istanbul was shortly after the deposition of Abdul Hamid, but this was no source of joy to him. On the contrary, he makes bitter remarks about the Young Turks, and the degradation which was to reach its culmination under the Kemalists, and he decided that this was no place for him. Indeed, by now he 'had no peace of soul until the day when [he] set foot on Algerian soil, and ... praised God for the ways of (his) people and their remaining in the faith of their fathers and grandfathers and following in the footsteps of the pious'. Here the autobiography ends. If, following Berque's epithet, the Shaikh was a modernist, he clearly was not an extreme one. One wonders what he would have thought of the F.L.N.

There are some important aspects of the Shaikh's religious career which are not discussed in his autobiography. One of them concerns his hiving-off from the system of Darqawi *zawiyas*. Mr Lings reports, plausibly, that the greatest jealousy the Shaikh had to face was from the heads of neighbouring Darqawi lodges, who were jealous of his success and influence, and that this was brought to a head when 'after about five years' (i.e. presumably five years after his succession) he made himself independent of the central Darqawi *zawiya* (in Morocco). This must have meant repudiating, or at least no longer observing, the kind of oath of allegiance which, as reported, he himself exacted from followers and heads of dependent sub-lodges of his own. The motive given for this declaration of independence was an innovation in mystical technique. (North African religious fraternities generally differentiate themselves from each other by the 'way' — i.e. to God — which they employ.) The Shaikh's innovation was to introduce the practice of *khalwah* — this being a cell in which a novice is put after swearing not to leave it for forty days if need be, and in which he must do nothing but repeat ceaselessly, day and night, the Divine Name, drawing out each time the syllable *ah* until he had no more breath left.

Mr Lings observes that the declaration of spiritual independence caused violent ill-feeling, and that he lost some of the disciples he had inherited, so to speak, from the Teacher. But new disciples came, and it appears there were even cases of whole *zawiyas* affiliating to him *en bloc*, leader and followers together. A major triumph for the Shaikh was to gain as a follower a descendant, a great-grandson, of the very founder of the order from which the Shaikh had seceded. This grandson had, it seems, been of no great significance in his own ancestral order, for he remarks (in a letter quoted by Lings), 'until [meeting the Shaikh] I had simply been an initiate of the order and nothing more'. The Shaikh opened his inward eye and led him to direct knowledge of God, as the cited letter observes. Of course, choosing freedom in this manner, so to speak, could not but cause indignation among his own betrayed relatives: but the great-grandson in question says he 'paid no attention to those of my family who blamed me for following [the Shaikh] ... '.

In Mr Lings's view the hostility of the rival lodges was short-lived, except for that of 'one or two hereditary marabouts who were in danger of losing their influence altogether'. But if in due course he escaped the hostility of his rivals on the right — of the 'Isawis whom he deserted early, of the Darqawis from whom he seceded with a whole lodgeful of followers, and from the hereditary marabouts — he had in due course to face hostility from the left, as it were, from the newer and more puritanical, rigoristic, anti-Sufi forms of Islam. This battle was fought in a rather modern form, by means of pamphleteering. The Shaikh answered an attack on mysticism by a teacher at the Religious College in Tunis, an attack which sounded the war-cry by its very title, *A Mirror to show up Errors.*

Mr Lings's sympathies are clearly with the mystics and he finds the arguments of the Tunisian religious teacher 'petty and childish' and manifests regretful surprise that the Shaikh should have bothered to reply at all. He excuses him by observing that the Shaikh must have realised that this attack had a significance going beyond that of their immediate author, being a crystallisation of a general hostility which could not be ignored. If the Shaikh did realise this he was quite right. The future — if not the very distant future — lay with these puritanical, more Protestant, so to speak, religious teachers: they laid the foundations of the modern North African national consciousness in their struggle against the religious particularism of those such as the Shaikh. (The generation of nationalists formed by these thinkers has since been replaced by another, whose thoughts wander to Peking or Belgrade rather than Mecca. But that is another story.)

The essence of the critic's argument is simple: 'Islam is nothing other than the Book of God and the Wont of His Messenger.' In other words, the ritual and other excrescences of the mystics are to be condemned. The Shaikh's answer was to claim that there was in the Book a wealth of hidden meanings which is beyond most men's attainment — in other words, that he was merely making explicit what is hidden (and must remain hidden for the majority), in the Book. He did not dispute the premiss that the Book and the Prophet's custom exhaust Islam: but there was more in these than could meet the uninitiated eye.

An interesting issue between the Puritans and the Mystics concerns *dancing*. The Sufi mystics generally make use of dancing in ritual contexts: the Puritans forbid it, and claim that the Prophet forbade it. Opinions differ on this point, as Mr Lings observes: he himself, sympathising as ever with the mystics, finds it difficult not to believe that the Companions of the Prophet did not make some spontaneous rhythmic movements of the body when reciting their various litanies . . . Mr Lings also goes on to remark, much more convincingly, that these practices incorporate 'traditional local dances which . . . as it were in the blood of [the] disciples . . . had . . . a more immediate appeal for them'. In the region of central Morocco where I worked, at about the same time as the Shaikh was practising in Algeria, two tribes (in the literal, kinship-and-territorial sense) of saints went to war on this issue of the permissibility of dancing, and it took their lay clients a long time to bring them to peace again. Those who were against dancing were closer to towns — i.e. to urban learned men who were more frequently of the 'reformist', i.e. puritan persuasion. The pro-dancing group were deeper in the recesses of the hills, where the local dances were more firmly embedded in custom.

The critic, the author of the *Mirror*, bluntly affirms that 'anyone who considers dancing to be legal is an infidel': the cautious Shaikh does not deny his position outright. He argues:

> Do you imagine that the Sufis hold dancing to be absolutely lawful, just as you hold it to be absolutely unlawful? ... It behoves the learned man not to pass any judgement about it until he knows what is the motive behind it, lest he forbid what God has allowed.

This seems extremely sound: unfortunately it leaves the believer without guidance between two risks, either to commit what may be forbidden or to forbid what God has allowed. The safest course would seem to be not to dance but not to forbid it to others either. Curiously, this is precisely what neither side to the dispute has done: some do dance, and some forbid it.

Another issue arising between the mystics and the puritans concerns the use of *rosaries*. Their use is indeed very widespread and so characteristic of the religious fraternities that one can refer to a fraternity, or its distinguishing spiritual technique, as a *wird* (rosary). For the puritans, the crucial fact is that rosaries were not used by the Prophet and his Companion. The Shaikh, replying to the *Mirror*, points out that the Companions did count with the help of date-stones and pebbles. He also argued from a tradition reporting the use of a knotted cord. From pebbles and knotted cords together, the argument by analogy to rosaries is surely powerful!

Another objection of the puritans to the rosary was that it is shaped like a cross. Here the Shaikh can hardly contain himself: 'By all that is marvellous, what has the form of a rosary to do with the cross? However, "the eye of hatred ferrets out faults".' Triumphantly, the Shaikh points out that the human shape has more resemblance to a cross than has a rosary, so that the critic would consistently have to put an end to his own existence, or at least take care never to see himself . . .

The critic had castigated as hypocrites 'all those who use rosaries', i.e. the religious orders. The content and tone of anti-order criticism is very similar to anti-popery criticism in Europe. The critic concentrates on the alleged hypocrisy, profit motive, scripturally unwarranted and sensuous innovations and additions in ritual, use of shrines, use of music (and dancing) and religious aids. Concerning shrines, the Shaikh defends his followers against the imputation that they believe that the dead shaikhs in shrines have powers to give or withhold: they merely believe, the Shaikh maintains, that they are intermediaries between the believer and God. Most interestingly, the Shaikh concedes that in a higher spiritual state 'all mediation is abolished', and defends the use of intermediaries only for those who have not reached this fuller state.

Thus we see him implicitly conceding the 'protestant' religious ideal, and

143

defending mediation by saints and shrines as merely a second best. We also see that he is by no means a mystic *only*, but that in dialectical self-defence he is willing to employ, with skill and vigour, scholastic arguments from analogy, etc.

In his struggle against the puritans of this Salafiyyah reform movement, the Shaikh also in 1922 started publishing a religious weekly newspaper, which in 1926 was replaced by another with a wider scope. Both were published in Algiers. The journal was used to rebut puritan charges at length. Even the sympathetic Mr Lings finds the treatment of the rival position unmerciful. Nevertheless, when the editors of the two rival papers and protagonists of two religious attitudes came to meet, in 1931, the meeting was cordial, and was reported as such in the puritans' paper. The report is worth quoting, to show that from the cells-of-solitary-confinement-with-the-Divine-Name aspect, the Shaikh's life also had its more homely, Pooterish side:

> A supper was given by Shaikh Sidi Ahmed Bin-'Aliwah and it was attended by some of the leading men of Mostaganem, together with about one hundred of the Shaikh's pupils. The Shaikh himself was exceedingly cordial and gracious to the point of serving some of the guests with his own hands . . . After supper verses from the Koran were recited, and then the Shaikh's pupils began to chant . . . The pleasure of the evening was further enhanced in between the singing by literary discussions . . . ; and among the many examples of courtesy shown us by our host the Shaikh, I was particularly struck by the fact that he never once touched on any point of disagreement between us . . .

It is difficult not to suspect that the style of this report has been influenced, not only by the mystic or puritan traditions, but also by the manner of reporting of social events in the near-by French provincial press.

The Autobiography and the other documents assembled by Mr Lings give us an excellent, if not wholly complete, picture of an Algerian religious personage of a given period, of the alternatives, opportunities, dangers facing him: the Shaikh was located somewhere in the middle of the spectrum ranging from the extreme 'right', so to speak — hereditary marabouts, practices such as snake-charming — and the extreme 'left', puritanical, rigorously devoted to the Word, to strict observance, denial of superstition, and equality of believers. He fought on both fronts; he had in his youth been further to the right, and in his age, merciless journalistic polemics notwithstanding, he took trouble to maintain at least courteous, if not cordial, relations with the 'left'. The religious spectrum had not yet acquired the political significance which it was due to have some decades later: though it is worth noting that a year prior to the dinner party reported above, the puritans in Fez had laid the foundation stone of modern Moroccan nationalism by organising a protest movement against French support of heterodox tribal practices . . . The various aspects of relivious life illuminated by his career are worth specifying individually.

Organisation: there is a clear hierarchy of Shaikh—moqadem—disciple. Discipleship varies in kind: the rural converts were not generally expected to become mystical initiates: 'when the shaikh stayed for a few days in the country, it sometimes happened that almost the whole countryside would come to him for initiation. If they did not aspire to follow the path, they came for the "initiation of blessing".'

Within the hierarchy, there was some division of labour. We have seen how, under the old Teacher, both the Shaikh and his business associates reached a high rank, but the associate continued to look after the business whilst the Shaikh neglected it for religion.

The hierarchy did not end with the status of Shaikh. The Shaikh is validated, as it were, by a spiritual lineage, which at the same time affiliates him to other centres, *zawiyas*, which perpetuate the same lineage and which are, spiritually and physically, descended from figures higher up on the Shaikh's spiritual lineage. Such affiliation implies subservience if the other centre is somehow on a 'straighter' line from the spiritual centre — if it is the original founding centre, from which the mystical practices radiated by conversion and initiation, and/or if it is led by a (literal) descendant of the founder. We have seen our Shaikh declaring his independence from such a system, giving as his reason an innovation in mystical technique. There can be no doubt but that some advantages are connected both with being independent, and with having dependent centres. It is a striking feature of these systems of spiritual allegiance that they are territorially discontinuous and comprise units within quite different social structures — e.g. urban clubs and rural communities.

The 'totems', as it were, of these spiritual lineages, i.e. their differentiating marks, are ritual and mystical specialisms. There can be no doubt about the 'esotericism' of these organisations: there is only an apparent contradiction between the appeal of specialised initiation by strenuous practices, and the desire to maximise the number of followers. In modern terms, this is the difference between party 'militants' and mere supporters. Nevertheless, there are theoretical difficulties about the claims to privileged access and special ways to God in Islam, and the claims are made cautiously and with some ambivalence.

The loyalties and solidarity of these hierarchical but voluntary organisations are reinforced by oaths of allegiance and obedience. The manner in which this oath is taken (e.g. whether by mouth or by hand-clasp) is itself one of the ritual differentiations of orders. These oaths do not appear to be totally effective: we have seen how the Shaikh lost, and acquired, disciples, and that on occasion whole lodges went over to his allegiance *en bloc*. One should add that in traditional North Africa, affiliation to some fraternity or other, at some degree of initiation, must have covered a very large part of, if not virtually the whole, population, so that conversion to a more or less exclusive brotherhood could on the whole be only at the expense of another one. We have also seen the fissions, fusion, and ambiguities of succession, which provide the raw material for the formal rules of these associations.

The texts assembled by Mr Lings in connection with the Shaikh do not

145

explicitly tell us much about the economics of the movement, but they do tell us a certain amount. How much wealth flows along the devotional lines? Enough, evidently, to allow a successful Shaikh to dispense with other forms of income. In his late years, the Shaikh does not seem to have carried on with trade, and even in his earlier years he could afford to neglect it. The land of his *zawiya* had been bought for him by a group of devotees, and the labour supplied free by volunteers, specialists and labourers, drawn from a wide area including tribesmen from the Rif. (This is described in a report by Dr Marcel Carret, a Frenchman who attended to the Shaikh and became his friend.) There are allusions to rules made by the Shaikh for his lieutenants and representatives not to accept more in the way of entertainment on their wanderings than is absolutely necessary; allusions to the failure on the part of devotees sometimes to perceive his material needs; and to the extent to which travel is facilitated by the existence of devotees in the area which is being covered. In brief, there clearly is a flow of goods and services upwards compensating for the spiritual flow downwards; but as with regard to esotericism and special practices, the spiritual recipient of the material flow is aware of the possibility of puritan criticism and adjusts himself to it and guards against abuses.

For classificatory purposes, one could arrange the phenomena exemplified or touched on by the Shaikh's life along a number of loosely correlated spectra:

(1) Kinship/voluntary association. There are hereditary marabouts, and within some of the voluntary orders (e.g. the one from which the Shaikh seceded) there is a kind of kinship-backbone of a dominant family, descendants of the founder, surrounded by voluntary converts. At the other extreme there are lodges of a newly prominent Shaikh, recruited voluntarily.

(2) Urban/rural centres. This opposition clearly has an intimate connection with the preceding one, in so far as in rural areas both saintly personages, and their devotees, as it were come in kin parcels. (Although there are numerous inter-tribal religious festivals, etc., nevertheless these festivals and pilgrimages are attended by groups rather than by individuals. There is no room for persisting religious associations cutting across kin lines.) Similarly, urban life, with its mobility and relative lack of kin groupings, is suited to genuine associations. Nevertheless, this correlation is subject to some qualifications: as we have seen, within one associated set of centres, the Shaikh's, there is room both for village grouping and for the central urban one. This is I believe a very typical situation. Secondly, rural or even non-rural hereditary saints may found, and remain the nucleus of, a genuine order (i.e. one recruited by individual conversion).

(3) Puritanism/others. I deliberately oppose puritanism by a residual notion ('other') rather than mystics or Sufis, for the following reason: at least two things are opposed to proper, rigorous Islam. One is mysticism, with its esotericism, extra ritual richness, mediation, etc. The other is rural, tribal heterodoxy, conscious or not. The notion of a North African saint has embraced the two: it covers mystics, specialists in ecstatic techniques, *and* specialised lineages within

146

tribal structures, magicians—arbitrators. Historically, it seems obvious that North African sanctity derives from *both*. (Historically, there is also a third root — warriors in the Holy War against infidels on the coast, especially Portuguese.) As Mr Lings rightly remarks, the dancing of the Sufis is both a mystic aid and something rooted in local customs. The saints arise to satisfy (at least) two needs — the need for an emotionally richer religion, and the requirements of tribal social structure. Leaving historical origins aside, the two forms now co-exist, barely distinguished conceptually, often within the same order. But the difference is still visible: on the whole, tribesmen come to saints for political leadership rather than mystical exercises, and townsfolk for spiritual rather than political reasons.

This distinction, between the puritans and the others, correlates with the preceding ones to some extent. Only urban life provides a good base for the puritans — for their rigorism requires literacy. The obverse does not hold: for the mystics and sometimes their (literal) lineages are also found in towns.

There is also a temporal consideration which is relevant here; the puritans have gained in importance very considerably in recent times, as a result of the Salafiyya movement. And although town-based, they do make their impact on the countryside. (Consider the little war, mentioned earlier, which took place about the turn of the century, about *dancing*, in the tribal recesses of the Atlas mountains.)

It is a corollary of the puritan's objection to esotericism and mediation that they are opposed to the role of lineages and privileges (other than those based on piety and learning) in religious life, and to this extent the puritan/others dichotomy correlates with the kin-groups/associations distinction.

In so far as sanctity is partly rooted in tribal requirements (arbitrators, mediators), one should not suppose that in characteristic life-histories of saintly 'ways', movements, a tribal episode necessarily comes in the beginning. I believe that the various religious movements do have characteristic life-histories — i.e. they generally do undergo structural transformation whilst maintaining nominal continuity. For instance, a movement may begin as a missionary one, devoted to spreading knowledge of purer Islam among tribes. Success may lead it to acquire such interests within the tribes, and such importance in the running of tribal affairs, that with time the original missionary impetus and function are lost: the movement becomes a kin group and segment within the tribes. The reverse story, of course, is just as liable to occur: a mountain lineage of hereditary saints may produce one who, starting with his local prestige, succeeds in founding a genuine and territorially discontinuous order. (This has occurred to the mountain saints whom I studied, intermittently, from 1954 till 1961.) More complex variants of such life-histories are of course possible and indeed likely. One might perhaps classify them in terms of their beginnings — whether they started as purifiers and missionaries, or as purveyors of mystical specialisms, as Holy Warriors, or as specialised tribal segments. In the nature of things, success must modify them, by altering the milieu in which they operate. And this is, of course, a corollary of the point made earlier, namely that different parts of the same order may also follow differing paths of development.

It would be difficult to offer any simple generalisation about the political role, in a wider sense, of the saints. Amongst their historical antecedents, as indicated, are the leaders in wars against the infidel. As long as there were tribes engaged in such wars, in the old sense, saints were found among them as their leaders. Modern, national opposition to European colonisation, on the other hand, was inspired by the puritans rather than the saints. Abd el Krim, who stands somewhere half-way between a traditional and a modern national resistance to Europeans, opposed the orders and marabouts on his territory. (Without definitive success, evidently: for Dr Carret reports, in his account of the Shaikh with whom we were concerned, that amongst the volunteers—builders of the Shaikh's *zawiya* 'the most humble of them all' were Rif mountaineers. To urban dwellers, whose judgement Dr Carret is presumably echoing, hill tribesmen would seem 'the humblest', if not worse: this is significant, for the contempt in which tribesmen, especially Berbers, are often held by townsfolk constitutes one stumbling block in their acceptance of purer, urban Islam. The saints are less fastidious socially, as it were.)

In the modern national struggle, the saints generally found themselves on the side of the French, or at any rate objects of hostility of the nationalists. The explanations of this normally offered are: the fact that the nationalists were formed by the reform movement, the Salafiyya (though this only pushes the question one step further back); and the fact that the saints found a place under the French system, the French often worked through them and, in nationalist eyes, encouraged obscurantism in the subject population. These factors no doubt operated, but one is tempted to seek a more fundamental sociological cause. Certainly, there were more prospects for the orders and saints amongst a subject population which, as our Shaikh put it, stayed in 'the faith of their fathers and grandfathers and [followed] in the footsteps of the pious', than in a free national and modernist state which is the aspiration of the nationalists. (We saw the distaste of our Shaikh for the Young Turks and Kemalism.) But his explanation too assumes they were acting from long-term rational foresight. The real clue is, I suspect, that the orders and systems of saintly allegiance were essentially far too segmented and particularistic to serve as bases or even vehicles for national feeling. They really were spiritual tribes, not spiritual nations. It is curious to reflect that both in Europe and in North Africa there seems to be a connection between nationalism and a 'protestant', i.e. anti-saintly or anti-religious-specialism and anti-ritual-richness movement: but in Europe the connection lay through Protestantism breaking up the unity of a spiritual super-state, whereas in North Africa it was through its overcoming segmented, minuscule spiritual tribes, substates.

148

6

The unknown Apollo of Biskra: the social base of Algerian puritanism

Modern Algeria bears various stigmata of radicalism. Its struggle for national liberation was one of exceptional severity, involving untold and incalculable suffering and sacrifices. Only Vietnam can surpass it; no other ex-colonial country can equal it. After independence, the commanding heights of the economy, and even a very significant part of the rural sector, passed into one form or another of socialist ownership, including the important experiments in *auto-gestion* (workers' self-administration), in both industrial and agricultural enterprises. In foreign policy, the hostility of its government to what it holds to be remaining forms of colonialism has been serious and sustained. Internally, the regime is relatively egalitarian and rather puritanical and earnest, by any standards. The Algerians look to their own efforts for the betterment of their condition. All these traits − a heroic struggle for liberation, followed by a good deal of socialism and a general earnest radicalism − ought to have made Algeria a place of pilgrimage for the international Left. It is well known that the promised land must be *somewhere*. Algeria has as good a claim as Russia, China, Yugoslavia, Cuba, Vietnam, to be at least considered for such a role. In fact, Algeria found in Frantz Fanon the thinker or poet of this vision. Though not a native of Algeria, he identified with the Algerian national cause and died whilst serving it, and became its internationally renowned theoretician.

All this being so, it is slightly odd that Algeria should have played the role of Home of Revolution and shrine of socialist pilgrimage only to such a very small extent. Of course, there have been pilgrims − but not so very many, and their reports have been, not disappointed, but muted. Somehow or other, Algeria isn't quite it. Why not?

The main reason why an eager socialist pilgrim, however willing to have faith, will find his ardour somewhat damped, is the prominence of Islam in modern Algeria. This does not look like the home of a secular socialist millenium. Islam seems alive amongst the people *and* is endorsed by the authorities. In fact, the man in the street is most unlikely to know the name of Frantz Fanon. No doubt, there is an Avenue Fanon, perhaps there is even a Square Fanon. But it is most unlikely that there is a Boulevard Fanon, though there is, for instance, a

149

Boulevard Franklin D. Roosevelt. Fanon is hardly known in the country whose struggle he celebrated. Neither his person nor his ideas have caught the popular imagination. The pilgrim may feel that Fanon is for export only. In fairness to the Algerians, it must be said that they did not encourage the international romantic public to make a cult of him; they cannot be accused of having practised a kind of deception. But whereas virtually no man in the street in Algeria knows the name of Fanon, he can be relied upon to know the name of another thinker, Ben Badis — who, however, is totally unknown abroad, other than to specialists. Yet he was a theoretician and a social thinker, and one who *was* capable of making a profound impact on the minds of the masses of a Third World country.

During the student troubles in developed countries, you could be sure of finding the name of Fanon or at least slogans from his work amongst the graffiti on university walls. You could be just as sure that you would not find the name or ideas of Ben Badis. Why did one thinker, internationally renowned, find no echo amongst the people about whose struggle he wrote? Why did another thinker, who really did know how to reach the masses in a Third World country, fail to be noted by the international public which is so eager to hear the true voice of the oppressed?

This is the question. Before it is answered, one must return to the mildly disappointed and somewhat bewildered socialist pilgrim wondering just why this near-socialist country, which had passed through the severest of ordeals of fire, should not be what he was seeking. He will note the prominence and importance of Islam. He will be struck by the frequency of the veil, by the pervasiveness of religious themes both at governmental and popular level. In all probability, he will argue as follows: Muslim traditions have a profound hold on the minds and hearts of this people. Millennial customs and traditions are not easily broken; one cannot expect them to crumble after a first contact with the ideas of the Enlightenment. A secular modernism cannot emerge until their hold has weakened; and that is something that cannot happen easily and quickly.

Our hypothetical (not really hypothetical) socialist pilgrim will be in error: there is little that is perennial, old, rigid, immemorial, about that particular, somewhat puritanical, Muslim atmosphere which can be sensed throughout contemporary Algeria. It may, indeed, have a strong hold on the country: but that strength is not rooted in antiquity. Its authority is not that of ageless custom. The reverence it inspires is not the unreasoning respect evoked by that which was never known to be different. On the contrary: that religiosity which stands between Algeria and the socialist pilgrim's dream has specific and, above all, very *recent* roots. The kind of Islam which is, in effect, the official religion of Algeria, is not older, but on the contrary, much *younger* than the Enlightenment.

Gide's saints

Western ideological pilgrims have visited Algeria before, and not always in search of the true revolution. The liberation they sought may have been personal and moral rather than political. In literature, the most distinguished of such pilgrims, and one who not merely sought, but also found his shrine, was André Gide. He is an eloquent and an accurate witness to the true erstwhile religious condition of Algeria, a condition which needs to be known before one can understand the present religious mood.

André Gide embarked for Africa in October 1893. That was a year of famine in Algeria, but Gide does not comment on this. After some time in Tunisia, he moved on to Algeria, and the culmination of this trip, as of the novel *L'Immoraliste* which describes it, was the Algerian oasis of Biskra. As he also tells us in *Si le grain ne meurt*, which is an avowed, rather than a thinly disguised, autobiography, he was no mere tourist in search of a new land, but a pilgrim in search of self-knowledge. He found it.

my puritan education had formed me thus, gave such importance to certain things, that I could not conceive that certain issues which troubled me, did not bother humanity at large ... I was Prometheus, astonished that men could live without the eagle and without being devoured. And yet, without knowing it, I loved that eagle ... but began to haggle with him. The problem remained the same ... which problem ... ?

In the name of God, what ideal forbids me to live according to my nature?

Till now I had lived according to the morality of Christ, or at least according to a certain puritanism which had been taught me as the morality of Christ ... I had succeeded only in causing a grave disturbance in my whole being ... the demands of my flesh did not know how to dispense with the consent of my spirit.

... I came to doubt whether God requires such constraint ... whether, in this struggle in which I bifurcated myself, I need ... put the Other in the wrong ...

I saw at last that this discordant dualism might resolve itself into harmony. At once it became clear to me that this harmony should be my supreme aim ...

When in October '93 I embarked for Africa, it was ... towards this golden fleece that my drive precipitated itself.[1]

It was this Apollonian unity and harmony which Gide found in North Africa. Its discovery and attainment involved various stages. In Algeria, Gide met Oscar Wilde and Lord Alfred Douglas. In due course he naturally had a row with Bosie, who then departed. But Wilde passed on to Gide a young man in whose arms Gide was to know ecstasy five times in one night (Gide indulges in some ingenious pleading with the reader to make him accept this figure), and through whom he found his own normality, which his previous ethic had prevented him from accepting. Gide's attempt to convince the reader of the statistical, Kinsey-esque aspect of his liberation has a curious logic; if I wanted to fib, he says, I could make my fibs so plausible that you would not even suspect anything. So the fact that I need to plead at all shows that I am really telling the unadorned truth. The truth of the matter is no doubt of importance for literary history. For our purposes, however, what matters is Gide's use and invocation of the local social background of that liberation which turned him into a professional ex-puritan for the rest of his life.

Gide's road to his anti-Damascus culminates in the oasis which he describes well both in the novel and in the autobiography, and it is there that he composes the poem of his liberation, the hymn to the unknown Apollo of Biskra, whom he credits with his deliberance. Why Biskra? The beauty of the oasis played its part: 'spring touched the oasis ... I listened, I saw, I breathed, as I had never done before ... I felt my heart freed, tearful in its gratitude, melting in adoration for this unknown Apollo ... ' In part, the richness of the classical remains in the countryside around Biskra, notably to the north of it, must have suggested such associations. But Gide's acute observation of the local ritual life is also relevant.

Biskra was a centre, amongst others, of prostitution. The girls were drawn (or were supposed to be drawn) from the Ulad Nail tribe. The flocks of these Ulad Nail roamed two *holy* streets, where the holy men had their lodges, and the Ulad Nail themselves were much in evidence there. This conspicuous presence of such profanity in the holy streets at first startled Gide. Was the appellation 'holy street' an ironic inversion, an *anti-phrase*, in view of the blatant goings-on which were to be observed there? He decides, rightly, that it was not: no irony was intended. The Ulad Nail take part in many of the local ceremonies, half profane, half religious. The most venerated holy men are to be seen in their company. Local piety does not view them ill ...

No doubt all this was so. Gide's religious ethnography of Biskra in 1894 can be corroborated from many other observations of North African folk religion. Biskra is a date-growing oasis, strategically located between the nomads of the arid desert to the south and the high hills of the Aures to the north. No doubt, here as elsewhere the market was also a fair, a festival guaranteed by saint and shrine in whose honour it was held, and those who came to the fair came for the joys of life, not for their denial. The living saints or holy men who underwrote such multi-purpose pilgrimages had little incentive to be censorious, and it would have been odd indeed had they been so. Here there was a social base for Apollonian unity, such as Gide sought and found. It was typical of North Africa, and especially typical of Algeria. Ben Badis, the great Algerian reformer, and fountainhead of that new puritan religiosity which marks the Algeria of today, himself admitted and stressed that prior to his own Reform movement, no one (in Algeria) supposed that Islam could be anything other than the cult of holy men, of marabouts.[2] The saints whom Gide saw in the holy streets of Biskra were indeed typical marabouts. These personages were common throughout North Africa, but in Algeria they enjoyed a near monopoly of religious leader-ship: their natural rivals are the *ulama*, the learned theologians—jurists, who stand contrasted to the tribal thaumaturges. But these generally require an urban basis, which nineteenth-century Muslim Algeria largely lacked:

The towns had been destroyed or occupied by the French; the burghers annihilated, ruined, or had fled ... Moreover, there are various indications suggesting that the urban bourgeoisie had been numerically unimportant, economically weak, and politically null, already under the Turks.[3]

What Gide saw was evidently the essence of Algerian religious life of the time. The profanity was as typical then as it would be untypical now. This fundamental transformation is our main topic. But when Gide prayed to the unknown Apollo of Biskra, he was not merely addressing his own projections, or the local pre-Islamic ruins; he had, for his time, chosen the earthly home of his faith with discernment. It is worth quoting Gide's hymn to the unknown Apollo of Biskra at greater length.

Take me! Take all of me — I cried. I belong to you. I obey you. I surrender myself. Decree that all in me should be light; yes! Light and lightness. In vain did I struggle against you till this day. But now I recognise you. Thy will be done: I resist no more; I surrender to you. Take me.

His heart, he tells us in these passages of *Si le grain ne meurt*, was sobbing with gratitude, dissolving in adoration of this unknown Apollo. The hymn certainly conveys such a state of mind.

The literary antecedents and consequences of this passage are curious. One might suppose, especially in the light of 'Thy will be done', that we have here a lapsed puritan's inversion of the Lord's Prayer. Not so. A perusal of d'Holbach's *System of Nature*, that compendium of the wisdom of the French Enlightenment, makes clear that we have here an eroticisation of d'Holbach's hymn to Nature:

Be happy, seek happiness, without fear. Do not resist my law. Vain are the hopes of religion. Free yourself from the yoke of religion, my proud rival. In my empire there is freedom ... Make no mistake; I punish, more surely than the gods, all crimes of the earth. The evildoer may escape the laws of man, but not mine.[4]

This plainly is the call to which Gide is responding so warmly. There can be no doubt about the literary echo. He eagerly reports how much he had already been punished for striving to resist his own nature, and hence Nature. But the aptness of his choice of locality for the incarnation of his Apollo, is confirmed not merely by the social historians of nineteenth-century Algeria, but also by much later ethnography of North Africa. In 1955 there appeared a volume by Jacques Berque, now professor at the Collège de France, which is the most intimate and detailed account we possess of the inner structure and life of a North African tribe.[5] On page 314, we find an account of a group of marabouts or saints, rather like those Gide saw in Biskra half a century earlier:

These saints ... help us to understand the specific traits of the style of life resulting from a 'saintly origin'. Their prestige is unconnected with any idea of merit, any moral evaluation ... [they have] fewer inhibitions. The saint is he who lives fully. One allows nature to speak through him, even in the form of unbridled desires ... One seeks through him a kind of complicity with heaven.

153

There can be no doubt but that Gide and Berque saw the same phenomenon, *and* that the language in which they noted it was drawn from the same pool of ideas and expressions. Nature − *qui est donc cette dame?* − who issued her edicts to d'Holbach, and to whom Gide later surrendered so fulsomely and voluptuously, now speaks through the *igurramen* (Berber holy men) of a lost valley in the western High Atlas, and is overheard by Monsieur le Controlleur Civil Berque. The manifest continuity of the literary tradition which records her activities does not make the perception itself any less accurate. But if one had any doubt that Berque is here echoing Gide, the doubts would be silenced by the sentences following the previous ones: 'This saint can turn his life into a kind of carnival. Paraphrasing Nietzsche, one may say of him that he can be the warmest of all warm beasts.'

The allusion is clear: Gide's pilgrimage half a century earlier was avowedly under the influence of Nietzsche. Thus North African religious life was an appropriate place for those seeking Apollonian harmony and acceptance of nature. But today, socialist pilgrims to Algeria find themselves disappointed, not through undue Apollonism, but on the contrary by an excessive denial of it, by a puritanism not so very unlike that which Gide then fled from in Europe. How did this change come about?

Ben Badis and the reform movement

The religious reform of Algeria was the work of the Reform movement. To say this is not enough: it is more important to know why the soil was so ready for this seed, than to know just who did the sowing when and how, and why this seed prospered. Nevertheless, it is as well to begin with the well-documented story of the sowing. The Reform movement in Algeria has found, in Ali Merad, a brilliant and painstaking historian.[6]

Merad places the effective beginning of the Reform movement in 1903, with the visit to Algeria in September of that year of the influential Egyptian reformer, Muhammad Abduh. So, ten years almost to a month since a European pilgrim had gone to seek Apollo in North Africa, an Oriental visitor came whose destiny it was to repudiate him. Shortly after this date, Merad finds the first signs of Reformist ideas. Already in 1904, a small volume appears whose very title conveys the slogan − the need to reform. The followers of the new trend notably included the teachers in the official religious schools, which trained interpreters and officials of state-controlled Muslim institutions. By 1913, a weekly journal begins to appear, and the editorial of its first issue declares it to be apolitical, but concerned with reform, with the combating of Satanic innovations. If this hostility to corruption and innovation includes opposition to the gallicisation of Algerian youth, it includes, with at least as much emphasis, violent opposition to the marabouts, to those holy men whose lack of fastidiousness in the holy streets of Biskra so agreeably surprised Gide, and whose willingness to allow nature to speak through them, even in the form of unbridled desires, was noted half a century later by Berque in the Atlas. It was *this* struggle above all, a fight against what to the proponents of Reform appeared as rural deformations and superstitions, which gave the movement its special character.

As Merad stresses,[7] the conflict between traditional and reformed Islam was not restricted to Algeria: on the contrary, the wave of Reform had reached Algeria rather late. But 'probably in no other country did the conflict attain the dimensions which it assumed in Algeria, in consequence of the specific social, cultural and political conditions of that country' (Merad). This is indeed the crucial fact, and those conditions deserve to be singled out. Very roughly: probably no Muslim country was more completely dependent on the rural holy men than was nineteenth-century Algeria, and it is doubtful whether any other country has swung more violently against them. It is the mechanisms of this swing of the pendulum which are fascinating.[8]

The account of the development of the Reform movement so far takes us to the First World War. War against Turkey and hence against the Khalifate naturally constituted a moral problem, and the French authorities obtained declarations of loyalty from influential Muslims. Ali Merad sees in this a part of the explanation of the decline of the marabouts. Merad observes that the francophilia of the marabouts did not shock anyone, but that the declaration of hostility to Turkey was seen as moral treason. At a moment when France and Turkey were at war, this would seem an oversubtle distinction. But above all, the simple 'reactive' theory is inadequate. No doubt, all occupants of recognised social positions, maraboutic leaders and others, had no choice but to be associated with the colonial state. When nationalist criteria came to be applied, retrospectively this could be held against them. But there were more immediate, concrete reasons why the current began to flow against the holy men and in favour of the reformers.

The man who emerged as undisputed leader of Reform, and whose spirit moulded that of modern Algeria, was Ben Badis, a member of a great Constantine bourgeois family. (At the moment, one of the larger churches in central Algiers is about to be transformed into the Ben Badis mosque.) But amongst his lieutenants, the most turbulent, aggressive and probably the most influential was Tayyib Uqbi. He often acted autonomously, and had started his own preaching of Reform in Biskra in 1920, five years prior to joining Ben Badis's movement. He was, as Merad says, the spearhead of the movement, and was in the end chosen to represent it in the capital, Algiers itself, whilst the leader remained in the relatively provincial city of Constantine. (But in consequence, Constantine is now a kind of religious capital of Algeria, with a Muslim university alongside an ordinary one. The technocracy/puritanism dualism of Algeria is symbolised by the relationship of Algiers to Constantine.)

By an irony of history, the centre and base of Uqbi's mission was that very oasis of Biskra which had been, for Gide, the symbol of the Apollonianism of

155

North Africa.[9] Uqbi's name derives from a village near Biskra, whose shrine commemorates Sidi Uqba, one of the early Muslim conquerors of the Maghreb. Uqbi was born in 1888, and spent much of his childhood in the Hejaz, and came under the influence of Wahabism, one of the last of the, as it were, pre-modern waves of Muslim reformism and fundamentalism, and the basis of the Saudi Arabian state. He at any rate did not view the goings-on of the holy streets of Biskra with the benevolence of Gide. Quite the reverse.

Uqbi and Ben Badis were in full agreement concerning the basic outlines of the reforming doctrine of the *salafiyya*: the struggle against blameworthy innovations, and mainly maraboutic innovations . . .
. . . the sheikh Uqbi was the least prudent of the Algerian reformist leaders . . . he could not find a modus vivendi with the official representatives of Muslim worship in Algiers . . .
. . . Uqbi . . . spoke of the partizans of maraboutism in an intransigent manner, as one convinced that right was on his side, and sure of his victory.
. . . for him . . . all who lacked the reformist . . . faith were in error, and should renounce their beliefs as soon as 'notified' by the reformers. Those who . . . persist in their 'error', should be treated as infamous tools of Satan. The greatest part of Uqbi's preaching consists of bitter invectives against the opponents of reformism (i.e. marabouts and supporters of official Muslim clergy) . . .
. . . he made himself noted by an anti-maraboutic zeal virtually unequalled in Algeria between the wars. His powerful diatribes against the marabouts and their supporters went beyond religious refutation . . .
. . . the so-called saints [he taught] are not superior beings holding all in their power . . . they should not be invoked . . . they themselves are incapable of defending themselves against the petty miseries of daily life . . . he denounces those who build . . . 'temples of error and ignorance' to the glory of saints. He pronounces his malediction against marabouts, and declares himself their opponent whether one takes them 'individually or in general' . . .
'I invoke no-one but God . . . Invoke whom you will, I shall never surrender to your idolatry . . . I have never performed the circumambulation [of a shrine] . . . I place no tissue on sepulchres . . . nor make pilgrimages to tombs . . . nor propitiatory sacrifices . . . I do not invoke the dead . . . that constitutes *shirk* . . .'[10]

One wonders whether Knox's Scotland or Calvin's Geneva would surpass this fervour. The centre of his attack is indeed the heresy of *shirk*. Ali Merad translates this as 'associationism'. What is meant by this term here is not the psychological doctrines of David Hume, but the view that saints and the dead and other beings or objects can through association with God partake of His sacredness — that the divine is diffused or refracted in the world by some kind of association.

This firebrand from Biskra claimed to be apolitical. His fury was directed against corruption of and within the faith: but the movement of reform should, he claimed, eschew politics. How this could be so in logic, given the enormous social content of Islam, we need not ask. Ali Merad observes that 'Uqbi's prudence consisted of formulae without meaning'.[11] He also tells us that it is 'relatively easy to establish a connection between the expansion of reformism in Algeria and the progress of nationalist ideas among the Muslim masses'.[12] The subjective sincerity of Uqbi's apolitism, in those difficult conditions, would be difficult to investigate now. But there can be little doubt about the powerful and inflammatory nature of his pronouncements and activity, and they did indeed have dramatic consequences.

In 1936, an official, so-to-speak collaborationist Muslim cleric was murdered, after being ferociously denounced as a traitor in a journal under Uqbi's influence. 'Henceforth, no traitor will remain unpunished', the journal had declared. Uqbi was accused of incitement to murder, and arrested. Though ultimately released, neither his morale nor his relations with the fellow-reformers ever recovered from this, and he died, an embittered and relatively isolated man, in 1960, two years prior to Algerian independence. Yet the uncompromising fervour and rigour of this Saharan John Knox had evidently done as much for the transformation of Algeria as the more subtle, moderate preaching of the grand bourgeois, Ben Badis. Biskra now spoke with a voice quite other than that of 1894.

The most interesting question about the Algerian Reform movement concerns the amazing *speed* of its impact. Ali Merad tells us:

the Algerian reform movement became, in the space of a mere ten years, a veritable religious party ... it organized an effective propaganda machine, and ended by forcing itself on the attention of the whole country (and of the Administration), as a movement endowed with a conquering dynamism.[13]

Or again, we read:

By 1931, the province of Constantine in its totality was for practical purposes won over to reformism. Kabylia was in the process of conversion to the Badisian doctrine ...[14]

As Merad also observes, such rapid success would not have been possible at *any* time. The soil was ripe. This seed at any rate was not due to perish, but to prosper.

It is probable that, had it come sooner, the Badisian propaganda would not have aroused any enthusiasm amongst the Arabs and Kabyles of Algeria.[15]

The precise starting point of the change of religious mood is perhaps in doubt. The historian Ch.-R. Ageron quotes the ethnographer Doutté, as saying in 1899 that 'maraboutism is the real religion of the natives of Africa Minor'; but Ageron goes on to express certain reservations about the uses to which this view was put.

That conception when formulated without any nuance ... had an incontestable polemical value: it denied the depth of Islamization, and justified or encouraged certain assimilationist or anticlerical tendencies. Insisting on pre-Islamic survivals, it attached itself to the Berber myth which it helped to revive.[16]

In *that* sense, the insistence on the pervasiveness of maraboutism does indeed contain a grave error: the cult of saints is not in the very least a sign of the weakness of Islamic identification. The saint-worship, on the contrary, is a means of achieving that very Muslim identification, on the part of rustic populations who cannot so easily approach the faith through the Book, and prefer that the Word should be flesh. But if one sees it as a rival though fervent form of Islam, rather than as a near-negation of it, then Doutté's observation would seem prefectly valid.

One might add that there also existed what might be called a traditional anti-maraboutic sentiment, noted by European observers of Algeria in the first half of the nineteenth century, such as General Daumas, who was French consul at the court of Amir Abd el Kader, or Charles Henry Churchill, Abd el Kader's English contemporary and biographer. Daumas quotes a significant saying, 'There is always a snake in a *zawiya*' (maraboutic lodge) — and Churchill reports similar feelings. But these were the sentiments of secular warrior chiefs, competing for tribal leadership with the marabouts, but who themselves expressed, and indeed owed their position to, an ethic of conspicuous consumption centred on themes such as raiding, falconry, etc. The presence of irony in the reverence has also been noted in the attitude to marabouts in the Moroccan Atlas. But this kind of partial hostility or ambivalence is quite different from the puritanical and urban *rejection* of marabouts, which was to come in with the Reformers.

Anyway, it is odd that members of a Catholic nation should have held saint-worship to be a sign of lukewarmness. Ageron expresses doubts about the progress of anti-maraboutic purification for the period up to 1914: 'Muslim Algerians . . . remained as faithful to their brotherhoods and indulged with the same good conscience and even enthusiasm the cult of their saints, as according to all indications they did prior to 1830.'[17] For the period prior to the First World War, no doubt this is true, except perhaps for some very small minority. Those who seek the start of this movement earlier, admit that its beginnings were numerically small: 'the emergence of a full-fledged reforming movement in the 1920s needs also to be connected to the sprouting of the first seeds of Islamic reformism among a small number of intellectuals in Algiers in the 1890s.'[18]

Given these small beginnings, whatever their starting date, and the exiguity of their impact prior to 1914, the rapidity of the impact of Reformism from the 1920s onwards is all the more remarkable.

A few decades earlier, Islam was co-extensive with maraboutism, according to Ben Badis himself as well as Doutté. Careful investigation may yet succeed in locating some orthodox or reforming elements here and there during that early period. However, it will need to be painstaking research: what was in evidence everywhere were the marabouts. Today the situation is reversed. No doubt research can easily locate survivals, or even new forms of maraboutism. Rumour has it that they are active.[19] In April 1974 I visited a hilltop saintly lodge overlooking what is now the bustling industrial town of Tizi Ouzou in Kabylia. The lodge claimed to be providing continuous round-the-clock therapeutic services for pilgrims, by means of a shift-work system operated by the four brothers who were the local inheritors of *baraka*. But these activities are much diminished. Why was the reversal so great? Why was the soil so very ready, so very receptive to the new message?

The two styles of religious life*

The basic answer I believe to be this: within Muslim societies, there is a permanent, if sometimes latent, tension and opposition between two styles of religious life. On the one hand, there is a puritanical, unitarian, individualist, scripturalist ideal of a single deity, which has disclosed its final message in a definitive Revelation available to all who care to read it. This version spurns mediation, and neither requires nor formally allows clergy: it presupposes only a literate class of scribes who act as guardians and exegetes of the revelation. This is an open class, accessible through learning, and not a caste or a priesthood. In contrast to this vision, there is the 'associationist' ideal, to use Merad's term, which allows mediation, propitiation, ritual and devotional excess, and religious hierarchy.

A community or an individual does not choose between these two visions simply through some idiosyncratic or arbitrary caprice, a kind of religious penchant. Each of these styles serves different social needs, and the urgency of one need or another depends on social circumstances. This is not, of course, an all-or-nothing matter: there are prolonged periods when the two styles co-exist peacefully and indeed inter-penetrate each other. At other times, they and the groups which stand to profit from them or have their position or life-styles ratified by them come into conflict; and there are times when the pendulum not merely swings, but swings violently. Algeria in this century was such a case. Under the impact of modernity, the pendulum swings more violently and becomes unhinged. But the pendulum does not swing for purely intellectual reasons: the erstwhile clients of the holy streets of Biskra did not become eager listeners to the preaching of Uqbi simply because they found his logic or his invective irresistible. Something had happened to Algerian society within this period to cause one style, which had been almost totally dominant, to lose its appeal, and be replaced by another which had been, not absent, but latent.

By coincidence, we happen to possess an account of the pre-modern and pre-Reformist social structure of that very village near Biskra which was the origin of the firebrand Uqbi and which gave him his name.[20] The population of the oasis consisted of a series of groups or clans, with no belief in a shared common ancestor, but led by the one clan of sharifian status (i.e. supposedly descended from the Prophet). According to legend, the first local representative and general

---

*This subject has been more fully dealt with in chapter 1.

ancestor of this dominant holy group made it his condition, prior to accepting leadership of the oasis, that each of the other groupings should link itself to him by providing him with a bride. (His brother and predecessor, who had failed to take such a precaution, had found his death at the hands of the very people who had previously invited him to govern them ...) This legend and the shared veneration of the shrine of Sidi Uqba gave the oasis the charter of its unity. The pilgrims to the shrine provided it with contacts and links as far afield as the city of Tunis.

All this is altogether typical of traditional North African life. Whatever the theological errors of *shirk*, an attack either on the shrine or on the holy lineage of the oasis would in effect have been attacks on the preconditions of its political and economic existence, on its mechanisms for the maintenance of order and its trade relations. In such circumstances, Tayyib Uqbi, however vehement and eloquent, would have wasted his breath in trying to persuade the inhabitants of his own native village to change their customs. But Captain Simon saw the oasis in the first years of this century. By the 1920s and 1930s, one may suppose that a centralised administration, labour migration, trade by lorry, not pilgrim, had made both the hereditary religious hierarchy and the shrine far less important to the inhabitants of the oasis. Now they could listen to the preachings of Uqbi.

The major and obvious function of maraboutism is to serve illiterate tribal populations in anarchic conditions. Providing mediation in cases of feud, organising festivals which are at the same time markets, guaranteeing frontiers, witnessing collective oaths, offering a personal incarnation of the sacred for tribesmen who have neither access to nor a penchant for learning – these are but some of the services which marabouts performed, and performed well. This applies equally to isolated holy lineages, and to those religious leaders linked by a complex and long-distance organisation which are called religious 'orders' or 'fraternities'.

The distinction between religious orders and holy lineages is a loose one. Religious orders are led by holy lineages, and in turn successful holy lineages may expand their following into a *tariqa*, an order. An order is a saint with an organised following; every saint is a potential order. If his offspring and/or his followers multiply, he, or rather they, will become an order. The reason why in Algeria this form of religion was specially dominant seems obvious: urban life had been relatively weak even prior to the French conquest, and had been destroyed or disrupted by the French. The surviving tribesmen needed saints, and the saints had few ideological rivals.[21] Sufism is the opium of the tribesmen, reformism of the townsmen.

But the situation changed. The colonial state, unlike the previous Turkish regency of Algiers, was not weak. It maintained effective order over its territory. The Pax Gallica eroded tribal organisation, and in due course there was also much migration to the towns and to France. Where once there had been tribesmen, there was now a proletariat and, in some measure, a petite bourgeoisie.

160

The unknown Apollo of Biskra

Under these circumstances, the marabouts, like nobles of the *ancien régime*, were losing their functions, but not their privileges. Worse still, such privileges as they did retain were now endorsed by the colonial power which saw in them the natural or the only intermediaries with the indigenous population. Under such circumstances, they became most vulnerable to the kind of propaganda which the Reform movement mounted against them.

A tribesman from the Aures mountains, come to Biskra or Sidi Uqba to sell a sheep and buy dates, combining the visit to the market with a participation in profane rituals in holy street, and having his trip both enlivened and made safer by the marabout — such a tribesman can be relied upon to remain deaf to any propaganda accusing the saint of *shirk*, of associationism. A religion without associationism, without living local incarnations of the holy, would be useless to him. The more associationism the better.

The situation is quite different for a detribalised townsman, or at any rate one possessed of a minimum of economic standing. A marabout is unlikely to fulfil any important function in *his* life: but what remains visible and what now becomes offensive is the marabouts' perks and privileges, their underwriting by an alien ruler, and those scandalous goings-on in holy street, which, the townsman notes, are viewed by the alien ruler with derision even or especially when he exploits them for political purposes. (Gide's enthusiasm for them was a bit eccentric and not altogether free from a tacitly patronising attitude: it is only because Gide has internalised puritanism only too well that he can enthuse about the supposed Apollonianism of a pack of Saharan dervishes.) Moreover, the marabouts are local and segmented; they cannot be carriers, let alone creators, of a national consciousness.

The Reform movement, on the other hand, can be just that. Its repudiation of 'associationism', of intermediaries, is the repudiation of the local form of the sacred. Its preaching of 'pure' Islam is in effect the preaching of an Islam equally accessible to all literate Muslims, the preaching of something which all Muslims generically share, but which also distinguishes them from the non-Muslim ruler. This is highly relevant when a nascent nationalism can hope to recruit all Muslims, and no others, in a given territory. The Reform movement does not need to be overtly nationalist in order to be a form of proto-nationalism; its proclaimed apolitism could be subjectively sincere, or opportunist — it does not matter. At the same time, the fact that its main activity was the battle with rural superstition made it that much harder for the authorities to proscribe it.[22]

The Reform movement not only preaches something which all Muslims share and which distinguishes them from others, but also something in which they can take legitimate pride. A purified, theological, scholarly Islam is not something manifestly inferior, or indeed inferior at all, to other world religions: it is only those goings-on in holy street which make one feel ashamed. It is all very well for a European romantic, sure of his civilised status, to idealise those excesses and write hymns to them: he can take a strong, orderly society for granted, and

161

pride himself on his own rebellion against its puritanism. But a Muslim artisan or shopkeeper, seeking identity and dignity, will hardly find them in prostrations before Apollo. On the contrary, puritanism spurned by Gide will seem to him a desirable distinguishing mark of urban civilisation, separating him from the rural life he has left behind. Ali Merad writes:

the creation of a petite bourgeoisie converted to European civilization, diminished the field in which maraboutism could operate. That petite bourgeoisie (teachers, civil servants in central or local government, entrepreneurs) was almost cut off from the people ... Moreover, the use of its leisure (and no doubt its concern with respectability) prevented it from taking part in collective religious and folklore displays.[23]

Not for them, clearly, that *mélange* of the profane and the sacred which warmed the heart of the pilgrim of 1893.

The interesting thing is, however, that these sacred-and-profane activities are alien not merely to a petite bourgeoisie attracted by European civilisation, whom Merad notes in this passage, but at least equally so to a petite bourgeoisie which aspires not to European urban life, but simply to traditional Muslim or Arab town styles. An urban stratum of this kind has a double reason for being attracted by reformism: not only does its own rigour distinguish it from the non-respectable excesses of the rustic tribesman, it at the same time also legitimates such a stratum against those who aspire to or possess privileges in virtue of gallicisation, westernisation. Reformism is a double-edged sword; it defends pure Islam against the internal corruption of marabouts and against the external corruption of westernisation. The first theme was initially the most prominent, but the other was always clearly understood, and in due course came to be very important.

We possess some interesting evidence on this social boundary between the villages and the small towns — a social frontier which is perhaps the most important dividing line in North African social life. Consider, for instance, a recent book by Dr Vanessa Maher,[24] in which the author examines both a small market town and nearby villages:

Everyone [in the village] goes to the *hedra* [ecstatic dancing under maraboutic patronage] except the Shurfa [descendants of Muhammed] who say that it is a scene of licence ... Although cultivated Arabs and Arabised Berbers come to [the village] from [the town], they regard the proceedings with explicit contempt and call them barbarous.

The author also observes that

the *hedra* ... can be viewed as an assertion of the validity of Berber cultural forms, which wherever they come into contact with Arab values, are demeaned ...

She describes how well the *hedra* is both profane and sacred, involving as it does deliberate and conscious sacrilege; all this is presumably similar to what Gide witnessed in Biskra some eighty years earlier. The only thing one need not accept here is the reference to Berbers: in Dr Maher's region, townsmen happen to be Arab and villagers Berber, and therefore it seems that the affirmation of rural values is an affirmation of Berber cultural forms. But the Berberism is irrelevant: Arab tribesmen, or for that matter arabophone townsmen below a certain socio-cultural level, will also gladly participate in these activities, as her own material suggests. Whether or not you revere morally ambiguous saints and participate in profane-sacred festivals relates to the most important social boundary in North Africa, between the life-styles of the petty bourgeoisie and of the countryside, which she does much to illuminate: but it is not, other than incidentally, an ethnic or linguistic boundary. Dr Maher's thesis is important in showing how very much hinges on this boundary: attitudes to work, kin, women, government, as well as to religious style, depend on whether you live in a tribally articulated rural community, or a more atomic and mobile urban one. Roughly speaking there are two dominant life-styles. In one of them, your womenfolk work in the fields, are not secluded or veiled, bride-price is low or nominal, brides are in effect exchanged between social groups, social groups are very well defined and visible, religious life is centred on public festivals in which women play a very definite part, and which reaffirm the identity and boundary of groups, and which are ecstatic or at least expressive rather than scripturalist. By contrast, there is on the other hand a more urban style, based on commercial or bureaucratic employment, in which womenfolk are secluded, and veiled when they come out, where the marriage market is (for the family if not the bride) relatively freer and less kin-constrained, where bride price is high and indeed the object of inflationary pressure, where groups are more ambiguous and ill-defined, and where ritual life is more sober, rule-bound, scripturalist, individualistic, anonymous and has a much more marked tendency to exclude women.[25] The former style of course produces much less docile subjects of the state than the latter.

Members of rural society seeking prestige or positions of authority will of course emulate this or that aspect of the urban style, to the best of their understanding of it, and, on occasion, at some economic cost. Some urban dwellers at the bottom of the social scale, with no prestige to lose and some economic advantage to gain, may specialise in catering to the wilder religious needs of the less fastidious or more deprived or badly stricken townsfolk.[26] The central fact of modern North African history, however, is the shift from the rural to the urban style, in numbers *and* in authority. The Reform movement reflects this shift.

The revulsion of the townsman for the rustic and the tribesman is of course old and antedates the Reform movement: reformism merely provides it with a theological sanction and a programme. An interesting expression of it is a proclamation of the Muslim burghers and scholars of the city of Constantine in 1871, urging firmness on the French authorities when dealing with rebellious tribes: 'the bedouin will not abandon their traditional conduct and the traditions of their mountains, unless struck by a severe and energetic repression which will fill them with fear and terror'.[27] As Ageron observes in his admirable study, this proclamation was no doubt officially inspired: nonetheless, the form of words and ideas chosen to express bourgeois loyalty to authority in a critical situation is deeply symptomatic. It was signed amongst others by two members of the Ben Badis family. There is a consistency rather than a contradiction in the family attitude: when, some five decades later, *the* great Ben Badis himself was to preach reform, its central aim was, precisely, to persuade those tribesmen to give up the traditional conduct and habits of their mountains.

Dr Maher's book gives us a synchronic snapshot of the religious difference between villagers and townsfolk in recent Morocco; but the same contrast may also be found diachronically within a small town, during the period of reformist expansion. Even if urban life and respectability have an inherent and perennial tendency towards the 'purer' type of Islam, during periods when urban styles, especially in Algeria, constituted a submerged authority, this tendency remained latent, and even small towns organised their religious life around saints and orders. Gilbert Grandguillaume's sociological history of a small Western Algerian town, Nedroma, describes the transformation admirably.

In Nedroma the presence [of religious orders] was very ancient. The town was even celebrated for their number and vitality . . . Today, only one has maintained itself . . .

In the 1900s, the orders controlled the totality of religious life . . .

As from the 1930s, the orders began to mute their dissensions so as to make common cause against a shared enemy: the Association of Ulama [reformist theologians] . . . whose aim is the purification of Islam from blameworthy innovations, the cult of saints, the basis of the orders . . .

During the period of maraboutism, the model [of Muslim behaviour] included membership of an order, and assiduity in its practices. He who did not take part was held to be that much 'less Muslim'.[28]

Western Algeria was conquered by reformism later than other regions, and its firm implantation in the town of Nedroma appears to date only from 1949. And the victory is not yet complete: as late as 1969, a progressive anti-saint Algerian journal needs to fulminate as follows against the hysteria manifested at the interment of a saint:

It is impossible to imagine the hysterical mob opposing the inhumation of the deceased, to the great satisfaction of . . . his effective successor . . . How can they claim the appelation of Muslim, those primaeval, obscurantist beings, who are maintained in a state of ignorance . . .

What is one to think of those ignorant beings . . . offering, this one his only sheep, this one a goat, . . . flour, bread, sugar, even potatoes! The ignorance and obscurantism in which they have been maintained for decades constitute extenuating circumstances.

But what is beyond all comprehension . . . is when one also sees in this mob public prosecutors X., Y., Z., and central commissars of A. and B., and a chief of police . . .[29]

Monsieur Grandguillaume does not think that these officials should be so severely reprobated, evidently. He observes:

the personality of Sidi Ali [the deceased saint] was above . . . accusations of cupidity. He enjoyed a great reputation and the presence at his funeral of official personalities is not to be interpreted as an approbation of the system of saintly centres . . .[30]

One is glad to hear that officialdom in Western Algeria is sound, and on the side of purity not profanity. All the same, the scenes so well described and analysed by M. Grandguillaume contain indications that the victory of reformism, though impressive in its extent and speed, is not yet total.[31] But the important thing to note is the shift in the central, dominant ideal: in 1900, to be a full Muslim involved participation in the saintly rituals. Some five decades later, the dominant view is that such participation deprives one of the right to make such a claim.

The rejection of the ritual style

What is the explanation of this profound and dramatic shift (whether or not it is total)? The central explanation is that in this period, an overwhelming proportion of North Africans found themselves propelled from the style of life favouring local festivals, saint cults and so forth, to one which rejects them. Maher's book makes plain that the one kind of ritual style goes together with a whole syndrome, involving a type of occupation, location, the nature and significance of kin relations, mobility, pervasiveness of central authority. Within this period, tribal structures were either eroded (as in much of Algeria) or weakened (as in Morocco). The erstwhile tribesman was subjected to this impact, whether he remained in his region, or moved permanently to a town, or took part in temporary labour migration.

When the old style of religion predominated, and the countrymen who were its primary clientele were in a majority, it pervaded even the towns. In large centres, saints and orders peacefully co-existed with a scholarly bourgeoisie.[32] In smaller towns, as Grandguillaume's material shows, they may even have been virtually exclusive. At that stage, as he observes, 'Islam assumed, through the religious orders, a feudal organization within the framework of a commercial society.'[33] By 'feudal', what is evidently meant here is that the orders were hierarchically organised, with a pyramid of followers, each lower level committing its allegiance to its superiors and to their superiors in turn. But, he adds, 'The multiplicity [of the orders] in Nedroma reflects the egalitarian mentality of the old city, which apparently did not allow, in the pre-colonial period, the domination by any one group . . . ' Certainly: the world of the saints and of orders had been both hierarchical and also fragmented, pluralistic. The free competition between a large multiplicity of saints made domination by any one of them difficult. They both compensated for the absence of a strong central power, and militated against its emergence. But the imposition of a strong and well-centralised authority in due course undermined them in turn.

The shift from an Apollonian, pluralistic religion led by a (theoretically closed) stratum of saints, to a puritanical, mediationless faith led by a (theoretically open) class of scholars, is common throughout North Africa, even if there are marked local differences in the timing and completeness of the transition. But this transformation is particularly striking in Algeria. Why?

In religion, the reformers *replaced* the marabouts. But in other spheres — notably social leadership — their strength lay not so much in replacing a group that had lost its role and appeal, but in helping to *fill a vacuum*. Tunisia and Morocco, by contrast, were Protectorates, and benefited from a continuity in institutions and elites. Leadership was always available. But in Algeria the feebleness of the prior urban tradition, the weak and alien (Turkish) nature of pre-colonial government, the very much greater social disruption brought about by conquest and colonisation and by the form it took, all meant that the country was almost leaderless. Such major Muslim landowners and maraboutic leaders as remained were, by the end of the nineteenth century, tied to the old colonial authority. The pulverised Muslim lower strata, whether rural or urban, were constrained to look to religion for leadership above all by a lack of alternative, much as Maltese or Irish peasants were predisposed to look to their Church for lack of any other institution. The saints were, in modern conditions, useless: they were essentially local or particularistic. A shrine is tied to a locality, to specific patterns of pilgrimage; a saint is linked to the performance of this or that service, the curing of this or that ailment. Their magic has a functional and territorial specificity. For a tribal society well-articulated in terms of clans and segments, they were for this very reason admirably suited; and they were also well adapted for mediation between such tribesmen and the towns. But for an atomised, mobile, uprooted population, their usefulness was limited, at best. As a banner under which a whole large population, a latent nation, is to recognise its own identity, they were useless, both through their fragmentation and through the fact that the practices they stood for — ecstasies, rural festivals, the mingling of the profane and the sacred — are scarcely usable as a modern ideology or as a basis for national pride. By contrast, the purified, literacy-stressing Islam of the reformers was very well suited for this end.

Thus one need not even invoke the fact that the marabouts had compromised themselves with the colonial power. So had the reformers, who also declared their loyalty to the established order. For instance, Ben Badis wrote in his journal *Shihab* in August 1932 that his 'readers have no desire but to enjoy all the rights of the children of the tricolour whilst also assuming their duties . . . generous

France cannot but give them some day, which cannot be far, all the rights enjoyed by the French'.[34] Ali Merad in the work cited tries to solve this difficulty in part by stressing that the marabouts went further, and over and above declaring their loyalty to France, actually also condemned Turkey, then a Muslim power. But this is to attribute far too much weight to a logical nuance, a scholastic distinction. The real explanation lies not in the relatively accidental, situationally imposed and forgivable political alignment in this or that situation, but in the deeper, more permanent social changes, and the type of identification required and provided. What was also of importance was that the colonial power could not easily proscribe the Reform movement (though it did occasionally hamper it), just because it was primarily religious. (Overt political activity was both more difficult, and even more prey to internal dissension.) An official circular by the Secretary General of Algiers Prefecture, dated 16 February 1933, says:

Most heads of orders and main saintly families venerated by the natives are sincerely converted to our domination and see themselves threatened by a grouping which, by an active and skilful propaganda, recruits new adherents daily . . . It is not possible to tolerate a propaganda which, under the mask of Islamic culture and religious reforms, hides a pernicious orientation . . .

Hence I ask you to survey with the most careful attention meetings and lectures organized by the Association of Muslim Scholars presided over by Ben Badis whose accredited spokesman is . . . Tayyib Uqbi . . .[35]

All the same, it is hard to proscribe altogether a movement whose sincere primary concern is with the purity of faith and ritual. Colonial officials had few doubts about the justice of the reformers' case against the saints. Ali Merad quotes the comments of one of them on the marabouts:

Those great impostors who falsify religion, who enrich themselves by exploiting the naive credulity of the masses and who everywhere resist doggedly the new spirit of virtue and tolerance which will fatally erode their influence and fortune.

Thus wrote a French official destined to play an important part in Algerian developments.[36] The new spirit was certainly destined to sap their fortune and influence and, in a puritanical sense, it was also to be the champion of virtue. Whether it was also destined to be tolerant is less clear.

After Independence

When Independence came, Reformist Islam was virtually the only usable ideology deeply implanted and intelligible inside the country. During the revolutionary struggle, when there was still a possibility of some kind of compromise, and of the retention by free Algeria of its large non-Muslim minority, an element of secularism was at least discernible in the nationalist doctrine. The future Algerian republic was to be not merely democratic and popular, but also secular. With the virtually total departure of the non-Muslims, this word disappeared, though Algeria did not go as far as some newly independent Muslim countries and actually incorporate Islam in its name. Reformist Islam is there as a kind of established religion. During the struggle, a socialist element had also been present — inevitably so, given the historic period in which it took place. The abandonment of large-scale enterprises by the departing Europeans, and the importance of oil and natural gas, meant that a measure of socialism also became a reality, and not just a word, in post-Independence Algeria: the new oil, gas, and the large abandoned enterprises and estates could hardly be handed over to individuals. In a variety of forms, some of them experimental, they were socialised.

The socio-economic structure of post-Independence Algeria provides a further basis for the role of reformism, over and above the ideological monopoly which it came close to enjoying during the later parts of the colonial period. The phrase 'industrial-military complex' has a quite special applicability to Algeria. The really large enterprises are nationalised. The state machine is continuous with them, and has a military tone, having been forged in a bitter and prolonged liberation struggle, and having received its present form after the military coup of 1965. The administrators of the nationalised large enterprises and the state bureaucracy form one relatively continuous caste. They are selected by participation in the national struggle and/or by technical competence. They have a tendency to speak French to each other. Their technical competence was acquired through the French medium.

They have power but not, in the long run, any clear legitimacy. Participation in national liberation cannot be invoked for ever, and as time passes, it can hardly apply to the younger recruits. Grandguillaume is interesting about the new ideals:

During the first years of independence, the central authority attempted to impose 'socialist Islam' as the 'religious model'. In general, this attempt soon ended in failure. In the particular case of Nedroma, the urban population, traditionally attached to private property, could hardly admit such a model . . .

This model not being accepted, what other model is accepted? In Nedroma, it would seem to be defined as opposition to an excessively speedy westernization . . .[37]

Much of the ruling class of occupants of posts in the state bureaucracy and the large nationalised enterprises *is* westernised. Otherwise it has little homogeneity, being recruited in diverse ways from a variety of origins. It does not resemble that relatively tight network of families which dominates, for instance, neighbouring Morocco.[38]

Their so-to-speak atomic, one-by-one recruitment, their lack of previous homogeneity, and their possession of military and administrative skills and power, without other clear legitimacy, makes them the Mamluks of the modern world. They sit on top of a numerous petite bourgeoisie, augmented by natural growth, economic development and by the inheritance of all the small enterprises abandoned by the petty *colons* who left in 1962. This very numerous class does however have a plausible, identity-conferring, legitimating ideology close to hand. Reformist Islam had two planks: hostility to the old marabouts and, secondly, to westernisation. The marabouts are perhaps no longer a great threat, though no doubt self-respecting burghers continue to welcome good reasons which vindicate their own new style of life as against ignorant rural excesses and superstitions. The insistence on purity of Islam, not only against the internal corruption by 'saints', but also against external dilution, has now consequently acquired a new major significance.[39] It is these *petits Musulmans*, who have replaced the *petits blancs* of colonial Algeria, who set the tone. They need to define themselves both against rustic ignoramuses and against the values practised, but ambivalently held, by the Mamluks.

The central fact about modern Algeria seems to be that the relationship between the Mamluks and the bourgeoisie is one of co-existence, not hostility. According to an admirable book on the cities of the medieval Middle East,[40] this was so then and it seems to be so now. In the medieval levantine cities, Mamluks looked after government and war, and the bourgeoisie and its *ulama* provided legitimacy; the two classes in the end melded and intermarried. It appears to be so in modern Algeria: the Mamluks look after state, army, oil and gas, whilst the bourgeoisie and its *ulama* handle retail trade and legitimacy.

The extent to which the Mamluks acknowledge that legitimacy lies not with them but with the *ulama* is remarkable. It has as its consequence a most heroic *Kulturkampf*, waged by the Mamluks against themselves. More than its neighbours, Algeria practises a very serious arabisation programme. The feasibility of this, of arabising rapidly an entire educational system, including the university, may well be in doubt. Most of the teachers at Algiers University, even though native Algerians, cannot lecture in Arabic; and the psychological difficulties of switching to Arabic in Algiers are best illustrated by the fact that arabisation crash courses are planned *outside* the country, e.g. in Syria. Whether this *Kulturkampf* will or can succeed remains to be seen. That it is attempted, with such great earnestness and determination, testifies to the manner in which reformism is the established religion of the country.

The consequences of all this in a comparative framework are interesting. One continues to think of Kemalism as the paradigm of the modernisation of a Muslim country. The current Algerian *Kulturkampf* is just as painful, just as dramatic, and just as difficult. But it is a kind of mirror-image of Ataturk's shock therapy. The de-Islamisation of Anatolian peasantry goes against the grain, as does the de-gallicisation of an Algerian technocrat. In either case, one may well wonder whether it will be accomplished.

It is possible that the two attempts at drastic cultural engineering even have something in common. Once again, Ali Merad is interesting on this subject.

Speaking of the inter-war period, he says: 'paradoxical though it may seem, the young pre-reformers adopted an equal enthusiasm for the Turkey of Mustafa Kemal and for the Arabia of Ibn Saud'.[41] He goes on to say that this 'unreasoned admiration for two diametrically opposed aspects of contemporary Muslim life' was justified, in the eyes of these young reformers, by the simple fact that the then Algerian conservatives were equally hostile both to Kemalism and to Wahabi theocracy. Perhaps the young reformers were wiser than that. In formal doctrine, Muslim fundamentalism and Kemalism may indeed be opposed. When it comes to social substance, this is no longer so obvious. In our day Turks, looking back at Ataturk's work, are tempted to see its weakness precisely in the unconsciously *ulama*-like rigidity with which the new secular Koran of the West was imposed, and to feel tempted to try a new, liberal, as it were Mutazilite Kemalism.[42]

It was once supposed that Islam was incompatible with modernisation, or with the requirements of industrial society. This may well be true of the erstwhile Apollonian Islam of Biskra, which once was typical enough of a very great part of the rural and tribal Muslim world. But the severe discipline of puritan Islam may in fact be compatible with, or positively favourable to, modern social organisation.[43]

The obligatory prayers and the fast may be a bit of a nuisance, but, unlike ecstatic festivals or reliance on saintly intercession, they do teach a man a bit of discipline, which is a most desirable trait in an industrial worker. They teach him that rules in books are there to be obeyed, and that bringing donations to shrines will get him nowhere. Why not try orderly *literate* prayer and work, instead? For good Weberian reasons, it seems that modernisation may just as well be done with Islam as against it — provided it is the right kind of Islam, that of the Reformers and not that of the saints. In his interesting paper 'Some observations on the ethical teachings of Orthodox Reformism in Algeria', Professor Pessah Shinar stresses this aspect of the moral teaching of the reformers and writes:

The orthodox reformists . . . were emphatic in asserting that Faith and Works, in addition to their spiritual significance, were also of supreme relevance to mundane happiness, to the prosperity and success of the individual Muslim and the Islamic community . . .

The Islamic reformists in Algeria took a broader and more sophisticated view of the manner in which Faith and Observance engender moral qualities (in contrast to the 'associationist' theory of exchange of vows, invocations, offerings, pilgrimages, for material benefits) and through them influence the life and success of the individual Muslim and Islam as a whole. They stressed the psychological effect — the stimulating, invigorating quality inherent in the faith . . . Faith and rites, they asserted, act like a powerhouse in generating and accumulating vast energies, strength, will, endurance of hardship, complete dedication, hope, perseverance, single-mindedness, resolve, daring . . .[44]

The unknown Apollo of Biskra

The this-worldliness of the reformist ethic can also be illustrated by what Merad rightly calls an ingenious classification of men, expounded by Ben Badis in his journal *Shihah* in February 1939.[45] The classification works by means of a two-by-two table, generated by two simple binary oppositions: one may neglect one's duty to the other world or not neglect it, and one may neglect or not neglect one's material concerns in this world. The most blessed of men is he who does not neglect either concern: he will be happy in this world and in the next. The atheist who is also unmindful of his terrestrial needs is unhappy indeed, for he will suffer both here and hereafter. The logic of this casuistry seems impeccable, though it sins on the side of optimism, by neglecting the possibility that one may attend to one's concerns, but without success. What is interesting is that the adherents of maraboutism are apparently meant to correspond to the option of seeking to please God but without making a proper use of this world – thereby committing the impiety of not making good use of the possibilities offered by God in *this* world.[46] Such this-worldliness, conjoined to a puritanical stress on Koranic rule-observance, would seem a Weberian ethic indeed.

One may add that puritan Islam has a potential for favourable adjustment not merely to industrialism, but also to modern radicalism. In one sense, it may indeed be conservative: it is committed to the existence of a definitive, final blueprint of social life, and to its implementation. But the uncompromising rigidity of this view has a certain affinity with the radicalisms of our age. Colonel Gaddafy's ideology for instance looks like a remarkable conflation of free-floating revolutionary radicalism with such Muslim fundamentalism, a kind of Reformism–Maoism.

On 6 June 1973, Colonel Gaddafy purchased four full pages of *The Times*, and the first of these was devoted to his exposition of his own creed. Some of his ideas are striking:

Heaven has addressed the earth many times through the prophets. The last of these prophets was Mohammed and the last of these messages of God was the Koran.

We know that Science . . . has not found all the answers . . . The Koran provides those answers and refutes all the hallucinations of materialism and existentialism.

The Libyan Cultural Revolution aims at dismissing these hallucinations . . . and calls for a revival of Islam according to the teaching of the Koran . . .

. . . what matters is that people all over the world must worship God instead of worshipping mortals like Lenin or Stalin . . . or worshipping the cows and idols . . .

We too used to worship idols before . . . Mohammed . . .

This fascinating passage conflates the cult of personality in the specifically Soviet sense, with the rejection of anthropolatry which was the main effective doctrine of the Reformers – and throws in Hindu cows and the pre-Muslim Arab state of ignorance for good measure. Thus the repudiation of deviations from the

171

true revolutionary path is made to speak not only with the same voice, but in the same words, as the repudiation of Muslim heresy.

The social base of Libyan puritanism also seems similar to that which it has further west: the shift from tribal to urban milieux. An anthropologist working on a community of recently sedentarised Libyan Bedouin — who are hardly famed for Muslim rigour when in their natural habitat — reports that they display extreme, obsessional and unrivalled zeal concerning the seclusion of their womenfolk once the community is settled.

The Libyan way is more extreme, irresponsible, loud and impatient than the Algerian version — perhaps because the Libyan way to independence was effortless rather than purchased by a prolonged struggle. But in other ways, Libya went through stages analogous to Algeria: the primary struggle against colonialism had been led by one of the religious orders, whose leader was later to be made into a monarch by a departing European power — only to be deposed in due course by the puritan Colonel.

Gaddafy has gone far in the direction of fundamentalism:

... preaching a return to primitive Islam ... Libyans were denied their alcohol. Mini-skirts were made maxi by order. Street signs are in Arabic only ... In November 1972, it was announced that the ... punishment for theft and robbery, cutting off a foot and a hand respectively, were to be revived.[47]

Gaddafy had taken over from King Idris, who had been leader of the Sanusi religious order.

The map of the distribution of Sanusi lodges in Cyrenaica coincided with the main points in the distribution of power among the Bedouin. The ability to identify ... the powerful Bedouin sheiks had characterized the leadership of the Order for the 74 years of its life. Idris inherited this technique ...[48]

But the technique was hardly relevant any longer when, as Professor Peters shows, the Libyans left their tribal units and encampments under the impact of oil. The Sanusi Order's technique for providing leadership and identity was now far less usable than the fundamentalist, scripturalist one which was open to Gaddafy and which he employed. With fewer people and more oil revenue than in Algeria, it was also easier to exaggerate.

The contrast between Algeria and Turkey is however the most instructive one, even or especially after one has seen that the rejection and the reaffirmation of Islam may resemble each other. Turkey modernises against Islam, Algeria with it. Turkey endeavours to bridge the gap between elite and mass by changing the faith of the latter, Algeria by changing the speech of the former. Turkey's traditional state had been strong, Algeria's weak. The Ottoman empire had presided over a plurality of religious communities; traditional North Africa was relatively homogeneous. Turkey began to modernise in an age when liberal constitutionalism was held to be a key to the secret of the new technological power, and it seems that the Turks internalised this view; Algeria chose its path in an age no longer given to such ideas, and the Algerians, who had hardly benefited from an alien parliamentarianism, seem free of them. The Turkish elite is relatively continuous; the Algerian Mamluks are new men. Turkey escaped colonialism, Algeria suffered an unusually long period of it.

Somewhere in these contrasts, and not merely in the fact that Turks are not Arabs, there is presumably the clue to why Turkey enters the modern world under the banner of secularism, and Algeria under the banner of Islam; why the Turkish state is troubled by religious opposition, and the Maghrebin states are not. The sheer fact of having had a strong Muslim state, which associated the Ottoman *ulama* with its authority, deprived the latter of much incentive to purify and reform; whereas the relative absence of official temptations, and the need to fill a vacuum arising from the absence of any effective non-religious elite, gave the Algerian reformers both the incentive and the opportunity to mould a society in their own image.[49] Contemporary Algeria is certainly 'modern' in the sense of being unlike its own saint-ridden past: but it is modern in its Islamism, not in its secularisation.

7

Trousers in Tunisia

Tunisia is fortunate in the American scholarship which it has attracted. For instance, its early nineteenth century, the first period of transition and of failure to make a transition, can be followed and understood very well thanks to Carl Brown's excellent book, *The Tunisia of Ahmad Bey*,[1] which is complemented by the admirable volume which ought to be its companion, Arnold Green's study of the Tunisian *ulama* between 1873 and 1915.[2]

Muslim traditional political culture seems to come in two different editions: there is what I believe to be the standard or normal version, which might be called the Ibn Khaldun type, and there is the Ottoman variant. The former is marked by the pervasiveness of tribal organisation (i.e. kin-defined, local, order-maintaining and defensive groups trespassing on the violence-monopoly of the state), and the corresponding weakness of the central state, which is itself based on a privileged tribe or group of tribes. The Ottoman type, on the other hand, is one in which a higher proportion of the countryside is effectively controlled by the centre, and in which the central state by-passes the weakness noted by Ibn Khaldun, inherent in the tribal recruitment of the political elite, by using some alternative method or combination of methods — Mamluks, *devshirme*, phanariots, or what have you. Carl Brown sums up the sound anti-Ibn-Khaldun principle of Ottoman politics:

A recalcitrant mamluk could be deprived of all power and property at any time, and following his disgrace could not go back to his tribe and foment revolt. He had no tribe, no local support, no power or authority save that attached to the office he happened to be holding.

Nor, one might add, was he whilst in office molested by swarms of perk-demanding kinsmen, swaying him away from the stern call of duty. It seems that in pre-modern conditions, only eunuchs, priests, slaves or politically-emasculated minorities can behave in a proper bureaucratic manner. There is a pariah bureaucracy as well as a pariah capitalism.

Muslim states did not of course need to be pure examples of either type — indeed few, if any, were. It was a matter of degree or proportion. In North

174

Trousers in Tunisia

Africa, the Ibn Khaldun elements predominate in the West; the Ottoman-type features increase as one proceeds eastward. In Morocco, the attempt to organise a slave army in the early eighteenth century led to no very permanent results, though it has left its trace in the royal black slave guard. (A hilarious piece of symbolism during the French protectorate was to see this corps parading to celebrate 14 July.) Tunisia, at the other end of the Maghreb, was probably the most Ottoman in type of the North African states. As Carl Brown observes,

Since ... the thirteenth century, no force of nomads or mountaineers from within has overthrown a dynasty or created another, or even played a crucial role in political changes.

The ideological modernisation of Muslim societies also comes in two well-known forms: there is Secularism and Reformism. (In spirit if not in manifest doctrine, these need not be so very far apart. There was a fundamentalist, theological quality about first-generation Kemalists which may make them brothers under the skin of the Reformists, and Ali Merad has amusingly described how the early Young Algerians were attracted, simultaneously, by both the Young Turks and the Wahabis.) There may be some connection between the kind of traditional polity and of styles of intellectual modernisation. Where the old state was strong, the old clerisy is too well-heeled and well-entrenched to toy with Reformism, and hence those who wish for change take to secular banners and political means. Where the state was weak, on the other hand, local politico-religious centres, namely living-saint-cults, which are repugnant to puritan Islam and to the modern spirit alike, are correspondingly strong; hence those who strive for change can do so in opposition to such heterodoxy and in the name of the *purification* of religion, rather than of opposition to it.

This generalisation may not be without its exceptions, but Tunisia at any rate seems to fit in squarely within the Ottoman/Kemalist syndrome. The manner in which the traditional scholars were too well-entrenched in the old order to become the spearheads of the new (as happened in neighbouring Algeria, where they were *not* well-entrenched) is admirably documented in Arnold Green's book. The way in which, on the other hand, a relatively well-centralised state endeavoured to modernise itself is the topic of Carl Brown's *The Tunisia of Ahmad Bey*.

This volume does indeed contain two books at the price of one. The first half is an account of Ottoman society and its functioning in a minor, largely autonomous province, on the eve of the colonial period and of modernisation. The second half is a political biography of Ahmad Bey, who ruled Tunisia from 1837 till 1855, and was a kind of abortive mini-Mehemet-Ali. The first half of the book primarily sets the scene, and the second tells a story.

The first half is an extremely elegant and convincing portrait of a society, which should be of great interest not merely to historians of the region, but to students of the Ottoman Empire and indeed of pre-industrial political systems generally. As Brown observes: 'The genuis of Ottoman imperial rule lay in the ability of so few to control so many.'

Brown estimates the population of Tunisia at the time to have been 1½ million, and the military establishment towards the end of the eighteenth century to have averaged under 5000. This small army ruled over a population of whom a quarter or a third were nomads, whilst the rest of the countrymen were tribally organised and shared the usual Mediterranean honour ethos. The military equipment of the rulers could not have been outstandingly superior to that of the ordinary heads of households, responsible for a violent defence of family honour, and the population was not a mass of supine agricultural workers habituated to subjection, but, in large proportion, independent agriculturalists/pastoralists with a serviceable local organisation. So how was this political miracle achieved?

The elements which go into the answer are described in the book with very great skill. Political scientists such as John Waterbury have imported the notion of 'segmentation' from anthropology to describe certain traits of (e.g. Moroccan) ruling classes; but what one also needs is the idea of the segmentation-*using* state. The paradox of the rule by few over an armed and kin-organised countryside becomes much less paradoxical if one remembers that it was precisely the neat balancing of the local rivals, ensured by the segmentary system, which allowed the centre to rule with such economy in personnel. Brown observes:

Tribal revolts were *never* crushed . . . the government bided its time, relying on the weapons of bribery, economic reprisal . . . and divide-and-rule tactics (incitement of neighbouring tribes against the offender) . . .

This economy in turn presumably allowed the state to refrain from pushing its tax demands to levels at which they might have forced people to resist. The almost caste-like impermeability of the ruling group, which to modern eyes looks like a jealous protection of that group's privilege, was also a political precaution effective against the group itself, or against ambitious members within it. It made it harder for them to establish power-bases in the rest of the society, as Brown says. Though it does not prevent clique-formation inside the ruling group, it makes it that much harder for the rivalries inside the group to be linked automatically to other rivalries in the society outside. (That this danger existed is illustrated by the fact that up to within living memory, rural moieties in Tunisia were articulated in terms of a long-past dynastic succession struggle.) The whole system also illustrates — to cross-refer to an interesting dispute about the nature of traditional Maghrebin society — that the tribal segmentary system must have been in some measure a reality rather than simply a terminological cover for a patronage society. Had optimal, dyadic patronage been the norm, the system as a whole would have been highly unstable and unpredictable, and the insulation of the top ruling group could not have worked at all.

Brown indicates an interesting difference between Tunisia and neighbouring

Trousers in Tunisia

Algeria, which was (though he does not use this terminology) a much purer case of the segmentation-using state: in Algeria the small Turkish minority kept up its isolation and monopoly right up to the end — when the French defeated them in 1830, they were amazed at the small quantity of transport required to send a whole state machine back to Istanbul — whereas in Tunisia, countervailing forces were available within the political elite: Mamluks, Algerian Kabyles (whose appellation has given the French language the word *zouave*, in diametrical opposition to the original sense of *zwaya* as a religious non-arms-bearing tribe), and local cavalry. There is nothing to indicate that the Algerian system was changing prior to the colonial impact: by contrast, in Tunisia it was being eroded both militarily and culturally. Two revolts by Turkish soldiery (Turkish in fact or only in ascription, by this stage) were evidently suppressed in 1811 and 1816 without undue difficulty, with the aid of other units and even of the populace: and also, by the first half of the nineteenth century, the Ottoman language was on its way out. Ahmad Bey, the hero of Brown's story, actually wrote to the Sublime Porte in Arabic, and was the first local ruler to do so.

At the centre of Ahmad Bey's efforts at westernisation was of course the modernisation of the army, by means of the creation of Western-style units. Carl Brown's account of the difficulties involved in this has enabled me to understand at last a derisive line in a still vigorous and scurrilous Czech folk song ('Herzegovina'), commemorating the Habsburg occupation of Herzegovina and presumably composed by Czech infantrymen involved in the operation. It refers to the Muslim enemy:

> Tam na stráni jsou ukrytí Mohamedáni,
> Mohamedáni, hnusní pohani,
> Kalhoty maj' vykasaný, plivaj' do dlaní.

The last line refers contemptuously to the Muslim soldiers' habit of rolling up their trousers. I never knew hitherto why they did so, nor why it should be pejorative. Now I know:

The European-style . . . uniforms were resisted by the recruits . . . who . . . disliked the jibes of . . . *Bu Sarwal* ('the trousered one'). They would carefully roll up the trousers over their knees when off duty and if caught by one of the officers attempt to justify their action . . .

The issue of the rolled-up trousers evidently resounded on both shores of the Mediterranean and constitutes one of the less well-known crises of modernisation. Trousers were not the only problem

The greatest break with past military tradition was the recruitment of native Tunisians. The troubles and popular resentment this caused . . .

The resentment was evidently not restricted to those whose erstwhile monopoly of such service was now being breached.

Though Brown says that in general there was a parallelism in the pattern of

177

military modernisation in Turkey, Egypt and Tunisia, it does not seem to be a complete one. The military reforms in Egypt were evidently effective enough for Mehemet Ali to do very well indeed against his nominal Ottoman sovereign. The testing time for the new Tunisian army came on the side of the Porte, not against him, in the Crimean war, and Brown does not seem to think that the test was passed very successfully. The Tunisian expedition against the Czar must certainly be among the more bizarre episodes of history. The evidence about what happened seems thin. On page 308 the author is presumably echoing Western views when he says, 'The troops never saw combat duty and presumably never rendered any other service.' But on page 309, however, we are told:

The Tunisian troops apparently experienced some combat in the Batoum area and perhaps elsewhere as well. Others served garrison duty in the Sebastopol area after the fall of that city.

Though the passages quoted are not clear, the author seems to be more inclined to endorse the latter version. In any case, as he says, this must have been one of the last military expeditions to be financed by the private wealth of a ruler. Ahmad Bey sold his personal jewellery hoard to pay for the adventure.

Carl Brown certainly does not succeed in establishing Ahmad Bey as one of the great heroic modernisers, pulling a reluctant country by the scruff of its neck into the modern world: nor does he intend to do so. He considers his fatal flaw to have been in the field of financing the whole enterprise, or in a misplaced trust in the man to whom he delegated this aspect. The man in question founded a state bank, which was meant to promote commercial capitalism. Apparently he committed fraud, and then successfully fled to Europe. It is amusing to reflect that about a century later, when the fashionable path to development was through collectivisation, rather than through commercial banks, another able Tunisian temporarily secured the trust of the ruler, tried the New Way forward, and then also successfully fled to Europe.

8

The sociology of Robert Montagne (1893–1954)

The modern state — territorial, national, secular, centralised — is taken for granted by its citizens. If they theorise about it at all, they are generally concerned about the precise extent of its proper powers and responsibilities, rather than about its basic nature or existence. That the maintenance of order should be the responsibility of specialised agencies, acting under the law and not in pursuit of private ends, and that it should recruit its personnel from the governed population and remain culturally continuous with it — all this seems *so* self-evident that to spell it out in ordinary discussion appears pedantic. Liberals add the right to associate with a view to reforming society; socialists insist on the need to prevent economic oppression; egalitarians, on the need to ensure equality. But the traits we have specified stand outside most current debates and seem axiomatic. If people find themselves obliged to redress wrongs by private use of violence, if their rulers belong to a quite different community, are culturally alien, and run the state machine openly for the own private advantage — then we are, by our contemporary standards, in the presence of some blatant aberration, a veritable political *scandale*.

Such is the conventional wisdom of the day. But, whatever authority it may have, it can hardly spring from some statistical normality. A survey of the forms of political association found throughout human history would hardly bear out the view that the effectively centralised, 'national' (culturally homogeneous) state is so prevalent that any deviation from it must be considered pathological. Quite the reverse.

Our tacit and self-evident norms may indeed be good ones, but their authority cannot be rooted in some near-universal pervasiveness of what they enjoin. To understand them, we should know their specific social roots and preconditions; and to do that, we need to know a little about those social forms that *differ* from them. Here we are somewhat hampered by the seeming self-evidence of our own assumptions. More specifically, we are hampered by the lack of any good typology of social and political forms.

Our failure to acquire a good, useful classification of types of society is both conspicuous and strange. We possess a shared and reasonably illuminating ter-

179

minology for categorising architectural styles or painting, not to mention plants or insects. Neither the existence of borderline cases nor the fact that important principles of classification (e.g. origin and structure) cut across one another really hampers the taxonomical enterprise in other fields. But when it comes to what concerns us most – human societies – both our ingenuity and our drive seem to desert us. The classifications we use tend to be either crude (industrial/ pre-industrial), or *ad hoc* and unsystematic, or tied to archaic theories we no longer hold and to questions we no longer ask. No doubt there are various reasons for this failure, but they can hardly be diagnosed, let alone remedied, in an article.

However, if someone should attempt this task, he will need to use one book that appeared in French in 1930 and that has never been translated: Robert Montagne's *Les Berbères et le Makhzen dans le Sud du Maroc, Essai sur la transformation politique des Berbères sédentaires* (*groupe Chleuh*), published in Paris by the Librairie Félix Alcan. While it deserves to be known as a classic, in fact, outside the ranks of North African specialists, it is virtually unknown. One can easily see the reasons why. The title is unfortunate and misleading, and hardly calculated to whet the curiosity of someone browsing through a library or a catalogue. It mentions a mysterious and unidentified entity, the *Makhzen*, and it appears to be about the relationship of this entity, whatever it may be, to one particular region, the south, of one particular country in Africa. The matter becomes even worse if one looks at the subtitle. It suggests that the book is concerned with a sub-group of tribes, the Chleuh, whoever they might be and however that word might be pronounced. Clearly a book for specialists. Perhaps it contains fascinating information for someone interested in sedentary tribesmen in the south of one particular country, but for the rest of us, whose human sympathy and curiosity extend impartially to tribesmen and townsmen, nomad and sedentary, east, west, and north as well as south, clearly this book of over four hundred pages has little to offer. Perhaps a summary of its findings . . . ?

Anyone arguing in this manner on the basis of the title would be committing a complete, albeit a natural, mistake. The book in fact contains a superb analysis of an important and widely diffused *type* of society, one which for lack of a better name (and without prejudice) one could call the Muslim or the Ibn-Khaldunian type: the kind of society in which a weak state co-exists with strong tribes, in which the tribes have what might be called a 'segmentary' structure, and in which the lack of political cohesion is accompanied by a striking degree of cultural continuity and economic interaction. This kind of society is especially common within Islam – although this is not to say that necessarily all Muslim countries exemplify this syndrome or that no non-Muslim country does. But the type extends far beyond the southern Moroccan case studies which inspired Montagne's book, and indeed Montagne draws on a far wider range of material than the title suggests. The book has remarkable sociological breadth and historical depth.

The sociology of Robert Montagne

Apart from the misleading title, there may perhaps be another reason for Montagne's neglect. Robert Montagne was a liberal rightist, in the sense that he was not opposed to the colonial system as such, nor to the French presence in North Africa, however sensitive and perceptive his understanding of the indigenous society might have been. From a historical viewpoint this is hardly important. His claim to our attention rests on the fact that he represented the high point of French colonial ethnography, and not on his direct participation in events; the dilemmas of French policy are reflected and illuminated in his work, though his ideas do not explain French policy. But his political position does explain the kind of reception his work received.

To a very considerable extent, French sociological and ethnographic work in North Africa was carried out by military officers and administrative officials. It accompanied conquest, it was a kind of reconnaisance in depth, and it was the handmaiden of government. In consequence, there was surprisingly little inter-action between the French university and North African research. Emile Durkheim's and Marx's and Engels's views on primitive society were influenced by Algerian Berber material. But, as time progressed, the North African world of *colon* and officer became increasingly separate from the mainstream of French and European intellectual life. Notwithstanding the facts that one out-standing French historian of North Africa, Ch.-André Julien, was an early friend of the nationalists and that an outstanding human geographer was a Communist, by and large the world of research into North African tribal societies was a closed one, with rightist and military associations ignoring and ignored by the wider world of scholarship. Montagne's own masterpiece is inspired by ideas drawn from his knowledge of classical Greek politics, by the rejection of the medieval analogy, by a good knowledge of Ibn Khaldun and North African his-tory, and by another unjustly forgotten French scholar E. Masqueray, who in 1886 published a study which attempted to do a kind of Fustel de Coulanges for North Africa, by tracing the evolutionary pattern of its social forms. But he seems to draw little inspiration from the main currents of sociological and anthropological thought. Conversely, when, for instance, Lévi-Strauss deploys his extraordinary erudition and lists the societies that exhibit binary or moiety organisation, he ignores Montagne, despite Montagne's almost excessive pre-occupation with moieties among the Berbers.

So long as North Africa was dominated by France, interest in its tribal populations tended to be a preserve of military or civilian servants of French authorities, and an interest in the apparently archaic aspects of these societies seemed suspect to other scholars. With independence, the old right lost interest, scholarly or other, in North Africa; while the left, rediscovering this world, had little inclination to dig up the works of a naval officer assigned to political intelligence in the interests of establishing a colonial pro-tectorate. In this it was mistaken. The sociological importance of Montagne's work, which is enormous, is quite independent of whatever assessment one might make either of colonialism in general or of the French record in North Africa in particular.

Montagne was born in 1893 and entered naval college in 1911. He came to Morocco as a naval officer after the First World War, and apparently some of his spare-time sociological inquiries attracted the attention of the great French pro-consul, Marshal Lyautey. The major problem facing the French, who had estab-lished a protectorate over the monarchy in 1912, was the highly effective resistance, not yet either of the elite or of the towns, but of the unsubdued tribal populations, both in the Rif and in the Atlas mountains. Montagne later wrote:

France was . . . able, after thirty-two years' endeavour and thanks to the efforts of our own military and political personnel and to the cooperation of the tribes that submitted to our rule, to achieve the political unification of Morocco, prob-ably for the first time in history. She was determined, at the same time, to inte-grate the defeated tribes into the Sherifian Empire that the Protectorate had restored and reorganised.[1]

Montagne was assigned to ethnographic work, which was in practice insepar-able from political intelligence. He did not return to the sea. In the French empire, the army had developed under Gallieni and Lyautey a tradition of con-quest and administration by political rather than military means through an understanding and utilisation of indigenous institutions. This was in many ways parallel to the ideas of 'indirect rule' developed by the British. But there was a difference. On the whole, the British did not simultaneously deal with princes *and* with dissident tribesmen. It tended to be one or the other. The peculiarity of the Moroccan situation was that the indirect rulers were simultaneously utilis-ing native institutions at quite different levels — a theocratic, nominally absolutist but effectively enfeebled sultanate, and anarchic but militarily effective tribes-men, with petty local tyrants emerging in between. The result, in Montagne's work, was to be a remarkable portrait of a total and highly complex society, a study combining anthropological detail with historical sweep. The academic fruits of his labours led eventually to a professorship at the Collège de France. When the new proletariat of the shanty-towns replaced the tribes as the main political problem for the rulers, Montagne's sociological interests reflected the change, and he was thus also the author of one of the first studies of the new Moroccan working class. He died in 1954.

So, in colonial days, his work tended to be the property of a closed circle of soldiers and administrators concerned with its practical application rather than its wider circulation, while in the days of independence and the age of the Third World, it seemed part of a repudiated past. But the time is ripe for rediscovering it.

Through Montagne's work, we can come to understand a certain type of non-Western state, very unlike that national centralised state which we so much take for granted. The misleading title of his masterpiece already singles out the main

The sociology of Robert Montagne

dramatis personae in this political structure; the *Makhzen* is the traditional North African term for the central power, and the Berbers are paradigmatic *tribesmen*. The type of political information with which he was concerned is above all characterised by the co-existence of these two main elements: a central authority, nominally if not effectively recognised by an entire society, which thereby acquires a kind of moral unity, and the tribes. The circumstances of the French conquest of Morocco, which took place in the early decades of this century, were such that neither of these elements could possibly be ignored. This was not so, for instance, in neighbouring Algeria: when the French arrived there in 1830, they dismantled the central structure, which had indeed been a very elegant and economic one, and thereafter found themselves facing in the main a chaotic patchwork, or, under Abd el Kader, a new formation. In Morocco, this could not be so: the international treaties and horse-dealing that allowed the French entry into Morocco obliged the French to treat it as a 'protectorate' – to be there as protectors and renovators of the central power – so they could not ignore it. Commenting on these dilemmas, a French general, P.J. André, who took part in the conquest of Morocco, reminisces:

The author of these lines remembers particularly Marshal Lyautey's first visit to Taza, recently occupied by our troops . . . His attention was drawn to the distinctiveness of the local Berber chiefs, of the tribes, of the local religious orders, who claimed to accept French authority but refused their submission to the Makhzen. One of the officers present was not too afraid to say: 'This is the moment to establish in Taza a Berber republic which will be loyalist to us . . . ' The Marshal replied: 'No doubt you are right, but I am in Morocco for the purpose of restoring the authority of the Sultan throughout the land, and I can do no other.'[2]

At the same time, the only effective military opposition the French encountered came from tribesmen. It was not a trivial opposition. In the nineteen-twenties, tribesmen from the Rif decisively defeated one European power, Spain, and very nearly defeated France herself. In central Morocco, small mountain tribes defied France for decades.

The relationship between a weak, town-based, religiously charismatic dynasty, respected but not obeyed, and tribes which were remarkably cohesive and militarily effective, yet often devoid of any centralised permanent leadership – this relationship could not, in these circumstances, fail to be at the very centre of interest and attention. Thus the circumstances of the French conquest of Morocco virtually imposed a certain highly illuminating sociological perspective on its political intelligence officers, of whom Montagne was one.

It was also a perspective that other students of Oriental state formations generally missed. One can only speculate why there is so relatively little scholarly work on this topic. Oriental societies are the subject matter of Oriental studies; but the Orientalist's definition of reality is whatever is attested by a text, and texts are generally written by scribes at courts with a view to pleasing rulers, and rulers do not normally relish being reminded of insolent tribesmen who defy their authority. Moreover, the European vision of the Oriental state may inevitably have been overly influenced by the Ottoman Empire, untypical in that it had an unusually strong state structure, based on a rather special principle of organisation and cohesion. In Africa and in the South Seas, it is true, scholars and anthropologists did look directly at tribes; but sub-Saharan tribes, when not stateless, generally had tribal states, i.e. political structures emerging from within the ethnic group rather than superimposed on it or opposed to it. In brief, anthropologists tended to look at tribes that were more or less islands unto themselves, rather than unrefined members of a literate civilisation, while Orientalists tended to look at literate civilisations through the eyes of their texts. In neither case were they led to consider the relationship between tribal groups and an urban-based central power. If, as I suspect, this is the heart of the matter, it follows that they tended to miss the main theme of at least one important type of non-Western polity.

Of course, it would not be true to say that there are no studies of this topic. Owen Lattimore's work on the relationship between the centralised Chinese state and the nomads of the Asian steppes is a good example and is strictly parallel to Montagne's work; the two should stand side by side on the shelves. Still, it is remarkable how little is available on this subject. British India might have been expected to provide a stimulus for research in this direction. Perhaps the Mogul state was too decrepit by the time Western scholarship looked at India; perhaps the key theme in India was the relationship of state to peasant and caste rather than to tribe; the 'tribal' populations surviving in the subcontinent were either far too marginal to the system, or, where they constituted a political threat, as on the north-western frontier, belonged to a different cultural tradition altogether. Or again, the emirates of Northern Nigeria might have stimulated interest in this topic; but in Northern Nigeria the British dealt with the Fulani or Hausa emirs and not with the humble tribesmen, and again one element in the picture was lacking.

Here we come to a further crucial feature of the Moroccan political situation at the time of the French conquest which was favourable to the correct phrasing of the sociological question: the *dramatis personae* on the scene were not merely the Sultan and the tribes. There were also the tyrants, *les grands caids*. Or to put it another way, the French encountered two radically different forms of political organisation in the tribal highlands. Some tribes were ruled by fairly egalitarian tribal assemblies, composed of heads of households, and in fact organised in whole hierarchies of such assemblies for tribal groups of diverse sizes, the larger incorporating the smaller units. Others were ruled arbitrarily by autocratic robber-baron figures, tyrannising over their subjects from romantic-looking mountain castles.

The grip of the republican or anarchic tradition is not so strong that there do not constantly emerge in North Africa, within several of the five or six thousand little elementary states which cover the mountain regions of the Maghreb, ambitious and energetic men capable of setting themselves above the councils of notables. These leaders establish states of varying sizes, by violence or by political manoeuvring; and there are even those who manage to build chiefdoms, kingdoms and empires ... We observe also that the decline of the states that they found is often as swift as their emergence is sudden.

The French conquerors and administrators of Morocco could not conceivably remain insensitive to these striking differences, for their concrete policies had to take note of these diverse elements, and indeed they made use of them in diverse ways. In fact, French policy in Morocco invoked a variety of contradictory principles.

(1) The French presence in Morocco was based on a treaty with the Sultan, and the promise to provide protection to the central government and to strengthen it.

(2) At the same time, the French formed alliances with the great robber-barons of the south, notably the famous Glawi, Pasha of Marrakesh, and some others. Sometimes they created tribal rulers, caids, where none had previously existed, or had only existed in embryonic form.

(3) As a means both of securing, if possible, the submission of the tribes and of facilitating their subsequent administration, they underwrote tribal custom, allowing the tribes to retain their assemblies and to govern themselves by tribal customary law.

Each of these elements may have been essential for the attainment of French ends — the first legitimated French entry, the second secured powerful allies, notably in the south, and the third neutralised or diminished opposition in the largest and most intractable block of tribal lands in central Morocco, where the High Atlas and the Middle Atlas meet each other and also join the nomadic area of the borderlands. Logically and sociologically, however, there was an inevitable tension between these policies.

Nominally, the Sultan was an absolute ruler; hence, the toleration or support of *de facto* independent principalities on his territory was, in theory, in conflict with the protecting power's obligation to sustain his authority. At the same time, he was also the religious leader of the country, obliged *qua* Muslim ruler to promote good and suppress evil, good and evil being delimited by Koranic law in the keeping of the scribes who interpreted the Koran and perpetuated the traditions of the Prophet and his companions. But the customary law of the tribes deviated from holy law; hence to underwrite it was to underwrite heresy and schism. (It was this particular conflict that provided the first issue for modern nationalism.) Thus, there was also a conflict between obligation to the Sultan and commitment to the tribesmen. Finally, there was, of course, also a conflict between baron and tribesmen. The baron stands for local order and tyranny; the tribal assembly, for anarchy and freedom.

The dilemmas of French colonial policy in Morocco arose from efforts to satisfy diverse allies and appease potential enemies. (In due course, a settler lobby was to complicate the game further.) The ultimate importance of Robert Montagne lies in the fact that he was both a great sociological theoretician and a superb ethnographic observer. But he is also of interest as a historical document, through whom we can gain insight into the French options in the Morocco of that time. Was one to support the Sultan and his court — archaic, Oriental, ineffectual, corrupt, but with a great hold on the symbols of ultimate legitimacy? Was one to support the robber-barons — effective, brutal, repulsive, yet possessed of a certain barbarous splendour and capable of providing military backing? Or was one to support the tribal republics, attractive in their Swiss-style participatory democracy, but also archaic in their own way, intractable, prone to feuds, addicted to anarchy, procrastination, fission? Reading Robert Montagne, there is no doubt in my mind where his deepest sympathies lay — with the tribal republics.

> ... one is tempted in one's heart of hearts to take the side of the Berber repub-
> lics. It seems as though all the goodness and right is on their side. Why, then, are
> we so deeply associated with the qaids? Is this proof of a Machiavellian conspiracy
> on the part of the Makhzen and of the French authorities? In fact the rationale
> behind this collaboration ... is quite simple. It is that it is practically impossible
> to deal with a Berber republic ... It requires years of patience to get a council
> to take a decision about such things as the reorganisation of a region, the build-
> ing of roads, the payment of taxes and the exercise of justice. All the time one
> would be held up by continual discussion and countless insignificant complaints.
> There is no place for the ordered anarchy of the Berber cantons in a modern
> state.

Montagne saw lucidly the social forces which also favoured the other, rival participants. The emotional and policy dilemmas faced by administrators and policy-makers were reflected in his work. It is sociology's gain that the choices highlighted exactly those elements that need to be singled out if we are to understand this type of polity.

What does his work tell us about these elements and their interrelations? There are, in fact, several connected themes to be found:

(1) the internal organisation of the tribesmen in what may be called their normal political condition;

(2) their alternative organisation when subjected to the tyrants, and the highly important thesis of the tendency of such tribal societies to oscillate between a republican and a tyrannical constitution; and

(3) the relationship of both forms of organisation to the central state and a theory of state formation.

On each of these points Montagne combines brilliant abstract theory with fascinating and detailed description. He had his material underfoot: the man who wandered around the western High Atlas and saw the great baronies of the Glawi, Gountafi, and Mtouggi knew how power could occasionally crystallise in a tribe; a man involved in the Rif war could see, through the great adventure of Abd el Krim, the man who defied two European states at a time when colonialism was still triumphant and seemed invincible, just what the process of state formation was in a tribal world. The man involved in the slow and finally uncompleted French conquest of central Morocco also knew how egalitarian tribal republics functioned and the manner in which assemblies and religion combined to maintain order where no sovereign kept the peace. Montagne had a certain advantage over the British functionalist anthropologists who were, at about the same time, transforming anthropology by their thorough and sustained fieldwork. He felt no obligation whatever to be ahistorical. On the contrary, while much of his material was underfoot, he made, at the same time, remarkable use of history. North Africa may be (or may have been until very recently) a tribal world, but it is not one without well-documented history. In addition Montagne had the fourteenth-century scholar Ibn Khaldun – a superb historian–sociologist, who had both documented and schematised the medieval period of the region – as a predecessor. One of Montagne's conclusions was precisely a kind of continuity thesis: the medieval political dramas of the Almoravides and the Almohades and the contemporary politics of Abd el Krim, or of the Pashas of Marrakesh, or the petty chiefs of the Middle Atlas, were variations on the same themes and moved within the same structure.

What were his specific conclusions? One may usefully begin with a negative conclusion about the great 'robber-barons': this was *not* a form of feudalism.

The term 'feudal' has sometimes been used to refer to this form of political system created by Berber leaders in the Atlas ... [But] we do not find in Morocco that hierarchic power structure which characterises European feudalism ... nor is there any equivalent of the feudal courts ... there is nothing like the bonds which tied subjects to the land ... the precarious nature of this system of domination should rule out the use of the term 'feudal' which in the West at least refers to a very stable form ... In Berber society the tribal rebellion is rarely long delayed and the absolute power of the rulers never lasts for more than two or three generations. In fact the only term which really could be applied to this form is ... 'the despotic regime'. It drains the life from a region and is not able, because of its own fragility, to establish lasting institutions.

The superb, romantic, crag-top, crenellated castles, the violence, squalor, corvées, ethos of honour, the tangled intrigues of the barons with one another and with their nominal overlords, the brutality, the household servants, the complex households, the medieval-style Jews – all these immediately suggest a return to the European High Middle Ages. Over and above this, there is the regrettable tendency, springing perhaps from Marxism but now part of daily French political terminology as well, of using the expression *les féodaux* for any strong rural power-holders with a local, rather than a centrally ordained, power-base. This is the appearance; the conventional political wisdom confirms it, and literature consecrates it by speaking of *les seigneurs de l'Atlas*, 'the Lords of the Atlas'.

So much for appearance. Reality is different. This is no feudalism. There is no stability in the system. There is no separate estate of warriors and fief-holders, endeavouring to monopolise military and political functions. There is no code of reciprocal obligations.

Montagne prefers to compare the great chiefs, such as those who dominated much of the western High Atlas during the early part of this century, to the tyrants of ancient Greek cities, tyrants in the original sense of usurpers who succeeded in emerging from the complex political struggles of an oligarchic republic and who precariously and brutally hung on to their power — though not for very long.

the Berber *amghar* must not be confused with the king or chief in other primitive societies. The social relations that he has with the tribe and the mechanics of his rise place him rather with the 'tyrant' of Greek society in the eighth century B.C., before the cities had developed their political constitution.

They emerge from a triangular struggle, in which the other participants are both local rivals and the central power. A significant step in the emergence of the greatest of the southern barons occurred when the rising chief permitted a royal progress of the Sultan's peripatetic court and dubious army to cross his mountain passes, and was rewarded with a Krupp canon, which the royal retinue was with great difficulty lugging across the mountain fastnesses. With this, it was much easier to reduce the collective storehouse forts, the *agadirs* and *ighirmen*, of recalcitrant tribesmen. Less distinguished chiefs could, on their own account, owe their position to no more than having been the first local lineage to own a fast-loading rifle.

Thus, in Montagne's view, the seeming feudalism of the Moroccan south of the early twentieth century was not a stable social form. It was not even *a* social form at all, in a certain sense; it was one *stage* in an oscillating social form.

This is one of Montagne's main theses about Berber politics: it oscillates between two inherently unstable forms. The precarious balance of power in the tribal republics occasionally allows an ambitious leader of one segment to assert his supremacy and expand his power. But the tyranny that emerges is at least as unstable as the one before, and after a time it disintegrates again and the original near-egalitarian system reappears. This thesis has a striking resemblance to the one quite independently proposed by Edmund Leach for Highland Burma over two decades later.[3] The mechanisms and the details of the analysis were not the same: Leach's account was linked to a subtle theory of the relationship of mind to society derived from Durkheim and to a dissection of the tensions within the Burmese hill tribes' principles of kinship, whereas Montagne on the whole remained within the bounds of political anthropology.

This brings one to Montagne's account of the internal mechanics of the alternative condition of this unstable, oscillating tribal world. Here the relevant point of comparison is the work of the great British social anthropologist, the late Edward Evans-Pritchard, and, above all, his work on the Nilotic tribe of the Nuer.[4] Each faced the same theoretical problem, the nature of politics in seemingly anarchic tribal conditions. Westerners tend to hold two opposed and equally mistaken views of tribal politics: one, that in the absence of an effective sovereign, it consists of a Hobbesian war of all against all, and the other, that the benighted savage, with his closed tribal mind reinforced by an abject fear of the supernatural, slavishly conforms to social requirements, barely able to conceive of defying them, let alone summoning courage to do so. Whatever their merits as ideal types for use in political philosophy, these visions have little applicability to concrete ethnography. In tribal societies, social control is neither absent nor automatically enforced through mental rigidity and superstition.

The circumstances in which the two men worked were both similar and different in equally interesting ways. The internal mechanics of Nuer and Berber politics are very similar. In fact, I believe that the principles discovered at work among the Nuer by Evans-Pritchard apply with greater purity to the Berbers than they do to the Nuer themselves. On the other hand, the various Nilotic tribes whom Evans-Pritchard studied in the southern Sudan lived beyond the pale of the Muslim Arab civilisation to the north of them. They were raided or attacked by the Arabs, but they were not Muslims and had not become part of the same civilisation (a fact destined to be full of grave consequences for the post-colonial Sudanese republic). The British had destroyed, rather than protected, the relatively centralised Mahdist state in the Sudan. The Berbers of the Atlas, on the other hand, combined dissident and turbulent independence with a wholehearted, unambiguous internalisation of Islam, in terms of which the central state was legitimated. The French had not dismantled that state, but were acting, at least officially, in its name.

So much for the background of the two studies. There were also differences in the conclusions. These two great students of tribal politics agreed on one central point: the order which *was* there to be found in an anarchic, ungoverned social environment was produced by balanced opposition, by a balance of power. But beyond this shared point, their analyses begin to diverge, and I happen to believe Evans-Pritchard's to be the better one. Evans-Pritchard concentrated on the fact that in this kind of society units of different size are, as it were, nested in each other; the tribe divides into clans, clans into sub-clans and so on. Montagne was in error when he sought *the* crucial unit in Berber society, overruling its own and fully appropriate habit of using the same term for units at diverse levels and of diverse sizes. He even invented a name — canton — for it. No particular level of size is in fact very much more important than any other. At each and every level, there is opposition between groups of that particular scale, and the rivalry and opposition of two sub-clans, which keeps each of them internally cohesive, does not preclude co-operation as fellow-units of the full clan, and so forth. Balanced opposition can only be something like an adequate

189

explanation of the maintenance of order, if units do indeed exist at every level of size at which conflict is liable to arise.

Montagne did not hit upon this theory (though I believe it to be valid for traditional Berber society), notwithstanding the fact that its conceptual preconditions had been prepared by the classical French sociologist Emile Durkheim on the basis of Algerian Berber ethnographic documentation with which Montagne was familiar and which, through Masqueray's work, had greatly influenced him. Instead, he stressed one particular form of balanced opposition, namely, that manifested in a kind of tribal two-party system, the opposition of two great tribal leagues to each other in a given territory, known as *leffs* in Morocco and as *soffs* in parts of Algeria. In the western High Atlas and elsewhere, he maintained, such opposed leagues were arranged along neat chess-board principles, with neighbouring tribal units belonging to opposed leagues. One's neighbour was of the opposing party, but one's neighbour-but-one belonged to one's own league.

When a canton enters into a state of war with one of its neighbours,

it receives assistance from the next canton but one, and step by step there develops a sort of vast political chequer-board in two colours. These blocs are very stable and it is considered a great dishonour if a canton changes allegiance.

Maps are found in Montagne's work tracing such chequer-board patterns.

This part of Montagne's theory is open to criticism on both theoretical and empirical grounds. Jacques Berque, a successor of Montagne at the Collège de France and an outstanding specialist in North African and Berber societies, investigated — and administered — the Seksawa, a tribe at the very heart of the region which Montagne had known best, and he did not find that the *leff* theory applied.[5] Also, although Berber tribes are segmented and subsegmented into constituent parts, the divisions are not always binary. At a theoretical level, one can apply the following criticism: suppose that these *ilfuf* (plural of *leff*) do indeed exist. This then provides an explanation — i.e. the balance of power — for why some degree of order exists, notwithstanding the absence of any specialised order-enforcing agencies, *at the level of size in terms of which these leagues are articulated*. Suppose, for instance, that the units which join these leagues are valley-sized. This then helps to explain why one *valley* will not attack another valley, when a temporary weakness of that neighbour offers a good chance of, say, seizing an upland pasture: the temporary advantage will not be seized for fear of activating the entire system of alliances.

So far so good. But how about conflicts *within* the valley, concerning, say, the division of the pastures it already possesses, or the allocation of water to the irrigation ditches? For there is no sovereign to impose his will *inside* the valley, between its constituent villages or clans, any more than there is one *between* valleys or groups of valleys.

Conflict occurs at every level: about a garden inside a village, about a couple of sheep between two neighbouring hamlets, about a forest between two clans, about a huge upland-plateau summer pasture between two large tribal con-federations. A theory of order-maintenance that invokes leagues whose members are, say, villages, can only explain the preservation of peace at that level, i.e. between villages, but not at any larger or smaller level. Evans-Pritchard's theory succeeds at this very point — in fact, it succeeds *particularly* at this point and highlights the crucial difference between modern society and segmentary tribal ones. In our world, one particular level of organisation — the national state — is crucial for the purpose of order-enforcement and, indeed, in the words of the famous Weberian definition of the state, monopolises legitimate violence. In a segmentary society, on the other hand, the various nested levels are of roughly equal importance, and violence is equally legitimate throughout.

It is also possible to criticise the theory of binary leagues from the opposite viewpoint, by an argument which, if valid (I do not hold that it is), strikes at it and at the 'segmentary' theory equally. It is possible to say that either theory is far too neat, that both endow social reality with an orderly logic which it does not really possess. Situations are far too varied and far too opportunistic for their alignments to follow such tidy lines. The idiom of either binary leagues or of segmentary organisation is indeed only an idiom, in terms of which the participants speak and perhaps even think, rather than act, and which covers a far more complex and fluid reality. Ian Cunnison, studying the nomadic Arabs, the Baggara, wandering in the north-east Sahara, found them using segmentary terminology, while their actual organisation was far less tidy and clear-cut.[6] Clifford Geertz, turning toward North African Islam after his previous work on Indonesia, seems inclined to think that the segmentary idea is imposed by the observer rather than rooted in things.[7] The question is interesting. Those who (like myself) hold the segmentary theory to be true (even if perhaps not the whole truth) are inclined to suspect that some of the fluidity noted by later observers is due to the more effective centralisation of recent decades. When the state at last does take over the task of maintaining order, the mechanisms and units that had previously performed this role as best they could tend to atrophy; they then survive as a terminology rather than as a reality.

This is an interesting question, but one which need not be answered for the purpose of assessing the intellectual significance of Montagne. If he was not quite the equal of Evans-Pritchard in the account of the inner mechanisms of tribal life, he had an advantage over him when it came to tribal relations with the central state. The advantage sprang, as we have already indicated, from the context of his work. In general, the European conquest of the colonial world was, so to speak, sociologically inelegant: sometimes the Europeans dealt with monarchs and spurned the tribes, sometimes they destroyed the monarchy and looked at the tribes in isolation, and sometimes, of course, they dealt with tribes that had in any case been isolated in their prior condition. Morocco was an exception. Here, for once, the conqueror employed a scalpel which exhibited the anatomy or morphology of the society in its entirety, for it wanted at the same time to preserve the monarchy and to make use of the tribes. The dissection was not even lethal; the monarchy is still there, and so are the tribes.

This brings us to Montagne's third theme, the relationship of tribes to the state and to state formation. It is here that he is closest to his great predecessor in North African sociology, Ibn Khaldun. It is here also that the description and the theory in his work merge into each other most closely. There is perhaps no way in which one can theorise and sum up in one formula the inevitably tortuous path by which some mountain marabout or elective tribal leader slowly worms his way up to great power, first in his own segment, then in its rival segments as well, and who finally, with luck, astuteness, opportunity, and ruthlessness, manages to expand and make absolute his authority. But when he does succeed, it is still kinship that provides him with the principles of organisation and cohesion.

... let us set out clearly ... the simple mechanism by which [a tyrant's] emergence and rise to power take place. In a canton the aspiring amghar gains control thanks to the support of a loyal faction based on his own patriarchal family ... In a tribe he triumphs because of the strength of his leff ... In a larger field still, the great caid subdues tribes ... with troops provided by his tribe. He gives the remunerative task of collecting taxes from remote tribes to fellow members of his canton and tribe. It is essentially the exploitation of a whole area by a single tribe.

This concentric structure of the Berber state founded by force explains the facility with which it is established and organised, but it also explains, at the same time, the speed of its disintegration.

When the authority of Abd el Krim snowballed in the Rif after his great victory over the Spaniards, in deference to the spirit of the times he called his state a republic and his government a cabinet — but this cabinet was still composed of his longstanding village companions. The state is only a successful, conquering tribe, and it owes its ephemeral cohesion to its tribal roots. Montagne derives evident satisfaction from tracing the underlying similarities of medieval dynasties and the successful political adventurers of twentieth-century Morocco. It is in this area that his debt to Ibn Khaldun is greatest: cohesion and civilisation are seen as antithetical. Cohesion is the fruit of the hardships of tribal life; hence tribes can on occasion form major political units, but they do so only in the image of their previous tribal existence. In so doing, they lose their cohesion in the end, and the unit disintegrates. Thus all political centralisation is unstable and ephemeral.

This pessimistic political sociology is not universally applicable, even within Islam. There is at least one other model, one brought to its highest level of perfection by the Ottomans: a model in which a ruling elite is recruited not *en bloc* from a successful conquering tribe by, as it were, human bulk purchase but, on the contrary, is brought or conscripted one by one, on the slave markets of the

Black Sea or as a tax levy on Balkan peasants. In such a society, kinship appears not as the sole (albeit fragile) source of cohesion, but as an obstacle to it. Where rulers elsewhere recruited their administrative and executive officers from priests or eunuchs, this society achieves similar ends by taking them from what is technically a class of slaves. Lack of ancestry in a Mamluk, bought, or brought in as tax revenue, can be almost as good an inducement to administrative loyalty and effectiveness as the lack of hope of progeny (real or avowable) in a eunuch or priest. Anyway, this is a different model, and one not so typical of North Africa, even though the Turks brought elements of it to Algeria and Tunisia. The model which *is* illuminated by Montagne's work is the one in which government is primarily a matter of tribes which support the dynasty governing or containing the rest.

This is an important type, well represented among the traditional polities of Africa and Asia, and present as a partial or regional element even in such states as the Ottoman Empire that also exemplify other principles. For the understanding of this model, Montagne remains an important — perhaps the best — source. He constitutes an invaluable corrective to the more popular models of 'feudal' or 'Oriental' society. This last in particular has been overrated of late for various reasons: it may have applied in some cases; it may be a useful parable on Stalinism; it may receive confirmation from what the scribes wrote, if one ignores the fact that they often wrote what the ruler wished for rather than what was in fact the case. But reality was generally more fragile and unstable, and the nature of that precariousness was perhaps best seized, thanks both to the highly specific circumstances of his time and to his own particular genius, by Robert Montagne.[8]

9

Patterns of rural rebellion in Morocco during the early years of independence

Since Moroccan Independence in 1956, there has been a number of relatively minor rural rebellions, in the main in Berber regions. Morocco is an independent country which had undergone a fairly brief colonial period (1912–56), and with a social structure which is a strange amalgam of a pre-industrial but partially urban society, with a modern sector which had emerged rapidly during foreign rule. Its present population is 11½ million, of whom something under a half (no one knows exactly) are Berber-speakers, rural tribesmen whose tribal organisation is fairly well preserved. The rest are Arabic-speakers, urban and rural (disregarding Jewish and European minorities).

This chapter will attempt to throw some light on the place of such tribesmen, whose language is not that of the state in which they live, within the wider society of which they are now part. It will do this through trying to explain the odd and surprising features of the tribal risings mentioned above. These oddities are considerable:

(*a*) The uprisings collapse fairly easily. This is very surprising in view of the past history of Morocco.

(*b*) Its leaders, when captured, are treated with leniency. Though generally imprisoned for indefinite periods, they are not killed. This, likewise, is odd.

(*c*) The uprisings generally simply do not make sense, quite literally. For instance: tribesmen who proclaim themselves supporters of X, stage a rebellion — *whilst X is in office* as Prime Minister. Or again: a rural leader who proclaims himself a supporter of dynastic personage Y stages a rebellion — which is then suppressed *by Y himself*, whose supporter the rebel claims to be, and in whose very support the rebellion was made.

Feature (*c*) is manifestly and genuinely puzzling. We should be puzzled if we found a bona fide Fidelista rebellion against Castro, a Titoist uprising suppressed by the Marshal himself, etc.

Features (*a*) and (*b*) may not seem quite as puzzling to someone not acquainted with Morocco's past: but, at least for the sake and duration of the argument, I must ask that it be accepted that, in the light of even very recent

194

Moroccan history, these features are *most* odd, and indeed just as odd as the self-contradictory feature (*c*).

Some superficial and mistaken explanations:

(*a*) The listener or reader may suspect that where alleged or self-proclaimed followers of X rebel whilst X himself is in power, or where Y suppresses a rising made on his own behalf, all is not what it seems: that the supposed followers of X are not such really, but only falsely claim the appropriate label. Or, that Y is suppressing rebels who only wished to use his name, but who are in fact his enemies. The movements invoking the name of X or Y, he may suspect, are not united but profoundly divided internally.

Now it is certainly the case that all is not as it seems. But it simply is not the case that the followers-of-X are not such really, or those proclaiming allegiance to Y do not really feel it. I must ask that this to be accepted as a fact,[1] and in any case, I propose to put forward an explanation which does not require the assumption of the spuriousness of apparent loyalties.

(*b*) A favourite explanation with journalists commenting on the Moroccan scene: do not attempt to make consistent sense of Moroccan affairs. It *never* makes sense. It is all a matter of personalities, irrational passions, accidents, etc., etc. No explanations are possible or required for the conduct of these people.

This is facile and false. But the frequency with which journalists are forced to invoke such pseudo-explanations, when pressed to attempt any kind of coherent account, is significant.

(*c*) Another favourite explanation, particularly amongst European residents in Morocco: the tribes have gone soft. Their fathers, a mere twenty-five years or so ago, fought fiercely against all comers; and the central power had to stick their heads onto the ramparts of Fez, *pour encourager les autres*. But today . . . the fact that tribal revolts collapse, and that when they do, no heads adorn the walls of the new Ministry of the Interior — whose modern plaster and extensive glass windows are admittedly ill-suited for such decoration — simply indicates degeneracy all round. This explanation is also false.

(*d*) There is an explanation which is often favoured by observers from outside Morocco, and which is also enshrined in a serious study of post-Independence Moroccan politics,[2] and which sees in these occasional rural risings attempts by tribesmen to recover their erstwhile tribal independence. This explanation owes its superficial appeal to fitting in with a widespread and popular stereotype of Berbers, and tribesmen generally, as ferocious near-Noble Savages devoted to tribal ways, anxious to preserve them in their purity for a kind of ethnographic zoo, and resentful of all outside interference. In part, this explanation also appeals to those who are hostile to the new independent Morocco (though this is not true of the author of the volume cited), and who would welcome a demonstration of its incapacity to retain the loyalty of its subjects.

In fact I am confident, in the light of the characteristics of these rural risings, of field observation, and of general considerations, that this explanation is false.

When, in connection with the biggest of the risings, the Rif tribesmen submitted a list of complaints to the central government, the list contained the complaint that the region was *under*-administered and neglected. When confronted with the alternatives of tradition and of the benefits of modernity and industrialism, Moroccan tribesmen behave in conformity to the views of Sir Charles Snow rather than those of Dr Leavis: given the option, they prefer modernity. These risings, whatever they are, simply are not atavistic movements.

(*e*) There is also an explanation very popular with Moroccans themselves. It runs as follows: Morocco is a monarchy. Hence, any rebellion is really an act against the King. But all Moroccans love their King. Admittedly, they neverthe-less, in moments of folly and forgetfulness, commit rebellion. But when they realise what they are doing, they are sorry, and desist. (This explains the early collapse of rebellions.) The King, however, loves all his subjects, and is all too glad to forgive. (This explains the relative leniency towards the culprits.)

I do not propose to discuss the merits of this explanation.

Before an adequate sociological explanation can be offered, the background must be sketched in. Moroccan history, and hence also the history of its urban/ rural, governmental/tribal relationships, has gone through three phases: [I] tra-ditional society, till about 1912 (later for some regions); [IIA] the French period; [IIB] the period of independence, since the winter of 1955–6. IIA and IIB can be lumped together for many purposes as two substages of the 'Modern' period. They have far more in common with each other than either has with I.

Traditional Morocco [I]. Islam obtains throughout (with only a Jewish minority, which can be disregarded for the present purpose). A dynasty rational-ised in terms of Islam: the monarch is a descendant of the Prophet. (This how-ever is not a very strong validation in so far as Morocco is full of people believed to be so descended.) In name, religious unity is complete: not only are all Moroccans Muslims, but they are all *Sunni* Muslims, and moreover, they are all Sunni Muslims of the Maliki rite.

The central power was dynastic. It was based on the walled towns – garrisons as well as centres of learning and trade – and on varying kinds of supporting sheepdogs: foreign mercenaries, slave armies, but above all on privileged (tax-exempt) tribes (which in earlier times were often also the tribe from which the dynasty had sprung: but later, dynasties had non-tribal, Prophet-originating genealogies). Apart from these special, tax-exempt and tax-extracting tribes, the rest of the country was divided into tax-paying and tax-resisting areas: into *blad makhzen* (land of government) and *blad siba* (land of dissidence). The latter fluc-tuated in size but covered something close to half the territory of the country. The loose and fluctuating division of the land into *makhzen* and *siba* was the central fact of Moroccan history: the United States had its moving frontier, Morocco had a static one. Most mountainous and desert terrain, and most but not all Berber areas, were *siba*.

One might well ask whether a country, about half of which is permanently outside the political order and moreover speaks in the main a different language, should be called *one country* at all. Although of course the modern nationalist territorial notion of 'country' was absent, nevertheless I think the answer is Yes. The lands between the Sahara, Atlantic and Mediterranean have a considerable geographic unity (only to the East is the frontier somewhat more arbitrary), and they were united by Islam. Dissidence, though accounting for one half of this territory, was geographically discontinuous, and it was selfconsciously a *dissidence from* something, something which was tacitly recognised in various ways, including the use of the notion of *siba* in self-characterisation.

The relationship between the central power and the tribes of this kind of 'external proletariat' were as follows: the latter were in a permanent *state* of dissidence. (Rebellion, in the language of linguistic philosophers, was a dispositional, not an episodic concept.) They were a threat to the central power; a kind of political womb of potential new dynasties; a moral scandal, being addicted to brigandage, heterodox practices and, allegedly, sexual licence, etc. Similarly, central power was a threat to them: a strong monarch would periodically mount expeditions against them. The essence of government, in fact, was a highly peripatetic court and army, with a multiplicity of 'capitals', and local officials, who were really local power-holders who were ratified by the monarch and had made their submission to him.

Nevertheless, the political bifurcation of the country (*makhzen/siba*) was compatible with unity in other senses. Economic and religious life moved across the (often vague and fluctuating) border between the two kinds of area. Regular pilgrimages took pilgrims across it; markets existed on either side; religious orders had lodges on either side, and local 'saints' had followers drawn from either side. Indeed an important function of the various local religious centres was precisely to facilitate and guarantee contact across septic frontiers, not merely between *makhzen* and *siba*, but also between various tribes.

This aspect of Moroccan history — the existence of a large penumbra of anarchy surrounding the political community — is very well documented, for the following reason: the French policy in Morocco was accompanied and supported by high-powered and highbrow historiography and sociology, and the French case was not so much that modern Morocco was a colonial creation, like some tropical African states, but rather that the overcoming of *siba*, and hence national unification, was a French achievement. Whatever the ideological uses of the historic fact of *siba*, there can be little doubt that it was indeed a fact. Moroccan nationalist writers who react against French interpretations do not deny it, but merely re-interpret it (as indicative, for instance, of democratic rather than absolutist traditions).

To sum up: the traditional power set-up was a mildly unstable stalemate between dynastic central power, based on towns and the plain, and hill and desert tribes who successfully defied it.

The French period [IIA]. This situation changed with the coming of the

French in this century. The colonial period in Morocco took the form of a 'protectorate', i.e. the French ruled 'in the name of' the old dynasty. The *ancien régime* continued, in name. The French *nouveau régime*, however, which effectively ruled, did not also perpetuate the old stalemate with the marginal tribes. It subdued them. (As we have seen, the territorial unification of the country, for the first time, was one of its proud claims.) *All* the tribes were now, by 1934, incorporated in the state. And although the *nouveau régime* had taken some time to subdue the tribes, it was fairly successful in coping with them and administering them subsequently. The antithesis, and the ultimate doom, of the old *makhzen*, i.e. the tribes, was not an insuperable problem for the new, French *makhzen*.

The *nouveau régime* found its doom elsewhere. This part of the story is pure Marx. With the French administration providing security and an infrastructure of transport, communications, etc., a modern economy mushroomed at great speed and generated a typical proletariat of an early stage of industrialisation — recently sucked off the land, uprooted, unspecialised, extremely ill-housed, severely underemployed, and politically explosive. *This* was the dissidence of the new regime. The termination of French rule came when this new internal proletariat went into active dissidence ('terrorism') in the early 1950s, led by a new intelligentsia and in alliance with the symbolic head of the *old* regime. They were joined, when the battle was virtually won, by parts of the countryside as well. They were, of course, helped by the favourable international situation, and in particular by the situation in neighbouring Algeria.

It is interesting to note that each of the two successive regimes was quite capable of coping with the doom, the generated antithesis, of the *other*: like pawns in chess, each could 'take' diagonally, but not straight. The new power could cope with tribes through superior technology and organisation; the old could always cope with an urban mob, mainly by not needing it — rather the reverse, for townsfolk needed the government for defence against the tribes.

But the new proletariat and the recent political history of Morocco as such are not our concerns here: tribal/governmental relations are.

One feature of the French Protectorate period was that the previous wolves-beyond-the-pale became the latest sheepdogs: the central power used the Berber tribesmen to keep order, both through native troops and through tribal tyrants such as the famous Glawi, Pasha of Marrakesh. This was a fairly good way of controlling one of the traditional, walled towns: an *ad hoc* levy of tribesmen would be camped under the walls, and let inside them unless rioters inside desisted. But it was not usable against the new dissidence, the new proletariat, in its shanty-towns, *bidonvilles*. Bidonvilles have no walls, so that there is no way of using a levy as a threat without letting it loose, and in any case, there is not much to loot inside.

Another important feature of this period was that, in one sense, the tribesmen continued to be insulated. It is true that the Pax Gallica prevailed, and tribesmen could go and seek work in the plain, etc. But for those who remained in their villages and encampments – who, after all, were the majority – political life remained, in a new way, as local and circumscribed as before, perhaps more so. This was for a number of reasons:

(1) The *Dahir berbère* And All That. This is one of the most well-worn themes in the discussion of modern Morocco: it is not, in fact, as important as some other associated factors, but in view of its notoriety I shall take it first.

This *dahir* (decree) was promulgated in 1930, and underwrote the retention by Berber tribes of their tribal customary law, if they chose to retain it, as opposed to Koranic Law administered by Koranic judges and to centralised, national law. Tribal law is differentiated from Muslim law by being, of course, secular; and (contrary to a widely held stereotype of the tribal mind) it is seen and held to be secular, as emanating from the traditions of the tribe and changeable by consent. It differs from Muslim law in content on various points, of which the most interesting perhaps are (*a*) method of proof, tribal law recognising and favouring proof by collective oath with supernatural sanctions at traditional shrines, etc., and (*b*) concerning family matters, notably by frequently excluding female inheritance in these severely patrilineal tribes, whereas Koranic law, *in theory*, ensures that the daughter inherits one half of the share of the son. But the most important differentiation of tribal law is not to be found in its content or in its meta-legal theory, but in (*c*) the fact that it invoked local lay tribunals rather than trained, specialised, individual judges.

The historic significance of the promulgation of the *Dahir berbère* was that it triggered off modern Moroccan nationalism, and bridged the gap between old Islamic feeling and the modern national one. The *Dahir* provoked violent protests from the learned guardians of Islam in the old towns, and these protests were echoed in Muslim lands as far as Indonesia. It was seen as the official underwriting of scandalous heterodox practices; it was also seen as a prelude to an attempt at converting the Berbers to Christianity; and it was *also* seen as a Divide and Rule measure destined to alienate the mountain tribes from the national community. The history of modern Moroccan nationalist movements begins with the protest movements against the *Dahir berbère*.

(2) The tribal regions were now administered by military officers or civilians (according to region) and, in practice, every region lived a political life fairly insulated from the others. It is true that all regions were united with each other in one political system; but unifying links between them were modern, not only on the physical plane (cars, jeeps, and telephones, which in rural areas were most precarious), but, more significantly, they were such on the human plane. They were connected by a network of bureaucrats, Frenchmen, in French, related by a modern bureaucratic hierarchy and procedures. All these were of course a mystery to the tribesmen: as far as they were concerned, the local district officer was the representative of a power whose principles and inner mechanics they did not understand and could not hope to influence. There was

hardly any question of playing off someone at the centre of the hierarchy against its local representative: the tribesmen would not have known how to find, how to approach, or how to influence such a personage at the centre. Hence each administrative district was, for the tribesmen, a complete world on its own, whose battles and problems were worked out locally.

All this is a slight exaggeration. Some exceptional, really big tribal chieftains could play a political game at a more than local level. The Glawi, friend of Winston Churchill, lived a cosmopolitan life in the political as well as other senses[3] with town houses in Paris and Casablanca as well as a palace in Marrakesh and a castle in the tribal homelands amongst the Glawa tribe. Occasionally, and notably under the Glawi's leadership, local rural leaders might form a political movement active on the national level. Again, a local tribal dignitary might resist the French administration's pressure on a point of national policy;[4] but these were exceptions. Basically, local life was local life, self-enclosed and self-sufficient. The links which united the regions were beyond the reach or the comprehension of illiterate tribesmen.

The theory of power during this period was that of *reduplication*: just as, at the top (in theory), power was shared by the Sultan and the French proconsul, so at each level a Moroccan and a French official were paired off (excepting, of course, at the lowest levels − village headmen did not have an attendant Frenchman − and in technical services). The reality was, however, affected by different factors. Take any administrative region: at its head, a French captain and a tribal caid, such dignitaries being imposed on (and chosen from) even those tribes who did not traditionally have any permanent chiefs, but elected them annually. The two men, captain and caid, faced each other: but their positions were very different. The captain was at the bottom end, at the end of the antennae, as it were, of a hierarchy reaching up to the proconsul, assisted by many specialist technical agencies, and endowed with genuine means of communication, moral and physical, and a discipline. The caid, on the other hand, was at the top of a local hierarchy, leading up from village or clan headmen to himself, with whom he in turn could communicate perfectly. One of the men, the caid, was as it were, at the ceiling of his world, the other, the captain, on the floor of his: yet they were at the same level, both supervising the same number of people and the same area, and even, roughly, with similar power. The consequence was this: for the tribesmen, political life was the conflict of local groups, alignments, lineages, families, for local power, and the game was played out within the region: it was of course important, indeed crucial, to gain the support of the administration, but this meant, essentially, its one local regional representative. There was not much point − nor the means − to look towards the provincial or, still less, the national capital. Each administrative district was politically, very nearly an island unto itself − despite the fact that roads were clear of bandits and one could cross tribal frontiers in security.[5]

Transition from [IIA] *to* [IIB]. Independence came during the winter of

1955–6, as a result of a number of factors, including the international situation, urban 'terrorism', etc., and, towards the end, rural uprisings. Only these last concern us.

First of all, it is interesting that the rural troubles for the French came only towards the end, when the direction of events was becoming clear, and contained an element of band-waggon-jumping. I am not suggesting that the tribesmen were basically pro-French: but what does follow, I think, is that a reasonably intelligent and well-organised *nouveau régime*, a modern administration which is well-staffed, well-informed and well-trained, does not have too much difficulty in controlling tribal populations in areas where the tribal organisation is well preserved. These rural social structures, like some kind of scaffolding, are easy to perceive: there are no large anonymous, amorphous, uncontrollable masses. It is not difficult to operate a 'prefect system' which utilises internal local divisions and provides sufficient spoils for some to control the others. A squirearchy of caids was supported, and if necessary invented and created.

When rural troubles did come, they varied in kind, along a spectrum whose extremes were the following: (*a*) fully planned, 'modern' operations, based in this case on Spanish territory; these were in no sense tribal, but manned rather by 'politically conscious elements'; (*b*) totally unplanned, genuinely tribal and extremely violent outbreaks of hysteria, such as that of the Smala tribe on 20 August 1955, leading to the massacre (and multiple retaliatory counter-massacre) of Oued Zem. Other risings were between these extremes: for instance, they might be led by a nucleus of 'politically conscious' men who had received instructions from the underground political party, but who led men who still acted in local kin units.

Those groups of rebels who were at all organised continued to exist, and indeed to multiply, even after the French had given in and fighting had ceased. Indeed, the number of such groups multiplied, and many were by then locally organised and drilled. They were known as units of the 'Army of Liberation'.

An important fact for the present argument is the following: during the negotiations between nationalist leaders and the French in the autumn of 1955, and indeed earlier, an important argument on the French side — sincere or not — was to query the standing of the opposing negotiators, or would-be negotiators, and to cast doubts on their qualification to speak for their fellow-nationals. A frequent argument from the illiberal French Right was always that there are no valid representatives, that the 'agitators' are not entitled to speak for their contented or misguided fellow-nationals, that there are no *interlocuteurs valables*.

The answer on the part of the national leaders was this: we prove that we speak for our nationals, that *we* — and not this or that political rival or French stooge — are the recognised leaders, by the fact that *our* order for a cessation of hostilities will be observed. For, as stated, the countryside was full of growing armed or militant groups, some of them engaged in hostilities. Some of them were certainly organised by the nationalist leaders who claimed authority over them; others had arisen in all kinds of semi-spontaneous ways. It is doubtful whether anyone could be quite sure whose order they would take. In the end, these groupings were disbanded or incorporated in the new Royal Army: but only in the end, and after several years of continued activity.

The point which is crucial here is this: there was a situation where no one really knew clearly whose authority counted. There had been no election conferring a mandate on this or that man or party, and if there had been, it would not have been very relevant. The only demonstration — or, indeed, disproof — of a claim to leadership and authority by a man in the capital was that *his* voice was heeded by some reasonably formidable organised group in the countryside. Very crudely, the weight of a man's, or party's, voice in the capital was a function of the number of men willing to lay down their arms at his orders in the countryside. The self-identification of the *interlocuteurs valables* in the face of the French set up a model for the demonstration of influence in the subsequent years of Independence.

Independence [IIB]. Independent modern Morocco came into being in the spring of 1956. In theory, this was a restoration of the pre-French-protectorate, pre-1912 state. Theoretically all power was vested in the Sultan,[6] who however now, significantly, decided to have himself called king, (*'malik'*), thus hinting at the shift of image from theocratic empire to national state. So much for theory. The realities had changed since 1912. There were now modern towns alongside the old, and vast shanty-towns alongside the new towns, a modern administrative machinery and economic infrastructure, a small modern elite. Also, as indicated, there was no longer a penumbra of dissident tribes.

The political situation of the tribes was now determined by the following factors: abrogation of the *Dahir berbère*; the setting up of 'rural communes'; abolition of the 'feudal class'; the administration; the Separation of Powers; the emergence of political parties. Each of these must be considered in turn.

The abrogation of the *Dahir berbère*. Tribal customary law and tribunals were now abolished, and replaced by national law administered by appointed, non-local judges. As far as the actual content of law was concerned, this made a less profound difference than one might suppose. For instance, collective tribal lands (pastures, forests) were the concern of the Ministry of Interior, not of Justice, and its agents were free to adjudicate or decide disputes according to traditional local criteria. Judges were also aided by 'assessors' whose role was not all that different from that of members of Customary Law tribunals under the French. But it did mean the termination of the customary tribunals and their sessions — which used to be prolonged, regular, and canalised much local energy into cheap and enjoyable litigation — and this termination incidentally stimulated a greater recourse to informal arbitration, which in a sense was closer to the real, pre-French traditional situation than was the embalming of 'custom' in the ice-box of indirect rule.

Whilst tribal separatism was to be abolished, new 'rural communes' were to be set up, as forms of local democracy and aids for development. In fact, however, these were a long time coming, and when they were set up and elections held for them in 1960, they did not amount to much: their powers and resources are too limited. They may yet — especially if the Left come to power — become institutions of importance; but as yet they are not very significant.

The class of tribal caids was abolished. The *name* was transferred to the bureaucrat, a non-local official, who now replaced the French district officer. The only locally-recruited office-holders were headmen at village level, or at most clan level where the groups involved were not very large. This did have an enormously important consequence: there was no outlet, in the *official* hierarchy of the state, for the ambitious local who wished to operate locally, or whose local interests or lack of formal education prevented other than local activity. Admittedly, there were the village headmanships — but the power, prestige and perks attaching to these are not significant.

The essence of Independence was the continuation of the administrative machine, but with Moroccan personnel replacing the French. But: as indicated, the old dualism was gone. A district no longer had an official, representing central power, facing a tribal leader, representing the local groups: there was only *one* administrative hierarchy, which down to and including the level of district officer consists of appointed, non-local professional officials, and which below that level consists of local, non-professional, part-time headmen, etc.

But if the central/local duality disappeared, another form emerged. One of the big slogans of post-Independence Morocco was the 'Separation of Powers', a Good Thing which characterises all forward-looking nations. There are various reasons why this excellent eighteenth-century ideal should have been so much invoked in Morocco: opposition to the usurpation of powers by the French previously, the 'confusion of powers', as the Moroccan press called it; the fact that it was a slogan cherished by the Left as a future lever against royal power, and also by the monarchy against party power; and as a diversion of interest from the failure to implement some other anticipated reforms which were expected from a constitutional, democratic, progressive state. The separation of powers meant a number of things, and some of its manifestations were odd.[7]

But in the rural tribal areas it had primarily the following meaning: previously, the district officer, whilst facing the tribal leader, was himself the undisputed and complete master of the administrative outpost and all the important and manifold activities emanating from it. The administrative outpost, one should say, is a striking and important enclave in tribal lands, standing for the central power and modernity. Now, however, authority within it came to be divided: the administrator and the new judge were distinct, and each had his own Ministry to answer. Each tended to be 'modern' at least to the extent of understanding what went on in the capital. This opposition was not one between a man who could appeal to the centre and one who could not (but on the contrary based his power on a local following and understanding), but between two men neither of whom was a local and both of whom could appeal to the centre. Ironically, and inconveniently if they were in conflict, both these capital-oriented officials depended on the same solitary and highly precarious telephone line, the same telephone line operator, etc., and hence were liable to have some difficulty in keeping things secret from each other.[8]

The recruitment of the new administration was from: (*a*) men who had held subordinate positions as clerks, interpreters, etc., to the French, (*b*) men distinguished in the Resistance against the French, and (*c*) men literate in the traditional, Arabic-urban sense. It was the first of these classes, with their prior knowledge and experience of the administration that was to be kept going, who were the most important.

The political parties. These organised widely immediately after Independence, setting up cells throughout the country. In the immediate post-Independence wave of enthusiasm, recruitment was enormous, and it has been calculated that the total claimed membership of all the parties was larger than the total population of the country. But even subsequently, cells and organisation and affiliation survived. This is the crucial fact. The parties provided an organisation, a hierarchy, and a channel of information leading right up to the provincial and national capitals. The rural regions were now incorporated in the national community, and local politics were not, as under the French, locally circumscribed.

Hence it was now important to have a line to the capital, to have a friend at court. Moreover, there was no outlet other than political parties for the ambitious local: the official hierarchy was now single-track, or at least not divided on the local/central principle, and all posts in it at attractive levels, i.e. at all levels above the very lowest, were reserved for full-time non-local officials. These factors explain the incentives for the locals to be active in the parties; and there were equally incentives for 'men at court', i.e. politicians at the national level, to be willing and anxious to organise these channels and antennae leading into the recesses of the countryside. This was not merely because it was always possible that the much-announced national elections would really be held one day: but also, as explained earlier, influence at the centre was in part a function of what rural support a man could claim or mobilise. This was a game of poker in which generally hands were not shown, and in which frequently the participants themselves were not sure, and not in a position to be sure, what cards they held. What locals *said* was not of much consequence: they might proclaim a lot of things (notably an unwavering love of the King), or cautiously keep quiet;[9] what mattered was whom they would obey in a crisis, and this could not be ascertained in advance.[10]

This is not the place to trace the history of the parties. Suffice it to say that, by the end of the 1950s, three important parties emerged and had their antennae of patronage and organisation reaching out into the country: the Right, the Left, and the allegedly Berber-Separatist party.

The material must now be drawn together and set against its background.

Morocco is a transitional country, which means, amongst other things, that most of the people involved know that fundamental changes in society are coming, and that most of the present social environment — political, economic, social — is extremely precarious and temporary. Hence, the political struggle is played for enormous stakes: not for marginal advantages, or for top positions in a stable structure, but, on the contrary, for control of the direction of the fundamental changes: and the winner takes all. The struggle has not been played out: at present, the parties are jockeying for position and awaiting the suitable moment.

In the meantime, influence is a matter of followers, and followers are those who will follow you in a crisis, or when *the* crisis comes, rather than simply those who will vote for you. (There have in any case been no elections other than local ones.) The incorporation of the countryside in the political life of the nation has meant, in effect, the burgeoning of a number of systems of patronage and support, of a *number* of central nervous systems whose nerve ends reach into the villages. The systems rival the official hierarchies — those, in particular, of the Ministry of Interior, and of Justice — and indeed cut across them and intertwine with them: an official's political loyalty is, in the end, more important than his loyalty to his formal superior, at any rate in a crisis. This complex wiring does of course lead to short-circuits of the currents of power.

These systems of patronage and support are, however, necessarily in part covert, and also extremely loose-jointed, so to speak. They are anchored onto local situations by being connected with local rivalries: the local Montagues join party X, and the Capulets become the branch secretaries of Y. But the local issues dividing the Montagues and Capulets have a good deal of autonomy, and are not necessarily connected with national ones: *one* of the things which is liable to happen is that they erupt into violence, as local strife in rural Morocco habitually has done in the past, and take on the appearance of political violence. But this is not the only thing which happens. The local rural pressure-organisations must, if they are to be useful to their patrons at the centre, remain fairly ready to be activated for overt action at short notice. They are there, so to speak, with detonators in place and barely a safety-catch on. From time to time, they are triggered off: it may be, through one of the local quarrels which really have nothing to do with national issues; or again, it may be that some patron wishes for once to strike a match to see whether it will work when the day comes, or he may wish to show opponents what good matches he has.

When some of this politically explosive material in the countryside is set off in one of these ways, if it does not spread into a national conflagration and trial of strength — which, so far, has not happened — it is put out rapidly. The patron continues to sit in the capital, he may even have to take part in the suppression of a tribal rising which for the time being he cannot commend overtly; but when its leaders are brought to gaol it is his task to see to it that they do not face the full consequences of their transgression. And in as far as alignments at the centre are complex and manifold, it is generally not to the interest of those who could exact full retribution to antagonise some group definitively by doing so.

All this, I believe, explains the strange patterns of rural risings, with their rapid collapse and lenient aftermaths — relatively — since Independence. The national political battle has not been fought, and until it is, these little rural dress-rehearsals, the limberings-up of the limbs of patronage and support, are played with restraint: a flare-up, then everyone looks around for reactions, the positions held are analysed as in chess, and the weaker side resigns in a civilised manner — for the time being. Hence it is quite wrong to see these risings as atavistic reversals to tribal independence: they are the very reverse, being a participation in a national game. There is of course some historical connection between the lands of the old dissidence, and the areas of activation of 'armies of liberation', etc.; but the phenomenon is quite different.[11]

10

Saints and their descendants

Sidi Lahcen Lyussi was a noted seventeenth-century Moroccan saint. He was born in 1631 among the Berber tribes of the upper Muluya valley. Like other such saints, he was, or was credited with being, an arbitrator both between rival tribes and between the tribal world and the central power. An inter-tribal treaty dated 1642 (or rather, of course, the equivalent year of the Muslim era) invokes him as conciliator and guarantor in disputes between diverse People of the Shadow, i.e. various tribes of the northern slopes of the Atlas. This would make him eleven years old when he acted as an inter-tribal Kissinger, which suggests precocity even for a saint. A French commentator, Jacques Berque, tactfully observes in a footnote of his *Al-Yousi*[1] that *cet acte, daté de 1642 . . . semble prématuré . . .* People really should take more care about how they date their treaties.

The seventeenth century was an exceptionally turbulent and anarchic period, even by the standards of traditional Morocco. Rival authorities, generally claiming religious legitimation, disputed the land with each other and with the tribes. Two politico-religious issues were of importance, then as now, and our saint made his contribution to both of them. One concerns the standing, the rights and duties, of the central power, and the other deals with the position of the living saints, their power of intercession and their participation in mystical or popular practices. These two great issues are interconnected. It is possible to see the monarch as merely the greatest of the marabouts, or alternatively as that central authority which is impelled, both by the need to monopolise power and as a guardian of orthodoxy, to be at the very least wary of the rural thaumaturges.

Al Yussi seems to have been a careful moderate on both issues. During the latter part of his life he saw anarchy mitigated by the establishment of the present Moroccan dynasty. He dared address two reproachful letters to Mulay Ismail, the famous and brutal restorer of order. As Jacques Berque points out, in their implied hints at the right of rebellion against a ruler who fails in his duties, Al Yussi's admonitions went further than those of his contemporary Bossuet when addressing Louis XIV. But then, in his old age, Al Yussi took the precaution of not accepting invitations to come to court and remained with his

Berbers, or so the legends claim. Paul Rabinow oddly observes, in *Symbolic Domination*,[2] that 'Sidi Lahcen was bold enough to refuse the offer' to come to court; but it would have been more perilous and bold to *accept* such an invitation. He died on 11 September 1681, we are told by Professor Berque, who also notes the irony inherent in his folk canonisation:

> Miracles multiply around the shrine. In truly North African style, the scourge of spurious mystics, the aggressive champion of orthodoxy, himself turns into a rural saint. Would this have surprised him?[3]

Whatever fame Al Yussi acquired in the seventeenth century, he could hardly have had a better international reception in the twentieth. Western scholarship has so far accorded him at least three separate studies, and the quality of this attention is even more remarkable than its quantity. Professor Berque, professor at the Collège de France, is an outstanding French Islamicist, and Clifford Geertz not merely occupies a similar position among American anthropologists of his generation, but also constitutes the bridgehead of the social sciences at the Institute of Advanced Studies at Princeton. His *Islam Observed*[4] was a comparative study of the two geographic extremes of the Muslim world, Indonesia and Morocco, and, making extensive use of Professor Berque's book, it treated Al Yussi as the paradigm of Moroccan culture. So, the upstart Berber from the triste high savannah of the upper Muluya valley can hardly complain of his international audience.

Professor Berque and Professor Geertz are veritable *igurramen* in their own cultures, with loads of *baraka* — so much charisma as to excite both the admiration and the envy of others, as is the fate of *igurramen*. Dr Rabinow, on the other hand, is a young American anthropologist and thus an apprentice, and his work cannot properly be appraised without relating him to his spiritual lineage. As indicated, it is a formidable one. Professor Berque and Professor Geertz are, each of them, both conceptual and literary poets. Each of them has carried out massive and detailed ethnographic research, which somehow licenses their flights of interpretation. But in consequence, it makes them dangerous models to emulate.

Dr Rabinow does not replicate the work of his two predecessors. At the heart of his book lies an ethnographic study of the village community, a substantial proportion of which claims descent from the seventeenth-century saint. Neither of his predecessors had done this. Professor Berque's book was a piece of documentary political, social and intellectual history and interpretation — he had done his fieldwork elsewhere, as had Professor Geertz — while Professor Geertz's was an essay in comparative cultural anthropology. It is the ethnographic part of Dr Rabinow's book which is both new and valuable, and constitutes a genuine and useful contribution to the documentation of Moroccan social life. For instance, it is fascinating to learn about the anti-saint campaign in the village in 1967. The pendulum which had been swinging in Islam for a long time, between an egalitarian, scripturalist monotheism and a more mystical, ecstatic cult of saints, has tended of late to swing so far in North Africa that one wonders whether it will be permanently unhinged. The crucial connection between political centralisation and diminished reverence for saints and their progeny is noted by Dr Rabinow: 'By reinforcing and shoring up the courts [the French] undermined the mediation function [of the saints] . . . ' The post-Independence state is even more centralised than the colonial one. But, most strangely for one who takes 'culture' so seriously, Dr Rabinow does not discuss the pan-Maghreb and pan-Islamic Reform and anti-saint movement, only barely mentioning 'questions of Islamic Reform'. One might get the impression that the conflict is either a local thing, or emanates from a mysterious entity called culture. Qui est donc cette dame?

The non-ethnographic part of the book is less than convincing. For instance, it asserts as a fact that the saint 'demanded and received a . . . decree from the sultan testifying to his legitimate status as a [descendant of the Prophet]'. But two pages later it emerges that the evidence for this is a *local* legend. Now local legends which describe the saint's moral victory over the monarch are of course profoundly significant — they say, in effect, that our local saint is of top quality because he once bested the king himself in a contest of holiness! Our home team is good, it once actually scored against Leeds — by using the sultan as the ultimate yardstick, the local legend naively endorses his authority. *That* it should do so is of course of the utmost significance. But *what* this shows is something totally different from the implications of a historic document, signed by the sultan and endorsing the saint. I know of no evidence of such a document, and Dr Rabinow offers none; he merely treats the local story as its equivalent, when in fact its sociological significance is almost diametrically the opposite. What is at issue is not the relative historical reliability of document and oral tradition, but *motive*: who says what to whom for what end, is enormously important. If locals say that the king endorsed their village-pump shrine, and that he was in fact spiritually compelled to do so, this indicates something quite different from a situation in which the king himself says so, quite irrespective of whether either party speaks truly.

Dr Rabinow seems at this point to be echoing *Islam Observed*: '[The sultan's] answer to maraboutism was to license it; or anyway, to try to'. Perhaps this was his answer, and no doubt sultans did issue certificates of 'sherifian' descent. But all we have been offered, in the context of Lyussi, is evidence that a local holy lineage, by anchoring its legend to an alleged encounter with the monarch, unwittingly licensed *his* authority, by implication making its own legitimacy derivative from it. This sheds no light at all on the sultan's policy, though it sheds a great deal on that of the lineage.

Or take again the question, so crucial for Islam, of the use of the hereditary principle in religion and in the choice of leaders. There are indeed fascinating parallels between the issues of Yussi's own life in the seventeenth century, about which we learn from the documents cited in Professor Berque's book, and the village-pump battle in 1967, well described by Dr Rabinow. But Dr Rabinow goes too far: 'The rise of the genealogical principle and its successful institutionalization occurred at the time of Sidi Lahcen.' The idea that the hereditary principle had to wait for the seventeenth century is weird. This also seems to be an echo of *Islam Observed*:

Two major classes of answer were, sometimes separately, sometimes simultaneously, given [to the question of the sources of sanctity]: what we may call the miraculous and the genealogical . . . though the two principles were often, after the seventeenth century perhaps most often, invoked together, they were yet separate principles, and in the tension between them can be seen reflected much of the dynamic of Moroccan cultural history.

Now it seems to me most doubtful whether the seventeenth century was such a watershed, whether there is any such tension, whether magic and ancestry were opposed, and whether indeed either of them could, for any length of time, operate on its own. Ancestry alone either over-produces leadership and thus brings about an inflationary devaluation of its currency (as often happens), or, in conjunction with primogeniture or some other form of restrictive rule (not much in evidence in Morocco), becomes too rigid. Magic on its own is too liberal: by permitting free entry into the market — no guild can impose restrictive practices on charisma — and granting a *carrière ouverte aux talents maraboutiques*, it leads to excessive instability and goes against the grain of a kinship-oriented society. The most viable mix is a judicious blend of magical powers and ancestry (especially when the latter is adjustable *ex post*, whether by oral tradition or written charters). Such a mix contains the socially required proportions of constraint and free play.

The change which may really have occurred at that time is quite another one: perhaps it was then that the *idiom* of prestigious ancestry came to be articulated in terms of links with the Prophet. It is still possible to find saintly lineages not claiming such a link, for instance in southern Arabia. Clearly the conversion to the specifically 'sherifian' idiom of prestigious ancestry must be a datable historical event, whether or not we know the date, though of course the date may vary from place to place. But this change of idiom of genealogy is something quite different from the alleged confluence of previously separate magical and genealogical principles, an idea which seems both implausible and speculative.

Incidentally, the political or constitutional implications of the 'sherifian' idiom of sanctity-conferring ancestry are ambiguous. It is true that they imply a kind of recognition of the monarchy: we are meritorious because we are *shurfa*, says the local holy lineage, and the sultan is a *sherif* too. So by the same token the sultan is meritorious. All *shurfa* are *shurfa* but the sultan is more so. But equally, when convenient, it can be read the other way: we too are *shurfa*. So, Our Lord King, do not try any urban holier-than-thou one-upmanship on us, or at least don't overdo it. And incidentally, is it not wrong of you to tax your own kin? So there are certain psychic and tactical advantages to be gleaned from these genealogical links with the monarch, even when they stop short, for the time being, of claiming complete autonomy or equality.

While the allegations of tension between genealogy and magic seem to me questionable, there seems to be another competition, better attested in history and ethnography, between sanctity (ancestry plus magic) on the one hand, and moral merit and scriptural learning on the other. (This may of course be mistaken for the other tension, when moral merit is held to be a cause of magical powers, or ancestry a cause of both.) It is also true that the modern world tends to force the saints to retrench, and they often now shed their various attributes separately and in succession. Magical powers may go first (district officers generally have a strong aversion against the practice of magic by their parishioners, whatever cultural anthropology may say), while genealogy may linger on. But when in full use, were they distinct?

Whatever the truth about these intriguing matters, Dr Rabinow's handling of them is far too culture-metaphysical to carry conviction. He is correspondingly slapdash when dealing with hard-core questions of social organisation. He dismisses the crucial question — what is a North African tribe? — by saying, there are no tribes, only *qabilah*. Is this a playful insistence on using only the local concept, on principle? No; for he gives us some reasons why, in his view, there are no tribes. The evidence is that the local term refers to a 'commonality [which] may have a variety of sources, and . . . can refer to groupings as small as a household or as large as the nation'. Indeed. It is precisely this 'nested' quality of the *qabilah* or the *taqbilt*, the fact that the terms can refer to any of a whole series of superimposed groups of quite diverse size, each activated by a different contingency, which has led other anthropologists to elaborate and accept the notion of *segmentary* tribes. If Dr Rabinow has good reasons for rejecting this notion, he has kept them to himself. But it would have been better to discuss its relevance to his own material, which appears consistent with it, than to dismiss the whole issue with a patronising aphorism. To be candid, it is the metaphysical aphorisms in the book which really deserve pruning.

Or take the absolutely crucial issue of the relationship of central government to tribal dissidence, of *makhzen* to *siba*. (For undisclosed reasons, Dr Rabinow also talks as if *siba* in his community had a definite commencement — an odd idea.) Referring to this contrast as allegedly handled in the 'French sources', Dr Rabinow dismisses it sententiously: 'This is a radically inadequate description. It is too spatial, too substantialist, and much too solid and corporeal a view . . . ' Here Dr Rabinow is simply perpetuating a myth, to the effect that French scholarship reified or over-formalised the government/dissidence distinction. On such a view, you'd expect a road-sign along the track from Fez to the mountains, saying ACHTUNG SIBA, or something like 'You are now leaving the American Sector.' Who ever held such a view? Dr Rabinow does not even mention the greatest of the French political anthropologists, Robert Montagne. If he consults his work, he will find that Montagne actually stresses that the boundary between central authority and tribal *fronde* was a matter of endlessly subtle and barely perceptible gradations: from the absolute power in the plain to the annual elective chief of the high mountains, one passed *par des transitions insensibles.*[5] Dr Rabinow does not cite the men whom he claims to correct, but only an American summary of them, one written entirely and openly on the basis of library research within the United States. As such a merely preliminary survey, Bernard Hoffman's *The Structure of Traditional Moroccan Rural Society*,[6] which firmly refrained from claiming to be anything else, was a good effort; but if one wishes to refute the authors whom he was summarising, it is better to consult their own words.

Marred by too much communing with ineffables — authenticities, galloping tensions, cultural categories, symbolic formulations which are the vehicles of meaning, and inevitably, alienation — and by inadequate attention to the concrete, Dr Rabinow's book is nevertheless useful for its ethnography, and one hopes that this will in due course be made more complete, as a prefatory remark promises. Amal Rassam Vinogradov's study of a lay tribe, not at all distant from Yussi's shrine, *The Ait Ndhir of Morocco*,[7] is far more successful and satisfactory, both logically and aesthetically. Her study is less ambitious, or perhaps one should say, ambitious in the right direction.

Her book is tightly organised and impeccably lucid. If it has a fault, it is that it is too brief — one would like to know more detail, even if it were anecdotal — and that it offers no novel interpretation. But within the terms of reference it sets itself, it is hard to fault it. Historical and ethnographic evidence is assembled and brought to bear on the same topic, without confusing sources and hence the significance of either. The data are related to existing issues concerning Moroccan society, with great clarity.

We learn from her, among other things, what kind of lay tribes and clients kept those saints and *shurfa* going, and had need of their services, and how they were rewarded. Where Dr Rabinow notes, convincingly, how centralisation undermined the basis of this role, Dr Vinogradov also observes an interesting temporary counter-current:

Despite the fact that the political roles of ... shurfa, as mediators and arbitrators, was undermined by the Pax Gallica, their socio-psychological function, if anything, increased during the early years of the Protectorate ... The anxious and insecure Ndhiri turned to the shurfa and marabouts ... By 1940, it was evident that the French had ... facilitated the cultural conquest of the Ait Ndhir by the urban Arab.

Her subject is an erstwhile pastoral but now sedentarised tribe to the south of the imperial cities of Fez and Meknes. Their tribal territory also includes, though Dr Vinogradov does not mention this, one of the more fashionable of Morocco's skiing resorts. The Aid Ndhir did not benefit much, either in the past or in the present, from the proximity to the imperial centre or to its modern playgrounds.

Saints and their descendants

They distinguish between tribes allied to the ruler, tribes too weak to resist him, and tribes who are free and independent, and in the past they were proud to belong to the wolves, rather than be either sheep or sheepdogs. They lived on this border between government and dissidence:

Whenever the tribe was at war with the government, it abandoned its cultivated territories and retired to the plateau; as things improved, they returned to the plain . . .

The consequence seems to have been collective ownership of land, with councils allocating plots to individual households. Unfortunately Dr Vinogradov does not or cannot tell us the frequency of reallocations. On the crucial issue concerning Berber social organisation, she takes a moderate view:

It is both arbitrary and unrewarding to conceive of the socio-political system of the Ait Ndhir in exclusively segmentary or alliance terms. A more realistic interpretation would be derived if one were to view the social order in terms of a dynamic interplay of the two models.

The Ait Ndhir, on her evidence — though she does not say so in these words — seem to have had fairly weak chieftaincies and much anarchy and looseness in organisation. Though familiar with the standard Berber institutional devices usable for such an end, they do not seem to have acted as one unit. Two factors distort the segmentary model: excessively great surrounding instability and internal stratification. They seem to have been affected by the first of these in the past, and by the second since the ending of tribal dissidence, which the old men recall with nostalgia.

About their present condition, Dr Vinogradov is both more pessimistic and more concrete than Dr Rabinow is about his saints. According to him, what the progeny of Sidi Lachen Lyussi want is 'authenticity'. The predicament of the humbler Ait Ndhir is more intelligible:

Massive acquisition of tribal land for agricultural colonisation and the forced introduction of private property . . . led to the breakdown of the tribal framework and the formation of a landless, anomic rural proletariat.

11

The marabouts in the market-place

Eickelman's *Moroccan Islam* and Brown's *People of Salé* are two very valuable and highly comparable books, which make a most significant contribution to our knowledge of Moroccan society and Islam in general.[1] Both authors are young Americans, though one of them teaches in England. No outsider would be able to guess, without benefit of blurb, whether either book is written by an anthropologist with a sense of history, or by a historian with a penchant for interview and oral tradition. There is no trace in either work of that synchronicity which used to characterise anthropology, with historical facts segregated into a kind of ghetto chapter. Neither author could conceivably be open to the stricture which John Davis levels at the failure of anthropologists working in the Mediterranean to make use of history, when he observes ironically in his excellent *Mediterranean People* that 'history is a kind of social change' (i.e. deals with those unfortunate social traits which are not properly functional and do not have the grace to be stable).[2]

Traditional Islam covers both urban life, which provides the cultural infrastructure for a scripturalist religion, and a tribal countryside — with a corresponding spectrum in religious belief and practice. The two authors have chosen complementary topics. Ken Brown deals with the old-established town of Salé, famous in English literature and popular consciousness through Robinson Crusoe and for its pirates; Dale Eickelman deals with an important holy lineage which has long dominated, politically and religiously, a very large part of the Atlantic plain of Morocco.

The fact that there is one single spectrum in Islam may be more important than that it stretches between two opposed poles, between saint and scholar. The scholar may aspire to saintly powers, and the saint includes scholarship amongst his sanctity-conferring attributes. Similarly, the social bases of the two Muslim centres explored in these works are not in total contrast. Mr Brown makes plain the deep involvement of the town of Salé with its rural hinterland. As for Boujad, the home of the Sherqawa saints who are Mr Eickelman's subject — it was no isolated monastery in a tribal wilderness. For instance, in 1883,

214

The marabouts in the market-place

Boujad ... served ... as a major market center. Some [members of the saintly lineage] participated in the market as merchants ... and as guarantors of the market's peace. The weapons of the tribesmen were deposited with the lord of the *zawya* or one of his kinsmen for its duration. Sherqawa also acted as escorts ... for caravans ...

This kind of political and economic role for sanctity in a semi-anarchic tribal milieu is entirely characteristic, and of its essence.

In general outline, this phenomenon is well known. Mr Eickelman's major achievement is to add a very thoroughly researched, sensitively interpreted, elegantly and readably presented case study, which combines meticulous attention to local detail with a convincing account of its wider context. He describes both the traditional situation, which he calls the period of 'maraboutic hegemony', and the subsequent erosion of the position of saints by political centralisation (mediators are not required for trade or feud, when the state protects the one and proscribes the other) and by the anti-saint, anti-mediation propaganda of the modern Reform movement.

Mr Eickelman seizes one aspect of the matter when he says that 'the core of belief in maraboutism is quite simple. It postulates that relations between men and the supernatural operate in nearly the same way as do relations between men only'. Maraboutism was indeed God's own patronage network. But in fact it both mirrored and complemented human relations: some tribesmen *avoided* having to bow to secular patrons by the use of spiritual ones, who being spiritual had to be pacific, and hence could not be too extortionate. Maraboutism as a relation to God has been undermined by the fact that relations between men have changed. Ironically a society which has probably, through centralisation, become *more* patronage-ridden in daily life than it had been previously, has at the same time tried to disabuse itself of patronage ideas in religion. Nowadays, as one of his townsmen informants told Mr Eickelman: 'Of course the radio says that everything comes directly from God.' Hence 'the clients of the marabouts ... are aware much more sharply than in the past that there are other conceptions of Islam in which there is no room for marabouts'. There is no paradox in the fact that patronage in the worldly sphere has gone up just when it declined in the religious sphere; for the old political functions of the religious patronage networks are now being usurped by plain politics.

It is possible, however, that Mr Eickelman, in common with other members of his particular school, exaggerates the extent to which the worldly sphere had, even in the past, been patronage-ridden. He holds that 'dyadic, personally contracted bonds of inferiority and superiority ... are thought to structure the Moroccan social order'. At present this may well be so. But in the past, dyadic and unequal relations, symbolised by a ritual sacrifice or an act of submission by one party to another, were only one of two types of possible significant relation between men or groups. The other kind was egalitarian kinship, symbolised by the equal relationship of brothers, whether in the present or between putative

215

brothers—ancestors. Now that Morocco is no longer predominantly tribal, while the state is not yet (if it ever will be) impersonally bureaucratic, patronage naturally flourishes, and hence dyadic unsymmetrical relations may indeed be the norm; but it is dangerous to to retroject this onto the past without qualification. At the very time when dyadic inequality was the norm in religion, it did *not* also have the monopoly of human relations in *this* world.

A tendency to underestimate the impact of the modern (colonial and post-colonial) state in diffusing patronage relations at the expense of the previous segmentary tribal ones, of Ibn Khaldun's *asabiya* if you wish, is one of the mistakes to which the school to which Mr Eickelman belongs is prone. It is a curious mistake for a school priding itself on its sensitivity to culture-change, in so far as the present contains ample evidence of past segmentary tribal organisation as a reality and not merely as an idiom. Mr Eickelman's account both of the past functioning, and of the decline, of the hereditary saints cannot be faulted; yet the role of saintly arbitrator and mediator could not have been performed, had there not been reasonably stable more-than-dyadic groups with which one could deal. There are of course other pervasive institutions, which do not involve the saints quite so directly, such as trial by collective oath, or feud, or a rational control of pasture utilisation, which simply would not have been possible had not kin-articulated, reasonably stable collectivities been a reality.

Mr Eickelman's account of, so to speak, stable-state maraboutism, and its decline, is excellent. But the book also contains a discussion of the so-called maraboutic crisis, stretching roughly from the fifteenth to the seventeenth centuries, when it is all supposed to have started. Mr Eickelman seems to vacillate in his attitude to this idea. He says on page 20, apparently endorsing it, that

this period [of the 'maraboutic crisis'] . . . is important as the formative period that shaped much of Morocco's prevailing religious and political style for ensuing centuries. This is of interest because . . . it is the inverse of that same style which concerns me . . .

The inverse, or rather the termination, of that style he describes admirably. Here he can tell us both when and how, and does so very well. But did that style really begin with the 'maraboutic crisis'? Mr Eickelman clearly has his doubts, referring to the 'general thinness of sources for the period', to the 'dubious accuracy of the assumption' (of continuity), to the fact that the scholar whom he uses most extensively for that period, Alfred Bel, gives 'almost no sociological context', and so forth. Moreover, the scholar in question works with a modern definition of religion, which separates it from politics; this then requires an explanation of how and when it was 'corrupted' by political involvement, which is somewhat misleading if such 'corruption' was the norm of the original condition.

Mr Eickelman is uneasy about all this, and seems to feel happier when he switches away from a substantive-historical use of the idea, and treats it merely as an interesting projection-test for the way in which contemporary and recent generations *see* Moroccan society. But the whole idea seems to me to deserve much more sustained scrutiny.

It is not in doubt that Morocco possessed strong dynasties in the Middle Ages; or that persons in the maraboutic style are prominent in the times of trouble which followed, and that they do not disappear or diminish in importance till the coming of modernism. What is in doubt is that a distinctive period of Moroccan history can explain an institution about which it has *not* been shown that it is in any way distinctively Moroccan. For instance, one of the factors invoked in Mr Eickelman's book for the then decline of the monarchy and consequent upsurge of marabouts is that the monarchy 'had constantly to compromise with [crusaders] and with the Christian powers of southern Europe. The Ottomans in Algeria ... played on this sentiment ... ' On this argument, maraboutism ought to be weaker in an Algeria under Ottoman tutelage, less compromised by collaboration with the infidel. There is nothing whatever to support such a conclusion, and a very great deal to contradict it.

Before maraboutism can be explained by distinctive episodes of Moroccan history, it must first of all be distinctively Moroccan. It is not distinctive in North Africa. And in the rest of Islam? It depends perhaps on which other regions one selects for comparison. My own inclination is to look for an *anti*-maraboutic crisis or cleansing operation when the saints are absent, rather than for a maraboutic crisis when they are prominent. Perhaps there are no maraboutic crises, only *anti*-maraboutic ones. Be that as it may: Mr Eickelman does not really consider this question. Abdalla Bujra's highly relevant work on southern Arabia, which shows hereditary saints playing a role very similar to the one performed in North Africa, or Ioan Lewis on Somalia, or Fredrik Barth on Swat − so extensively debated in anthropology − are not mentioned. At this point, it is very difficult not to suspect that a school which concentrates on Morocco, but draws its previous ideas from Indonesia, was perhaps misled into looking for local explanations for something generic to arid-zone Islam.

Is there such a school? Interestingly, Mr Eickelman denies this, while conceding the plausibility of the suspicion that 'it would have been easy to lapse into a "school" '. It seems that the shaikh of this *zawiya* would have none of it: 'Cliff [Geertz] quietly but vigorously insisted that each of us develop individually a style of thought and analysis.' To say 'I am of no school' is almost as suspect as to say 'I have no preconceptions.' This school (if it be allowed to exist) contains scholars of brilliance, and outstanding achievements can be expected from it. But for that very reason it would advance matters if its shared and debatable views could be specified and debated.

Some of the concrete ones which are of interest I have already mentioned. But there is a general one which perhaps matters most of all. It is a certain kind of culture-talk. Now it is indisputable that what men do and endure generally 'has meaning' for them; that these meanings come as parts of loose systems, which are tied both to languages and to institutions; and that in some way or other, these systems must be sustained by the collectivities of men who share them (or partly share them), and in turn, that they make their contribution to the perpetuation of the said collectivities. These 'cultures' both persist and change over time. Moreover, it may be necessary to spell all this out to first-year students, just in case it had not occurred to them, and it may also be necessary to stress it to behaviourists, who either deny it or deny its relevance. So far so good.

But what is not quite so good is to proceed to make ponderous statements, sometimes in beautiful Proustian prose, which amount to little more than an expansion of these loose insights, plus perhaps certain elaborations, such as that meanings are socially manipulated (e.g. a man who claims to be holier than thou is, if you like, manipulating the cultural notion of holiness to raise his status). Now the reason why this is dangerous is that it may give the impression, to speaker and listener alike, that some reasonably precise theory or explanation is being offered, when in fact such culture-talk tends merely to indicate a problem, not a solution. The more 'technical', academic-professional such talk becomes, the harder it is to follow, and the greater the risk of someone supposing that the reason why he cannot find a clear and definite explanation contained in it is not that there is not one there to be found, but that it is there, only dreadfully deep.

Mr Eickelman could not be accused of excessive generosity to his predecessors in the study of Muslim sanctity. For instance, he observes that:

Such myths serve as 'charters' through which individuals and groups of individuals legitimate ties . . . Because orientalists and ethnographers have long presumed that such myths do not exist in the Muslim world, at least outside the corpus of formal Islamic rituals, they have been almost entirely neglected by scholars . . .

Only the word 'almost' saves this statement from absurdity. Such questionable claims to ('almost') originality do not matter much, and Mr Eickelman is not personally ungenerous. But what is seriously worrying is that he may suppose that the originality lies in the cloud-culture-talk injected into what is otherwise a beautifully researched, well rounded-off, convincing, but also perfectly orthodox account of Moroccan sanctity. The danger also arises that interesting, genuine and arguable disagreements (e.g. about the pervasiveness of dyadic—unequal relationships, and hence presumably the allegedly mythical status of segmentary equality), get muddled up with a distinctly less interesting debate about the merits of some supposedly rival theory, which however exists only questionably, under that culture-double-talk. It is as true that we manipulate social meanings as that we talk prose, but we should not let this idea go to our heads, and quite especially ought not to suppose that we have a theory when we merely possess a style.

Ken Brown teaches anthropology in Manchester, but whatever intellectual clan-affiliation he has is not easy to discern in his work. At any rate, his book contains no paradoxes, and if he has experienced any Durkheimian immersion in collective representations at Old Trafford, he has kept it to himself. In other words, there are no obvious stigmata of the anthropological Manchester school (not to be confused with any other school of the same name).

The city of Salé is historically significant not merely in virtue of its pirates, who flourished at the same time, and perhaps partly for the same reason, as the alleged 'maraboutic crisis'. It was the exception to the usual generalisation about the supine submission of Muslim towns to the central power. The Saletins once constituted a vigorous city state, strong enough to fight it out with the most powerful maraboutic group of the time, the Dilaites. Commandant Coindreau, the French historian of the Sallee Rovers,[3] tells us that when they were at last subdued by the central state, piracy declined not because it was suppressed, but because it was nationalised. This perennial mismanagement of nationalised industries is something dreadful.

Mr Brown's book, unlike Mr Eickelman's, does not contain any excursions into the really distant past. This in itself is significant: the historic past of Salé as a city state, an autonomous community of citizens, does not seem alive in contemporary consciousness, though Saletins apparently do occasionally invoke sea-captain ancestors. Their values do not seem to be eccentric or dissident. During the colonial period, however, Salé enjoyed the reputation of being a virulently nationalist town. The basis for this attitude had been laid early.

As a description of Muslim urban life, Mr Brown's study certainly deserves to stand alongside the works of Roger Le Tourneau, Ira Lapidus, or Michael Gilsenan. It is, however, unfortunate that, in his effort to offer an overall description, he has not pursued any one of his themes to the point where a fully worked-out conclusion could emerge. This is not, so to speak, a *thèse à thèse*. If there is an underlying plot, it is that *plus ça change, plus c'avait déjà changé*. The changes which become most manifest and conspicuous in the twentieth century had already been in full swing in the nineteenth. For instance, the nineteenth century saw the decline in the pattern, long ago noted by Ibn Khaldun, of government based on privileged tribes. Instead, the bureaucracy, growing in importance, was manned by a kind of *bourgeoisie de robe*, drawn from towns such as Salé.

At the same time, Mr Brown is convinced that an increase in economic differentiation took place, associated both with greater centralisation ('patrimonialism') and with *comprador* trade. He quotes Le Tourneau's observation about traditional Fez, to the effect that conflict occurred not between classes but between clans, or rather 'changing and ephemeral oppositions of clans'. Mr Brown also finds no classes in any literal sense within Salé: 'until the 1870s the social structure of Salé appears to have been relatively undifferentiated in socio-economic classes or cultural categories'.

219

I found no evidence of collective action by any patrilineal group ... between 1830 and 1930. The elite were not leaders of powerful extended families but men who controlled clientele groups held together by mutual interests, not ties of consanguinity. A group of allies or clients centred around one man who promised no permanence beyond its effectiveness, or at most, the lives of the individuals concerned.

Mr Brown also notes how the national culture, promoted by nationalism, is in effect the old urban culture, but observes that 'the spread and conquest of urban culture and the national integration that it aimed at have not been realized to a very great extent in Morocco'.

While his overall description of Salé is excellent, the individual themes he deals with could have been taken further, and one trusts that he will yet do so, possibly in connection with his more recent work in other parts of North Africa. Clearly, the Saletins and the Sherqawis belong to the same world; patronage and fluid associations prevail, though the dominant saintly lineages in Boujad seemed to have had a greater saintly capital and a correspondingly greater continuity in time. Reformism seems to have hit Salé sooner — not surprisingly — and to have had more marked anticipations in the nineteenth century. Meritocratic scholarship, on the other hand, seems to have had better prospects in Salé. But, as if to underscore the continuity of social forms between Brown's and Eickelman's regions, when the Saletins met in political protest in 1930 and started the movement towards both nationalism and the purification of Islam from anthropolatry, they did so in the local lodge of one of the shaikh-revering religious orders.

12

Rulers and tribesmen

Danziger's *Abd-al-Qadir* and Dunn's *Resistance in the Desert*[1] seem to be inspired by the possibly questionable idea that there is some kind of continuity between modern anti-colonial nationalism and the resistance previously encountered by colonisers during the ascendancy period of European imperialism. Each of them deals with French expansion in North Africa. Danziger treats of Abd-al-Qadir, who led the resistance to the French during the first two decades of the French 'presence' in Algeria — though Danziger for some reason concentrates on the period between 1830 and 1839, confining the rest to a brief epilogue. By contrast, Ross Dunn deals with the far South-East of Morocco, a land of desert and oases caught between the Sahara, the Atlas and the (shifting) Algerian border, during the later part of the nineteenth and the early years of this century. Their subject matters are neatly contrasted: Danziger deals above all with one man, and with his attempts to build a state. Dunn treats of a barely governed region in which no state, in any very strong sense, arose during the period treated. His hero or subject is not a man but a tribal system. Danziger's book belongs squarely to the fashion for the scholarly study of state- or nation-building, and he has looked at Algeria of the 1830s to seek for its roots or antecedents. Ross Dunn is interested in resistance not merely to colonialism but also to non-European rulers, and the nuance he introduces into this set of questions can perhaps best be summarised in his own words:

In the context of black Africa, Ranger and others have argued convincingly for the existence of substantive connections between nineteenth-century resistance and modern nationalism . . . the slackening and troubled pace of national integration . . . following the ebullient decades of mass nationalism brings into sharper focus . . . also . . . the institutional devices and political strategies by which people grappled with . . . efforts . . . to push them down some . . . road towards millennial bliss or national consciousness.

So, where Danziger looks for a precursor of nation- and state-building, Dunn looks for precursors to armed resistance, whether to alien or to indigenous rulers. A romanticism of local independence may be more original than a romanticism of national independence — or perhaps one should say that the wheel has

221

turned full circle. Sympathy with the local community in its resistance to the central power was also once characteristic of some at least among the colonial administrators, and earned them the accusation of indulging in Divide and Rule tactics. As for the Tafilalet oasis and its surrounding desert, which was merely of some commercial and symbolic significance in the period studied by Dunn, it is now of supreme strategic importance in the struggle for Saharan resources. The hold of the Moroccan monarchy over it is no longer loose and delegated to weak *khalifas* and local assemblies, and one cannot imagine that the prospects for local autonomy are good. I am told by a recent visitor that the local population now eagerly displays the Moroccan national dress of blue-jeans, and carefully avoids the black turbans which have become a symbol of Polisario.

Danziger writes very much as a historian, and his account of the Algerian social structure and institutions is unconvincing and occasionally misleading. Like Ross Dunn, he relies above all on French sources, though Dunn supplemented this by extensive interrogations in the field. Danziger is described in the blurb as a consultant on Middle Eastern affairs at present working at an Institute in Haifa: if he had such institutional attachments at the time he was working on this book, he would not have been able to visit Algeria, which may help excuse his lack of feel for Algerian culture. He is by no means lacking in sympathy for his subject — quite the contrary — but his account of institutions does not have the ring of truth. On page 6 we are told that the entire rural population was classified into tribes (*qabilah*), whereas on the preceding page it is implied that the plural of this word designates Berbers as such. Both usages no doubt occurred, but to let this inconsistency pass without comment is to ignore the clue to something important — namely, that the ethnicity or speech of a tribal group was of no great concern to the rulers of the time, and required no orderly nomenclature. We are told that in 'the mountains . . . the Berbers lived in virtual isolation', having been told more accurately, a few paragraphs earlier, about frequent trade and employment contacts. In fact, there was, for instance, a Kabyle community in Algiers, and political autonomy of the mountain valleys went with economic/cultural/religious continuity, a combination which is crucial for the understanding of North African traditional society.

The account of tribal organisation on page 7 is not felicitous. In the case of segmentary tribes, it is fairly meaningless to speak of the 'vast difference' in size, in so far as a tribal segment (or fraction, in French terminology) *is* a tribe in very much the same sense as the total tribe. The most one can say is that the genealogical ceiling is reached sooner in some cases than in others, but its absence does not imply lack of co-operation, any more than its presence implies effective unity. Hence it is not clear what could be meant by saying that 'in general the clan was the basic social unit, while the fraction and the tribe fulfilled political functions'. The point is that there is no indigenous concept, singling out one level in the segmentary ladder, which could be the equivalent of 'clan' in the above sentence; and in fact, units at every level and of every size performed

222

political functions, e.g. acted in self-defence. It is not true that the 'clan's chief had absolute authority over clan members'. Some, not all, North African tribes have 'big men', and their authority is seldom absolute in fact or theory.

It is arguable whether the 'prominent members of each tribe . . . may properly be regarded as belonging to its nobility . . . in the sense of hereditary class . . .' The author is probably closer to the truth when he says that 'the martial nobility . . . were the principal beneficiaries of the Turkish system', i.e. leading members of tax-collecting, partially tax-exempt tribes. In so far as such men remained members of their tribal units, with whom they generally shared ancestors (putative or real), and indeed owed their position to their base in this kin-defined system, in which the use of arms was diffused and not restricted, it is misleading to assimilate them to a martial nobility which defines itself by distinctive birth. When the French arrived they naturally looked for a *noblesse d'épée*, and followed misleading scents in trying to find it, and Danziger seems to have attached himself to this pack. Even Tocqueville spoke a little in this manner, though Danziger unfortunately does not cite his very perceptive letters. There is a great irony in all this: the first ones to start this chase were looking for a culture untainted by the egalitarianism they disliked at home in France (General Daumas, consul to Abd-al-Qadir, was candid on this point): in our time, the hunt is perpetuated by Marxist historians determined to find a 'feudal mode of production'. It was one of Robert Montagne's achievements, in his definitive study of the very big men of the Moroccan western High Atlas,[2] to establish clearly the crucial differences between this form of leadership and feudalism — crag-top crenellated castles notwithstanding. Tribes are not altogether as egalitarian as the pure segmentary model suggests; and interference of the central act promotes inequality by creating the need for administrative intermediaries, who emerge from among the big men of the tribe. But such a group is not to be equated with a feudal estate.

It is not true that 'all indigenous Algerians (with the exception of the Jews) regarded themselves as Sunni Muslims of the Maliki school'. The Ibadi-Kharejite minority is socially and historically important, and from their oasis home in Mzab paid annual tribute to Algiers (including eight slaves a year), and were thus as much part of the pre-1830 Algeria as anyone. More subtly, it is not correct to argue that 'since it was the Arabs who brought Islam to North Africa and who converted the Berbers, it is not surprising that their descendants remained stricter Muslims than the Berbers'. This may sound plausible, but curiously enough the reverse obtains. Throughout a large belt of territory stretching from the Western Desert of Egypt to modern Mauritania, one finds a curious tribal division of labour, in which Arab tribesmen are the men of the sword, whilst tribes of Berber speech or ancestry are the religious specialists. (In practice this does not mean that they abstain from fighting, but only that men of the Book are customarily drawn from amongst their ranks.) Men from the Maghreb have a great reputation for religious wisdom amongst, for instance, Cyrenaican bedouin.

One can only speculate about the reasons for this paradoxical state of affairs. One obvious fact is this: the majority of those who in North Africa can claim a genuine Arabian ancestry at all, must have had forefathers amongst the Hilalian invasion around the eleventh century. That was no jihad at all, but a migration of nomads, clearly notorious for their religious ignorance in their own Arabian homeland, who had been urged on their way by reluctant host governments (such as the Fatimids) eager to be rid of them, or imported (after being defeated) for service in the local government (as in Morocco). At the same time, it is reasonable to suspect that holy lineages existed amongst Berbers prior to Islam, and that their religious virtuosity, passed on from father to son, assumed a Muslim idiom. Thus, oddly, it was the convert*ed* not the convert*ing* ethnic group which came to provide religious specialists.[3]

What is true is that townsmen see themselves as better Muslims than country-folk. But this has nothing to do with Arab or Berber origins. In any case an emphasis on urban and scholarly values and a corresponding contempt for rural saint-worship is probably anachronistic when applied to the Algeria of Abd-al-Qadir's time, as much of Danziger's own material clearly indicates. For instance, on his own evidence, at any rate in the countryside — and Algeria was not very urbanised — there simply was no institutional basis for any Islam other than that of the saints: 'there is no argument that instruction in the countryside was dispensed exclusively by marabouts and their disciples'.

Again, it is somewhat weird to say that 'the Turks had managed to find an ingenious solution for this problem [of tax-collection] . . . They chose powerful Arab tribes to collect taxes for them from other tribes . . . In return, they received . . . choicest lands . . . and a partial tax exemption . . . ' You might as well credit the Turks with inventing the wheel. Far from being an ingenious solution found by clever Turks, this is simply *the* traditional, conventional kind of state-formation in North Africa, well-documented for the Middle Ages by Ibn Khaldun. What the Turks did invent was exactly the opposite: they created a viable system which, at least at the top, *dispensed with* a tribal elite, securing its own members by purchase, public advertisement (by ambulant criers in Turkey proper), co-option or forcible individual recruitment, and systematically trained them, thus possessing a means of creating an *esprit de corps* which was *not* tribal. They thus evaded the bitter dilemma which, for Ibn Khaldun, constitutes the human condition — the option between tribalism and social dissolution. The Turks emerged from central Asia so as to refute Ibn Khaldun and to show North Africans (and others) that a state could have a basis other than a tribal one. That they *also* used the old, tribal devices at a lower administrative level is not surprising, but they can hardly be credited with having *found* this solution. On the contrary, it was they who relegated it to the lower echelons, as it were.

Or again, Danziger talks as if Abd-al-Qadir could, had he chosen, have abolished the tribal system. What else was there, and how could it conceivably have been abrogated at that stage, and with the means at his disposal? He also, I suspect, overrates the role of Abd-al-Qadir in Algerian folk consciousness. The urban-based, scholarly reformist movement of Ben Badis in this century (whom Danziger does not mention) is far more important, I suspect, in forming the Algerian national self-image, than the repudiated tribal and maraboutic world which Abd-al-Qadir represented.

These various mistakes of emphasis stand between the author and a sensible evaluation of Abd-al-Qadir. He rightly dismisses Marxist interpretations (' . . . the destruction of the bases of feudalism in Algeria . . . '), which are simple cases of Left Bank apriorism, and he is far too patient with the much-debated non-question − was he a patriot or a man of religion? His own conclusion is true enough as far as it goes − he 'was a pragmatic Islamic resistance leader and state builder' − but does this statement amount to much? He was indeed a Muslim; had he not been 'pragmatic' he would not have survived; he fought the French some of the time; and he built a state, of a kind. The question is − what kind, and how?

Here one must come to Mr Danziger's merits, which are very considerable, notwithstanding the above-listed disputable interpretations or background assumptions. His historiography is painstaking, detailed, rich, readable and orderly, and enables one to reach and document one's own conclusions, if one is not satisfied with his. It seems to me fairly obvious − from the book's own internal evidence − what happened in the case of Abd-al-Qadir. The French destroyed the Turkish carapace which had been superimposed on Algerian society, and were in no position, initially, to replace it. In the resulting vacuum, Algeria promptly reverted to its traditional, Ibn-Khaldunian condition. The tribes persisted, but the only possible supra-tribal leadership could be provided by the religious *noblesse de robe*, by the marabouts. Many marabouts were available, and one was chosen. It must have been an historical accident, resulting from an interplay of Moroccan, French and tribal intrigue and the fortunes of war, that the mantle fell on one of them. Naturally he used a theocratic idiom, for no other political language was available. His state was built on tribal support and privileged tribes, and was correspondingly fragile: in adversity, his closest supporters could and would turn upon him, as Danziger shows. Though Danziger quotes Pessah Shinar, he seems to ignore the conclusion of the Israeli scholar's comparative study of Abd-al-Qadir and Abd-al-Krim: notwithstanding the fact that he had to work with tribal material, the latter was a genuine state-builder and theocratic reformer, and displayed the combination of those two traits so characteristic of Maghrebin early nationalism. Abd-al-Qadir was nothing of the kind: he belonged squarely to the world of tribes and marabouts, and used the traditional political tools in the old way. The state he built belonged to the world of medieval Maghrebin dynasties, not to that of Mehemet Ali. Danziger admirably assembles the facts documenting this conclusion.

The most piquant fact in the volume, to my mind, is found on page 139. In 1837 Maréchal Bugeaud and Amir Abd-al-Qadir came to terms, at least for the time being. Bugeaud sold the Amir various arms, and received considerable funds, half of which he assigned to building roads in the department of the Dordogne, in the interests evidently of his own career as conservative deputy in the French assembly. So imperialism is not always inspired by the needs of monopoly capitalism. Monopoly capitalism, or any other I suspect, was not too conspicuous in the Dordogne of the 1840s. Some imperialisms seem closer to the politics of Clochemerle. Taxes or donations extracted from Algerian tribesmen by their Amir benefited the Dordogne peasantry, having also passed through the hands of their senator. Bugeaud, I imagine, would have made more sense to Julius Caesar than to Cecil Rhodes.

Where Danziger only looks at institutions as a means of telling a political story and interpreting the achievement of one man, for Ross Dunn the real dramatis personae are communities. In the Moroccan south-east, there are diverse communities, pastoral and sedentary, Arabophone and Berberophone, white and black, Muslim and Jewish, sacred and secular. But amongst this complex patchwork, never yet exhaustively studied (and it may alas be too late), two kinds of communities are of special importance: nomads and oasis-dwellers. To me at least, the most interesting part of Dunn's book is his account of the social organisation of these two kinds of community.

Danziger's book will be read for the story it has to tell; the institutional background has to be accepted as part of a package deal, and, though defective, it does not spoil the considerable merits of the story. Dunn's case is the opposite: lacking a personal carrier, so to speak, the narrative part of his book does not grip the imagination sufficiently in itself, and is likely to be of interest primarily for specialists. It is his dissection of his dramatis personae, the communities of the desert and oasis, which will deservedly attract a wider readership. The political, military, ecological and commercial threads in the tale are interwoven in a complex manner, and are well disentangled by Dunn. A French officer was obliged to study not merely the local map and ethnography, but also the relationship between the War Ministry and the shifting alignments in the Paris Assembly; the Berbers had to think about the state of the date harvest and the disposition of their flocks as well as about French fire-power. The narrative is based on painstaking research and is inherently important, but it is I suppose one of the disadvantages of acephalous systems, that, as long as they remain such, they generate no overall leaders and hence no heroes for their epics. In his conclusion concerning 'Patterns of resistance and leadership', Dr Dunn observes that

Resistance was stubborn, but it was also spasmodic and amorphous . . . There is no evidence that a guerrilla movement with a common strategy and leadership existed at any level. Moreover, the men who took part in small-scale raids were motivated not only by the desire to defend their land against foreign occupation but also by more mundane urges to make off with a share of the livestock, equipment and arms . . .

In a society in which raiding was an established institution, these 'mundane' motives might indeed furnish a perfectly sufficient explanation. If they do, this would provide a reason for doubting the idea which provides our authors with a starting-point — namely, the search for continuity between 'primitive' and nationalist resistance.

If any individual family story catches the reader's eyes, it will almost certainly be that of the Oufkir clan. A certain Mohammed ou Fekir owned 5000 palm trees in one of the smaller Berber-speaking oases located amongst Arabic pastoralists; this number amounted to one twelfth of the total trees of the oasis and, in conjunction with 4000 further trees elsewhere, probably made him the richest of the oasis's eighty-five notables. The oasis exchanged dates for wool, and the family wealth was also based on trade in woollen jellabas. Around 1900, Mohammed ou Fekir was elected shaikh of the Jema'a. He favoured co-operation with the French, impressed Maréchal Lyautey, and with his support ended as tyrant of the oasis. It was his very gallicised offspring who did so well in the French and subsequently Moroccan armies that he ended as Moroccan Minister of Interior, in which capacity he was personally involved in the murder of Mehdi Ben Barka in Paris, only to perish violently himself in 1972 when taking part in one of the unsuccessful coups against the King. His numerous kinsmen in A'in Cha'ir, now deprived of a cousin at court, are presumably still in the jellaba trade; there is a good tourist market for them these days. As they say in Lancashire, from jellabas to jellabas in three generations. One can only hope that the Oufkir family will find an adequate chronicler. The three pages accorded them by Ross Dunn will make a good start.

Dr Dunn also concludes:

it was only through 'maraboutism' that such resistance was undertaken ... resistance at the regional and local levels ... relied heavily on the leadership of saints. They were the only individuals in rural society, aside from a few extraordinarily charismatic tribal leaders, whose special role as arbitrators and brokers ... suited them for the task of orchestrating pan-tribal action.

The over-all conclusion is that resistance was continuous but fragmented, led by local saints and not by leaders capable of mobilising large populations and setting up a centralised state. Dr Dunn speculates why no genuine jihad, no real amir, arose in the South East. He comments on the fact that the concept of jihad contains not merely war against the infidel, but also the need to transform the community in accordance with Holy Law. Does not this contain the clue to the answer? The idea of puritanical reform presupposes a centralised state, with judges learned enough to know the Law, and a state machinery to impose it. The society of the far South East, as Ross Dunn's own material shows, provided no base for such an edifice.

One might add that, in consequence, the difference between the disunited resistance of the Moroccan South East between 1881 and 1912, and that of Abd-al-Qadir in the 1830s and 1840s, is not as great as sheer considerations of scale might suggest. Abd-al-Qadir represented the traditional Maghrebin state, just as the nomads of the Moroccan South East represented the traditional dissidence: and the two are built of similar elements. The former relies on privileged tribes and a maraboutic leader, the second, on equally competing tribes and maraboutic mediation. They can shade over into each other; the mediators are present in the state, the leader is normally recognised even by the dissident tribes. The presence or absence of towns seems decisive. The concentration of humanity which is called a town both requires, and is vulnerable to, effective government; and effective rulers build a town if they do not already possess one.

Ross Dunn's conclusions about the social organisation of the pastoralists are conventional and, to my mind, correct:

Southeastern Morocco was a region where political organisation was acephalous and segmentary. It was in general very similar to that found in the rest of rural Africa . . . and other societies commonly labeled as segmentary.

Dunn particularly describes two tribal groupings, one Arabophone and one Berberophone, which were specially prominent in the region: the Dawi Mani and the Ait Atta. He might have added that the Ait Atta must be one of the world's masterpieces in segmentary organisation. They occupied an enormous territory ranging from the Sahara to the northern slopes of the Atlas. Their pasture-rights and preferential bride-rights followed clan lines, and the dispersal of clan pockets on various boundaries helped ensure at least some measure of cohesion, despite the large numbers, dispersal, and lack of permanent hierarchy or governmental machinery. A man's right of access to diverse kinds of pasture − on the Sahara edge or at above 3000 metres in the Atlas − provided him both with insurances against climatic vagaries and an incentive to be mindful of his clan bonds. Thus a great deal was achieved without centralisation, and Dunn speaks with justice of Atta Imperialism.

Dunn's account of them does not diverge from that of other authors. What is, however, more intriguing is the question of the organisation of the oases, notably the great ones of Tafilalet and Figuig. His main conclusion about them is that they closely resembled the pastoralists in their acephalousness, other than that they were not capable of uniting in larger units embracing the total oasis, and were thus, so to speak, even *more* headless:

Tafilalet was an enormous, totally acephalous agglomeration . . . which in the face of many years of Ait Atta aggression had never put up anything approaching a united front.

The internal election of leaders was apparently the same in this oasis as amongst the pastoralists: rotation of the chiefly office amongst clans, such that one clan only provides candidates, whilst only the men of the remaining clans have the vote. Dunn concludes:

Tafilalet would have been devoid of overarching government were it not for the presence of the *khalifa* . . . of the sultan.

228

But he was not very powerful:

> The *khalifa* of Tafilalet . . . was never really a governor at all . . . [he] had only a few dozen . . . soldiers . . . He collected . . . koranic taxes . . . from those wishing to offer them voluntarily . . . He . . . mediated quarrels and feuds . . . stood outside the web of tribal and village relationship . . . therefore . . . was in an advantageous position to play a prominent mediational role . . .

At this point, I have some doubts, but also, I should stress, doubts about my own doubts: not about the weakness of the *khalifa*, which sounds convincing enough, but about the feebleness of or simplicity of oasis institutions and their similarity to those of the pastoralists. I cannot properly explain these doubts, and their qualifications, without a personal note.

In the opening 'Acknowledgements', the author is kind enough to say that I thoroughly criticised his thesis soon after its completion, and have 'inspired its rewriting far more than [I] probably realise'. I did indeed read his thesis, on which this book is based, with admiration, and did make various comments. I do not know just how I, and others interested in central Moroccan mixed pastoralists with whom Dunn was in touch, such as D.M. Hart, have influenced his rewriting: but I become worried when I see the oasis-dwellers of Tafilalet (not so much of Figuig) described as being so very similar to the transhumants of the central High Atlas.

Those of us who have taken an interest in Moroccan tribal organisation are not so very numerous, and we are an incestuous lot (even if we are also divided into hostile leagues), and we do pass our ideas around in the way in which our tribesmen circulate their girl parallel-cousins as brides. So we must be careful.

My memory is that in Ross Dunn's original version, the socio-political organisation of the Tafilalet looked far less like that of the central High Atlas pastoralists, and more like something semi-urban, as reported, for instance, of the Ibadi oases of Mzab of Algeria (which material however had not at the time influenced Dunn). It is possible that my memory is entirely at fault. It is also possible that my memory is not at fault, but that Ross Dunn has changed his mind in the intervening period for some very good and cogent reasons. It cannot be stressed too strongly that he has done research on Tafilalet, and I have *not*, and his assertions must be accepted against my doubts. My doubts are not primarily inspired by the fact that he has in the meantime been consorting with people with a central Moroccan interest.

They *are* inspired by certain general considerations. It would be very surprising if the socio-political organisation of oasis-dwellers were the same as that of pastoralists. Pastoralists are mobile; they can and do move with their flocks. This imposes both a limitation on social control — you cannot misuse or exploit a mobile person as easily as a chained one — and also a certain need for cohesion, for they can only acquire and protect pastures collectively, and they must (and do) collectively regulate the use of scarce pastures. By contrast, oasis-dwellers are more vulnerable — their palm trees cannot move, and they can be cut down;

they have to co-operate about water; are not mobile and are compelled to remain in close proximity to each other; by all accounts they are rather more severely stratified, with a stratum of oppressed share-croppers, identifiable by colour; and, according to Dunn, in their larger units they are further from, and not closer to, civic organisation than are the mobile pastoralists.

Given all these differences in type of social constraint, and given some factual data on actual organisational differences, I should expect either clear differences in organisational principles, or, if not, a sustained discussion of why this reasonable-sounding expectation is not fulfilled. But I should feel happier if Dunn had explicitly stated this problem and *then* given his reasons for rejecting the idea of differences between oases and pastoralists. In the absence of such an explicit discussion, one can only fear that the issue had been by-passed.

It is of course absolutely no argument against Dr Dunn's conclusions on this point, that I or anyone expected them to be different. But the whole question of the social organisation of autonomous oases is so fascinating, and has received so little sustained and comparative examination (unlike the organisation of pastoralists), that the question should at least be looked at again. Until there is such a re-examination, Dunn's well-presented conclusions should of course stand, and of course they may well also stand thereafter.

Ross Dunn is a historian who has thoroughly internalised the concepts of social anthropologists and made excellent use of the method of oral interviewing as a way of supplementing his written sources. His book is clearly a very major contribution to the documented knowledge of Moroccan traditional institutions and local history in the nineteenth and twentieth centuries. The fact that it raises questions as well as answering so many others is a measure of its worth.

Notes

1 Flux and reflux in the faith of men

1 Alexis de Tocqueville, *Oeuvres complètes*, vol. III, Paris, 1962.
2 Cf. papers by V. Ayoub and J. Oppenheimer, forthcoming.
3 This was a system by which various religious communities within the Ottoman Empire were recognised by the central state as autonomous units, allowed to administer themselves internally in certain quite extensive areas such as family law, with their own jurisdiction over these matters, and were allowed to deal with the central state as a unit.
4 Michael Cook, *Monotheist Sages*, forthcoming.
5 Sir James Frazer, *The Golden Bough*, London, 1971.
6 David Hume, *Treatise of Human Nature*, London, 1969.
7 T.S. Eliot, *The Waste Land*, London, 1972.
8 Louis Dumont, *From Mandeville to Marx*, Chicago, 1977.
9 Cf. B. Turner, *Weber and Islam*, London, 1974; M. Rodinson, *Islam et Capitalisme*, Paris, 1966; John Waterbury, *North for the Trade*, Berkeley, Cal., 1972; Peter Gran, *Islamic Roots of Capitalism*, Austin, Texas, 1979; Sami Zubaida, 'Economic and political activism in Islam', *Economy and Society*, vol. I, no. 3, 1972.
10 Jean-Paul Charnay, *Sociologie religieuse de l'Islam*, Paris, 1977; Pierre Bourdieu, *Algeria 1960*, Cambridge, 1979.
11 Marshall G. Hodgson, *The Venture of Islam*, Chicago, 1975.
12 Charles Taylor, *Hegel*, Cambridge, 1975, p. 492: 'Islam ... was rather inconveniently placed, coming after the birth of absolute religion.'
13 David Hume, *Natural History of Religion*, Oxford, 1976.
14 Sir Edward Evans-Pritchard, *Theories of Primitive Religion*, Oxford, 1965.
15 Bernard Williams, 'Hume on religion' in *David Hume. A Symposium*, ed. D.F. Pears, London, 1973. 'His *basic* thesis in this work is that polytheism is an earlier belief than monotheism ... polytheism is primary over monotheism ... ' This was not Hume's basic thesis.
16 Frank E. Manuel, *The Eighteenth Century Confronts the Gods*, Harvard, 1959.
17 On the emergence of saint-worship in late antiquity, see the works of Professor Peter Brown, esp. *Relics and Social Status in the Age of Gregory of Tours*, Reading, 1977; 'A Dark-Age crisis: aspects of the iconoclastic controversy', in *The English Historical Review*, vol. CCCXLVI, January, 1973.
18 Frazer, *Golden Bough*.

19 F.W. Nietzsche, *Beyond Good and Evil*, Harmondsworth, 1973.
20 David Hume, 'Of Superstition and Enthusiasm', in *Essays Moral, Political and Literary*, Oxford, 1963; also in *Hume on Religion*, ed. R. Wollheim, London, 1963.
21 David Hume, *History of England*, Chicago, 1975.
22 Cf. André Adam, *Histoire de Casablanca (des origines à 1941)*, Aix-en-Provence, 1968, p. 158, n. 58: 'The citizens were often *frondeurs*. Revolts never secured those franchises from their sovereign which, in mediaeval Europe, founded communal liberties. The main reason seems to me the permanent menace which tribes constituted for the towns and which forced them to seek the protection of the sultans. This phenomenon . . . reaches far beyond Morocco and . . . throughout Islam . . . one sees the flourishing of a fine urban civilisation, [but] the conception of public law was in conflict with the development of municipal life.' It seems to me that the conception of 'public law' reflected a balance of power which it could not change. The commercial and clerkly burghers were caught between state and tribe.
23 Plato, *The Republic*, ed. F.M. Cornford, Oxford, 1973.
24 Ibn Khaldun, *The Muqaddimah*, trans. Franz Rosenthal, London, 1958. All quotations from Ibn Khaldun in this chapter are from this source. On the relevance of Ibn Khaldun, see for instance Muhsin Mahdi, *Ibn Khaldun's Philosophy of History*, London, 1957, esp. chapter IV, H.R. Trevor-Roper, *Historical Essays*, London, 1957, chapter V, and A. Cheddadi, 'Le système du pouvoir en Islam d'après Ibn Khaldun', *Annales*, May–August 1980.
25 Tocqueville, *Oeuvres complètes*.
26 Jacques Berque, *Structures sociales du Haut-Atlas*, Paris, 1978.
27 It does not invariably do so. Leaving aside less-than-equal clients and dependants (religious or craft specialists), on occasion stratification arises amongst the pastoralists themselves. The outstanding example are the Tuareg. But as far as the various pastoral strata are concerned, one suspects that Tuareg ideology exaggerates the reality of inequality, and that the same was true for instance in Mauritania. Extreme or demonstratively symbolised inequality is normally prevented amongst pastoralists by the fact that the oppressed or insulted group can seize opportunities to move away with their herds. The brazen inequality among the Tuareg of the Hoggar may be explained by the extreme isolation of that area in the Sahara, which makes it hard or impossible to escape, not only for the occasional oasis cultivator group (this is not unusual), but also for pastoralists, *when in charge of the slower kind of herd or flock*. It is extremely significant that the upper strata monopolised the faster animals – i.e. the camels. Thus the 'people of the goat' could not easily escape domination. Cf. Marceau Gast, 'Pastoralisme nomade et pouvoir: la société traditionelle des Kel Ahaggar', in *Pastoral Production and Society*, ed. L'Equipe écologie et anthropologie des sociétés pastorales, Cambridge, 1979, and Jeremy Keenan, *The People of Ahaggar*, London, 1977. Cf. also C.C. Stewart with E.K. Stewart, *Islam and Social Order in Mauritania*, Oxford, 1973.
28 On the general social implication of literacy, cf. Jack Goody, *Literacy in Traditional Societies*, Cambridge, 1968. Paraphrasing Hegel, one might say that mankind passed through three stages. At first *none* could read. Then, *some* could read. Finally, *all* can read. Clearly, it is the second stage which lends itself to the extreme use of the Word for political legitimation. Only then can the Word escape the ravages of time by being recorded, but only

then it also becomes possible to monopolise and delimit its message.

29 On the political effectiveness or otherwise of supposed agnatic lineages in towns, cf. K. Brown, *People of Salé: Tradition and Change in a Moroccan City 1830–1930*, Manchester, 1976; C. Geertz, H. Geertz and L. Rosen, *Meaning and Order in Moroccan Society*, Cambridge, 1979; Sawsan El Messiri, *Ibn al-balad: A Concept of Egyptian Identity*, Leiden, 1979; Michael Johnson, 'Political bosses and their gangs', in *Patrons and Clients*, ed. E. Gellner and J. Waterbury, London, 1977; Fuad Khuri, *From Village to Suburb*, 1975.

30 Tocqueville, *Oeuvres complètes*.

31 Quoted in *Marxisme et Algérie*, ed. R. Gallisot and G. Badia, Paris, 1976.

32 Cf. Martha Mundy, 'Sana'a' dress, 1920–75', to appear in *San'a': An Islamic City*, ed. R.B. Sarjeant and R. Lewcock, forthcoming: 'Countrymen . . . emphasised the autarchy and autonomy of men and communities, excluding from tribal membership many of those dependent upon selling their services . . . ' Specialisation makes you dependent and morally suspect. Cf. T. Gerholm, *Market, Mosque and Mafrag*, Stockholm, 1977.

33 On minor sheepdogs, tribes privileged in return for service, cf. William Schorger, 'The evolution of political forms in a North African village', forthcoming; J. le Coz, 'Les Tribus Guichs au Maroc', in *Revue de Géographie du Maroc*, no. 7, 1965.

34 One of the differences between the Middle East proper and North Africa was that the former contained a more significant proportion of sedentary, dominated peasantry, in between the towns and the tribes. Cf. E. Burke, 'Morocco and the Middle East: reflections on some basic differences', *European Journal of Sociology*, 10, 1969. In fact, it is on occasion possible to discuss urban–rural relations in the Middle East with scarcely a reference to nomads and tribesmen, as if these hardly mattered, and as if domination were always urban. Cf. Gabriel Baer's 'Town and village – dichotomy or continuum?', *Asian and African Studies*, vol. 11, no. 1, 1976, which is a review of Richard Antoun and Ilya Harik (eds.), *Rural Politics and Social Change in the Middle East*, London, 1972.

35 For a microscopic version of this kind of domination in our own time, cf. Philip C. Salzman, 'The Proto-State in Iranian Baluchistan', in *Origins of the State*, ed. R. Cohen and E.R. Service, Philadelphia, 1978. It is not always and everywhere the case that the nomads raid the settled population. On occasion, man bites dog. Apparently, Chinese agricultural oasis-dwellers were known to raid successfully and brutally deplete the flocks of Mongolian nomads. Cf. Caroline Humphrey, 'Life in the Mongolian Gobi', *The Geographical Magazine*, 1971, vol. XLIII, no. 9.

36 Cf. 'The early state among the Scythians', in *The Early State*, ed. Henry J.M. Claessen and Peter Skalník, The Hague, 1978.

37 A.M. Khazanov, *Sotsialnaia Istoria Skifov* (The Social History of the Scythians), Moscow, 1975.

38 G.E. Markov, *Kochevniki Azii* (The Nomads of Asia), Moscow, 1976.

39 Germaine Tillion, *Le Harem et les cousins*, Paris, 1966.

40 E.E. Evans-Pritchard, *The Sanusi of Cyrenaica*, Oxford, 1949.

41 The noble savage others on occasion claimed to find among the Berbers. Tocqueville, *Oeuvres complètes*, observed 'If Rousseau had known the Kabyles . . . he would have sought his models in the Atlas.' Tocqueville noted that the Arabs were less egalitarian, and had something which could

perhaps be called a military aristocracy. But he also saw that a hereditary *religious* nobility was more important and characteristic of this world. One may distinguish the, so to speak, intensive and extensive uses of kinship and lineage, where the intensive use is *selective*, choosing individuals for *special* posts and positions, whilst the extensive employment allocates everyone to appropriate social groups, rather than to special positions within them. The intensive or selective use may be overt and formalised (e.g. primogeniture), or informal (e.g. further internal selection within the defined kin group by the deity in each generation), in which case it is a kind of compromise with the 'extensive' principle, which is nominally maintained but whose conse-quences are evaded. In this sense, Islam uses lineages intensively for one kind of religious elite (*shurfa, saada*), and extensively for the organisation of ordinary rural groups; European feudalism, on the other hand, used it intensively for a military elite, but not much for rural groups and not at all for the religions elite, recruiting it bureaucratically and denying it the right to an avowable posterity. Under feudalism, legitimate violence is not monopolised by the state but by an entire *estate*. In Muslim rural-tribal society it is not monopolised at all. (Only minority pariah groups are excluded from it. Customary law does not prohibit private group violence, it merely codifies its rules and provides procedures for its private ter-mination.) What follows from this of course is that you cannot define a nobility in terms of the right to bear and use arms. The status of warrior is too unselective. It would seem to follow that nobility can only be religious. No requirement of celibacy — rather the reverse — stands in the way of such an elite being hereditary.

42 P. Lucas and J.-Cl. Vatin, *L'Algérie des Anthropologues*, Paris, 1975.
43 For the study of such phenomena in areas other than the 'classical' regions of Ibn Khaldun, cf. F. Barth, *Political Leadership among Swat Pathans*, London, 1959; A. Bujra, *The Politics of Stratification*, Oxford, 1971; Ioan Lewis, *Pastoral Democracy*, London, 1961; Akbar Ahmed, *Millennium and Charisma among the Pathans*, London, 1976; Shelagh Weir, 'Social structure and political organisation in al-Nadhir, Yemen Arab Republic', forthcoming; N. Levtzion, *Muslims and Chiefs in West Africa*, Oxford, 1968; Emanuel Marx, *Bedouin of the Negev*, Manchester, 1967; G.R. Garthwaite, 'Khans and Shahs: a documentary analysis of the Bakhtiyari in Iran', forthcoming; B.W. Andrezejewski, 'The veneration of Sufi saints and its impact on the oral literature of the Somali people and on their literature in Arabic', in *African Language Studies*, vol. XV, 1974; Dominique Chevallier, *La Société du Mont Liban*, Paris, 1971; Samir Khalaf, *Persistence and Change in 19th Century Lebanon*, Beirut, 1979. For an account of the residue of a segmen-tary system surviving at village levels when the larger units have atrophied, cf. P. Stirling, *Turkish Village*, London, 1965.
44 Cf. Nikki Keddie (ed.), *Scholars, Saints and Sufis*, California, 1972; I. Lapidus, *Muslim Cities in the Later Middle Ages*, Harvard, 1967; A.M. Hourani and S.M. Stern (eds.), *The Islamic City*, Oxford, 1970; C.A.O. van Niewenhuijze, *Social Stratification and the Middle East*, Leiden, 1965; A. Zghal and F. Stambouli, 'Urban life in pre-colonial North Africa', *British Journal of Sociology*, vol. 27, 1976, pp. 1—20; R.I. Lawless and G.H. Blake, *Tlemcen*, London, 1976.
45 In India, the martyrdom and the passion play or ritual re-enacting it, are or were not a speciality of the Shi'ites, but came to be generally diffused

amongst Sunni Muslims as well, and only recent Reformist activity came to make it, once again, into a diacritical sectarian mark. Cf. Marc Gaboriau, *Minorités musulmanes dans le royaume hindou du Népal*, Nanterre, 1977.
46 Professor M. Rouholamini and Dr Ch. Bromberger, personal communication.
47 P.M. Holt, *The Mahdist State in the Sudan, 1881–1898*, Oxford, 1970; H. Shaked (ed.), *Isma'il b. 'Abd al-Qadir: The Life of the Sudanese Mahdi*, New Brunswick, 1978.
48 Gallissot and Badia, *Marxisme et Algérie*.
49 V.N. Nikiforov, *Vostok i Vsemirnaia Istoria* (The East and World History), Moscow, 1975.
50 M. Blincow, 'Class formation and patron–client ties in the Gharb Plain', forthcoming.
51 M. Gilsenan, *Saint and Sufi in Modern Egypt*, Oxford, 1973; V. Crapanzano, *The Hamadsha*, Berkeley, 1973.
52 Cf. John Paden, *Religion and Political Culture in Kano*, California, 1973; C.C. Stewart and E.K. Stewart, *Islam and Social Order in Mauritania*, Oxford, 1973; Jamil Abun-Nasr, *The Tijaniyya*, Oxford, 1965; B.G. Martin, *Muslim Brotherhoods in Nineteenth-Century Africa*, Cambridge, 1976; H.J. Fisher, *Ahmadiyyah*, London, 1963; I.M. Lewis (ed. with introduction), *Islam in Tropical Africa*, Oxford, 1966; J.S. Trimingham, *Islam in the Sudan*, London, 1949; M.G. Smith, *Government in Zazzau*, London, 1960; Raymond Firth, *Malay Fishermen*, London, 1946; Clive Kessler, *Islam and Politics in a Malay State: Kelantan 1938–1969*, Ithaca, N.Y., and London, 1978.
53 The same was largely true well into the nineteenth century in Egypt, despite (perhaps in part because of) the availability of the Wahabi counter-model. Cf. Gilbert Delanoue, *La Politique de l'état réformateur en matière d'instruction publique*, forthcoming.
54 John S. Habib, *Ibn Sa'ud's Warriors of Islam*, Leiden, 1978.
55 M. Morsy, personal communication. By contrast, colonial aggression a century later produced a different reaction in Abd el Krim's republic, though his tribal base was similar. Cf. D. Hart, *The Aith Wariaghar of the Moroccan Rif*, Arizona, 1976.
56 Cf. Albert Hourani, *Arabic Thought in the Liberal Age, 1798–1939*, Oxford, 1962; Clifford Geertz, *Islam Observed*, New Haven, Conn., 1968; Sylvia Haim, *Arab Nationalism – An Anthology* (esp. the introduction), California, 1962; Nadav Safran, *Egypt in Search of Political Community*, Harvard, 1961; G. Baer (ed.), *Asian and African Studies VII: The 'Ulama' in Modern History*, Jerusalem, 1970.
57 J.N.D. Anderson, *Islamic Law in the Modern World*, London, 1959.
58 W. Montgomery Watt, *Islam and the Integration of Society*, London, 1961.
59 L. Rosen's work on the actual functioning of courts in modern Morocco (forthcoming) seems to suggest that the Kadi's discretionary powers in effect allow him to take into consideration the local social realities and reputations in reaching verdicts. Whereas by contrast it is precisely the legally untrained local justices of the peace who indulge in rapid and arbitrary judgements, which illustrate Weber's pejorative notion of *Kadi Justiz*. If so, this would seem an interesting inversion of the old image of the relation between Holy Law and local custom – the former was supposed to be rigid, the latter supple and socially sensitive.

60 This way of schematising the manner in which the same themes are deployed differently on the two shores of the Mediterranean has been severely criticised in John Davis's witty and effective survey of Mediterranean anthropology, *Mediterranean People*, London, 1977.

61 The distinctiveness of the traditional Muslim state has now received official recognition in international law. In connection with the dispute about the Western Sahara, the International Court at the Hague observed 'in the view of the Court no rule of international law requires that a state should have some definite structure'. And evidently 'the Court willingly examines the specific forms of administrative organisation such as that of *blad Siba* (paragraph 96), and to pose questions about the practices of allegiance of Saharan caids'. *Blad Siba* was the part of Morocco which, bluntly, was not administered by the centre *at all* (thus constituting a somewhat limiting case of 'organisation administrative spécifique'), though at the same time remaining in some kind of moral/religious relationship to that centre. Caids were, theoretically, governmentally appointed officials. In practice, in outlying regions this nomination simply meant the confirmation of a local power-holder, or sometimes a possibly ineffectual attempt to create one.

The above quotation and the highlighting of the recognition by international law of the sociological distinctiveness of traditional Muslim political organisation come from Maurice Flory, *L'Avis de la Cour Internationale de Justice sur le Sahara Occidental* (16 Octobre 1975), in *Annuaire Français de Droit International*, XXI, 1975.

62 Captain Adolphus Slade in 1830, quoted in Elie Kedourie, 'Islam today', in *World of Islam*, ed. Bernard Lewis, London, 1976.

63 Cf. Amal Rassam Vinogradov, *The Ait Ndhir of Morocco*, Ann Arbor, Michigan, 1974, for the fate of some wolves under these conditions.

64 Paul Pascon, *Le Haouz de Marrakesh*, Rabbat, 1977. *Zaouias* are holy lodges, whereas caids are government officials.

65 K. Hopkins, *Conquerors and Slaves*, Cambridge, 1978.

66 Malcolm H. Kerr, *Islamic Reform*, Cambridge, 1966; Nikki R. Keddie, *An Islamic Response to Imperialism*, California, 1968; Jamil Abun-Nasr, 'The Salafiyya movement in Morocco', in *St Antony's Papers*, no. 16, Middle Eastern Series no. 3, London, 1963; E. Kedourie, *Afghani and Abduh*, London, 1966; H. Laoust, 'Le Réformisme orthodoxe des Salafiya', *Revue des études Islamiques*, VI, 1932; Sylvia Haim, *Arab Nationalism*, California, 1962; Ali Merad, *Le Réformisme musulman en Algérie de 1925 à 1940*, Paris, 1967; Claude Collot and Jean-Robert Henry, *Le Mouvement national algerien, textes 1912—1954*, Office des Publications Universitaires, Algiers, 1978; Riaz Hassan, *Islamisation: A Study of Religious and Social Change in Pakistan*, forthcoming; G.H. Jensen, *Militant Islam*, London, 1979. On rural puritanism, see K. Platt's forthcoming work on the Kerkennah islands.

67 S. Mardin, 'Religion in modern Turkey', in *International Social Science Journal*, vol. XXIX, no. 2, 1977.

68 Arnold Green, *The Tunisian Ulama 1873—1915*, Leiden, 1978.

69 S. Mardin, 'Religion in modern Turkey'. For the Balkan situation, see Alexandre Popovic, 'Sur la situation actuelle des ordres mystiques musulmanes en Yougoslavie', presented to a Conference in Amsterdam in December 1979, to be published, edited by E. Gellner and E. Wolf.

70 N. Yalman, 'Islamic Reform and the mystic tradition in Eastern Turkey', in *European Journal of Sociology*, vol. X, no. 1, 1969.

71   Cf. Hélène Carrère d'Encausse, *Réforme et révolution chez les musulmans de l'empire russe*, Paris, 1966. On the local ethnography, see A. Benningsen and C.L. Lemercier-Quelquejay, *Islam in the Soviet Union*, London, 1967. On Soviet ethnography of the area, see V.I. Basilov, *Kult Sviatykh v Islame*, Moscow, 1970, or *Domusulmanskie Vierovania i Obriady v Srednei Azii*, ed. G.P. Snesarov and V.I. Basilov, Moscow, 1975.

72   Personal communication from C. Souriau and T. Monastiri.

73   H. Bleuchot and T. Monastiri, 'L'Islam de K. El-Qaddhafi', in *Annuaire de l'Afrique du Nord*, Aix en Provence, 1980, and 'Le régime politique libyen et l'Islam', in *Pouvoirs*, P.U.F., 1979.

74   Cf. for instance Clifford Geertz, 'In search of North Africa', *New York Review of Books*, 22 April 1971, or Abdallah Hammoudi, 'Segmentarité, stratification sociale, pouvoir politique et sainteté', in *Hesperis Tamuda*, vol. XV, 1974. Cf. also Ian Cunnison, *Baggara Arabs*, Oxford, 1966; Talal Asad, *The Kebabish Arabs*, London, 1980; Emanuel Marx, 'Tribal pilgrimages to saints' tombs in South Sinai', presented to a Conference in Amsterdam in December 1979, in a collection to be edited by E. Gellner and E. Wolf; Clifford Geertz, Hildred Geertz, Lawrence Rosen, *Meaning and Order in Moroccan Society*, Cambridge, 1979; and Dale F. Eickelman, *The Middle East*, 1981. See the special issue of *Annales*, May—August 1980.

75   Dale F. Eickelman, *Moroccan Islam*, London, 1976.

76   Cf. John Waterbury, *Commander of the Faithful*, London, 1970; Rémy Leveau, *Le Fellah marocain — défenseur du trône*, Paris, 1976; Bruno Etienne, *L'Algérie, cultures et révolution*, Paris, 1977; Jean-Claude Vatin, *L'Algérie politique: histoire et société*, Paris, 1974; Lawrence Rosen, 'Rural political process and national political structure in Morocco', in R.T. Antoun and Ilya Hatik (eds.), *Rural Politics and Social Change in the Middle East*, Indiana, 1972; W. Quandt, *Revolution and Political Leadership*, Cambridge, Mass., 1969; Jean Leca and Jean-Claude Vatin, *L'Algérie politique: institutions et régime*, Paris, 1975; David Seddon, 'Local politics and state intervention', in *Arabs and Berbers*, ed. E. Gellner and C.L. Micaud, London, 1973, and Jeanne Favret's paper in the same volume; Anouar Abdel-Malek, *Egypte, société militaire*, Paris, 1962; Hanna Batatu, *The Old Social Classes and the Revolutionary Movements of Iraq*, Princeton, N.J., 1978; N. Safran, *Egypt in Search of Political Community*, Cambridge, Mass., 1961; Jean and Simone Lacoutoure, *Egypt in Transition*, London, 1958; P.J. Vatikiotis, *The Modern History of Egypt*, London, 1963; Richard P. Mitchell, *The Society of the Muslim Brothers*, London, 1969; Olivier Carré, *La Légitimation Islamique des socialismes arabes*, Paris, 1979.

77   Waterbury, *Commander of the Faithful*.

78   Cf. Bernard Lewis, *The Emergence of Modern Turkey*, Oxford, 1968; Halil Inalcik, *The Ottoman Empire*, London, 1973; Norman Izikowitz, *Ottoman Empire and Islamic Tradition*, New York, 1972; Stanford J. Shaw, *History of the Ottoman Empire and Modern Turkey*, 2 vols, Cambridge, 1976—7; Kemal H. Karpat (ed.), *The Ottoman State and its Place in World History*, Leiden, 1974.

79   Ibn Khaldun, *The Muqaddimah*.

80   Cf. L. Carl Brown, *The Tunisia of Ahmad Bey 1837—1855*, part one, Princeton, 1974; David Ayalon, *Studies of the Mamluks of Egypt 1250—1517*, London, 1977. On later forms of social organisation under the Mamluks, see André Raymond, *Artisans et commerçants au Caire*, 2 vols,

Damascus, 1973, or Roger Owen, Introduction to section II, in T. Naff and R. Owen, *Studies in Eighteenth Century Islamic History*, Southern Illinois, 1977. On Tunisia seen from below, see L. Valensi, *Fellahs tunisiens*, Paris, 1977. For taxation styles in Algeria under the Turks, see Peter von Sivers, *Economic Ethics in the Maghrib: Algeria and Tunisia in the Early Nineteenth Century*, forthcoming. For a comparative study of North African and Turkish development, see the forthcoming co-operative volume on this topic, edited by S. Mardin and W. Zartman.

81 Perry Anderson, *Lineages of the Absolute State*, London, 1974.
82 I. Lapidus, 'The evolution of Muslim urban society', in *Comparative Studies in Society and History*, vol. 15, no. 1, January 1973. See also Patricia Crone, *Slaves on Horses*, Cambridge, 1980.
83 R. Bendix, *Max Weber. An Intellectual Portrait*, London, 1960.
84 Hodgson, *The Venture of Islam*.
85 Cf. also, for evidence from other regions, Abner Cohen, *Customs and Politics in Urban Africa*, London, 1969; also Syed Hussein Alatas, 'Religion and modernisation in Southeast Asia', *European Journal of Sociology*, vol. XI, no. 2, 1970.
86 Cf. Said Amir Arjomand, 'Religion, political action and legitimate domination in Shi'ite Iran: 14th to 18th centuries A.D.', *European Journal of Sociology*, 1979; also his 'The Shi'ite hierocracy and the state in pre-modern Iran, 1785–1890', forthcoming; N. Keddie, *Iran: Religion, Politics and Society*, London, 1980; Ch. Bromberger, 'Islam et révolution en Iran', *Revue de l'Occident Musulman et de la Méditerranée*, vol. 29, 1980.
87 A scholar who has noted the great extent of this problem and endeavours to follow out the continuities in this moral domination by intellectuals is Gilbert Delanoue.
88 For instance, Dr Richard Tapper, working on nomads in Iran, was led by the paucity of other ritual to suppose that the state of high excitement preceding the annual migration was itself a *kind* of ritual, and served the Durkheimian purposes of ritual. Cf. *Pasture and Politics: Economics, Conflict and Ritual Among Shahsevan Nomads of Iranian Azarbayjan*, New York, 1979.
89 E. Peters, 'The proliferation of segments in the lineage of the Bedouin of Cyrenaica', in *Journal of the Royal Anthropological Institute*, vol. 90, part 1, 1960; Evans-Pritchard, *The Sanusi*.
90 Cf. Donald P. Cole, *The Nomads of the Nomads*, Chicago, 1975. Or again: 'The nucleus of the army with which Ibn Sa'ud originally expelled the Turks from Najd was composed of townsmen' (John S. Habib, *Ibn Sa'ud's Warriors of Islam*).
91 Professor R.B. Sarjeant of Cambridge drew my attention to this. Southern and Eastern Arabia altogether constitute an as yet not fully exploited sociological laboratory for checking whether formal doctrine or social organisation has greater effect on the actually practised religious style. One might expect the Ibadis of the Oman highlands to be impelled in a scripturalist-egalitarian direction by their doctrine, but D. Eickelman's preliminary researches suggest that the claims of lineage are not ignored. Ms Shelagh Weir's material on northern Yemen (to be published) suggests that Zaydism, at least at present, does not markedly differentiate its upholders from Sunnis. It may be that in the present ideological climate – prevalence of puritan Reformism, and the power of the Saudis in the peninsula – Zaydis are not eager to remind observers of their erstwhile dominance and

distinctiveness. The Sunnis at the other end of the Yemen, by contrast, are more willing to recollect the political significance of sectarianism. Cf. the work of C. Myntti, forthcoming.

92 Michael Gilsenan, *The Social Life of Islam*, forthcoming. At the same time, Bruno Etienne's researches (to be published) into popular religion in contemporary Casablanca suggest a powerful revival, sometimes encouraged from above, of folk Sufism — if only owing to the inadequacy of other therapeutic and supportive agencies.

93 Hugh Roberts, *Holy Lineages and Local Politics in Algeria*, forthcoming.

94 Robert Fernea, *Sheikh and Effendi*, Harvard, 1970.

95 Cf. A. Laraoui, *L'histoire du Maghreb: essai de synthèse*, Paris, 1970; Edward Said, *Orientalism*, New York, 1979; Y. Lacoste, A. Nouschi and A. Prenant, *L'Algérie passé et présent*, Paris, 1960.

96 David Ayalon, *Gunpowder and Firearms in the Mamluk Kingdom: A Challenge to a Mediaeval Society*, London, 1956.

97 John Hartley, 'The Political Organisation of an Arab Tribe of the Hadramaut', unpublished Ph.D. thesis, University of London, 1961.

98 For a valuable survey of classical orientalist interpretations of Islam, cf. J. Waardenburg, *L'Islam dans le miroir de L'Occident*, La Haye, 1969.

99 Hodgson, *The Venture of Islam*.

2 Cohesion and identity: the Maghreb from Ibn Khaldun to Emile Durkheim

1 This paper was written for a conference in Tunis on the theme of national identity and marking the fortieth anniversary of the Neo-Destour Party, and was also published in Tunisia in a volume of the Cahiers de C.E.R.E.S. entitled *Identité culturelle et conscience nationale en Tunisie*.

3 Post-traditional forms in Islam: the turf and trade, and votes and peanuts

1 Bernard Lewis, *The Assassins*, London, 1967 and 1970, p. 24.

2 *Ibid.*, p. 27.

3 H.S. Morris, *The Indians in Uganda*, London, 1968, p. 67. My account of the Ismailis is heavily indebted to this admirable book.

4 *Ibid.*, p. 68.

5 Donal B. Cruise O'Brien, *The Mourides of Senegal*, Oxford, 1970.

6 I.M. Lewis (ed.), *Islam in Tropical Africa*, Oxford, 1966.

4 Doctor and saint

1 The material used in this chapter is presented in greater detail in *Saints of the Atlas*, London and Chicago, 1969.

5 Sanctity, puritanism, secularisation and nationalism in North Africa: a case study

1 Martin Lings, *A Moslem Saint of the Twentieth Century*, London, 1961.

2 One is reminded of Kant's conviction that when Christ recommended love, He meant not what He said but a kind of abridgement of the *Critique of Practical Reason*.

3 The year was 1909. Mr Lings appears to have made a slip in the footnote

referring to this episode, when remarking that there was an epidemic in Saudi Arabia – meaning, presumably, in the territories which only became parts of Saudi Arabia much later.

6 The unknown Apollo of Biskra: the social base of Algerian puritanism

1 A. Gide, *Si le grain ne meurt*. All quotations from Gide are translated by Ernest Gellner.

2 Quoted in Ali Merad, *Le Réformisme musulman en Algérie de 1925 à 1940*, Paris, 1967.

3 F. Colonna, 'Cultural resistance and religious legitimacy in colonial Algeria', in *Economy and Society*, vol. 3, 1974, pp. 233–52. See also F. Stambouli and A. Zghal, 'La vie urbaine dans le Maghreb pré-colonial', in *L'Annuaire de l'Afrique du nord*, 1974, and also in *British Journal of Sociology*, 1976, p. 27, pp. 1–20.

4 d'Holbach, *Système de Nature*, first anonymous edition 1770, various subsequent editions.

5 Jacques Berque, *Structures sociales du Haut-Atlas*, Paris, 1955. See especially the expanded 1978 edition, in which Berque relates his study to subsequent research.

6 Ali Merad, *Le Réformisme musulman*. Also, by the same author, *Ibn Badis, commentateur du Koran*, Paris, 1971.

7 *Le Réformisme musulman*, pp. 53–4.

8 For a discussion of such Muslim 'scripturalism' and its appeal in other social contexts, see Clifford Geertz, *Islam Observed*, Yale, 1968.

9 By a further irony, Uqbi was in fact descended from the most prominent maraboutic lineage in the Aures region, the one maraboutic house which was of more than local significance and exercised a pan-Aures influence. I owe this piquant piece of information to Dr Fanny Colonna, who unearthed it in the course of her researches (to be published) on the social life of the Aures in the nineteenth century.

10 Ali Merad, *Le Réformisme Musulman*, pp. 97, 98, 99, 100, 262, 263, 264.

11 *Ibid.*, p. 100.

12 *Ibid.*, p. 147.

13 *Ibid.*, pp. 9, 10.

14 *Ibid.*, p. 141.

15 *Ibid.*, p. 83.

16 Charles-Robert Ageron, *Les Algériens musulmans et la France (1871–1919)*, Paris, 1968, vol. II, p. 903.

17 *Les Algériens musulmans*, p. 908.

18 E. Burke in *Middle Eastern Studies*, vol. 7, no. 2 (May 1971), p. 249. See also Malek Bennabi, *Mémoires d'un témoin du siècle*, Editions Nationales Algériennes, 1965, esp. pp. 75 and 76.

19 Since this was written, the following informative study of therapeutic and ecstatic folk practices in Algeria has appeared: A. Ouitis, *Les Contradictions sociales et leur expression symbolique dans le Sétifois*, Alger, 1977.

20 Capitaine H. Simon, Commandant Supérieur du cercle de Touggourt, 'Notes sur le mausolée de Sidi Ocba', *Revue Africaine*, Publiée par la Société historique algérienne, 1909, especially pp. 41–5.

21 Ahmed Nadir, in 'Les ordres religieux et la conquête française 1830–1851', in *Revue algérienne des sciences juridiques*, vol. IX, no. 4, December, 1972,

pp. 819–68, claims that Emir Abd el Kader, the leader of Algerian resistance during the early colonial period, was a kind of proto-reformer and predecessor of Ben Badis. By contrast, Pessah Shinar, in 'Abd el-Qadir and Abd al-Krim', in *Asian and African Studies. Annual of the Israel Oriental Society*, vol. 1, 1965, pp. 139–74, finds that Abd el Kader 'leans heavily on the maraboutic class'.

22   For a discussion of political developments and the role of these attitudes in it, see Clement Henry Moore, *North Africa*, Boston, 1970, or Elbaki Hermassi, *Leadership and National Development in North Africa*, London, 1972.

23   Ali Merad, *Le Réformisme musulman*, p. 74.

24   V. Maher, *Women and Property in Morocco*, Cambridge, 1974. For other comparative material and analysis of the position of women, see Lois Beck and Nikki Keddie (eds.), *Women in the Muslim World*, Harvard, 1978, and Nancy Tapper, 'Matrons and mistresses', *European Journal of Sociology*, 1980.

25   It appears that for instance the new Moroccan code of 1957 legally consecrates this social style (and there is no doubt that the dominant actual practice of Algeria does so). Cf. Fatima Mernissi, *Identité culturelle et idéologie sexuelle*, paper presented to the 24th International Congress of Sociology in Algiers, March 1974, pp. 3ff. The author notes 'the desire of the Moroccan legislator to use pre-colonial tradition as a guide for the future' (p. 3), but perhaps does not stress sufficiently that what is at issue is not the effective tradition of *all* pre-colonial Moroccans, but an ideal practised by some and merely respected, rather than implemented, by other social strata. Cf. also *Beyond the Veil*, Cambridge, Mass., 1978, by the same author.

26   Cf. Vincent Crapanzano, *The Hamadsha. A Study in Moroccan Ethnopsychiatry*, Berkeley, 1973, for an account of urban gangs of dancers/therapists of this kind.

27   Quoted in Ageron, *Les Algériens musulmans*, vol. I, p. 12n.

28   Gilbert Grandguillaume, *Nedroma. L'Évolution d'une Medina*, Leiden, 1976.

29   *Ibid*.

30   *Ibid*.

31   Reformism is on the ascendant throughout the Arab Muslim world, though the degree of its success varies. Correspondingly, saint cults are on the decline. But exceptions naturally occur: special circumstances or talents may lead to successful adaptation by some saintly movements to modern circumstances. One such unusual case is extremely well explored by Michael Gilsenan, in *Saint and Sufi in Modern Egypt. An Essay in the Sociology of Religion*, Oxford, 1973.

32   On the social history and structure of an important Moroccan town, the work of K. Brown, *People of Salé*, Manchester, 1977, provides admirable material. See below, pp. 214–20.

33   Grandguillaume, *Nedroma*.

34   Quoted in André Nouschi, *La Naissance du nationalisme algérien*, Paris, 1976, p. 66.

35   Quoted in *ibid*., pp. 69–70.

36   Quoted in Ali Merad, *Le Réformisme musulman*, p. 56.

37   Grandguillaume, *Nedroma*.

38   Cf. John Waterbury, *Commander of the Faithful*, London, 1970.

39   The situation has parallels with the appeal of Hellenism and of Orthodox

religion in Cyprus, where a petty bourgeoisie, without access to international circuits and anglophone education, finds in them a validation of their position against more privileged and westernised Cypriots. On this subject, see P. Loizos, *Bitter Favours: Politics in a Cypriot Village*, Oxford, 1974.

40 Ira Lapidus, *Muslim Cities in the Later Middle Ages*, Harvard, 1967.

41 Ali Merad, *Le Réformisme musulman*, p. 209.

42 This phrase is Professor Serif Mardin's. The idea can be found in his article, 'Religion in modern Turkey', *International Social Science Journal*, vol. XXIX, no. 2, 1977, or in Nur Yalman's 'Islamic Reform and the mystic tradition in Eastern Turkey', in the *European Journal of Sociology*, 1969, vol. X, no. 1.

43 In Soviet Central Asia, the Reform movement was known as Jadidism, literally New-ism. It was similar in spirit and inspiration to Ben Badis's movement in Algeria. The Russians saw its potentialities both for nationalism and for adaptation to modern requirements. So they suppressed the name and movement, but borrowed its ideas and doctrines for the officially controlled Islam. They pre-empted Reform, and did not repeat the French mistake of associating too long with archaic dervish forms of faith – except when writing local cultural history, when past achievements of Sufi mystics receive warm recognition. Only a dead dervish is allowed to be a good dervish.

44 Pessah Shinar, 'Some observations on the ethical teachings of Orthodox Reformism in Algeria', *Asian and African Studies*, Jerusalem Academic Press, vol. 8, no. 8, 1972, p. 269.

45 Summarised by Ali Merad, in *Ibn Badis*, p. 146.

46 *Ibid.*, p. 147.

47 Emrys Peters, 'Why Gaddafy?', in *New Society*, vol. 20, September 1972, p. 697.

48 *Ibid.*

49 The Tunisian case seems closer to the Turkish than the Algerian. The case of the Tunisian *ulama* has been extremely well explored by Arnold Green, in *The Tunisian Ulama 1873–1915*, Leiden, 1978. Apparently the Tunisian *ulama*, unlike most of the Algerian ones, were too well-heeled to be radical. In Morocco, Reformism was influential and made a major, direct and open contribution to both the ideology and the organisation of nationalism. But it never had anything resembling the near-monopoly of influence which it enjoyed in Algeria. The remarkable continuity of elites and institutions, from pre-colonial days through colonialism till independence, provided alternative leadership and legitimacy. In post-Independence Morocco, the Reformist fundamentalists do however have one achievement to their credit, not yet to my knowledge rivalled even by Gaddafy – they secured the passing of death sentences (though not their execution) for apostasy from Islam, in conformity with Koranic requirements.

7 Trousers in Tunisia

1 L. Carl Brown, *The Tunisia of Ahmad Bey 1837–1855*, Princeton, N.J., 1974.

2 Arnold Green, *The Tunisian Ulama 1873–1915*, Leiden, 1978.

8 The sociology of Robert Montagne (1893–1954)

1 To my knowledge, only two of Robert Montagne's works are available in English. The first is his inaugural lecture at the Collège de France, delivered in 1948, which was published as 'The modern state in Africa and Asia' in the *Cambridge Journal*, July 1952, translated by Elie and Sylvia Kedourie. This is interesting, though now perhaps dated: the flood of work on the Third World since it was published has made many of its general points familiar. The second is *The Berbers. Their Social and Political Organisation*, which was translated with an introduction by David Seddon, London, 1973, 93 pp. This translation of *La Vie sociale et la vie politique des Berbères* (1931) was based on a later and previously unpublished manuscript of 1947. All otherwise uncited quotations in the present article are taken from this translation by Seddon. This is a brilliant and succinct summary of his work on Berber political sociology, though it should not be allowed to stand between the reader and Montagne's untranslated masterpiece, *Les Berbères et le Makhzen dans le sud du Maroc*, Paris, 1930. Other works by Montagne include: *La Civilisation du désert*, Paris, 1947; *Naissance du prolétariat marocain*, Paris, 1951; and *Révolution au Maroc*, Paris, 1953. His most important predecessors in his field were Ibn Khaldun (1332–1406), most easily accessible in English in the translation by F. Rosenthal of *The Muqaddimah*, abridged edition, London, 1967, and the sadly unobtainable E. Masqueray, *La Formation des cités chez les populations sédentaires de l'Algérie*, Paris, 1886.
2 P.J. André, *Confréries religieuses musulmanes*, Algiers, 1956.
3 Edmund Leach, *Political Systems of Highland Burma*, London, 1970.
4 E.E. Evans-Pritchard, *The Nuer*, Oxford, 1940.
5 Jacques Berque, *Structures sociales du Haut-Atlas*, expanded edition, Paris, 1978.
6 Ian Cunnison, *Baggara Arabs*, Oxford, 1966.
7 Clifford Geertz, *Islam Observed*, New Haven, Conn., 1968.
8 The narrower topic of Montagne's work, the tyrannies of the western Atlas, is explored in a journalistic manner in G. Maxwell, *Lords of the Atlas*, 1970. This book is inaccurate in its details but gives a good overall impression. The setting of Montagne's work is explored in *Arabs and Berbers*, ed. E. Gellner and Ch. Micaud, London, 1973, a volume which in particular contains a discussion of French ethnography in North Africa by E. Burke, 'The image of the Moroccan state in French ethnological literature: new light on the origins of Lyautey's Berber policy'. The subsequent work in English on relevant themes includes John Waterbury, *The Commander of the Faithful*, London, 1970, and *North for the Trade*, Berkeley, Cal., 1972; Clifford Geertz, *Islam Observed*, 1968; Ernest Gellner, *Saints of the Atlas*, Chicago, 1970; E.E. Evans-Pritchard, *The Nuer*, 1940; Edmund Leach, *Political Systems of Highland Burma*, 1954, 1965, 1970; Vanessa Maher, *Women and Property in Morocco*, Cambridge, 1974; Amal Rassam Vinogradov, *The Ait Ndhir of Morocco*, Ann Arbor, Michigan, 1974; Paul Rabinow, *Symbolic Domination*, Chicago, 1975; William Zartman, *Morocco: Problems of New Power*, New York, 1964; Clement Henry Moore, *Politics in North Africa*, Boston, Mass., 1970; Elbaki Hermassi, *Leadership and National Development in North Africa*, Berkeley, Cal., 1972; Robin Bidwell, *Morocco under*

Colonial Rule, London, 1973; Edmund Burke III, *Prelude to Protectorate in Morocco*, Chicago and London, 1976; C.S. Coon, *Caravan*, New York, 1975.

9 Patterns of rural rebellion in Morocco during the early years of independence

1 When the Royalist Governor of Tafilalet province, Addi u Bihi, rebelled and was suppressed by the Crown Prince and the Royal Army, the explanation was not that he was not really Royalist after all. When the members of the Ait Abdi tribe, affiliated through their leader Haddu u Mha to the Leftist party, rebelled at the time when the Leftist leader Abdallah Ibrahim was Prime Minister, the explanation was not that they were not 'truly' Leftist, i.e. genuine and loyal clients of the Leftist party. (Of course, in a sense they were not truly 'Leftist', i.e. they have no idea of what 'Left' and 'Right' mean in the contexts from which these terms are borrowed. But that is hardly relevant. They do not need to understand to be loyal: and that they were.)

2 Douglas Ashford, *Political Change in Morocco*, Princeton, 1961.

3 One of his mistresses was a French actress of distinction, who was duly rewarded by a handsome piece of landed property in Morocco. In her declining years, in an administrative theatrical post in France, she charged one of the district officers, an army captain, to look after her Moroccan landed property. In her case, gallantry, if not Muslim Law, ensured some female inheritance, as it were.

4 The chief of the Ait Atta of the Shadow (i.e. of the northern slopes of the Atlas) did so in the early 1950s, and suffered exile in the south in consequence.

5 One of the factors in the decline in importance of rural holy lineages was precisely this: their settlements on intertribal borders lost their function of facilitating intertribal trade and movement.

6 There is a rival, Left theory which denies that this was traditionally the case. It maintains, instead, that traditional, pre-1912 Moroccan government was based on consent. Part of the evidence for this thesis is precisely the existence of dissidence, *siba*, of opting-out by regions and tribes, and of recognised ritual acts for opting-in, for submission. The thesis goes on to maintain that the absolutist interpretation of the past of the Moroccan state was a French invention, designed to rationalise the Sultan's abdication of power in favour of his 'Protectors'. Cf. M. Lahbabi, *Le Gouvernement marocain à l'aube du XXème siècle*, Rabat, 1958, and E. Gellner, 'The struggle for Morocco's past', in *The Middle East Journal*, Winter, 1961.

7 The police, for instance, remained under the direct control of the monarchy and not the Ministry of the Interior.

8 The matter was of course further complicated by the trilingual situation. The administration continued to work in French. Some administrators were Arab, some Berber. Some were literate in Arabic, some in French, some in both, and some in neither. Thus many needed interpreters, either to read documents in one of the two written languages (Berber is not written), or to communicate with locals. For instance, a document marked 'Confidential' would reach an administrator who happened to be illiterate. (The man I have in mind, I should add, is otherwise very able, and was given his post as a reward for ably organising a very daring rebellion during the final months of French rule.) He would, of course, be at the mercy of some of his sub-

ordinates when it came to reading the document: these subordinates might be politically opposed to him.

9   Locals were positively irritated when the fission in the major party forced them to make overt avowals of loyalty in one direction or the other, and often evaded this, certainly in the open. The political structure, both of traditional tribal organisation and of the present Moroccan state, makes anticipatory full political commitments, prior to the final result, undesirable and disagreeable. Tribal elections, for instance, end in unanimity, however hard-fought or hard-negotiated they may be. In the end it is a matter of sheer courtesy to vote for the victor.

10 There is an Arab story about a man who went into the desert. His equipment, carefully checked, included matches. To make sure that the matches would prove reliable, he tested and struck each one ... Similarly, those blessed with rural followers cannot test the loyalty of all of them in advance of actual use.

11 The contrast I am drawing is not the same as the one drawn by, for instance, students of Algeria, between old tribal and new national rebellions. That is a different contrast, and no doubt the crucial one for Algeria. But here we are contrasting old tribal dissidence with new revolts which are not 'national' either — they are not attempts at setting up regional independence, but are a move in a new national type of politics.

10 Saints and their descendants

1   Jacques Berque, *Al-Yousi; problèmes de la culture marocaine au XVIIème siècle*, Paris, 1958.
2   Paul Rabinow, *Symbolic Domination. Cultural Form and Historical Change in Morocco*, Chicago, 1975.
3   Berque, *Al-Yousi*.
4   Clifford Geertz, *Islam Observed*, New Haven, Conn., 1968.
5   Robert Montagne, *Les Berbères et le Makhzen dans le sud du Maroc*, Paris, 1930.
6   Bernard Hoffman, *The Structure of Traditional Moroccan Rural Society*, The Hague, 1967.
7   Amal Rassam Vinogradov, *The Ait Ndhir of Morocco*, Ann Arbor, 1975. See also John Chiapuris, *The Ait Ayash of the High Moulouya Plain: Rural Social Organization in Morocco*, Ann Arbor, Michigan, 1979.

11 The marabouts in the market-place

1   Dale F. Eickelman, *Moroccan Islam*, Austin, Texas, 1977; Kenneth L. Brown, *People of Salé*, Manchester, 1977.
2   John H.R. Davis, *Mediterranean People*, London, 1977.
3   R. Coindreau, *Les Corsaires de Salé*, Paris, 1948.

12 Rulers and tribesmen

1   Raphael Danziger, *Abd-al-Qadir and the Algerians. Resistance to the French and Internal Consolidation*, New York and London, 1977, and Ross E. Dunn, *Resistance in the Desert: Moroccan Responses to French Imperialism*

1881—1912, illustrated by Jeanne Dunn, Wisconsin, 1977. See also Edmund Burke III, *Prelude to Protectorate in Morocco*, Chicago and London, 1976.

2 Robert Montagne, *Les Berbères et le Makhzen dans le sud du Maroc*, Paris, 1930.

3 In other areas however, such as southern Tunisia and possibly adjoining regions, where Berber speech has some association with the Kharejite heresy, linguistic Arabisation probably went hand-in-hand with the imposition of religious orthodoxy. Cf. Michael Brett, 'Ibn Khaldun and the Arabisation of North Africa', in *The Maghreb Review*, vol. 4, no. 1 (Jan—Feb 1979).

Bibliography of Ernest Gellner's North African writings

Code (e.g. 1963 (*b*)) refers to the master bibliography in *The Devil in Modern Philosophy* (London 1974) and *Spectacles and Predicaments* (Cambridge 1979). Items marked * appear in this volume.

1956
(*a*) 'Berbers of Morocco', *Quarterly Review*, **294**, no. 608, April, pp. 218–23. Translated into French in Général P.J. André, *Confréries Religieuses Musulmanes*, Alger: Editions La Maison des Livres, pp. 345–50.
(*f*) 'The Sheep and The Saint', *Encounter*, **7**, November, pp. 42–6.

1957
(*c*) 'Highlanders of Morocco', *The Times*, 25 March, p. 11.
(*d*) 'The Summit of Azurki', *LSE Mountaineering Club Journal*, **4**, pp. 7–12. (Also in *Humanist*, **74**, no. 1, January 1959, pp. 16–19.)
(*f*) 'Independence in the Central High Atlas', *Middle East Journal*, **11**, no. 3, Summer, pp. 236–52.
(*k*) 'Beauty and the Berber', *Humanist*, **72**, no. 9, September, pp. 15–18.

1958
(*c*) 'The Far West of Islam' (review article on Jacques Berque, *Structures sociales du Haut-Atlas*), *British Journal of Sociology*, **9**, no. 1, March, pp. 73–82.
(*d*) 'How to Live in Anarchy', *Listener*, **59**, 3 April, pp. 579, 582–3.

1960
(*a*) 'The Middle East Observed', *Political Studies*, **8**, no. 1, February, pp. 66–70.
(*b*) Review of J.N.D. Anderson, *Islamic Law in the Modern World*, in *British Journal of Sociology*, **11**, no. 1, March, pp. 98–9.
(*f*) 'Allah & Caesar', *Hibbert Journal*, **59**, October, pp. 54–8.

1961
(*g*) 'From Ibn Khaldun to Karl Marx' (review of Donald E. Ashford, *Political Change in Morocco*), *Political Quarterly*, **32**, no. 4, October/December, pp. 385–92.
(*h*) 'The Struggle for Morocco's Past', *Middle East Journal*, **15**, no. 1,

Winter, pp. 79–90; reprinted in I.W. Zartman (ed.), *Man, State and Society in the Contemporary Maghrib*, New York: Praeger, 1973, pp. 37–49.
(*i*) 'Morocco', in Colin Legum (ed.), *Africa, A Handbook of the Continent*, London: Anthony Blond, pp. 43–60.
(*j*) Review of W. Montgomery Watt, *Islam and the Integration of Society*, in *British Journal of Sociology*, 12, no. 4, December, pp. 392–3.

1962
(*e*) 'Patterns of Rural Rebellion in Morocco: Tribes as Minorities', *European Journal of Sociology*, 3, no. 2, pp. 297–311; reprinted in 1973 (*b*), pp. 361–74.*

1963
(*b*) 'A Tunisian Visit', *New Society*, 1, 3 January, pp. 15–17.
(*c*) Review of Rom Landau, *Morocco Independent* in *Middle East Journal*, 17, nos. 1 and 2, Winter–Spring, pp. 174–5.
(*d*) 'Sanctity, Puritanism, Secularisation and Nationalism in North Africa', *Archives de Sociologie des Religions*, no. 15, pp. 71–86. Also in J.G. Peristiany (ed.), *Contributions to Mediterranean Sociology: Mediterranean Rural Communities and Social Change*. Acts of the Mediterranean Sociology Conference, July 1963, Paris: Mouton, 1965, pp. 31–48.*
(*e*) 'Thy Neighbour's Revolution', *New Society*, 1, 16 May, pp. 20–1.
(*g*) 'Saints of the Atlas', in Julian Pitt-Rivers (ed.), *Mediterranean Countrymen*, Paris: Mouton, pp. 145–57.

1964
(*b*) Review of C.F. Gallagher, *The United States and North Africa*, in *New Society*, 3, 30 April, pp. 28–9.
(*d*) 'Hume and North African Islam', in *Religion in Africa*, Centre of African Studies, University of Edinburgh, July, mimeo.
(*e*) 'Political and Religious Organization of the Berbers of the Central High Atlas', *Proceedings of the Seventh International Congress of Anthropology, Moscow, August 1964*, 4, pp. 314–21; reprinted in 1973 (*b*), pp. 59–66.

1965
(*b*) 'The Day The Pendulum Stood Still' (review of Sylvia G. Haim (ed.), *Arab Nationalism*), *New Society*, 5, 15 April, pp. 30–1.
(*d*) 'Tribalism and Social Change in North Africa', in W.H. Lewis (ed.), *French-Speaking Africa, The Search For Identity*, New York: Walker, pp. 107–18.

1967
(*a*) Review of *Asian and African Studies*, vol. 1, in *Middle Eastern Studies*, 3, no. 2, January, pp. 182–7.
(*b*) Review of I.M. Lewis (ed.), *Islam in Tropical Africa*, in *Cambridge Review*, 89, no. 2138, 28 January, pp. 180–1.

1968
(*b*) Review of Ian Cunnison, *Baggara Arabs: Power and Lineage in a Sudanese Nomad Tribe*, in *Middle Eastern Studies*, 4, no. 3, April, pp. 326–8.

(*c*) 'A Pendulum Swing Theory of Islam', *Annales Marocaines de Sociologie* (Institut de Sociologie, Rabat), pp. 5−14; also in *Philosophical Forum*, 2, Winter, 1970−1, pp. 234−44; and Roland Robertson (ed.), *Sociology of Religion*, Harmondsworth: Penguin 1969, pp. 127−38.*

1969
(*b*) 'Système tribal et changement social en Afrique du nord', *Annales Marocaines de Sociologie* (Institut du Sociologie, Rabat), pp. 3−19. French translation of 1965 (*d*).
(*c*) 'The Great Patron', *European Journal of Sociology*, **10**, pp. 61−9.
(*f*) 'Far West & Wild West' (review of André Adam, *Histoire de Casablanca des Origines à 1914*), *New Society*, **14**, 17 July, pp. 102−3.
(*j*) *Saints of the Atlas*, London: Weidenfeld and Nicolson; University of Chicago Press.

1970
(*c*) 'Pouvoir politique et fonction religieuse dans l'Islam marocain', *Annales: Economies−Sociétés−Civilisations*, **25**, no. 2, Mars−Avril, pp. 699−713. (Same as 1972(f).)
(*d*) Review of Gavin Maxwell, *Lords of the Atlas*, in *Middle Eastern Studies*, **6**, no. 2, May, pp. 224−7.
(*f*) (under the pseudonym 'Philip Peters') 'Tunisia: A System on Trial?', *New Society*, **16**, no. 408, 23 July, pp. 144−6.

1971
(*a*) Review of Talal Asad, *The Kababish Arabs: Power, Authority and Consent in a Nomadic Tribe*, in *British Journal of Sociology*, **22**, no. 1, March, pp. 110−11.
(*c*) Review of Robert E. Fernea, *Shaykh and Effendi: Changing Patterns of Authority Among the El Shabana of Southern Iraq*, in *Sociology*, **5**, no. 2, pp. 267−8.

1972
(*f*) 'Doctor and Saint', in Nikki R. Keddie (ed.), *Scholars, Saints, and Sufis*, Berkeley and Los Angeles: University of California Press, pp. 307−26.*
(*k*) Review of Magali Morsy, *Les Ahansala*, in *L'Annuaire de l'Afrique du Nord*, vol. xi, pp. 960−2, Aix-en-Provence.
(*j*) (under the pseudonym 'Philip Peters') 'Algeria After Independence', *New Society*, **20**, no. 497, 6 April, pp. 9−11.

1973
(*a*) 'Post-traditional Forms of Islam: The Turf and Trade, and Votes and Peanuts', *Daedalus*, **102**, no. 1, Winter, pp. 191−206.*
(*b*) Ed. with Charles Micaud, *Arabs and Berbers*, London: Duckworth. Contains an Introduction, pp. 11−21, and reprints of 1962 (*e*), pp. 361−74, ed. 1964 (*e*), pp. 59−66.
(*c*) Preface to the English translation of Robert Montagne, *The Berbers*, London: Frank Cass, pp. vii−ix.
(*h*) Introduction to Cynthia Nelson (ed.), *The Desert and the Sown: Nomads in Wider Society*, Research Series no. 21, Institute of International Studies, University of California, Berkeley, pp. 1−9.

1974
(*d*) Review of E. Daumas, *The Wages of the Desert, Middle Eastern Studies*, **10**, no. 1, January, pp. 99–100.
(*h*) 'The Unknown Apollo of Biskra', *Government and Opposition*, **9**, no. 3, Summer, pp. 277–310.*

1975
(*b*) 'Cohesion and Identity: The Maghreb From Ibn Khaldun to Emile Durkheim', *Government and Opposition*, **10**, no. 2, Spring, pp. 203–18.*
(*c*) Review of Bryan S. Turner, *Weber and Islam, Population Studies*, **29**, March, pp. 168–9.
(*f*) Review of Donal Cruise O'Brien, *Saints and Politicians*, in *Times Higher Education Supplement*, no. 191, 13 June, p. 16.
(*j*) Review of Vincent Crapanzano, *The Hamadsha: A Study in Moroccan Ethnopsychiatry*, in *Africa*, **45**, no. 3, pp. 336–8.
(*k*) Review of Vanessa Maher, *Women and Property in Morocco*, in *African Affairs*, **74**, no. 297, October, p. 497.

1976
(*a*) 'Comment Devenir Marabout', *Bulletin Economique et Social du Maroc*, double number 128–9, Rabat, n.d., pp. 1–43. French translation by Paul C. Coatalen of chapter 2 of 1969 (*j*).
(*b*) 'The Sociology of Robert Montagne (1893–1954)', *Daedalus*, **105**, no. 1, Winter, pp. 137–50.*
(*c*) 'Saints and Their Descendants' (review of Paul Rabinow, *Symbolic Domination*, and A.R. Vinogradov, *The Ait Ndhir of Morocco*), *Times Literary Supplement*, no. 3857, 13 February, p. 164.*
(*d*) Co-translator (with Diana Ferguson) of F. Stambouli and A. Zghal, 'Urban Life in Pre-Colonial Africa', *British Journal of Sociology*, **27**, March, pp. 1–20.

1977
(*f*) 'The Marabouts in the Market Place' (review of Dale P. Eickelman, *Moroccan Islam*, and Kenneth L. Brown, *People of Salé*), in *Times Literary Supplement*, 19 August, no. 3936, p. 1011.*
(*g*) Edited with John Waterbury, *Patrons and Clients*, London: Duckworth, with an Introduction by EAG.
(*j*) Review of John Waterbury, *North for the Trade. The Life and Times of a Berber Merchant*, in *Middle Eastern Studies*, **13**, no. 3, October, pp. 401–2.
(*k*) Review of Abdallah Laraoui, *The Crisis of the Arab Intellectual*, in *Journal of the Middle East Studies Association of North America*, **11**, no. 3, October, pp. 52–3.
(*o*) Foreword to Sawsan el Messiri, *Ibn al-Balad: A Concept of Egyptian Identity*, Leiden: E.J. Brill, pp. ix–xi.

1978
(*a*) 'Trousers in Tunisia' (review of L. Carl Brown, *The Tunisia of Ahmad Bey*), in *Middle Eastern Studies*, **14**, no. 1, January, pp. 127–30.*
(*e*) Review of David Montgomery Hart, *The Aith Waryaghar of the Moroccan Rif*, in *Man*, **13**, no. 1, March, pp. 151–2.

(*h*) Review of Harvey E. Goldberg, *Cave Dwellers and Citrus Growers*, in *Middle Eastern Studies*, **14**, no. 2, May, pp. 251−2.

(*l*) Review of Paul Pascon, *Le Haouz de Marrakesh*, in *Man*, n.s. **13**, no. 4, December, pp. 690−2.

1979

(*b*) 'Rulers and Tribesmen', review of Raphael Danziger, *Abd-al-Qadir and the Algerians*, and Ross E. Dunn, *Resistance in the Desert*, *Middle Eastern Studies*, **15**, no. 1, January, pp. 106−13.*

(*d*) Review of B.G. Martin, *Muslim Brotherhood in Nineteenth Century Africa*, *Middle Eastern Studies*, **15**, no. 2, May, pp. 285−6.

(*l*) Review of Hassan Jouad and Bernard Lortat-Jacob, *La Saison des Fêtes dans une Vallée du Haut-Atlas*, *Middle East Journal*, **33**, no. 3, pp. 374−5.

1980

(*c*) 'How the System Manages to Go On Functioning in War-Torn Lebanon', *The Times*, 1 February.

(*j*) 'State and Revolution in Islam', *Millennium*, **8**, no. 3, pp. 185−99.

Name index

Muslim names are indexed under the *first* name, except where they are cited western-style by initials and last name, i.e. Abd el Krim, rather than Krim, Abd el, but Zhgal, A., rather than A. Zghal.

252

Name index

Name index

Mustafa Kemal, 170
Myntti, C., 239 n. 91

Nadav, Safran, 235 n. 56
Naff, T., 238 n. 80
Napoleon, 20
Nasser, Gamal, 82
Nikiforov, V.N., 235 n. 49
Nietzsche, F., 11, 13, 154, 232 n. 19
Nouschi, André, 239 n. 95, 241 n. 34

O'Brien, Donal Cruise, 110, 239 n. 5
Ohmish, 124
Oppenheimer, T., 231 n. 2
Ouitis, A., 240 n. 19
Owen, Roger, 238 n. 80

Paden, John, 235 n. 52
Pahlevi family, 43
Parkinson, C.H., 139
Pascon, Paul, 236 n. 64
Pears, D.F., 231 n. 15
Peter, St, 42
Peter the Great, 108
Peters, Prof. Emrys, 172, 238 n. 89,
    242 n. 47
Pius XI, Pope, 135
Plato, 17–18, 19, 22–6, 28, 30, 31, 73,
    232 n. 23
Platt, K., 236 n. 66
Pontius Pilate, 42
Popovic, Alexandre, 236 n. 69
Prenant, A., 239 n. 95
Prometheus, 151
Proust, Marcel, 218

Quandt, W., 237 n. 76

Rabinow, Paul, 208–13, 243 n. 8, 245 n. 2
    (ch. 10)
Ranger, T.O., 221
Raymond, André, 73, 237 n. 80
Rezette, Paul, 57
Rhodes, Cecil, 226
Roberts, Hugh, 239 n. 93
Robinson Crusoe, 214
Robinson, M., 231 n. 9
Romanoff family, 43
Romulus, 11
Roosevelt, Franklin D., 150
Rosen, L., 233 n. 29, 235 n. 59, 237 n. 74,
    76
Rosenthal, Franz, 232 n. 24, 243 n. 1
Rouholamini, Prof. M., 235 n. 46
Rousseau, J.-J., 92, 233 n. 41
Russell, Bertrand, 23

Sadat, Anouar, 63
Said, Edward, 239 n. 95
Salzman, Philip C., 233 n. 35
Sarjeant, Prof. R.B., 233 n. 32, 238 n. 91
Satan, 156
Sawsan El Messiri, 233 n. 29

Schorger, William, 233 n. 33
Seddon, David, 237 n. 76, 243 n. 1
Service, E.R., 233 n. 35
Shaked, H., 235 n. 47
Sharif, Omar, 67
Shaw, Stanford J., 237 n. 78
Shinar, Pessah, 170, 225, 241 n. 21,
    242 n. 44
Simon, Capt., 160, 240 n. 20
Sivers, Peter von, 238 n. 80
Skalnik, Peter, 233 n. 36
Slade, Capt. Adolphus, 236 n. 62
Smith, M.G., 235 n. 52
Snesarov, G.P., 237 n. 71
Snow, Lord, 196
Souriau, C., 237 n. 72
Stalin, J., 108, 171
Stambouli, F., 234 n. 44, 240 n. 3
Stern, S.M., 234 n. 44
Stewart, C.C., 232 n. 27, 235 n. 52
Stewart, E.K., 232 n. 27, 235 n. 52
Stirling, Paul, 234 n. 43

Tapper, Nancy, 241 n. 24
Tapper, Richard, 238 n. 88
Taylor, Charles, 231 n. 12
Tayyib Iqbi, 155–7, 159–60, 167,
    240 n. 9
Theseus, 11
Tillion, Germaine, 33, 233 n. 39
Tito, Marshal, 194
Tocqueville, Alexis de, 1, 16, 19, 28, 68,
    93, 223, 231 n. 1, 232 n. 25, 233 n. 30,
    41
Trevor-Roper, H.R., 232 n. 24
Trimingham, J.S., 235 n. 52
Tuda Lahcen, 124
Turgot, A.R.J., 8
Turner, Bryan, 231 n. 9

Uqba (Ocba), Sidi, 156, 160, 240 n. 20

Valensi, L., 238 n. 80
Valentino, Rudolph, 38
van Niewenhuijze, C.A.O., 234 n. 14
Vatikiotis, P.J., 237 n. 76
Vatin, Jean-Claude, vii, 39, 234 n. 42,
    237 n. 76
Victoria, Queen, 106
Vinogradov, Amal Rassam, 212–13,
    236 n. 63, 243 n. 8, 245 n. 7 (ch. 10)
Virgin Mary, 11

Waardenburg, J., 239 n. 98
Waterbury, John, 72, 176, 231 n. 9,
    233 n. 29, 237 n. 76, 77, 241 n. 38,
    243 n. 8
Watt, W. Montgomery, 54, 235 n. 57
Weber, Max, 5, 14, 16, 78, 87, 89, 109, 132,
    170, 231 n. 9, 235 n. 59
Weir, Shelagh, 57, 234 n. 43, 238 n. 91
Wesley, John, 67
Whitehead, A.N., 13

Subject index

Subject index

222–4, 227, 233 n. 41, 243 n. 1, 8, 244 n. 8
Berbers, The, 243 n. 1
Beyond Good and Evil, 232 n. 19
Beyond the Veil, 241 n. 25
big man, 38, 40, 223
Biskra, 149–73
Bitter Favours, 242 n. 39
Black Sea, 193
blad (land), 236 n. 61
  blad siba, 196, 197, 211, 244 n. 6
  blad makhzen, 196, 197, 211
Bombay, 105, 106, 107, 108
Boujad, 214, 215, 220
bourgeoisie, 15, 41, 48, 162, 163, 165
Britain, British, 65, 107–8, 109, 184
  Raj, 66, 107–8
  social anthropology, 187–8
B.P. (British Petroleum), 67
Bu Sarwal, 177
Buddhism, 60
bureaucracy, 77
burghers, 63, 67, 80, 152, 232 n. 22
Burma, 188, 243 n. 3, 8
Byzantium, 2

caids, 56, 192, 200, 203, 236 n. 61, 64
Calvinist, 78
canton, 189, 190, 192
Caravan, 244 n. 8 (ch. 8)
Casablanca, 232 n. 22, 239 n. 92
caste, *see* India
Catholicism, 11, 13, 97
charisma, 14, 16, 40
  routinisation of, 14, 16
Childe Harold, 51
China, Chinese, 5, 78, 135, 149, 233 n. 35
Chleuh, 180
Christendom, Christian, Christianity, 1, 2, 4, 6, 42, 43, 54, 99, 103, 181–2, 199, 217
Church and state, 54–6, 100
Circassian, 75
cities, *see* towns
Civilisation du désert, La, 243 n. 1
class conflict, struggle, 34, 46, 47, 66, 219
clerks, lawyers, scribes, theologians, 103
  see also literacy, scholars
Clochemerle, 226
cohesion, 33, 86–98
  see also group solidarity
collective oath, 41, 68, 121
Collège de France, 153, 182, 190, 208, 243 n. 1
colonialism, 58, 66, 173
  and Islam, 66
Commander of the Faithful, 72, 237 n. 76, 77, 241 n. 38, 243 n. 8
communal consensus, 101, 103, 115–16
Communist Party, 60, 181
concepts, 23, 123
Confréries religieuses musulmanes, 243 n. 2
Confucianism, 4
Conquerors and Slaves, 236 n. 65

consanguinity, 27
Constantine, 155, 157
contradiction, 11, 12, 15, 32
Contradictions sociales et leur expression symbolique dans le Sétifois, Les, 240 n. 19
corruption, 66
Corsaires de Salé, Les, 245 n. 3 (ch. 11)
Crete, 22
Crimea, Crimean War, 32, 178
Critique of Practical Reason, 239 n. 2 (ch. 5)
crucifixion, 42
Cuba, 149
cultural diversity, problem of, 94–5
cultural specialisation, 90
culture theory, 209–12, 217–18
Customs and Politics in Urban Africa, 238 n. 85
Cycle of Equity, 75
Cyprus, 97, 242 n. 39
Cyrenaica, 81, 140, 172, 223, 238 n. 89
Czar, 178
Czech, 177

Dahir berbère, 199, 202
Damascus, 152
dancing (*ahaidus*), 125–6, 127, 142, 143, 147, 162
Darqawi, 141, 142
David Hume. A Symposium, 231 n. 15
Dawi Mani, 228
Dekkilé, 110
Delphi, 13
democracy, 60
dervish, *see* saints
despotism, Oriental, 82
devshirme, 75, 76, 174
Die Neue Zeit, 46
Dionysiac, 53
division of labour, 29, 33, 87, 90, 94
  and industrialisation, 90
Djerba, 132
Domusulmanskie Vierovania i Obriady v Srednei Azii, 237 n. 71
Dordogne, 226
Drang, 11
Druzes, 2
Dutch, 13

Early State, The, 233 n. 36
education and industrialisation, 91
Egypt, Egyptian, 52, 63, 72, 73, 74, 75, 82, 154, 178, 223, 233 n. 29, 235 n. 53, 56, 237 n. 76
Egypt in Search of Political Community, 235 n. 56, 237 n. 76
Egypt in Transition, 237 n. 76
Egypte, société militaire, 237 n. 76
Eighteenth Century Confronts the Gods, The, 8, 231 n. 16
El Azhar, 82
Elect of God, 6
Elementary Forms of the Religious Life, 92

Subject index

Subject index

inner light, 16
international politics and tribes, comparison, 96
Iran, Iranian, 32, 43, 45, 59, 63, 66, 69, 108, 233 n. 35, 234 n. 43, 238 n. 86, 88
Shah of, 43, 63
Iraq, 83, 237 n. 76
Ireland, Irish, 97, 166
'Isawi Tarika, 137, 142
Islam
bounded v. unbounded, 102
completion of, 23, 100
egalitarian scholarly, 5, 103
hold of culture of, 55−6
internal differentiation: folk v. scholarly, 5; egalitarian (left) v. hierarchical (right), 101−2; religion and social, 69
'church', 48, 54−6, 99−100
norms, 22−3
post-traditional forms, 99−113
purification/modernisation, 5, 130
Reformism (including Jadidism), 58, 60−1, 64, 67, 125, 132, 154, 158, 161, 163, 169, 171, 175, 234 n. 45, 236 n. 66, 70, 237 n. 71, 238 n. 91, 241 n. 31, 242 n. 42, 43, 49; traditionalism, 155, 165−7 (*see also* modernity); two styles of religious life, 159
Islam and Politics in a Malay State, 235 n. 52
Islam and Social Order in Mauritania, 232 n. 27, 235 n. 52
Islam and the Integration of Society, 235 n. 56
Islam dans le miroir de L'Occident, L', 239 n. 98
Islam et Capitalisme, 231 n. 9
Islam in the Soviet Union, 237 n. 71
Islam in the Sudan, 235 n. 52
Islam in Tropical Africa, 235 n. 52, 239 n. 6
Islam Observed, 208, 209, 210, 235 n. 56, 240 n. 8, 243 n. 7, 8, 245 n. 4 (ch. 10)
Islamic City, The, 234 n. 44
Islamic Law in the Modern World, 235 n. 57
Islamic Reform, 236 n. 66
Islamic Roots of Capitalism, 231 n. 9
Islamisation, 236 n. 66
Isma'il b. 'Abd al-Qadir, 235 n. 47
Ismailis, *Shia Imami Ismailia*, 63, 104−9, 113
Israel, 27
Istanbul, 140
Italy, Italian, 78

Jadidism, 60, 242 n. 43
see also Islam, Reformism
jellabas, 227
Jema'a, 227
Jews, Judaism, 1, 5, 16, 78, 112, 113, 118, 124, 132, 187, 194, 223, 226
jihad (holy war), 66, 82, 147, 224

Journal of Peasant Studies, 73

Kabyles, 28, 157, 177, 211, 222, 233 n. 41
Kabylia, 82, 157, 158
Kanun, 2
Kathmandu, 78
Kayor, 110
Kebabish Arabs, The, 237 n. 74
Kemalism, 58−60, 68, 141, 148, 169, 175
Kerkennah Islands, 236 n. 66
Khalifate, 83, 155, 228−9
Khalwah, 141
Kharejite, 7, 82, 102, 223, 246 n. 3
Khartoum, 46
kibbutz, 112, 113
kin, kinship, 27, 40, 87−8, 101, 131, 146, 216, 234 n. 41
see also lineage, segmentation
Knights of Malta, 134
Kochevniki Azii, 233 n. 38
Koran, Qur'an, The Book, Holy Writ, 6, 21, 50, 62, 63, 67, 68, 80, 81, 99, 101, 102, 103, 115−16, 123, 124, 132, 136, 144, 170, 171, 185, 199, 223, 240 n. 6, 242 n. 49
Korea, 68
Kult Sviatykh v Islame, 237 n. 71

Lancashire, 227
language, 32
law, 1, 42, 50, 55, 61, 64, 65, 71, 80, 185, 199
see also nomocracy, divine
leadership, ix
Leadership and National Development in North Africa, 241 n. 22, 243 n. 8
Lebanon, 2, 59
Leeds, 209
leff, ilfuf, soff, 190
legitimation, 115−16
Légitimation Islamique des socialismes arabes, La, 237 n. 76
liberty, 15
Libya, 62−4, 65, 69, 171, 172
lineage, 25, 44, 49, 52, 82, 116, 119, 122, 129, 131, 145, 160, 233 n. 29
succession, 121−2
see also segmentation, tribes
Lineages of the Absolute State, 238 n. 81
literacy, 5, 21−9, 41−2, 61, 89, 93, 104, 116, 132, 147, 166, 170, 184, 204
Literacy ... Traditional Societies, 232 n. 28
lodges, orders, brotherhoods, 48−9, 235 n. 52, 227 n. 76, 243 n. 2
'Lords of the Atlas, The', 187, 243 n. 8
Lords of the Atlas, 243 n. 8
Lord's Prayer, The, 153
luxuries (salt, sugar, tea), 126

Maghreb, 47, 72, 84, 86−98, 117, 134, 156, 173, 175, 176, 209, 223, 225, 240 n. 3
see also Africa

259

Subject index

Subject index

religion, theories of (*cont.*)
  and state, 54
  Weber's, 89
Religion and Political Culture in Kano,
    235 n. 52
Republic, 18, 232 n. 23
Resistance in the Desert, 221–30, 245 n. 1
    (ch. 12)
ressentiment, 12
revelation, 6, 45
Revolution, 62, 63
Revolution and Political Leadership,
    237 n. 76
Révolution au Maroc, 243 n. 1
Rif, 146, 148, 182, 183, 187, 192, 196
Roman Empire, 3, 4, 57
rosaries, 143
rules, 1
*Rural Politics and Social Change in the
    Middle East*, 233 n. 34, 237 n. 76
Russia, *see* Union of Soviet Socialist
    Republics

Sahara, 21, 50, 81, 119, 127, 161, 184, 191,
    197, 221, 222, 228, 232 n. 27,
    236 n. 61
St Andrews, 132
St Tropez, 132
Saint and Sufi in Modern Egypt, 235 n. 51,
    241 n. 31
saints, the, 40–1, 44, 50, 56–7, 58,
    114–30, 131, 132–3, 147, 153, 154,
    164, 175, 197, 207–13, 214–20,
    234 n. 44, 241 n. 31
  dervish, 40, 242 n. 43
  functions of, 119–23
  and modernity, 58
  pacifism of, 41, 122
  roles of, 41
  see also marabouts, *igurramen*
Saints of the Atlas, 239 n. 1 (ch. 4),
    243 n. 8
Salafiyyah, 144, 147, 148, 156
Salé, 214, 218–20
San'a': An Islamic City, 233 n. 32
Sanusi, 81, 133, 172, 233 n. 40
Sanusi of Cyrenaica, The, 233 n. 40,
    238 n. 89
Saudi Arabia, 62, 64, 65, 69, 156, 238 n. 91,
    240 n. 3 (ch. 5)
scholars, 43, 44, 79, 214
Scholars, Saints and Sufis, 234 n. 44
Scotland, 156
scripturalism, 21, 24, 31, 42, 50, 52, 55,
    61–2, 65, 76, 100, 209, 211
  completed, 23, 100
Scythians, 32
secularism, 60, 68
segmentary society, segmentation, 33,
    36–41, 69, 70, 72, 83, 86, 117–19,
    138, 176, 180, 189–93, 211, 222,
    228, 237 n. 74, 238 n. 89
  as explanation, 36, 85
  and leap-frogging, 119

masterpiece of, 228
rotation and complementarity in, 118
symmetrical and egalitarian, 118
Seksawa, 21, 190
Senegal, 109–13, 239 n. 5
Sermon on the Mount, 122
Shaikhs, 19, 51, 63, 106, 111, 133–4,
    135–49, 217, 220
  'A disciple must be in the hands of his
    shaikh as the corpse in the hands of
    the washers of the dead', 50, 111,
    134
Sharif, Sharifian, Sherifian, Shurfa, 57, 136,
    159, 162, 182, 210, 212, 234 n. 41
Sheikh and Effendi, 239 n. 94
shepherds, 33
Sherqawa, 214, 215, 220
Shi'a, Shi'ite, Shi'ism, Ismailis, Zaidis, 1, 2,
    42, 43, 66, 79, 82, 102, 103, 104–9,
    112, 113, 116, 234 n. 45, 238 n. 86
Shihah, 166, 171
shirk, 156, 160, 161
Si le grain ne meurt, 151, 153, 240 n. 1
sidi, 132–3
silsila, 68
slaves, 57, 73, 77
Smala, 201
'small nation', 95
Social Life of Islam, The, 239 n. 92
social order, 1
Social Stratification in the Middle East,
    234 n. 44
socialism, 48, 64, 112, 149, 168, 179
  and Zionism, 112
Société du Mont Liban, La, 234 n. 43
Society of the Muslim Brothers, The,
    237 n. 76
Sociologie religieuse de l'Islam, 231 n. 10
sociology, 86–7, 89
  of religion, 2, 13, 30–1
  origins of, 89
  and types of society, 179–80
solidarity, mechanical and organic, 86–8,
    90, 94
Somalia, Somalis, 62, 68, 217, 234 n. 43
Sotsialnaia Istoria Skifov, 233 n. 37
South Seas, 184
Soviets, 59
Spain, Spaniards, 18, 46, 133, 183, 192
specialism, 23–4
Stalinism, 193
state, 20, 47, 54–6, 59, 68, 76, 94–5, 125,
    132, 179, 191, 192, 221
  culturally diverse, 94–5
  moralistic, 47
  powers of, 55–6
  robber, 47
  weakness of, 20, 55–6
status, 93
*Structure of Traditional Moroccan Rural
    Society, The*, 212, 245 n. 6 (ch. 10)
Structures sociales du Haut-Atlas, 232 n. 26,
    240 n. 5, 243 n. 5
Studies of the Mamluks of Egypt 1250–

Subject index

Cambridge Studies in Social Anthropology

Editor: Jack Goody

266